D0917329

BY THINGS SEEN:
Reference and Recognition in Medieval Thought

Printed and bound in Canada

Frontispiece: "Alpha and Omega" — Bib. Nat. MS. Lat. 9438

Christ in majesty is here set within a frame of several significant dimensions. First, we see that he is seated in a mandorla which contains two interlocking circles, symbolic of the two realms, uncreated and created, eternal and temporal, which cohere in him. He holds a book, symbolic both of the Book of Life and the *evangelium*, his Gospel of which the gospels of the four evangelists in the corners are a translation. The evangelists have their traditional symbolic characterizations from Ezekiel — man (Matthew), lion (Mark), ox (Luke), eagle (John), and are the visible witnesses to the supreme authorship of the Creator himself, the Alpha and the Omega, who alone commands the story from beginning to end. The vaginal shape of the mandorla itself may, in this instance, not unfairly be related to the subject, which, as Bonaventure puts it for example, in his *Reductione artium ad theologiam*, is "the eternal incarnation of the Son of God".

BY THINGS SEEN:
Reference and Recognition in Medieval Thought

Edited by

DAVID L. JEFFREY

The University of Ottawa Press
Ottawa, Canada
1979

DEUS SCIENTIARUM · DOMINUS EST

UNIVERSITAS OTTAVIENSIS

ERRATA

By Things Seen, ed. D.L.Jeffrey

m. 1:20 -	"ipsius...quae..."
eface	"historians'"
5	"worldly city"
22	footnote sections 3 and 4 are inverted in text
23	end of first para. "significance"
25	"Manichaean"; "ungoverned wildness"
26	last para. "aversion or perversion"
28	"Augustine's criticisms"
76	3. "where"
94	"liturgy"
98	"consonant"
101	"reconcileable"
103	"or who follow the old art"
109	"1285-1290"
114	"vehicle" for "vehicule"
116	"when an artist is painting..."
118	"and hardly could..."
126	γραψα ; auxiliaries
136	"idle talk"
140	"responsibility"
143	"fairly"; "whether"
148	"glorified"
151	"sublimity in the lofty"
181	(notes 26 and 27 are inverted)
196	"Nicea" (also 205)
230	"philosopher"
269	"Laurence"; "hermeneutic"

Invisibilia enim epsius, a creatura mundi, per ea que facta sunt intellecta conspiciuntur.

Epist. ad Rom. 1:20

Preface

Ideals are what we chiefly associate with the Middle Ages perhaps more than with any other period of western European history. Seldom has the idea been so apparently important, the material so immaterial. Yet an awareness of this essential truth has sometimes led to a view of medieval life and thought which too readily disassociates the vital connection between the idea and its translation, between theory and experiment, or between spiritual and worldly knowledge.

In the present volume our intention is to examine aspects of one of the simplest and most basic features of medieval thinking: the principle of referral for understanding. No medieval idea is more important to an understanding of other medieval ideas, and no medieval idea, perhaps, is more distinctly a property of that period. It is the basic feature of medieval epistemology, and provides a structure for medieval aesthetics, as for political and even scientific theories. For all that, and probably because it is so different from comparable basic ideas in our own culture, it is not often itself the focus of studies of the period. For one thing, there is always a great danger that, while setting forth what appears to be a foundational concept, the generalization, however significant, will utterly fail to do justice to individual facts — a peril against which historians are justly set on their guard. For another, the really captivating feature of a given episode or epoch is often, in fact, a product of stresses set against its dominant ideas, so that it is the resulting clashes and skirmishes which occupy our attention, and the incongruities and crises with which we more readily identify.

The great struggle of medieval culture, nevertheless, was to comprehend, express, and maintain a unified view of reality. Between St. Augustine's *City of God*, with its avowed intention of justifying God's ways to man, and the confident dedication of merchant Francesco Datini "In the name of God and profit" (presumably a justification of the ways of man to God), lies a continuous chain of attempts to find significant coherence for the divergent elements of human experience. Throughout the period there grows an increasing tension between a "platonic" desire to harmonize God's universal truths with man's relative understanding, and what may be thought of as an Aristotelian awareness of the contingency of human understanding upon physical data and logical process. It is clear enough that at the beginning of the Middle Ages the principle of referral for understanding is rooted in the "platonic" and biblical instinct. But where the comprehensive discussions of Augustine and Boethius on questions of the nature and utility of knowledge had once seemed to reconcile satisfactorily man's place and God's purpose, under subsequent analysis ambiguous definitions and mutually exclusive compartments of thought began to be discovered.

The purpose of this collection of essays is to provide an introduction to the dynamic of relationship between the medieval idea of referral and its application, both at times when it seems to have worked fruitfully and at times when it did not, as the relationship can be traced in various significant arenas of cultural activity. In the pages which follow, eleven contemporary scholars have set about to describe how this central premise of medieval Christian thought shaped and ordered — and in turn itself was modified by — centrifugal forces of cultural experience and a characteristically centripital and ideal pursuit of understanding.

The essays, therefore, explore various medieval adaptations of idea and experience to the desire for a unified view. They introduce the student to the traditional Augustinian ordering of inquiry and explore in some detail the rich implications of a referential epistemology. They also illustrate practical challenges to the referential model as natural causes became more subtly acknowledge and understood. The principal focus of this study is the civilization of twelfth through fourteenth century Europe, for it is in this period, opened by a wide-spread celebration of Augustinian tradition but closed with a critical challenge to that philosophy, that one can most readily appreciate how dynamic was the struggle of medieval culture to maintain its traditional models.

There seemed no better place to begin a study of this kind than in what Hugh of St. Victor called "the liberal and mechanical arts" (*Didascalicon*, II.20). For according to Hugh, it is with the arts that the weakness of man, naked from Eden, may clothe itself and rightly order the mind (I.9). The arts not only mirror the parts of nature, but Nature's whole design, exploring both its tangible and intelligible image (I.10). Thus, the goal of the several arts is still, for the twelfth century, the goal of education itself, a moving from signs to things, from the *eloquentia* of the *trivium* to the practical theories of the *quadrivium* upon whose art coheres whatever unified measure of reality there is to be discovered. Typically, the ordering of experience, whether in Boethius' *Consolation of Philosophy*, John of Salisbury's *Policratus*, Hugh of St. Victor's *Didascalicon*, or Roger Bacon's *Opus Majus*, becomes a trial of perspectives, a dialectic of distinctions leading to the informed referral and "right proportioning" of things.

The essays in the second section ask questions about the nature of cultural diffusion, and pose historians queries concerning the counterpoint to vertical reference afforded by the exigencies of terrestrial experience. The third section asks what happens when various branches of philosophy break away from premises based upon revelation to ones based upon empirical observation and Aristotelian systems of logic. In the postscript, the editor gathers some implications of an increasingly horizontal organization of reference for late medieval traditioning of the concept of referral, and sees in the old contest between Platonic and Aristotelian modes of enquiry a vocabulary by which thinkers at the end of the Middle Ages attempted to describe an untenable synthesis of transcendent and terrestrial reference.

In all of these medieval efforts, it is the principle of reference for understanding which undergirds intellectual enterprise, and leads toward a unified understanding. The Editor and the various authors of this volume are aware that any selection of focal points for this study may prove disproportionate. Nevertheless, they hope that their present efforts will serve to illuminate the principle and to illustrate something of its development through to the end of that long period we still think of as the "Middle Ages" of our western culture.

Finally, the Editor would like to take this opportunity to thank each of the contributors for their patience, and for their personal commitment to the volume. Our work together began with their contributions to an interdisciplinary course directed by me at the University of Rochester Medieval House in 1972, and it is no exaggeration to say that I could not have initiated this task without their cooperation and attunement. Patrick Grant deserves a special word of acknowledgement — his conversation has been a salutary influence at many points of my preparation. Laurence Eldredge graciously consented to prepare his essay after the fact, an act of generosity which has been much appreciated. The volume has greatly benefited from the helpful suggestions of my colleagues Raymond St. Jacques and Thomas McAlindon, both of whom cheerfully undertook to read sections of the manuscript at unduly short notice. Katherine Brown contributed an earlier reading of the manuscript and offered many helpful suggestions. Finally, I am above all indebted to my friends and former colleagues Russell Peck and Richard Kaueper, who from the beginning laboured long and arduously for the book. Russell Peck, especially, contributed a substantial share of the early editing. Few members of the academic profession are better informed than he on the subject matter of this volume; none could have been more generous with that knowledge and understanding.

D.L.J.

TABLE OF CONTENTS

III. **Turning to Analysis**

Postscript

Introduction

The Self and the Book:
Reference and Recognition in Medieval Thought

The witness of records makes it evident that medieval thought is, summarily, Christian thought. It will be recognized that Christian thought (whether of biblical, medieval, or modern times), is based upon a theory of limited understanding. The medieval formulation of this point, however, should not be regarded as a mere *caveat*, but as the foundation to a responsible epistemology. Two notions governed its application. First, there was the fact that Christian thought holds also, and always, to confidence in an ultimate fullness of understanding. In the representative words of St. Paul:

> For we know in part .... but when that which is perfect comes, then that which is in part shall be done away.

> When I was a child I spoke as a child, I understood as a child, I thought as a child, but when I became a man I put away childish things. For now we see through a glass darkly; but then face to face; now I know in part; but then shall I know even as I am known.

> (I Corinthians 3:9-12)

Second, Paul encouraged his readers to observe a referential character in the created world:

> For the invisible things of him from the creation of the world are clearly seen, being understood by the things that are.

> (Romans 1:20)

From these tenets derive three of the most important practical aspects of Christian thought in the Middle Ages: 1) an acceptance of the natural as, in the root sense, significant; 2) a tendency to see any element of created order as nevertheless known only in part and therefore (explicitly or implicitly) to look for and refer it for understanding to a more perfect model; 3) an increasing emphasis on, and optimism about, the processes of learning. Epistemologically, medieval Christian thought was limited by its acute awareness of man's place in the middle — of his limited perspective on the whole of experience, even of his own personal experience, in pursuing the possibility of understanding. At the same time, it was liberated by its being premised upon a confidence in the comprehensive reality of a larger framework in which, though the reality may be encompassed by no individual human perspective, nevertheless in it all individual human perspectives are seen to participate. This confidence in man's "participation" generated a keen desire to explore elements of the "seen" in order that the truth of the larger order might be lived more appreciatively.

I. — THE CREATION OF MIDDLE EARTH

For these reasons no very illuminating pursuit of medieval thought-life can be undertaken without some appreciation of what is usually called "the doctrine of Creation". We need to guard against too swift a sense of satisfaction that as modern persons we really grasp this idea. The principle importance of the doctrine of creation for medieval theory is not to be found in credal affirmations of the Judaeo-Christian belief in God's once-in-time creation of the universe, *ex nihilo*. Nor, even, does it lie with that appreciation and acknowledgement of the power and plenitude of the Creator's providence which is commonly expressed in worship. In fact, the chief effect of "in the beginning God created" on medieval thought is its construal of human perspective as inextricably middled: whereas we tend to view history from the "stage" or "state" of "present knowledge" usually imagined as a kind of evolutionary mountain top — medieval man believed he saw from a point "in between", middle earth, somewhere along a route with definite limits — with an end as well as a beginning. The various forms of expression which were given to this sense of partial perspective reminds us that, historically, Christians have believed in a *finite* universe.

The biblical model for history thus had an enormous impact on medieval thinking in all areas. From the bargain struck between Adam and Eve and God in the Garden, on through the covenant from Noah's rainbow to Abraham's promise and the eschatological promise which descends through David's kingship and lineage to Christ, biblical history looks forward. From the very beginning it is eschatological — it "thinks" from the end. Unlike the basic character of that Greek philosophical literature which was so profoundly to influence the men of the renaissance — a literature given to the abstraction of principles, to rational process, to considerations of concepts such as "space" and the study of physics and cosmology — literature in the scriptural tradition, with its historical perspective, is very much interested in personal, historical experience and therefore in the meaning of time. And because it insists on there being an end "in the fullness of time" it finds it necessary to speak also of the beginning.

That the Scriptures should speak of the beginning has often seemed, even to such an apologist for Christian thought as Augustine, a real provocation. In his *Confessions* (XI) he reminds us eloquently of the frustration that arises from this awkwardness. For we cannot by ourselves adequately deal with "the beginning": existentially, to use the modern term, where the beginning begins our thinking stops, it comes to an end.[1] From the middle, and acutely conscious of the passage of time "that will not come again" we most urgently seek to know the beginning, and yet realize, existentially, empirically, that this is beyond our scope, the fractional reach of our mortality. We live only such a short while.

The other aspect of the Creation story which figures here, unavoidably, is the Fall. Once again, the modern reader needs to distinguish very carefully between what the Fall means and does not mean in medieval Christian thought. In terms of the biblical texts, most concisely what the Fall implies is that man's intellect, memory and will are impaired (Augustine), in need of education, reformed perception, and ultimately an identification with God's will and a return to the original intention of the Creator. What the Fall does not imply is that man's will and intellect are totally corrupt and incapable of response to the originals of Divine intention.

If, for a moment, we consider the Genesis story in its mythic aspects, as they are treated, for example, in the twelfth century Anglo-Norman play about it, the *Jeu d'Adam*, certain significant features emerge. When Eve and Adam enact their will to be separate, their consequent "fall" is probably less well translated in current English by the common term as by words like "fragmentation", "alienation", or "separation". The estrangement from Eden constitutes the opening of a great gap, a breach between "now" and "the beginning", between the Creator and his created beings, which places us inextricably, on our own account, beyond the power of thinking — *in medias res*, in the middle, beyond the grasp of beginning and end. In the *Jeu d'Adam* Adam and Eve look backward to paradise and ahead in vain, Adam saying:

"Jotez en sui par mon pecchié, parvoir del recovrer tot ai perdu l'espoir!"[2]

Myth after myth, in and out of Christian literature, describe this situation as one of lostness in the middle, where a command of structure, narrative and progress are beyond the reach of thinking — out of the grasp of mere words. The fall represents almost a division of conscious from unconscious states of mind. Even in its name, the "tree of good and evil" suggests a kind of reflective capacity which can seem to be both the origin and the fruit of the hopeless circularity and "subjectivity" of fallen thought.[3] Thus, the death which follows Eden is not only the loss of communion, the dissolution of the body and the estrangement of the soul, but, as for St. Augustine in the *Confessions*, the loss of a possibility of relationship to the whole story — time's full narrative. "Men perish," said the pre-Socratic philosopher

---

[1] D. Bonhoeffer re-expresses, in a modern European context, the Augustinian point of view in *Creation & Fall* (N.Y.: Macmillan, 1969), pp. 1-14.

[2] *Le Jeu d'Adam*, ed. William NOOMEN (Paris: Honoré Champion, 1971), p. 51, line 525-6. See also the edition by Lief Sletsjöe (Paris: Klincksick, 1968).

[3] Paul RICOEUR, *History and Truth*, tr. C.A. KELBLEY (Evanston: Northwestern University Press, 1965): "Objectivity and Subjectivity in History," pp. 21-40.

Alcaemon of Crotona, "because they cannot join the beginning with the end."[4] This old Greek statement might have been understood by medieval men as describing a literary problem, a problem of narrative. But in Christian thought down to the Middle Ages it is in fact the problem of joining which is seen to be the essential human problem, and its most immediate metaphors are often narrative, story, book metaphors.

Augustine provides a convenient entry point into medieval thinking on this subject, not only because he formalizes many of its central paradigms, but because his pre-Christian objections, as recorded in his *Confessions*, tally so well with perspectives of our own world. For Augustine the convert, our thinking, the thinking of those who must turn to the middle to know anything about the beginning, to Christ to know about God, is the thinking of fallen man, and has no beginning because it is necessarily circular. We think, exist, feel and will in a circle, and without the possibility of reference to something beyond itself our thinking wants to take this circle for the infinite and original reality and thus hopelessly entangles itself.

But for Augustine before his conversion, the thing which makes the opening words of Genesis so objectionable is in fact the same crux, the reader's consciousness of his basic inability to construct the whole of his own narrative, to rewrite the "book". For no one can speak of "the beginning" except One who was in the beginning. No ordinary man in the middle reaches from *alpha* to *omega*, even in the span of his own life. (See frontispiece). And so it is this very dilemma which highlights the importance of reference for understanding. The real question posed by Genesis 1:1 for the reader, and it is the ultimate question in all forms of Christian thought, is: "in what sense will we let our author be our Author?"

The relationship of authorship to authority ("auctoritas" as Chaucer puns with it) is thus a critical one for medieval Christian thought. The real problem posed by man's "middleness" in reading Scripture — or indeed any other text — is the degree to which he will allow his author authority, or credibility, while the story is unfolded. For the Christian thinker of the Middle Ages, there is ultimately only one answer: to read the story intelligently one must grant to authorship its integrity, must be willing to accept, even *pro tempus*, the author's viewpoint. This comes to be as true for reading the Book of Nature as for a painting, as apt to books of words as to the book of God's Word.[5]

But from Augustine forward, the idea that the Book of God's Words essentially accords with the Book of his Works is a keystone of Christian thought and particularly of the "doctrine of Creation". Although man's perspective is limited, both qualitatively and quantitatively, still he can see

---

[4] Sir Gilbert Burnet, *Early Greek Philosophy* (N.Y.: Meridian, 1968), 195.

[5] See Bonaventure's *Retracing the Arts to Theology*, ed. and trans. Emma Thérèse Healy (Franciscan Institute: St. Bonaventure, N.Y., 1955).

I.   "Tower of Babel"

The confusion of all languages as a result of the determination to penetrate the realm of "things unseen" by one's own devices is the explicit theme of the story of the tower of Babel. While the New Testament mirror to the story is the *glossolalia*, speaking in tongues at Pentecost, its opposite structure in Hebrew scripture is the story of Beth'el, where Jacob has his dream of the ladder to heaven, with angels ascending and descending. In this biblical illustration we are reminded that truth descends to man from above, as revelation or grace. An effort to ascend to the light of divine knowledge by our own devices, as from Plato's cave, is an act of pointless pride doomed to conclude only in a more hapless fragmentation of meaning than before. Ironically, Babel means, in Babylonian, "Gate of God" — the place at the top of a ziggurat, where one worships — but in Hebrew, it is also the word for Babylon, the prototype of the wordly city, which leads to a symbolic conflation of the two names. In the Middle Ages this symbolic identification was extended, leading Gregory the Great, for example, to speak of Babylon as the image of that sterility and disorder which follows from a rejection of the *auctoritas* and creation of God.

the correspondence, and may verify it, generally speaking, in an existential way.

> Omnis mundi creatura
> quasi liber et pictura
> nobis est in speculum:
> nostræ vitæ, nostræ mortis,
> nostri status, nostræ sortis
> fidele signaculum.[6]

All the world's creatures, as a book and a picture, are to us a mirror: in it our life, our death, our present condition and our passing on are faithfully signified.

As opposed to an aboriginal culture, in which idols may be made from elements of the world to 'image' a god, what happens here is that the created world is seen as already "imaging".... not God's "appearance," but rather, and most explicitly, his divine imagination. We see that the original biblical idea, despite resemblance, is not itself platonic, in the sense that one is not invited by the process of an education in such things to ascend to a mastery of the realm of pure forms. Indeed, that would be regarded as the pride of Babel (see plate I). Rather, the things of this world are seen as an insight, as informed by the glory of God which descends into the world, and of which glory the created order is, literally speaking, a lively "imagination."

After the Augustinian revival of the twelfth century, there is a great burgeoning of encyclopedias and dictionaries of symbols, in which the world of objects is systematically referred to as an imagination of higher things. In Vincent of Beauvais, Ridewall, or Bersuire, one may find spiritual meanings for anything from a nightingale to a cardinal number.

II. — IDEAL AND FALLEN ORDER

Though creation is a dark glass, it is, nevertheless, a glass: something through which we can see. Man is invited, in medieval Christian thought, to taste and to see, to compare, to evaluate, to read, to interpret, and then to grow toward understanding. That is, granted his middleness, he is invited to begin where he is in the middle, and to come by exploration and discovery to a place where, by reference to another text, he can read and affirm the design of the Book which is written, not merely his own small part in one limited chapter.

One sees here that Christian thought could be construed as inevitably historicist. But once again it is necessary to urge caution against a modern, post-Christian understanding of the term "historicist". Rather than the thesis-antithesis-synthesis dynamics of an Hegelian view of history, thinkers in the Judaeo-Christian tradition until at least the eighteenth century believed in history that unfolded, like a triptych, or the pages of a book, in a

---

[6] ALANUS OF INSULIS, pr. in *Psalterium profanum*, ed. and trans. Joseph EBERLE (Zurich: Manesse Verlag, 1962), p. 126.

pre-determined narrative, having the balance and the symmetries of story rather than the counterforces of physics.[7] In this story, like all good stories, meaning is not fully revealed until the ending. The structural prototype, the narrative model for the story of history, was, of course, the Bible. But the implications, epistemologically speaking, of a biblical rather than Hegelian historicist view of history is that historical judgements — just as personal experience judgements — are not construed in terms of a contest of forces and counter forces moving toward temporal compromise and a new synthesis. In this sense the popular term "medieval synthesis" is often misleading to students and, on occasion, to more mature scholars. Medieval historical judgements are interim statements, process statements, construed in terms of contrast between ideal and fallen order.[8] Or we could say that to some degree all historical actions constitute from a medieval perspective either affirmations or negations of creational models.

In such a view, though, there are clearly absolute qualities, there are not absolute quantities. Though there are fundamental and absolute realities — such as good, and God, and creation, as well as evil, and Satan, and destruction — there are no actual earthly bodies which absolutely represent one of these utter polarities, no simple embodiments of black or white. Instead, we are met in the world with admixtures, with a fallen creation to be sure, but with a creation in which countless transformations and recreations (as well as negations and destructions) are constantly taking place. Chaucer's Alice of Bath may represent a fairly extensive admixturing of qualities, but she remains redeemable — his Nun's Priest may express more understanding of love (or love of understanding), but as he himself seems to be aware, he too is capable of falling, and can witness in himself the disintegration of memory, intellect, and will; he can envision the possibility of personal disfigurement.[9]

Because there are not, in a fallen world, signal embodiments of absolute quantity, there is not, in most medieval Christian thought, a simplistic opposition between flesh and spirit. Salt routes and saints' lives, as Professor Lopez shows us, are inextricably intertwined. Flesh and spirit are different media of human experience, to be sure, and the medium of the flesh may appear to be more susceptible to fallen order than that of the spirit more available to ideal order. But there is much less dualism here than is popularly supposed, and little absolute opposition between flesh and spirit. The two are seen, in fact, as reciprocal and mutually profitable provisions of creation, both of which are necessary for a full realization of creation's purpose.

---

[7] Cf. the essay by C.S. LEWIS, "Historicism", *The Month*, N.S. IV (1950), 230-43; reprinted in *God, History and Historians* (New York: Oxford University Press, 1977), 225-38.

[8] To blame the fault of a creature, according to St. Augustine, is, in effect, to praise its essential nature — *On Free Choice of the Will*, tr. A.S. BENJAMIN (N.Y.: Bobbs-Merrill, 1964), III, xiii.

[9] *The Complete Poetry and Prose of Geoffrey Chaucer*, ed. John H. FISHER (N.Y.: Holt, Rinehart & Winston, 1977).

Even Cistercian monastics of the twelfth century will argue for respect for the reciprocity and interdependence of body and spirit,[10] and in the next century the Franciscans are using the referential relationship of creation to Creator and body to spirit to develop the richest application in aesthetics of the idea that the Middle Ages was to enjoy.[11]

It would be difficult to overestimate the centrality of the principle of referral for the development of style in medieval art. One good late pictorial illustration is provided by Titian, in a painting usually referred to as "Sacred and Profane Love" (Plate II). There was a time when modern critics (unduly influenced, perhaps, by post-Victorian instincts) assumed the clothed woman to be a figure for Sacred Love and the naked lady to be Venus. Working out of contemporary artistic vocabularies, the great art-historian Panofsky, however, was able to show that it is actually the unclothed figure who represents ideal love, the clothed figure physical love. We learn to see that the clothed lady has about her iconic attributes of sensuousness — a golden bowl and roses — as well as signs of conjugal relationship (her belt, and the wisp of myrtle). The posture assumed by the nude is discovered to be that of a nereid, often depicted on Roman sarcophagi of the type on which she sits, a nymph-like creature who often helps the deceased to attain a blissful hereafter.[12] Accordingly, her gesture is not that of any known Venus portrayal. Her flaming lamp, held upward, is an index to her spiritual reference, and the sarcophagi filled with water, is a pool or font in which she has just bathed. The little angel stirring the waters of this pool (cf. the angel of the pool of Bethesda, John 5:2) and the fact of the sarcophagi itself indicate the relationship of the painting to the idea of baptism, a transforming passage from imperfect and fallen order toward an ideal state. Panofsky notes for us that the face of the bather looks down in compassion on her counterpart: there is not an "altercation" here, but a spirit of gentleness.[13] The subject of the painting is the relation of flesh and spirit to the process and experience of re-creation. We see that we have also moved from a closed jar (a receptacle for jewels and ornaments) to an open vessel — a laver. A close examination of the focus of the two women thus reveals this identity: perhaps, as Panofsky suggests, they were twins. Or, to put it in another way, perhaps Titian wanted us to see them as the same person (or the same love) transformed in being brought through physical to spiritual perfection.

The development is analogous to what St. Paul speaks of when he describes his own developing spiritual psychology in terms of a contrast

---

[10] E.g. WILLIAM OF ST. THIERRY, *Golden Epistle* (Spencer, Mass.: Cistercian Publications), 35-7; 52-3.

[11] See John V. FLEMING, *An Introduction to the Franciscan Literature of the Middle Ages* (Chicago: Franciscan Herald Press, 1977), esp. chs. IV, VI; D.L. JEFFREY, *The Early English Lyric and Franciscan Spirituality* (Lincoln: Univ. of Nebraska Press, 1975), ch. III, and bibliography.

[12] E. PANOFSKY, *Problems in Titian* (New York, 1965), 111.

[13] PANOFSKY, 116.

II. "Sacred and Profane Love" — Titian

The background to Titian's painting is a helpful commentary on the transformation which is its main subject. On the left is a fortified city, with travellers coming to it. On the right is another city in a tranquil setting, dominated by a church steeple — the transition between the city of the world and the spiritual community thus corresponding to the baptismal movement of the main subject. Similarly, on the left near background two rabbits cavort — common symbols for natural sexuality or even lechery. In the near right background the cupidinous rabbit is being hunted by men with dogs, while nearby sheep graze contentedly, by still waters, in the presence of their shepherd.

between the "Old Man" and the "New Man", a development whereby in
the perfection of Love and Understanding the "New Man" is elevated,
when the ideal ascends over the limitations of fallen order (Ephesians 4).
The purpose of this process of transformation, as Paul reminds us, is
recreation — the restoration of creation: "If any man be in Christ he is a
new creation: old things are passed away; behold, all things are new" (2
Cor. 5:17). The beautiful creation on the right in Titian's painting is not that
old familiar Venus, but in every full and proper sense, a new Eve. And by
virtue of the principle of reference, the emphasis in Titian, as with Chaucer
or St. Paul, is on the process, an in-time moving away from imperfection
and toward perfection, from the moment of vision toward a lasting
encounter with the perfect object of our Love.

III. — RE-CREATION

It is this same movement, or process of learning, as well as its
contextual system of reference, which provides both the structure and the
vocabulary of a classic poem of the Middle Ages, Dante's *Vita Nuova*. Both
elements are made clear even in the book's opening words, in which Dante
cast himself as a student searching a book — "the book of my memory" he
says. From this book he wishes to take the "words" which he intends to
"recollect" in the book he is writing — if not completely, then at least "in
their meaning".[14] This very Augustinian notion of the human writer as a
scribe and translator is the characteristic posture of a great number of
medieval writers, not just Dante, and the use of the book-scribe metaphors
alert the medieval reader to such a writer's view of himself as a kind of
student, and of his work as text with a context, with reference for meaning
to another text. That is, the Book of Memory which Dante studies has as its
Author God himself, to whose writing in history the poet responds, as a
scribe. For Dante, in the *Inferno* (XV,88-90), the poetic tradition extending
from Homer to himself bears a kind of collective witness, as an anthology of
scribal translations, to God's continuous narrative presence in the reality of
temporal human experience.

That the poet's ostensibly autobiographical witness in the poem should
be thus retrospectively construed, that the story of his love for Beatrice
should be recollected as a series of transformations whereby he is led from
the limitations of carnal affection through a series of new understandings to
a higher love, is completely in accord with the context to which he refers.
From the topical dream vision in which the authority of the God of Love is
first mysteriously apparent (Sonnet I) on through the conventional reactions
and responses of love, the poet traces the course of his ardour to the point
(Sonnet VII) where begins a transformation of his love for Beatrice. In this
transformation he begins to see her in more than her physical aspect; now
with reference to those qualities of her person which "Love himself"

---

[14] A convenient translation is: DANTE, *The New Life*, tr. W. ANDERSON (Baltimore:
Penguin, 1964), 37.

admires. Gradually his attention moves, in parallel fashion, away from his own frustration and self-pity toward that sort of praise of his Lady which shares her beauty with others, and refers her beauty to God (and to Love, who by this point begins to be seen as identified with God [*Canzone I*]). The effect of this sharing and referral is a "humbling", so that "all sins leave his memory" — his older memory begins also to be transformed.[15] The purpose of *Canzone I*, Dante now informs us, is itself reference — to incline all men to Love. Beatrice is seen as renewed expression of God's creation:

> Dice di lei Amor: cosa mortale
> Com' esser può si adorna, e si pura?
> Poi la riguarda, e fra se stessa guira,
> Che Dio ne 'ntende di far cosa nova...
>
> Love says of her, 'How can a mortal thing
> Have beauty and purity in such wealth?'
> He looks at her, declaring to himself:
> 'God meant her as a new creation.'[16]

The effect of the new creation on Dante is to cause his old memory to begin to pass away and thus to cause him in this *canzone* to seek fresh counsel: "Tell me my way!" he pleads through his poem, as poetry now openly becomes both a plea for understanding and its envoy. Referral becomes more and more explicit, until Beatrice is identified with Christ himself in Sonnet XIV, and Love is retrospectively identified with God's Holy Spirit. The apparent restatement of *Canzone I* in Sonnet XVI is thus to be interpreted in a fuller sense of what has sometimes seemed to modern readers a blasphemous identification:

> Vede perfettamente ogni salute
> Chi la mia donna tra le donne vede:
> Quelle che vanno con lei, son tenute
> Di bella grazia a Dio vender merzede.
>
> He sees all salvation perfectly
> Who beholds my lady among her companions:
> Whoever walks with her must be constrained
> To thank God for the beautiful grace she is....[17]

The liturgical reminders provided by the use of texts from Jeremiah which follow ("O vos omnes") are all ones which invite participants through an identification in Christ's sorrow (as penitents) to a full appreciation of his Love, to the resurrection of a transformed Spirit and to an apprenticeship in the whole story of God's creation.[18] It is in connection with this point that Dante carefully explains his repeated use of "Nove", the number nine, which has to do with the time he first met Beatrice as well as with the hour of her death; but we are reminded that this is also the hour of Christ's death on the Cross. Also, Dante adds in Ch. XXX, and speaking of

---

[15] ANDERSON, p. 65.
[16] Quotation from *Opere Poetiche*, I. (Parigi, 1836), 55, tr. from ANDERSON.
[17] *Opere Poetiche*, I, 67.
[18] *Prose*, XXIX.

all that Beatrice is, that *nove* means "a new thing, that is, a miracle, whose root was solely in the Trinity".[19] Sadly for Dante, it is only after Beatrice's death that he is able at once both to refer her fully to the Love of God, where she resides, and to love first the God of Love who led him through her to Himself. His "memory restored" (Sonnet XVIII), a new spirit is born within him, and he here joins those who understand that this chapter of their present life in the world is not their true country, and who thus become pilgrims in search of a better understanding of Love. These *romei* are the ones to whom he addresses his poem.[20] The *New Life* is thus, as autobiography, witness to a conversion, to a transformation through Love, and it is understood through its application of the witness of The Book of God's Words (the Bible) to the Book of Memory (God's unfolding creation as discovered in human experience). That creation is a process and not a state is thus made most clear in the poem: the plot of history is simply a movement from creation through disintegration to a new creation and ultimately to creation reinformed. When the structure of personal experience is made conformable to the design of the Author of history, then Love's new creation may bear fruit in a personal re-creation, here also the re-creation of Dante's poems. Elsewhere, in the *Paradiso*, Dante will show us that the full blessedness of Beatrice is but partially seen, to be made known when, as the nereid on the other side of Death's baptism, she welcomes her pilgrim into that place where all faces are turned to gaze "in rapture on the face of Him 'who is *beatrice* (blessed) throughout all ages' ".[21] Accordingly, as Professor Freccero shows us, that poem's ultimate reference turns us toward that historical and ultimate ingathering of all chapters in the Book of Memory, those lives and poems whose singular and collective meaning will become clear in the light of our Author's own last chapter, his reading and judgement from that "other text" to which all human poems in time's anthology have been the privilege of a diverse and present gloss (*Paradiso* XXXIII,85-   ). Beatrice emerges in a new perspective: she herself is not the goal of the pilgrims quest for happiness, but when rightly "referred" she can help to lead him there.

IV. — THE IDEA OF A BOOK

We are reminded that one of the most striking witnesses to the non-monolithic character of Christian thought is contained in the literary character of its chief text. For the Bible is not an ostensible *summa*, the product of the thought of one human author, but is itself an *anthology*. The tremendous diversity in temperament and culture of its writers spans a period of something more than one thousand years, and subsequent Christian tradition has usually valued the diversity and richness of perspective on the Bible's overall structure which has been thereby obtained. Writ large, this

---

[19] See the translation in ANDERSON, p. 90. Cf. Professor PECK's essay on Number, which follows.

[20] *Romei* are, literally, "pilgrims to Rome" — cf. 'Romeo'.

[21] The last line of the *Vita Nuova*.

diversity is an illustration of one of the Bible's most common themes, one which pertains much to medieval literature and art. This theme is the integration of creation, that is, of the creation which is still being finished. Its metaphors in Biblical literature are almost always simple creational figures: "I am the vine, you are the branches" (John 15:5), or Paul's extended model for the Christian community (in Cor. 12:12 ff.) in which the community is seen as a human body with diverse but complementary and unified members.

From each of these metaphors emerge two principles, analogous to our early points about optimism about learning and *reference*. The first of these is that one consequence of our collective middleness and existential realization of fallen order is made known in the variety of imperfections that constitute the community of life. Also, because of the plenitude and complementarity of creation, life offers a lot of sheer physical diversity. Chaucer's "sondry folk" from the *Canterbury Tales* provide us with a memorable plenitude of illustrations — folk who, in the way of the world, find themselves on the road, at an inn, "by aventure", by chance, and who try to form a community, a common body. Clearly some of these characters are much less "perfected" than others. Yet all are heading toward a place of true communion, of the ingathering and sanctification (making whole) of their diversity, and this sense of an ultimate ingathering produces both an acceptance (e.g. for the Miller) and an affectionate good humour (e.g. toward the Wife of Bath) which is one of the most attractive characteristics of Christian thought in the Middle Ages. A practical rejoinder to the popular modern misconception that medieval Christian thought avoided the body for the sake of the spirit is found even in the names people lived with, quite contentedly, until after what we call the Enlightenment.[22] That people could and did live with names like Letcher, Gotobed, Grosseteste, Pryketayle, Clawcunte, Cunteles and Shakespeare suggests an attitude of acceptance for the body and the often humorous aspects of some of its members that utterly escapes the prurience and self-preoccupation of our own popular culture.[23] Medieval thought loves the diversity of creation, including human creation, and it is not prompted to scorn any member.

Not that medieval Christian thought did not find some members of their inevitable antics funny. It did. In fact, the grostesquerie and foolishness of sin were usually found to be funny.[24] But the perspective on humour was not a modern one, such as from "enlightenment" satirical writing down to the present has tended to acquire its sense of humorous incongruity from a sense of the self as superior to or distant from the object of humour. Medieval humour is based upon a sense of identification. The laughter is a

---

[22] Percy Hide REANEY, *The Origin of English Surnames* (New York, 1967), 289-95.

[23] See the excellent article by Russell A. PECK, "Public Myth and Private Dream", *PMLA*, 90 (1975), 461-68.

[24] D.W. ROBERTSON, Jr., *A Preface to Chaucer* (Princeton: Princeton University Press, 1963), 89, et seq.

laughter with, not at, and it arises because the one who laughs does so knowing that he shares in laughter his like propensities for laughable behavior. There is a sense, therefore, in which Chaucer's pilgrims laugh themselves (and the reader) into a more perfect reconciliation.

But medieval humour is based also on reference. Reconciliation is made possible by the fact that the standard against which the incongruity is measured is not the otherness of any individual observer: it is the perfection of God's original and new creation against which *all* observers are measured and found incongruous. Found in the middle together, in such a world we acknowledge our humorous (or not so humorous) imperfections, and travel through love and understanding toward the end of the story, where these social and literary problems of the One and the Many are resolved by our Author: in Biblical terms, "In my Father's house [one, and the book's ending] are *many* mansions [provisions for creation's diversity] — if it were not so I would have told you" (John 14:6); in Chaucer's terms:

> Then shall men understonde.... and after the word of Jhesu Crist, it is in the endeless bliss of hevene.... there as is the blisful companye that rejoysen hem evermo, everich of otheres joye, ther as the body of man, that whilom was foul and derk, is more cleer than the sonne; ther as the body, that whilom was syk, freele, and fieble, and mortal, is inmortal, and so strong and so hool that no thing apeyren it; ther as ne is neither hunger, thurst ne coold, but every soule replenyssed with the sighte of the parfit knowynge of God.[25]

That is, the model for integration derives its integrity from acknowledgement of its reference to an ultimate Authorial Design.

For a medieval writer, the patterns of creation, especially those patterns within man himself, ideally reflect the mind of the Creator. Happily, this enables him to learn about both God and creation at the same time. For Augustine the *universe*, that is, all created things which turn toward the One (*unus + versus*) is like "a great book", to be read and studied.[26] As St. Bonaventure will explain it again eight centuries later:

> The whole world is a shadow, a way, and a trace; a *book* with writing front and back. Indeed, in every creature there is a refulgence of the divine exemplar, but mixed with darkness; hence it resembles some kind of opacity combined with light. Also, it is a way leading to the exemplar. As you notice a ray of light coming in through a window is coloured according to the shades of different panes, so the divine ray shines differently in each creature and in the various properties.... Is is a trace of God's wisdom. Wherefore the creature exists only as a kind of imitation of God's wisdom, as certain plastic representation of it. And for all these reasons, it is a kind of book *written.... without.*[27] [my italics]

Creation is a book — the Book of God's Works. History (personal or

---

[25] *Parson's Tale*, 1075-80 (ed. FISHER, p. 396).

[26] Sermon on Matt. 11:25, 26 — in *Selected Sermons of St. Augustine*, ed. Quincy HOWE, Jr. (New York: Holt, Reinhart and Winston, 1966), 224.

[27] BONAVENTURE, *Hexämeron: Collations on the Six Days*, Coll. 12, par. 14, in *The Works of Bonaventure*, trans. Jose DE VINCK (Paterson, N.J.: St. Anthony Guild Press, 1970), V. 179.

III.   "St. Augustine vs. Felicianus"

Augustine debates with Felicianus in the *theatrum* of this world, while Felicianus' book has as its reference his own authorship. (Thus he points to himself.) Augustine's posture indicates both his own and a higher *auctoritas*. With two fingers, Augustine makes the case for authority on the grounds that his own words inhere in the higher truth of the Word, the uncreated logos incarnated in Christ and translated in His Book. Christ's hand points upward in the traditional reference, with two fingers side by side indicating the ultimate unity of divine Truth: "Verily, verily I say unto you...."

universal) is a book — the Book of Memory. Added to this is Scripture — the anthology — the Book of God's Word. Wherever in Christian thought men write books about personal learning, about coming to understanding or to love, these metaphors are usually implicitly or even explicitly present. Professor Grant reminds us that in Book VIII of Augustine's *Confessions* — the famous conversion chapter — Augustine puts off the old man and takes on the new in a garden, and through the medium of a book understood in reference to the Book of Creation, affirms his middleness and the authority of Creation's Author. Here Augustine combines the advantage of the "book written *without*" with God's Book to produce his own book — a book "written within". The model, itself biblical (cf. Isaiah, John, Revelation), is foundational to the structure of medieval Christian epistemology — indeed to all Christian thought. It is the criteria of reference for every other book. (Plate III)

From a modern perspective, the limitations of such a system are not inconsiderable. For one thing, we may be irritated by it in a way at once complementary but opposite to the young Augustine. That anyone should suggest that full meaning shall remain hidden until revelation of an ending which is not of our own device might seem to us, as moderns, the real provocation proposed by the Book. But the Christian view of history is a view of history with a definite conclusion. It sees both beginning and ending as beyond our empirical grasp — for their comprehension we are subject to our need for a joining device, something which can knit each middle chapter into the sense of the whole unfolding book. The notion that "Men perish because they cannot join the beginning with the end," for Christian thought in the Middle Ages as well as for certain Greeks, describes a critical problem in epistemology.[28] Its ultimate solution in medieval thought is concisely set out for the reader in the last book of the Bible. The conjoiner is not just the complete narrative of the great "book that had writing on back and front" (Rev. 5:1) but the word of the One who dares to read it — the Author himself — who in the opening words of St. John the Divine, as the closing, proclaims "I am the Alpha and the Omega.... who is, who was, and who is to come, the Almighty" (Rev. 1:8). That is, the ending is seen to be really an ingathering of every thing, even the original beginning. Its interim appreciation is the principle of reference for understanding to the Great Book — a principle that makes history and creation alike more readable.

Dante's *Vita Nuova* ends, not untypically, on a tantalizing note — with allusions to a miraculous vision which binds Dante to silence and to a life of study leading to translations of such vision as he has been granted. But the full vision itself is withheld. This restraint, however, does not prevent us from seeing in his poem a genuine integrity. On the one level, while conclusion can be anticipated, we find that it can never be fully "imagined". On the other, the value of the referential epistemology is that

---

[28] It is there, of course, in Hebrew thought as well — cf. Isaiah 46:10.

even though we see only in part, and not in whole, we may come to see truly. There are few attempts to paint paradise in the right panel of medieval triptychs — that vision remains mysteriously poised beyond the farthest reaches of the imagination, something which may not be discovered, but rather, is to be *revealed*: "Eye hath not seen, nor ear heard, nor hath it entered into the mind of man all that God has prepared for those who love him" (I Cor. 2:9). For the medieval Christian thinker, the total meaning of history remains inaccessible to the limitation of our understanding. Yet for an Augustine or a Dante the true meaning of history has been already made known, from Creation to New Creation, and thus it may be studied and responded to with joy, until, as in the words of Isaiah (34:4) and Revelation (5:14) "the heavens shall be folded up like a book."

The referential model thus bears by design a timeless aspect, and indeed it retains a truly amazing vigour throughout all of what we think of as the Middle Ages, right up until the 15th century. Then, and only then, does an increasing focus on things seen for themselves obscure the old relationship, and ideals in the mind begin to be absorbed among the objects of creation.

D.L.J.

I

CREATION AND CREATIVITY

There is yet another kind of person who reads in books that he may find God. But the very countenance of creation is a great book. Behold, examine, and read this book from top to bottom. God did not make letters of ink by which you might know him. He placed before you eyes all that he has made. Why do you seek greater testimony?

St. AUGUSTINE, *Sermon on Matthew 11:25, 26.*

The whole world is…. a book with writing front and back.

ST. BONAVENTURE, *Hexämeron*, XII, 14.

Redeeming the Time: The *Confessions* of St. Augustine

PATRICK GRANT

St. Augustine of Hippo was born in 354 and died in 430. A generation before his birth, in the year 324, Constantine had become sole emperor, and, for the first time, the Roman empire was officially Christian. Yet by the year 410, a generation before Augustine's death, Alaric and his Visigoths had sacked Rome, and in the year 430 the Vandals had set siege to the African seaport town of Hippo from where Augustine, as bishop, administered his see. In that same year, in the town of Hippo, Augustine died.

The prospect of a mighty Roman empire thus recently emerged (officially at least) into the era of grace and now so promptly taken over again by pagans caused some plain difficulties for the Christians, St. Augustine among them, who were convinced of a benevolent design in God's providence. Certainly the burden of interpreting such events on the grand scale remains evident throughout Augustine's writings, and even though he engaged with unusual perceptiveness the intimate problems of salvation he always did so in the context of challenges dictated by larger political events of his day. Augustine's career is consequently often charted in terms of the three main controversies, the timely challenges from the arena of contemporary history, through which his life and work evolved.[1] The first dealt with the Manichaeans (from about 387-400), the second with the Donatists (400-412), and the third with the Pelagians (412-430).[2]

It is important to see the *Confessions* in this general context, because although the book essentially recounts the story of Augustine's early life up to his conversion, it also reflects strongly his special concern with the Manichaean heresy during the time when he was writing (about the year 397). So, for example, there is a certain preoccupation in the *Confessions* with the abstract question of the nature of evil, for the Manichaeans had suggested an unorthodox dualism of two eternal and basically opposed metaphysical principles, unalterably good and bad. There is also a strong Neo-Platonist flavour, because Augustine had found especially in the Neo-Platonists an effective means of rebuking these Manichaean claims. We should therefore not lose sight of the fact that contemporary events remain

---

[1] See especially Gerald BONNER, *St. Augustine of Hippo, Life and Controversies* (London, 1963); Peter BROWN, *Augustine of Hippo: A Biography* (Berkeley, 1967).
[2] These, and the following approximate dates relating to Donatism and Pelagianism, are from Henri MARROU, *Saint Augustin et l'augustinisme* (Paris, 1955), p. 50.

very important even in the *Confessions*, where Augustine first of all tells us a fascinating and particular human story.

The account begins with the author considering his infancy, but admitting that he cannot remember anything of it. Rather, he reconstructs his earliest years from observations of other infants, noting that selfish greed and envy afflict even babies (I,vii,11). He then tells of his boyhood and early schooling at Thagaste and the neighboring town of Madauros, and how he found sinful delight in going to "vain shows" (I,xvii,30),[4] how he thieved food out of pure greed from the cellar of his parents' house, and how he lorded it over his companions "by vain desire for pre-eminence" (I,xvii,30). When he turned sixteen, he says, "the madness of lust.... took rule over me" (II,ii,3), and he fell into bad ways with girls. Then, the event everybody remembers, he recalls robbing an orchard of pears, and flinging the unripe fruit to hogs (II,iv,9). The story continues by recounting Augustine's wanderings as a student and teacher through the Middle East and Italy, telling of his eventual conversion and reconciliation with his mother before her death at Ostia, and ending with Book IX. Book X then provides a treatise on memory which develops into an extended examination by the author of his own conscience under the threefold heading of *"lust of the flesh, lust of the eyes, and ambition of the world"* (X,xxx,41).[3] Books XI and XII are an elaborate examination of the first chapter of Genesis, and contain an equally elaborate meditation on the nature of time. Book XIII, the last book, contains a further examination of Genesis, and develops into a prophetic statement on the church in the world.

The story of the *Confessions* is of course interesting at face value, yet its unity is not at all obvious. Those last four books comprise almost half of the whole work, and there have been many, sometimes odd, suggestions about what Augustine intended by this kind of structure. Perhaps the verb *confiteri* (to confess)[4] provides the clue. Perhaps the book is a sacrifice of praise applied to three topics corresponding to main divisions in the work.[5] Perhaps "pilgrimage" is the key motif,[6] or perhaps Augustine was adapting a catechetical method outlined in his *On Catechising the Uninstructed*.[7]

---

[3] All quotations are taken from The *"Confessions"* of St. Augustine, trans. E.B. Pusey (London, 1907). The translation is, as John J. O'Meara points out, not altogether satisfactory, "but it is difficult not to prefer it to others of more recent date, and for many it has the charm of an Authorized Version." [The Young Augustine (London, 1954), p. ix.]

[4] O'Meara, *The Young Augustine*, pp. 2-3; Bonner, *Life and Controversies*, p. 48.

[5] J. Stiglmayr, *Das Werk der augustinischen Konfessionen mit einem Opfergelübde besiegelt*, in Zietschrift für Aszese und Mystik, V. (1930); and *Zum Aufbau der Confessiones des hl. Augustin*, in Scholastik, VII (1932), pp. 386-403.

[6] Robert J. O'Connell, *St. Augustine's Confessions, The Odyssey of Soul* (Harvard, 1969), pp. 11-12.

[7] M. Wundt, *Augustins Konfessionen*, in Zietschrift für die neutestamentliche Wissenschaft, 22 (1923), 185. Wundt's idea is developed by P. Courcelle, *Recherches sur les Confessions de saint Augustin* (Paris, 1950), pp. 20-26. Courcelle's opinions that the most important part of the *Confessions* was to be the commentary on Genesis, that the autobiographical section ran away with the author, and that Book X was inserted at a later date at the request of readers, are dealt with by O'Meara, *The Young Augustine*, pp. 14-17.

Perhaps it is just a badly made book.[8] But whatever their point of view,[9] most critics agree that Augustine approaches his story in a very deliberate and artificial manner. It is not simply autobiography. Writing after the event, he chooses details carefully selected to demonstrate a total theory of man in relation to providence, and the story is thus not wholly a personal history; it is in large part also typical.[10] In this concern to make timely narrative embody such universal significance Augustine consequently leaves out numerous particular details which a biographer today would deem essential. He never tells us, for example, the name of the concubine who was the mother of his child, or of the dear friend whose death moved him so much in Book IV. The symbolic signifiance of his mistress as a certain type of woman, and of friendship as a certain kind of personal encounter have become the important thing.

All this naturally raises questions about the validity of the book as autobiography at all. Perhaps the whole work is a fictitious pastiche of typically edifying situations based in only the loosest way on fact. At the end of the nineteenth century critical fashion claimed for the *Confessions* (as it did for much ancient literature) that the historical truth had indeed been heavily written over. The debate was long and involved, but today, most scholars agree that the story is factual enough, even though the selection and interpretation of the events is wrought from the point of view of their symbolic signifiance. The point of Augustine's "selection" is simply this: events can have different meanings at different times. There may be a difference between their significance as they actually happen, and as they are recollected and judged. The question of memory, therefore, in relation to time becomes one of the most important themes, and a realization of this point should satisfy critics who are disturbed, for instance, by the intensity of Augustine's self-recrimination concerning the theft of pears. The event itself does not cause the recrimination so much as the judgement on what the event, in retrospect, signifies, and whereby a providential implication is disclosed.

Certainly one of the most important things that Augustine wants to convince us of throughout the *Confessions* is that God's guiding hand was there from the beginning, even in the author's utmost foolishness. Yet at the same time he wants to recreate the problems as he encountered them, so that they will be problems for us, the readers, as well, and we will be drawn into the work and into Augustine's pilgrimage, which in a sense will become our pilgrimage too. The very first words of the *Confessions* are a prayer which puts God at the center of the action:

> Great art Thou, O Lord, and greatly to be praised; great is Thy power, and Thy wisdom infinite. (I,i,1)

---

[8] O'MEARA, *The Young Augustine*, p. 13.

[9] There are useful summaries of the problem and of critical reaction to it in O'CONNELL, *Confessions*, pp. 3ff.; O'MEARA, *The Young Augustine*, pp. 13 ff.; and COURCELLE, *Recherches*, pp. 21 ff.

[10] COURCELLE, *Recherches*, pp. 21 ff.; O'MEARA, *The Young Augustine*, p. 18.

But God is described soon after in the following terms:

> Most merciful, yet most just; most hidden, yet most present; most beautiful yet most strong; stable, yet incomprehensible; unchangeable, yet all-changing; never new, never old. (I,iv,4)

The presence that Augustine praises here is paradoxical, and God is represented in terms we cannot understand. We are assured of his presence, but we are invited to be baffled by the fact. We share Augustine's knowledge as author and bishop that God is present, yet also the point of view of the sinner who does not at all see God's presence in the events as they occur in time.

Indeed as Book I continues it is difficult to see what God's presence has to do specifically with the particular events in the story — for instance, the gluttony of little babies, the delight in "vain shows", the desire for pre-eminence in school, or the stealing of the pears. But the answer is there even though we only discover it clearly when we look back. Recall the threefold examination of conscience in Book X under the headings of "lust of the flesh, lust of the eyes, and ambition of the world." These headings correspond to the sins of concupiscence, curiosity, and pride, and as Augustine says succinctly in his commentary on Psalm 8, "these three sorts of vices, the pleasure of the flesh, and pride, and curiosity, comprise all sins."[12] Now we can reconsider why Augustine tells us what he does about his boyhood. The gluttonous baby, the boy who raids the cellar, and the incontinent youth are examples of concupiscence. The boy so taken with stage plays and spectacles exemplifies the sin of curiosity. The envious child and the arrogant schoolboy are clearly proud. The theft of pears, which to some has seemed disproportionately emphasized, is now seen to warrant that emphasis because this sin, if properly understood, represents the mystery of iniquity in general (II,viii,16), thus encompassing the other three types of transgression. That the sin was trivial and motiveless makes it more appalling. It is the archetype of all sin, a pointless theft of fruit from a garden.

Now all this is not terribly obvious, especially to the modern reader, but the plan is there, and ought to become unmistakable from the vantage point of Book X. In retrospect, we might say, not only do we, the readers, see the earlier events of the story in an increasingly clear light, but Augustine's own recollection of those events has revealed their significance. The memory of events in past time from the point of view of present regeneration reveals that God has always had an eternal plan for the individual (or everyman) in the larger scheme of history. God's eternal plan

---

[11] The crucial point is the apparent difference between the dialogue written at Cassiciacum in 386, just after Augustine's conversion, and the account of the conversion itself. The *Contra Academicos, Beata Vita*, and *De Ordine* show a philosophic detachment which is quite different from the spirituality of the *Confessions*, Books VIII and IX. For a useful summary of the debate, see BONNER, *Life and Controversies*, p. 42 ff.; J.J. O'MEARA, "Augustine and Neo-Platonism," in *Recherches augustiniennes*, I (Paris, 1958), 91-111.

[12] Translated by PUSEY, *The Confessions*, p. 229, note 2.

is what redeems the time, and we can thus also appreciate why Augustine engages in that peculiar examination of memory in Book X as a preface to the threefold examination of conscience: through memory the meaning of time is discovered.

The *Confessions* is full of details which prepare us for the important discussion of memory. Early in the story, for example, a host of leading questions are deliberately left up in the air simply to provoke our curiosity. "But what speak I of these things?" (IV,vi,11); "What is it to me that my declamation was applauded above so many of my own age and class? Is not all this smoke and wind?" (I,xvii,27). The point of view is very complex here. The questions are not at all unimportant, though the answers to them cannot be made too clear so early in the work. Only by appreciating fully the selective power of memory, as we do in Book X, do we come to understand how the deeds of an obscure past can vivify and inform the present. We are thus led easily to the ensuing examination of conscience itself, for the threefold heading under which it is conducted (concupiscence, curiosity and pride) corresponds in turn to the three main faculties of man's mind. For Augustine, man has a higher reason (*sapientia*), a lower reason (*scientia*), and senses (*sensualis animae motus*).[13] It follows that the sin against higher reason is pride, against the lower reason is curiosity, and against the senses is concupiscence. And since the creation of the human individual involves also by implication the meaning of the entire creation, this constitution of man's mind is reflected in the heavens and in the earth:

> And let the day, lightened by the sun, utter unto day, speech of wisdom (*sapientiae*); and night, shining with the moon, shew unto night, the word of knowledge (*scientiae*).... Let the sea also conceive and bring forth your works; and let the waters bring forth the moving creature that hath life. (XIII,xix,25-xx,26)

The lower animals themselves are a book wherein man can read the structure of his consciousness as well as his sinfulness:

> Contain yourselves from the ungovernment wildness of pride, the sluggish voluptuousness of luxury, and the false name of knowledge: that so the wild beasts may be tamed, the cattle broken to the yoke, the serpents, harmless. For these be the motions of our mind under an allegory; that is to say, the hautiness of pride, the delight of lust, and the poison of curiosity, are the motions of a dead soul. (XIII,xxi,30)

Man thus sees himself symbolically in the heavens above him as in the earth beneath him, and it should now become more clear why Augustine expends so much effort in those final books on an exposition of Genesis, for the young man's particular story leads him inevitably, as we see, to enquire after the meaning of the whole temporal creation, an event related in Christian revelation especially by Genesis I. Here we should recall again Augustine's preoccupation with the Manichaen heresy which had both rejected the validity of the Old Testament revelation and also denounced the physical world as evil. By using the opening chapter of Genesis Augustine is able not only to expound his own psychological theory (that man's mind is

---

[13] *De Trinitate*. XIII.3.4.

reflected in creation), but to confirm also the orthodox Christian teaching on creation against the Manichaean heretics. Such considerations, partly extrinsic and partly internal, can do something to explain how the last four books on memory, time and Genesis contribute to Augustine's plan. Yet all depends on our clear acknowledgement that these books function not as a logical extension, but as a thematic or spiritual amplification of the autobiography.

It is customary to point out that the Latin verb *confiteri* from which Augustine takes his title has also a thematic significance, for it too encompasses a threefold significance which in turn relates to the author's concern for time. *Confiteri* denotes not only the admission or confession of past sins, but also the confession of faith and confession of praise,[14] and Augustine clearly and ubiquitously uses the word in all these distinct senses. ["Thou.... art merciful to their sins who confess" (III,viii,16); "I will now declare and confess unto Thy name" (VIII,vi,13); "Thou commandest me to praise Thee in these things, to confess unto Thee" (I,vii,12).] Given what we have already established about the importance of memory, time, and eternity, we might now suggest that the confession of past sins corresponds to the first nine books, the memory of Augustine's past life up to his conversion.[15] The confession of faith corresponds to the present examination of conscience in Book X. And the confession of praise looks to a future of eternal rest, for the promise of rest and the intuition of eternity are stressed throughout the concluding chapters. Thus we have a journey not only of a young man through the Middle East and Mediterranean in search of salvation, but a journey from past to present to future, through the divisions of time to eternity. Yet both journeys turn out in the end the same: the young man wanders on his particular way in sinfulness through time which, in the larger arena, is a condition of fallen humanity itself and of the history which human civilization must endure as a prologue to the consummation of eternity. The soul, "whose pilgrimage is made long and far away," is fallen into "changeableness of times" (XII,13), and man, both as individual and species, must return to the timeless condition from which he is fallen. His times must be recollected to be redeemed.

Redemption, however, depends on conversion, and for Augustine *conversion* has the fairly precise meaning simply of "turning towards", as distinct from *aversion* or *preversion* which mean the opposite, "turning away." Consequently the young man, the sinful soul, having initially turned away from home, wanders and is lost in the multiplicity of times, until, by the grace of God, he is turned around and enabled to journey back. The wanderings of an Aeneas thus may culminate in the return of a prodigal son: "I wandered further from Thee, into more and more fruitless seed-plots of sorrows" (II,ii,2), until you "didst turn me round" (VIII,vii,16). Throughout the *Confessions* the Latin verb *vertere*, "to turn" (root of the English

---

[14] See O'MEARA, *The Young Augustine*, p. 2.
[15] Cf. O'CONNELL, *Confessions*, p. 7.

"convert"), is played with persistently, and is easy enough to catch in translation. Here is a description of some subversive students whom Augustine encounters during his stint as a teacher at Carthage:

> I.... was sometimes delighted with their friendship, whose doings I ever did abhor, i.e. their "subvertings," wherewith they wantonly persecuted the modesty of strangers.... What then could they be more truly called than "subverters?" themselves subverted and altogether perverted first. (III,iii,6)

The play on "vertere" is as obvious in Latin as in English and shows something of the rhetorical artifice of which Augustine the orator was fond. But again, even this seemingly specific recollection of student radicalism which, when we read it for the first time seems simply part of the story of events, turns out also to have a significance within the theological scheme of the *Confessions* because under the guise of word play it intimates the mysterious action of conversion concealed analogously in the multiplicity of time. Here are two more examples of the verb "vertere," which confirm Augustine's persistence on the motif of turning and bring me also to my next main point. At the beginning of Book II, Augustine writes:

> I was torn piecemeal, while turned from Thee, the One Good, I lost myself among a multiplicity of things. (II,i,1)

And at the beginning of Book V:

> Thou alone art near, even to those that remove far from Thee. Let them then be turned, and seek Thee.... Let them be turned, and seek Thee; and behold, Thou art there in their heart, in the heart of those that confess to Thee, and cast themselves upon Thee, and weep in Thy bosom, after all their rugged ways. Then dost Thou gently wipe away their tears, and they weep the more, and joy in weeping. (V,ii,2)

These examples illustrate clearly the different senses of turning (aversion and conversion), but they also describe the process according to quite different modes. The first passage derives from the Greeks; its meaning is metaphysical. Augustine turns from the "One Good" to enter a "shadowy" world of multiplicity, and this is the fall into time discussed in philosophical terms. The second, by contrast, is the turning of a human head to a comforting bosom, and the return of a wandering son to a kindly father whose care is almost maternal: "thou dost gently wipe away their tears, and they weep the more, and joy in weeping." The inspiration here is Biblical rather than philosophical, but the two examples together serve nicely to introduce the sophisticated quality of the synthesis at the heart of his *Confessions* and throughout his work between Neo-Platonist metaphysics and Hebrew religion.

There has been controversy about which of the Greeks Augustine had read, but modern opinion generally agrees upon some of Plotinus's *Enneads*, particularly *On Beauty*, and on some books of Porphyry, particularly *Return of the Soul*.[16] In these authors Augustine found an

---

[16] Key positions were established by W. THEILER, *Porphyrios und Augustin* (Halle, 1933), and P. HENRY, *Plotin et l'Occident* (Louvain, 1934). Theiler thinks that Augustine had read

admirable quality of spiritual elation as well as a sophisticated vocabulary which especially enabled him to reply, as I have pointed out, to the Manichaeans on the question of evil. Briefly, Augustine seized on the Neo-Platonist idea that evil is not a real substance, but an absence of perfection in a being. The following passage shows the alacrity with which he wielded the philosophical vocabulary which providence had provided him so effectively to rebuke his opponents:

> So long therefore as they [things] are, they are good: therefore whatsoever is, is good. That evil then which I sought, whence it is, is not any substance: for were it a substance, it should be good. For either it should be an incorruptible substance, and so a chief good: or a corruptible substance; which unless it were good, could not be corrupted.... Therefore are all things; because each is good, and altogether very good, because our God made all things very good. (VII,xii,18)

Although the philosophers thus helped to provide some important answers to serious problems, still, Neo-Platonism by itself was not enough wholly to effect Augustine's own conversion. The most intense part of the *Confessions* is in consequence Book VIII, when the Christian teachings of Bishop Ambrose on the Old Testament have cancelled out the Manichaean heresies of Bishop Faustus, and the Neo-Platonists have freed Augustine's mind of intellectual doubts arising from the problem of evil. He then discovers that although he knows all these answers he still cannot submit in a complete act of faith, for his will remains recalcitrant:

> Thus did my two wills, one new, and the other old, one carnal, the other spiritual, struggle within me; and by their discord, undid my soul. (VIII,v,10)

The final answer he finds is not in philosophy, but in a personal relationship which involves the whole man, intellect and will, and which is to be found uniquely in Jesus Christ who contains in himself both the transcendent Good of Plotinus and the particularity of an individual human nature.

As a Christian, Augustine's criticims of the Neo-Platonists centers simply on the fact that they do not know this mystery of incarnation: "that the Word was made flesh and dwelt among us," he writes, "I read not there" (VII,ix,14). In terms of the triadic sin, theirs is pride, and as one consequence the philosophers are ignorant that time is redeemed by the coming of Jesus in the fullness of time. By contrast, Christians in St. Paul's words will "walk circumspectly, not as fools, but as wise, redeeming the time" (Eph. 5:15-17), and commenting on this passage, Augustine enjoins, "let us *redeem the time*; because the days are evil,"[17] warning specifically that the good are persecuted not only by sticks and stones, but by the

---

only Porphyry; Henry that he had read only Plotinus. A useful summary is in O'MEARA, *The Young Augustine*, pp. 133 ff. The most notable recent contributions to the Neo-Platonist debate are Robert J. O'CONNELL'S two books, *The Confessions* and *St. Augustine's Early Theory of Man*, A.D. 386-391 (Harvard, 1968).

[17] Sermon CXVII, *On the Words of the Apostle, Ephes.V.*, "See that ye walk circumspectly, not as fools, but as wise, redeeming the time, because the days are evil," in A Library of the Fathers: *Homilies on the New Testament* (Oxford, 1845), II, 847.

example and "conversation" of false counsellors.[18] Because "perils from false brethren can never cease even unto the end of the world," the Christian must continually give himself over, personally and wholly, to Christ, and even "lose something of his own for redeeming the time."[19] Here Augustine makes clear that the sacrifice demanded by faith involves especially the renunciation of self-will and the aspirations to autonomy for which he suspects the philosophers. Moreover, the context of such faith is time itself, which, as long as humanity endures in the fallen state, will continue to provide the trials by which faith is to be tested. Thus, in accord with the second of our two "vertere" passages and with Augustine's insistence on the personally transforming nature of faith there runs through the *Confessions* a further set of non-philosophical and highly personal images which attempt to catch the sense in which conversion is less a matter of abstract reasoning than total relationship.

These images have been well described by one critic in terms of the Latin verb "fovere,"[20] which means "to care for," but has the added implication of "warming" or even "burning." "Fovere" conveys God's care of a little child, as a father or as a mother (or through a mother), protecting, nourishing, gentle, and sometimes cruel. It is also associated with the fire of charity, by which alone we can turn to our father's bosom. Examples are plentiful: "or what am I even at the best, but an infant sucking the milk Thou givest, and feeding upon Thee, the food that perisheth not?" (IV,i,1); "nor can man's hard-heartedness thrust back Thy hand.... and nothing can hide itself from Thy heat." Man in his human weariness must turn back to God for "refreshment and true strength" (V,i,1). Not surprisingly, a child directs Augustine to "take up and read" the passage of the Bible which finally effects his conversion. (The highly symbolic nature of this event, indeed, has led some critics to regard it as totally fictitious)[21]. Certainly, throughout the *Confessions*, the "fovere" motif of maternal-paternal care of the straying and wanting child is consistently set against the other passages impersonal metaphysics, often to the enormous enrichment of each, and indeed the best-known passages of the *Confessions* are perhaps those where the Neo-Platonist elation and the Biblical spirit actually converge. For instance:

> Oil poured below water, is raised above the water; water poured upon oil, sinks below the oil. They are urged by their own weights to seek their own places. When out of their

---

[18] *Ibid.*, p. 846.

[19] *Ibid.*, p. 848.

[20] O'CONNELL, *Confessions*, pp. 34-36.

[21] The most elaborate argument, subsequently defended in a series of articles, is that of COURCELLE, *Recherches*, pp. 190 ff. Courcelle claims that Augustine is using a) the commonplace literary motif of Heracles choosing between Virtue and Pleasure; b) a rhetorical debate between the Vanities and Continence; c) certain passages from Persius; d) the fig tree as a symbol for the shadow of sin, based on a figurative reading of John 1:47-50. A variant reading of the text "de vicina domo" as "de vinina domo" proves that the child is a voice within. The debate is usefully summarized in O'MEARA, *The Young Augustine*, pp. 182 ff.

order, they are restless; restored to order, they are at rest. My weight, is my love; thereby
I am borne, whithersoever I am borne. We are inflamed, by Thy Gift we are kindled; and
are carried upwards; we glow inwardly, and go forwards. We ascend Thy ways that be in
our heart, and sing a song of degrees; we glow inwardly with Thy fire, with Thy good
fire, and we go; because we go upwards to the peace of Jerusalem. (XIII,ix,10)

Christian charity, the personal gift of God which inflames us inwardly with
love, unites here in an inspired metaphor with the Neo-Platonist chain of
being and theory of weights whereby things tend towards their proper place.
It is appropriate that charity, as fire, should rise upwards, and through the
extraordinary combination of weight and love the total image is both cosmic
and at the same time intensely personal, moving as it does in terms of
conversion from the restlessness of the lower creation in time to the peace of
the eternal Jerusalem.

At its best the *Confessions* in this manner can continually hold up the
seemingly opaque and concrete events of Augustine's story and show them
transparent in the light of eternity. Yet in recounting one of the most
significant concrete relationships of his life, Augustine is often hard pressed
to achieve the transparency of symbolic writing he so clearly desires.
Monica, his mother, is one of his most important characters, but sometimes
it is not easy to reconcile her individual complexity with an obvious typical
significance. Although the treatment of his mother remains characteristic of
Augustine's symbolic method, some problems of the method itself become
obvious in his manner of dealing with her.

First of all, Monica is not idealized. At Milan she brings offerings of
food and drink to the martyrs' tombs and is rebuked by Ambrose for doing
so (VI,ii,2), and her attempt to engineer a marriage for her son is not at all
successful. Still, Monica obviously represents something of God's maternal
care of his children. This is true in an intimate way ("for neither my mother
nor my nurses stored their own breasts for me; but Thou didst bestow the
food of my infancy through them" (I,vi,7), just as, in a more general sense,
Monica is also something of the church, *mater ecclesia*, to whose bosom the
faithful must return. Thus Augustine writes of "the pious care of thy mother
and Thy Church, the mother of us all" (I,xi,17). Our faith should be in
"our spiritual mother, Thy Catholic Church" (VII,i,1). Again, the reunion
of Augustine and Monica, which is heavily stressed in Book IX and
culminates in the shared mystical vision at Ostia (IX,x,24ff.), stands as a
figurative reply to the spiritual superiority of the Neo-Platonists, whose way
of salvation Augustine had recently rejected. Only when Augustine has
found grace can he share again his mother's simple faith.[22] By contrast, for
example, Porphyry in his biography of Plotinus tells us that the master was
so ashamed of his body that he never revealed his parentage or origins.[23]
For Augustine the Christian attitude toward created nature is more positive,

---

[22] Cf. O'CONNELL, *The Confessions*, pp. 110 ff.
[23] PORPHYRY, *On the Life of Plotinus and the Arrangement of His Work*, in PLOTINUS, *The
Enneads*, trans., Stephen MACKENNA (London, 1969), p. 1.

and the point against the philosophers is well made by the long account of Christian fellowship with his mother.

One fairly obvious problem with all this suggestion and symbolism is simply its multivalency, but the confusion is much increased because Augustine's attitude towards his mother is so often itself plainly ambiguous. She loved him with (as the book everywhere attests) an intensity which on the individual psychological level threatened as much as precipitated his maturity, and the symbolic correlative for this deeply personal and ambivalent influence is consequently difficult for him to find. Augustine casts his line in many directions, but his uncertainty reflects in the very diversity of the symbolic lures he supplies to hook Monica securely to the scheme of his book. She remains elusive, yet there is a fascination too in her son's very ambivalence which we would not want to surrender but which would surely dissipate within a successful trite analogy of ectype to archetype.

There is a final, and most important theme, however, to which Monica also directs our attention, namely the psychology of human love which Augustine describes in one of the most significant distinctions of his entire theology as a choice between *caritas* and *cupiditas*.[24] These two loves are characteristically seen in relations with women. On the one hand is the concupiscible and ultimately selfish love of whores. On the other is the true love of God, selfless, which is seen reflected in a proper love of women. So Augustine loves his concubine in a wayward passion which is without understanding, and when his mother encourages him to send the concubine away, she wishes to turn him from *cupiditas* to *caritas*. At one point Augustine even beseeches God in the name of "our mother charity" (XIII,vi,7) and throughout the *Confessions* the charitable and loving care of Monica contrasts the unruly concupiscence of her wandering son "severed amid times," as he says, "whose order I know not" (XI,xxix,39).

The dealings between Monica and Augustine with regard to his unnamed concubine are, as generations of readers have complained, not altogether satisfactory, even despite the symbolic import, and this again reflects Augustine's ambivalence concerning his mother. Admittedly, putting away the concubine occurs at the nadir of his spiritual career, but the mixed motivations which seem to underlie the action are not squarely faced or resolved, even in retrospect. Still, the issues broached in these relationships remain some of the most significant of Augustine's thought: the cupidinous love of women represents fallenness itself and the condition of wandering into time and multiplicity; the love of women in charity with reference to God suggests the return to the father, to Jerusalem and eternity. As far as man is concerned, he therefore faces in one of two directions, either looking down, or looking up: he either loves God or he loves the world. He cannot love both, and is either faced towards Babylon or towards Jerusalem. His love is either charity or cupidity. He is either converted, and

---

[24] A most concise account occurs in *De Doctrina Christiana* III.X.16.

reaching towards his eternal home, or his face is turned away, and he wanders unredeemed in the multiplicity of times.

But it is also in history, in time, that man can find redemption. The second Adam, born into time, will redeem the sin of the first Adam, with which human history began. The mystery of all human sin (hinted at in the theft of pears) is contained in that first sin in the Garden of Eden, and man continues to bear it with him. Just as we have seen human nature endowed with higher reason, lower reason, and senses, so it has also in correspondence to these three elements a principle of Adam, Eve, and serpent. Man is a sensual creature, but he "is set over all irrational creatures" by "the power of reason and understanding" (*scientia* and *sapientia*):

> And as in his soul there is one power which has dominion by directing, another made subject, that it might obey; so was there for the man, [Adam] corporeally also, made a woman [Eve]. (XIII,xxxii,47)

In his book *On the Trinity*, Augustine pursues this parallel at some length and with more clarity than in the Confessions, telling us plainly that whenever the animal nature introduces to his thinking (*scientia*) some inducement to enjoy itself without referral to the higher reason (*sapientia*) the "serpent discourses with the woman. And to consent to this allurement is to eat of the forbidden tree." [25] In this first sin in the Garden of Eden, every subsequent human sin is therefore contained, and as a result man suffers death, being thrust forth into history and fallen time. Yet just as the first Adam is redeemed by the second, by God born into time, so everyman may be redeemed from the dissipation of his own personal history, his biography, by God being born into his life.

Augustine's *Confessions*, then, is first of all a book of its times, not only in terms of the general history of the period, but of the timely controversies to which the author addressed himself. As autobiography, the work clearly attempts to tell an actual story which occurred at a particular time and in special circumstances, but it contrives to do so in a way which will make clear also the timeless significance of what actually happened. The baffling construction of the *Confessions* is due mainly to the difficulty of combining the materials of current controversy with the recollected incidents and the conviction also of providential deliverance through conversion. An underpinning which provides a co-ordinating principle for such diversity, and which emerges only slowly but with increasing brightness as the work proceeds, is nothing less than an entire theory of man fallen by original sin into time, into history, and redeemed in the fullness of time, by the Son of God, the Word made flesh. Augustine's attitude is thus never far from that of St. Paul who asked of the Colossians that they pray "also for us, that God would open unto us a door of utterance, to speak the mystery of Christ": the word is made manifest by the grace of the Lord to his servants, and only with the Word in his heart may a man "walk in wisdom toward them that are without, redeeming the time" (Coloss. 4:3-5).

---

[25] *On the Trinity*, XII.xii, ed. Philip SCHAFF, *A Select Library of the Nicene and Post-Nicene Fathers of the Christian Church* (Buffalo, 1887), III, 162.

Dante's *Medusa:* Allegory and Autobiography

John FRECCERO

For St. Augustine, language provided the paradigm for all human understanding, for it seemed to derive timeless truth from an utterance in time. This mediation between time and eternity made language, the *word*, a perfect symbol of the relationship of God to the world. Christian reality was neither the Platonic dream of a disembodied logos, an intellectual reality totally divorced from the world, nor an unintelligible nightmare irredeemably lost *in* the world: it was rather, like syntax, time pressed into the service of eternity. History was the unfolding of God's word in time. The elements of history, men and events, were as syllables linked together, striving toward closure and significance, the end term which, in Christian language, was the Word made flesh. As a sentence derives meaning retrospectively from its last term, so process was to be understood only from the ending: death gave meaning to life and apocalypse gave meaning to all that went before until, in the words of Isaiah, "the heavens shall be folded together as a book" (34:4).

This linguistic metaphor, an example of what has been called "logocentrism," provides a basis for an understanding of Christian allegory. Men use signs to signify things, but God uses things to signify other things. To continue the metaphor, all of reality is God's book, of which allegory in the strict Christian sense is quite simply the syntax. Allegory is thus not a way of writing at all, but is rather a theory of history, the master code in a universe of signs where things both *are* and signify. From a naturalistic standpoint, we may say that the reinterpretation of past events in the light of a new and definitive event, the essence of allegorical interpretation, is a way of *reading* concrete events as though they were written down in a book, in which the ending casts its light on what went before. Far from being the enormously complicated machine imagined by some exegetes, Christian allegory is simply the sentence structure of God's past, present and future utterance to man.

In the medieval view, the essence of God's Book was revealed to man in the form of the Bible, a translation of God's syntax into the syntax of human discourse. The two "books" are therefore not the same, for the

---

¹ The word was coined by Jacques DERRIDA, *De la Grammatologie* (Paris, 1967).

Bible is quite literally a book, whose words signify things as do all words.
The uniqueness of the Bible, however, resided in the fact that the things it
signified, men and events, in turn signified other things (the men and events
of the New Testament) as though they themselves were signs. To put the
matter another way, men require words in order to signify, whereas God
"writes," so to speak, with men and things. The Bible communicates God's
meaning, His "writing," to man. From the standpoint of a non-believer, we
may say that the relationship of the Bible to Christian reality, the ideal
"book," was a feedback, a mirror image wherein it is impossible to
distinguish the reflector from the reflected. Whether the human discourse of
the Bible is a pale reflection in words of the nature of God, as Christians
believed, or whether God Himself is a metaphoric projection of the nature of
language, the literary interpreter remains within the realm of verbal
discourse without deciding its ontological status. Applying the principle of
what Kenneth Burke has called "logology,"[2] if reality is God's Book, this
may mean either that the totality to which the books of men aspire is a pale
simulachrum of the Divine totality, or that the very notion of God is a
reflection of the idea of a book as it might be imagined without the
mediation of time and space. In either case we remain in a linguistic world,
subtended by silence, not knowing whether it is the silence of Being or of
nothingness. All literature, for the Middle Ages, remains a present gloss on
an absent text or, in Dante's words, shadowy manifestations of the vision of
God's Book.[3] The rest is idolatry.

Strictly speaking, God's Book ends, as does the Bible, with the Christ
event, the fullness of time. The New Testament ends the message begun by
the Old and the message is definitive. Our time, the time between the
coming of Christ and the Apocalypse, was considered to be a kind of
waiting period during which the message given to men interpreted the hearts
of all men. The experience of Christ was expected to be recapitulated in the
lives of men by the conversion experience, what St. Paul referred to as the
death of the Old Man and the birth of the New. To return to the linguistic
metaphor, all literature, at least for the Augustinian Christian, was literary
"testament" of the application of the New Testament to life. So in Dante's
words, the poetic tradition extending from Homer to himself bore witness of
God's continuous glossing of the "Book of Memory," individual human
experience "chiosata da altro testo" — glossed by another text — until the
ending of time.[4] This gradual unfolding of the Word binds literature and
history together, until the time when, Augustine says, there will be no need
for words: "Justi et sancti .... fruuntur Verbo Dei sine lectione, sine
litteris."[5]

Autobiography, for the Christian, is thus the application of God's

[2] Kenneth BURKE, *The Rhetoric of Religion: Studies in Logology* (Boston, 1961),
introduction.
[3] *Paradiso* I, 22.
[4] *Inferno* XV, 88-90.
[5] Quoted by Maurice PONTET, *L'Exégèse de S. Augustin* (Paris, 1954), p. 96.

syntax, allegory, to one's own life, the "Book of Memory" glossed by "God's Book." In contemporary terms, it is an attempt to reduce Sartrian words (*les Mots*) to the Word (*le Verbe*). Augustine's *Confessions* in this respect is the first of a tradition that extends, however ironically, even to Sartre in our own day and that includes, perhaps most illustriously, the Dante of the *Vita Nuova* and of the *Divine Comedy*. The constant theme of Dante's literary effort, that he is simply a scribe copying down his Book of Memory in words, suggests a relationship between the poet's life and his work that is exactly analogous to the relationship of God's Book to the Bible: God's Book and the Book of Memory are metaphors — just as it is impossible to say whether God's presence is the reality of the Bible or the illusory projection of it, so it is impossible to say whether the conversion experience is the cause or the creature of the poem that we read. We have only words upon words, approaching the silence of the ending as a limit; the words, the exemplum, says Dante, must suffice for him to whom grace reserves the experience.

In professional Dante circles there is seemingly endless debate about the nature of Dante's allegory in the poem and the extent to which it reflects (or *imitates*, some have said) the allegory of the Bible. To what extent is his fiction not a fiction and how, in this respect, does his poem relate to other allegorical poetry of the Middle Ages?[6] The disagreement among scholars seems to suggest that the debate has reached an impasse and that perhaps more enlightenment is to be gained by a modern restatement. Thus far, I have outlined as succinctly as possible what seems to me a different approach to the problem. I should like to turn now to an instance of Dante's allegory in the poem in order to illustrate.

I have deliberately chosen what would appear to be unpromising ground. The Medusa passage of the *Inferno* would at first glance appear to be the purest example of sterile personification allegory thoroughly uncharacteristic of the kind of dramatic realism Erich Auerbach and others have led us to expect from a close analysis of Dante's text. In Canto IX, as the pilgrim and his guide are halted in their infernal descent by the fortified gates of the City of Dis, the three Furies appear at the embattlements and threaten the pilgrim with petrification:

> Con l'unghie si fendea ciascuna il petto
> Battiensi a palme e gridavan sì alto
> Ch'i' mi strinsi al poeta per sospetto.
> 'Venga Medusa, sì 'l farem di smalto,'
> Dicevan tutte riguardando in giuso:
> 'Mal non vengiammo in Teseo l'assalto.'

---

[6] The most useful bibliography may be found in Robert HOLLANDER, *Allegory in Dante's "Commedia"* (Princeton, 1969). Charles Singleton, whose by now classic thesis is that the poem is written according to the "Allegory of Theologians," had expressed the opinion that even the episode of the Medusa would, upon further study, reveal the Biblical nature of Dante's allegory. It is my hope that the present work bears out that opinion. See SINGLETON, *Dante Studies I: Commedia: Elements of Structure* (Cambridge, 1954), "Allegory".

'Volgiti in dietro e tien lo viso chiuso;
    Chè se il Gorgon si mostra, e tu 'l vedessi
    Nulla sarebbe del tornar mai suso.'
Così disse 'l maestro; ed elli stessi
    Mi volse, e non si tenne a le mie mani
    Che con le sue ancor non mi chiudessi.
O voi c'avete li 'ntelletti sani,
    Mirate la dottrina che s'asconde
    Sotto il velame de li versi strani.

[Each was tearing her breast with her nails. They were beating themselves with their hands and crying out so loudly that in fear I pressed close to the poet. "Let Medusa come and we'll turn him to stone," they all cried, looking downward. "Badly did we avenge the assault of Theseus." "Turn your back and keep your eyes shut; for should the Gorgon show herself and you see her, there would be no returning above." Thus said the master, and he himself turned me round, not trusting to my hands, and covered my face with his own hands as well. O you who have sound understanding, mark the doctrine that is hidden under the veil of the strange verses.]

The passage has proven to be both baffling and — because of the imperious address to the reader — somewhat embarrassing. Commentators are usually content to dismiss it as a vague sort of allegorism, not subject to certain interpretation, referring to some capital-letter vice or other and therefore of no great poetic importance. Others, like Erich Auerbach,[7] have recourse to the mythographic tradition extending back to Fulgentius, according to which Medusa would represent some kind of terror or, perhaps, according to a related tradition, *oblivio*, as described by the second Vatican mythographer. The difficulty with such an approach is that it offers no way of rooting a background text in the poem. Medusa may well represent terror or *oblivio*; she may also represent despair, heresy, wrath, ignorance, malice, incontinence or idolatry, all of which have from time to time been suggested, yet none of which seem to possess that concreteness which Auerbach was later in his career to identify as peculiarly Dantesque.

The most startling thing about traditional efforts to discuss the passage is that they have missed what to a modern reader is most obvious about the Medusa whenever she makes her oneiric appearance: whatever the horror she represents to the male imagination, it is in some sense a sexual horror. From Freud and Ferenczy to the present, the Medusa has been a recurrent theme in psychoanalytic literature. In Dante criticism, we have been so aware of the need to insert the poem into its proper historic context, so wary of superimposing modern preoccupations upon a medieval poem, that we have been blind to the obvious. Nor would Dante have had to anticipate the findings of psychoanalysis to sense in the figure of the Medusa a sensual ambiguity, for ancient mythology already suggests that the threat is of that nature. It was precisely because of her feminine *beauty* that the Medusa came to be regarded as a horror. Whatever the interpretive context, the threat of the Medusa has a peculiar temporal dimension, an initial sensual

---

[7] Erich AUERBACH, *Dante: Poet of the Secular World*, trans. R. MANHEIM (Chicago, 1961), p. 188 n. 26.

fascination that then turns to horror. In the text itself, it would be difficult to imagine why Virgil does not trust the pilgrim's ability to shield his own eyes, were it not for a suggestion of initial fascination.

By themselves, these are mere suspicions, but there is an explicit reference in the text to suggest that the subject matter here is specifically erotic rather than abstractly moral. The previous assault of Theseus, mentioned by the Furies as in some way analogous to the pilgrim's attempted entry into the City of Dis, was virtually a sexual assault. Theseus descended into the underworld with his friend Pirithoüs in order to carry off Persephone and, unlike his hapless friend, was rescued by Hercules, the traditional exemplar of male virtue. The theme of the search for Persephone is not merely anecdotal, but is of some structural importance in the poem, for Dante himself is in a sense in search of a prelapsarian Persephone, an erotic innocence which he recaptures, at one remove, in his encounter with Matelda at the top of the Mountain of Purgatory:

> Tu mi fai rimembrar dove e qual era
> Proserpina nel tempo che perdette
> La madre lei ed ella primavera.

> [You remind me of where and what Persephone was in the time her mother lost her and she lost the spring.]

The two references to Persephone in the poem, the first implied and the second clearly stated, suggest that the figure of the Medusa and the encounter with Matelda are somehow coordinate. Whatever else Matelda may represent, the pastoral landscape and the erotic feelings of the pilgrim would seem to indicate the recapture, or near recapture, of a pastoral (and therefore *poetic*) innocence, a return to Eden after a long *askesis*. For the moment, I should like to suggest that the Medusa represents precisely the impediment to such a recapture. The search for Persephone in the fallen world and in the world of the *Inferno* is avenged by the Medusa, if the Furies have their way. Short of the Earthly Paradise, there would seem to be no erotic (or poetic) innocence.

A generation later, Geoffrey Chaucer was to use the Furies in a way that is quite consistent with my hypothesis about the passage in Canto IX. The invocation of *Troilus and Creseyde*, that bookish tale of woe, addresses the Furies, rather than the Muses, as the proper inspirers of the dark passion that is the subject of the *Romance*.[8] Indeed, the insistence on the Furies would seem to foreshadow the "anti-romance" quality of Chaucer's poem, a deliberate undercutting of a genre that had been the poet's own. The *Troilus* is in many ways a palinodic auto-critique: the language with which it begins, with its address to "Thesiphone.... cruwel Furie sorwynge," may even be an allusion to the passage under discussion here. Had it not been for our preconceptions about Dante's penchant for moralizing, interpreters would have found, both in Dante's text and in literary history, support for

---

[8] *Troilus and Criseyde*, I, 6-11.

what seems a reasonable hypothesis: the threat of the Medusa proffered by the Furies represents, in the pilgrim's askesis, a sensual fascination and potential entrapment, precluding all further progress. At the top of the Mountain of Purgatory, after the encounter with Matelda and the naming of the poet, Beatrice chastises the pilgrim for his former fascination and accuses him of having been petrified by "vanità": "io veggio te ne lo 'ntelletto fatto di pietra... s˜che t'abbaglia il lume del mio detto" — [I see that your intellect is turned to stone, so that the light of my speech dazzles you]. Thus, by a neat parallelism, Beatrice attributes Dante's interpretive obtuseness to his petrification — in short, to the fact that, like an obtuse reader of the Medusa passage, his *intelletto* is not yet *sano*, that he is unable to see the truth beneath the veil of her accusatory verses.

Once it is established that the episode exists as a dark counter-statement to the celebration of a poetic eros, it is perhaps easier to come up with the kind of poetic analogue that medievalists feel they need to bolster their interpretive self-confidence, a "source" of the kind that Dantists have been searching for in order to give the Medusa the specificity that is lacking in most moralising interpretations. Such a text is to be found, I believe, in the *Roman de la Rose*. Recent study has shown that the first step along the road of the poetic askesis that was to culminate in the *Divine Comedy* was Dante's poetic paraphrase in Italian of the *Roman de la Rose*. Chaucer too was too educated in love poetry by this poem, as were indeed a whole generation of poets.[9] The *Roman* was the quintessential type of which both the *Troilus* and, in a sense, the *Divine Comedy* are anti-types, *anti-romans*. It happens that the *Roman de la Rose* offers us a precise, if inverted, parallel of the action in Canto IX, an illusion, in Dante's view, of which the Medusa is the disillusioning reality.

At the ending of Jean de Meung's poem, as the lover is about to besiege the castle in what is one of the most scandalous episodes in Medieval Literature, an image is presented to him from the tower of the castle, a sculptured image far surpassing in beauty the image of Pygmalion, fired by Venus' arrow. Of great interest to us is that in some versions of the poem that might have been available to Dante, the image is contrasted for some fifty lines with the image of the Medusa:

> [Tel ymage n'ot mais en tour;
> Plus avient miracle entour
> Qu'onc n'avint entour Medusa...]
> Mais l'ymage dont ci vous conte
> Les vertux Medusa seurmonte,
> Qu'el ne sert pas de genz tuer,
> Ne d'eus faire en roche uer.
> Ceste de roche les remue,
> En leur forme les continue,
> Voire en meilleur que devant n'orent

---

[9] For Chaucer's translation of the *Roman*, see *The Works of Geoffrey Chaucer*, ed. F. N. ROBINSON (Boston, 1961), p. 564.

Ne qu'onques mais avoir ne poront.
Cela nuist et ceste profite,
Cele ocit, ceste resouscite,
Cele les eslevez mout grieve
Et ceste les grevez relieve;
Car qui de ceste s'aprochast
Et tout veist et tout touchast
S'il fust ainz en roche muez
Ou de son droit sen remuez,
Ja puis roche ne le tenist,
En son droit sen s'en revenist,
Si fust il a touz jours gueriz
De touz maus et de touz periz...[10]

[But the image of which I speak far surpasses the power of Medusa, for she neither killed men nor did she turn them to stone. Indeed, she rescued them from stone and restored them to manhood's form, even better than they were before. Medusa harms and this one profits men. Medusa kills and this one resuscitates; that one makes the light heavy and this one makes the heavy light. Whoever can approach, see and even touch this image, were he transmuted into stone before and not in his right senses, stone would no longer contain him. Recovering his previous strength, he would be forever cured of all evil and all harm.]

Langlois rejected this passage as an interpolation, although it is contained in several manuscripts, some of which are Florentine, dating from the XIIIth century. Whatever its authorship, it provides us with an extraordinary parallel to the action in Canto IX of the *Inferno*. It presents us with an ironically optimistic view of the power of Eros, a view of which Dante's Medusa seems the dark and reversed counter-image.

In the *Roman de la Rose*, the Medusa does not appear, any more than it does in the *Inferno*, but exists only as an anti-type of Venus's idol. The presence of mock-epic machinery in this erotomachia has a counterpart in the pointedly non-Christian fortifications of Dante's infernal city. Furthermore, petrification is described in this passage as analogous to the condition of one who is "de son droit sen remuez," much as it is in the *Comedy*. Finally, the insistence on the fact that this is a *sculptured* image and its proximity in the text to the *exemplum* of Pygmalion convey unmistakeably the sense in which this image is artifact, the work of an artist. Exactly the same impression is conveyed in Canto IX by the use of the word "smalto," stone that is *worked*,[11] suggesting that the threatened petrification of the pilgrim would, in a bizarre sense, amount to a work of infernal art. We shall see that these hints of an association between entrapment and art are not merely rhetorical but are rather part of a larger palinodic pattern in which the poet acknowledges the suggestive power of art and thereby vindicates his own. For the moment, we may say simply that Dante's Medusa is, so to speak, Venus's idol stripped of its ironic charm and seen, or almost seen, under the aspect of death.

---

[10] *Roman de la Rose*, ed. E. LANGLOIS (Paris, 1914), vol. V, p. 107. The interpolation occurs at vv. 20810-11.

[11] See the remarks on the word by C. S. SINGLETON, *The Divine Comedy: Inferno*, vol. 2, Commentary (Princeton, 1970), pp. 137-38.

Thus far, whatever the merit of my suggested reading of the threat of the Medusa, there can be little doubt that it remains in the realm of what Dante would have called the allegory of poets, a representational moralization. The example that the poet gives in the *Convivio* of the allegory of poets, a truth hidden under the veil of a beautiful lie, would seem to reinforce the impression. He quotes the fable of Orpheus moving rocks and trees with his song, by which we are to understand that "the wise man can move according to his will those who do not live according to knowledge and art, for those who do not live a rational life are indeed like stones."[12] Nonetheless, there remain some details which are worth further consideration. First of all, there seems to be inherent in the figure of the Medusa a kind of temporality, a curious diachronic quality. In the myth, for example, Medusa begins as a beautiful woman who later becomes a gorgon. Again, in the perhaps interpolated passage of the *Roman de la Rose*, the duality of the Medusa, at once fascinating and horrifying, is what evokes the negative comparison with the lover's idol. So too, as we have noticed, in Dante's text. If the Medusa were an unequivocal horror, what would account for the fact that the pilgrim requires Virgil's help to shield his eyes from the sight of her? The Medusa would rather seem to be a figure like the Siren of the *Purgatorio*, a stinking hag whom the pilgrim, under the influence of song, takes to be a ravishing beauty. Finally, if the passage of the *Roman de la Rose* is related to Dante's episode, the two stand in sharp symmetric contrast, a before-and-after relationship thoroughly reminiscent of the dialectic inherent in the myth.

It is for this temporal dimension of meaning that a simple abstraction of personification allegory seems least able to account. The allegory of poets, as Dante defines it, suggests a vertical movement, from the particularity of the text to the capital-letter quality that lies somehow above it and beyond, in some eternal world. The story of Medusa, however, both in its mythological form and in its literary expression, seems to stress historicity, a temporal change: before and after, then and now, the beauty of the lady changed to ugliness, fascination turned to horror. This horizontal dimension of significance seems to suggest a different allegorical mode.

In a very different connection, Paul De Man has observed that, among the Romantics, "the prevalence of allegory always corresponds to the unveiling of an authentically temporal destiny." Unlike the symbol, which is a spatial presence or coincidence of both signifier and signified, allegory "designates a distance with respect to its own origin," a temporal void separating the text from an ideal anterior significance, itself a kind of prior "text," which can never be reached since its essence is to be pure anteriority. For De Man, the secularized allegory of some of the Romantics renounces "the nostalgia and the desire to coincide [and] establishes its language in the void of this temporal distance." On the other hand, the celebration of the symbol in Romantic esthetics, at the expense of allegory,

---

[12] *Convivio*, II, I, 2-5.

bespeaks a deliberate self-mystification, an evasion of the authentic human destiny which, like its allegorical expression, is established in the temporal void.[13]

When we extend De Man's categories to an analysis of Christian allegory, we find that the yearning for a coincidence of signifier and signified, characteristic of allegorical interpretation, is not an infinite regression toward an ideal text forever out of reach, but rather finds its satisfaction in the Word made flesh, the ultimate coincidence of signifier and signified upon which all of Christian theology is founded. In other words, all allegory reveals a temporal dimension, but authentically Christian allegory surveys the temporal void retrospectively, apocalyptically, from a point of closure which is the Christ event, the utlimate significance of God's Book. The coincidence of the Logos with its expression in time is the *given*, which then serves to gloss all of the apparently heterogenous details of other expressions.At the same time, this perspective is privileged, for it can be gained only through an askesis analogous to Christ's, a death and resurrection. All poets may begin with the allegory of poets; the yearning for ultimate significance, if it is satisfied, transforms that search retrospectively into the allegory of theologians. If it is not satisfied, it runs the risk of idolatry, a worship of the man-made sign for its own sake. It is just such a threat that is posed by the Medusa.

In the figure of the Medusa, the temporality that we sense is not the yearning for a perfect representation of vice for which these verses would be the mere representation; the profusion of generic "solutions" to the crux testifies to the uselessness of such a search. Nor is the alternative to remain content with the letter, however, for the address to the reader clearly suggests that therein lies a critical petrification, a danger as immediate as that facing the pilgrim. I should like to suggest that the temporality we sense in the threat is rather the temporality of retrospection, of a danger narrowly averted, of a former illusion seen for what it is. Such a temporality is the essence of the descent in Hell.

Whatever its mythological ancestry, the pilgrim's catabasis is a kind of descent into the self, the medieval equivalent of antiquity's "know thyself." Such a journey is in fact a retrospective taking stock, a glance backward in memory from a totally new perspective. The perspective of the pilgrim is separated from the perspective of the poet by the span of memory, the "then" and "now" of the interpretive glance, two moments separated by conversion. Nostalgia, on such a journey, would on the contrary imply a continuity with a former self, the threat of no return. In connection with the Medusa, the text mentions clearly, not merely petrification, but *no return*, as if to suggest a threat of the past, a retrospective delectation, like that of Lot's wife. Such a temptation to evade an authentically temporal destiny

---

[13] Paul DE MAN, "The Rhetoric of Temporality," *Interpretation: Theory and Practice*, ed. C. S. SINGLETON (Baltimore, 1969), pp. 190-91.

faces St. Augustine just before his conversion, when his former mistresses seem to appear behind him, tempting him to turn and look at them, *respicere*, as they pluck at his fleshly garment.[14] In the medieval allegorization of the journey of Orpheus to the underworld, a similar significance is given to the irreparable loss of Eurydice. According to Guillaume de Conches, Orpheus's descent into the underworld represents the sage's effort to find himself, his Eurydice, and he is defeated by nostalgia for his own former sin.[15] At this point in his descent, the pilgrim faces a similar temptation: the Furies, a traditional representation of guilt and remorse, urge him to confront what is, in effect, his own past as poet. Dante did not have to read the *Roman de la Rose* in order to learn of a lady who turned her lovers to stone, for he had in fact celebrated such a lady in his *Rime Petrose*, the stony rhymes, written for the mysterious *Donna Pietra*. The temporality inherent in the representation of the Medusa is the novelistic dimension of meaning for which several other episodes in the poem are famous: the Dante who is, in retrospective judgment on the Dante who was, the duality that is resolved in the poem's ending.

The *Rime Petrose*, the dazzling virtuoso pieces of Dante's youth, celebrate a dark, violent passion for the "Stony Lady" whose hardness turns the poet, her lover, into a man of stone. In the survey of the progress of Dante's love and of his poetry from the *Vita Nuova* to the *Comedy*, the *Rime Petrose* constitutes a surd element; radically fragmentary, Contini has called them,[16] finding no place clearly identifiable in the poet's development. At one point in the *Purgatorio*, when Beatrice castigates the pilgrim for his infidelity, she seems to accuse him of a love for "vanità," a "pargoletta," a little girl, using precisely the same word that the poet has used somewhat disparagingly of his *Donna Pietra* in one of the *Rime*: The poet asks, what will become of him in springtime, when love rains down from heaven and only within him does frost remain? "Saranne quello ch'è d'un uom di marmo/ se in pargoletta fia per core un marmo" [I will be like a man of stone, if that little girl has a stony heart]. The recall in the *Purgatorio* of this word has given rise to endless speculation about the identity of the woman whom Dante denoted with the code-name of "Donna Pietra". Critics have been right, I think, to wish to see biography in the poem, but they have been incorrect to imagine that the words of the poem were simply vehicles for communicating true confessions. The biography of a poet, as poet, is his poetry, and it is in this sense that the *rime petrose* are present and relevant here. In the same poem that has given rise to speculation about the 'pargoletta" there appear some verses of potentially much greater significance. They describe a wintry scene in which the despairing lover seems to have lost his beloved forever. They should be compared with the *versi strani* of Canto IX:

---

[14] *Confessions* VIII, cap. xi.

[15] See John B. FRIEDMAN, *Orpheus in the Middle Ages* (Cambridge, 1970), pp. 104-9.

[16] Gianfranco CONTINI, "Introduction to Dante's *Rime*," in *Dante: Twentieth Century Views*, ed. J. FRECCERO (Englewood Cliffs, N.J., 1965), p. 36.

Versan le vene le fummifere acque
per li vapor che la terra ha nel ventre
che d'abisso li tira suso in *alto*;
onde cammino al bel giorno mi piacque
che ora è fatto rivo, e sarà mentre
che durerà del verno il grande *assalto*
la terra fa un suol che par di *smalto*
e l'acqua morta si converte in vetro...

Con l'unghie si fendea ciascuna il petto
Battiensi a palme e gridavan sì *alto*
Ch'i' mi strinsi al poeta per sospetto.
'Venga Medusa, sì 'l farem di *smalto*,'
Dicevan tutte rigurdando in giuso:
'Mal non vengianmo in Teseo l'*assalto*.'

[Streams pour forth their waters steaming for the heat that the earth contains within it, which brings them up from the abyss, so that the path I used to like in warmer weather has become a stream and so will remain while the assault of winter lasts. The earth is soil turned to stone and still water has become like glass...]

This description of a world without love, matching the poet's winter of the soul, contains exactly the rhyme words contained in Dante's description of the Medusa: *alto, assalto, smalto*, sibilants and *rime aspre* that might well qualify as the *versi strani* of the address to the reader. Thus, in a passage which threatens petrification, is recalled, in a reified, concrete way, precisely the poem that celebrated such a reification at the hands of a kind of Medusa. The words themselves reflect each other in such a way that they constitute a short-circuit across the temporal distance that separates the two works, a block that threatens to make further progress impossible.

The verses in the ninth canto of the *Inferno* are a reflection, quite literally, of the poet's former self. The threat is of literary self-satisfaction, a delectation of a former poetic virtuosity and an evasion of continued askesis. For the reader, the parallel threat is to refuse to see the allegory through the letter, to ignore the double-focus of the *versi strani*. The appearance of a recall to the *Rime Petrose* is an invitation to the reader to measure the distance that separates the *now* of the poet from the *then* of his *persona*; in the fiction of the poem, the Medusa is, like the Lady of Stone, no historic character at all, but the poet's own creation. Its threat is the threat of idolatry. In terms of mythological *exempla*, petrification by the Medusa is the real consequence of Pygmalion's folly.

The point is worth stressing. Ever since Augustine, the Middle Ages insisted upon the link between Eros and language, between the reaching out in desire for what mortals can never possess and the reaching out of language toward the significance of silence. To refuse to see in human desire an incompleteness that urges the soul on to transcendence is to remain within the realm of creatures, worshipping them as only the Creator was to be worshipped. Similarly, to refuse to see language and poetry as continual askesis, pointing beyond themselves, is to remain within the letter, treating it as an absolute devoid of the spirit which gives meaning to human discourse. The subject matter of love poetry is *poetry*, as much as it is love, and the reification of love is at the same time a reification of the words that celebrate that passion.[17]

---

[17] For the adaptation of Augustinian theology to the Medieval Love Lyric, see Frederick GOLDIN, *The Mirror of Narcissus in the Courtly Love Lyric* (Ithaca, 1967), pp. 207ff.

The search for the self which is the quest of the poet can only be accomplished through the mediation of the imagination, the Narcissus image which is at once an image of the self and all that the self is not. For a Medieval poet steeped in the Augustinian tradition, the search for the self in the mirror of creatures, the beloved, ends with a false image of the self which is either rejected in favor of God, the light which casts the reflection, or accepted as a true image, an image which is totally other. Seeing the self in otherness and accepting the vision as true reduces the spirit to something totally alienated from itself, like a rock or a tree, totally deprived of consciousness. Like language itself, the image can only represent by pointing beyond itself, by beckoning the beholder to pierce through it to its ultimate significance. Idolatry is a refusal to go beyond, a self-petrification.

Virgil is the mediator between Dante's former dark passion and verbal virtuosity on one hand and the restless striving of the pilgrim on the other, at least until his guidance gives way to the guidance of Beatrice. He is defined as a lamp to Dante's feet by Cato in the *Purgatorio* and again by Statius, who adds that he is as a lamp held behind by one who goes by night, lighting the way for others but powerless to help himself. Virgil must finally yield to Beatrice, the light of grace, who, as we have seen, definitively frees the poet of his sensual bonds, most dramatically in the episode of the Siren.

It may seem somewhat strange to think of Virgil at all in the context of love poetry, except insofar as every poet is a poet of desire. Yet it was Virgil's vision of passion overcome that was part of the portrait of Aeneas. At the opening of the fifth book, as Aeneas sails away from Carthage, he looks back at its burning walls and leaves Dido forever behind him. The chaotic force of *folle amore* — mad passion — was epitomized for Dante by the figure of Dido and of Cupid who sat in her lap. Further, it is under the sign of Dido that Paolo and Francesca bewail their adulterous love in Hell. In the great struggle between individual desire and providential destiny, Virgil's Aeneas is the man whose life is shaped by a higher destiny, at the expense of his own individuality. It is Virgil's way to avert his glance and to continue on the *fatale andare*. It is for this reason that he comes to the pilgrim's aid, until Beatrice shows the way to a reconciliation of human love with the Divine plan. Just as the historic Virgil, in Dante's reading, had pointed the way out of the erotic impasse toward *lo bello stilo*, so in the poem, at precisely the moment where the pilgrim passes from the realm of incontinence to the realm of malice, it is Virgil who helps him to avoid the pitfall facing all poets of love. To do more than this is the work of Divine Grace, which is a question I hope to explore in a future study.

I have said that the characteristic of Dante's treatment of erotic themes is diachronic: then and now. Indeed, the entire story of his love for Beatrice might be summed up as a kind of double focus on erotic passion, a nascent erotic passion, abandoned, to which the poet returns with a redemptive recapture of the past. So too with the figure of the Medusa, whose redemptive counterpart in the poem is, as I have suggested, Matelda. Critics have long since noticed the erotic language with which Dante describes Matelda and the pilgrim's longing for her. Her pristine innocence represents the recapture of the erotic in poetry and a redemption of it as a preparation for transcendence. At the same time, it is a going beyond Virgil, a reconciliation of individual human love and of providential destiny which was perhaps unthinkable before the Incarnation. Perhaps for this reason in Canto XXX of the *Purgatorio*, Dante marks the return of Beatrice with the words, "conosco i segni dell'antica fiamma," echoing the despairing words of Dido, while the angels sing "Date o manibus lilia plena," echoing the funereal gesture of Anchises in the Underworld, but transforming the purple lilies of mourning into the white lilies of the Resurrection. At this point, Virgil definitively disappears, when death, before which even he and the Rome he celebrated had to bow, gives way to transcendence, in the person of Beatrice.

To return to the passage of the Medusa, we are now perhaps in a position to answer some of the fundamental questions it raises. Doubtless, one can find an abstract moral meaning in the dramatization as one might expect of an allegory of poets. At the same time, however, we have seen that the passage is charged with the double focus of Dante's own life, the Dante who is, looking back at the Dante who *was*, through the medium of words. This is the very essence of Biblical allegory and, therefore, of the allegory of theologians. The Christ event was the end term of an historical process, the fullness of time, from the perspective of which the history of the world might be read and judged according to a meaning which perhaps even the participants in that history could not perceive. The "then" and "now", the Old Testament and the New, were at once the continuity and discontinuity of universal history, the letter and the spirit respectively of God's revelation. Christian autobiography is the application of this dia-chronism to one's own life as witness, or "confession," of the continual unfolding of the Word.

If Dante's allegory is that of the theologians, this is not to say that his story need be accepted as literally true, as though he were a prophet or madman. The allegory of theologians is God's way of writing and therefore not writing at all, but a way of viewing history, the experience of the world and of the poet in it. This experience cannot be directly recaptured except through a translation into words, as in the Bible or in the poem we read. Such a "translation" is sometimes literal, sometimes figurative, according to what St. Thomas referred to as the "allegory of the letter."[18] The Book of Memory has as its Author God Himself, while the poet is a faithful scribe. In this sense, Dante's poem is neither a copy nor an imitation of the Bible. It *is* the allegory of theologians figuratively applied to his own life.

Nonetheless, the passage from the events of Dante's life to the words

---

[18] See P. SYNAVE, "La Doctrine de St Thomas d'Aquin sur le sens littéral des Écritures," *Revue Biblique*, XXXV (1926), 40-65.

and images he uses to signify them is one that we cannot make. This is why it is impossible to guess at the identity of *Donna Pietra*, just as it is impossible to see in the verses of the Medusa some event of the poet's life. We must be content with words on words, the juxtaposition of two poetic expressions, beyond which it would take an act of faith equal to Dante's to go, beyond which indeed, there is no Dante that we can ever know.

Finally, in order to suggest a last poetic implication of the passage we have been discussing, I should like to go beyond the confines of Dante's text and look ahead to a very different poet, who nevertheless used many of the same motifs. I refer of course to Francesco Petrarch, whose very name is for him an occasion for stony puns. In the course of his *Canzoniere*, I think he provides us with the definitive gloss on Dante's Medusa. Like Pygmalion, Petrarch falls in love with his own creation and is in turn created by her: the pun *lauro/Laura* points to this self-contained process which is the essence of his creation. He creates with his poetry the Lady Laura, who in turn created his reputation as poet laureate. She is therefore not a mediatrix, pointing beyond herself, but is rather enclosed within the confines of his own being as poet, which is to say, the poem. This is precisely what Petrarch acknowledges when he confesses in his final prayer to the sin of idolatry, adoration of the work of his own hands. Speaking of Laura no longer as the infinitely beloved, he calls her a Medusa:

Medusa e l'error mio m'han fatto un sasso[19]

[Medusa and my sin have made me a stone].

For all of his tears of repentance, however, there seems to be a consolation for a more secular age. Petrarch's enduring fame as the weeping lover seems to suggest that, if he was turned to stone because of his idolatry, at least a stone lasts forever. If it is devoid of the spirit linking it to reality and to the life of the poet, it is nevertheless immune to the ravages of time, a monumental portrait of the artist. In the same poem, Petrarch sees the problem of reification as inherent in all poetry, including that of his illustrious predecessor. This, I take it, is the point of his address to the Virgin as the only true mediatrix: "vera beatrice," where the absence of capitalization drives the point home more forcefully. For Petrarch, the precursor of Romanticism, the implication seems to be that every mirror of love poetry contains the Medusa, even when it looks like a lamp.

---

[19] PETRARCH, *Canzoniere* CCLXVI, 111.

Number as Cosmic Language*

RUSSELL A. PECK

"Perfection is common to all numbers, for in the progress of our thought from our own plane to that of the gods, they present the first example of perfect abstraction."

— MACROBIUS, *De Somnium Scipionis*

"To ascend the path towards Wisdom, we discover that numbers transcend our mind and remain unchangeable in their own."

— St. AUGUSTINE, *De Libero Arbitrio*[1]

Because medieval cosmology is thoroughly mathematical in its conception, the rhetoric of numbers permeates all areas of medieval learning. Philosophy and aesthetics, theology and considerations of the soul (what we would call psychology), the various divisions of the quadrivium and creative arts, all become colored with conceptual and procedural similarities through number lore. Whether the end sought be the Oneness of God through the correspondent accidents of the many, the perceiving of likenesses in different modes of human endeavor through analogy, or exploration of the idiosyncrasies of nature within the generalizations of creation, numerology provides the language shared by all, a common denomination in that most characteristic of medieval mental excursions, the quest to relate particulars to universals. St. Augustine observes:

If you look at something mutable, you cannot grasp it either with the bodily senses or the consideration of the mind, unless it possesses some numerical form. If this form is removed, the mutable dissolves into nothing; do not, then, doubt that there is some eternal and immutable Form which prevents mutable objects from being destroyed and allows them to complete their temporal course, as it were, by measured movements in a distinct variety of forms. This eternal Form is neither contained nor.... spread out in space, neither prolonged nor changed by time. Through eternal Form every temporal thing can receive its form, and, in accordance with its kind, can manifest and embody number in space and time.[2]

---

* By permission of the author and Bucknell University Press. This essay appears also in *Essays in the Numerical Analysis of Medieval Literature*, ed. Caroline D. ECKHARDT (Lewisburg, Pa.: Bucknell University Press, 1979.)

[1] The epigrams are from MACROBIUS, *Commentary on the Dream of Scipio*, I.v.4, trans. William Harris STAHL (New York, 1952), p. 95; and St. AUGUSTINE, *De Libero Arbitrio Voluntatis*, II.xi.126, trans. Anna S. BENJAMIN and L. H. HACKSTAFF (Indianapolis, 1964), p. 64.

[2] *De Libero Arbitrio*, II.xvi.171 (*Ibid.*, p. 76).

As long as the Neoplatonic theory of Universal Forms is upheld, this argument of man's participation in the Creator's design, a design without which nothing would exist,[3] is relished with exuberant praise. From the late 11th century to the early 13th, during which period there is an intensive revival of Augustinian study, the theory is the genetrix of most epistemology. Even after Aristotelians, nominalists, and empiricists have seriously challenged the doctrine of universals in the later medieval period, the argument of knowledge through analysis of design continues to be explored and mathematics maintains its preëminence in epistemology, though in a somewhat altered form. Roger Bacon, for example, may insist that mathematics is a purely descriptive science which must be rid of metaphysical excrescences imposed by tradition. Even so, he relies heartily upon analogical arguments in his discussion of the Trinity and though a "scientist," is sensitive throughout his writing to the importance of correspondences in the meaning of God's created forms. Even so late a figure as Kepler, though now usually viewed as seminal in the history of our scientific disciplines, was an ardent numerologist.[4]

In my discussion of medieval number theory I shall concentrate on the Neoplatonic tradition and shall consider five interrelated topics: 1) Numerology and the theory of correspondent forms; 2) Mathematics as basis of all the arts; 3) Number and concepts of ethics and mental health; 4) Number and the utility of beauty; and 5) Number and concentric time.

I. — NUMEROLOGY AND THE THEORY OF CORRESPONDENT FORMS

During the twelfth century there was a revival and proliferation of discussions of a correspondent macrocosm and microscosm. With such discussion came a renewed interest in numerology, particularly as it had been understood and applied by St. Augustine. Numerology is crucial to Neoplatonic theories of correspondent forms in that it provides a language apart from things which can nonetheless measure and correlate what would otherwise be isolate. As Macrobius puts it, numbers are the primary

---

[3] E.g., see *De Libero Arbitrio*, II.xvi.164 (p. 73): "The sky, the earth, and the sea and.... whatever in them shines from above or crawls, flies, or swims below," have "form because they have number. Take away these forms and there will be nothing.... [They] exist only insofar as they have number." For a vivid restatement of Augustine's thesis see ISIDORE OF SEVILLE, *Etymologiæ*, III.iv.3 (*PL*, 82, 156): "Through number we are instructed in order not to be confounded. Take number from all things, and all things perish." Cf. MACROBIUS, *In Somn. Scip.*, I.v.5 ff. For later medieval views on the interdependence of matter and form see AVICEBRON, *De Fons Vitæ* IV.6 and GROSSETESTE, *Com. Post Analytica*, II, 2.

[4] See *Opus Majus*, pt. 6, trans. Robert Belle BURKE (Philadelphia, 1928), where is his plea for experimental science and exposition of correct method of scientific approach to solving natural problems Bacon insists on the importance of mathematics as a purely descriptive science. His eloquent discussion of Trinity and the perfection of 3 occurs in part 4 (Burke, I, 245). For a somewhat discursive discussion of Kepler as numerologist see Gunnar QVARNSTROM, *Poetry and Numbers* (Lund, 1966), pp. 16-17.

example of "perfect abstraction."[5] It was commonly asserted that the numbers of Creation exist apart from mutability and human error and are closest to the language of the Creator Himself. St. Augustine explains that if a man comprehends number it is not changed; yet if he fails to grasp it, its truth "does not disappear; rather, it remains true and permanent, while man's failure to grasp it is commensurate with the extent of his error."[6] So pure and absolute is number that it was held to exist even before form, time, or space, preëxistent in the mind of God.[7]

Because of its purity of abstraction, number offered the cosmic theorist a bridge between the corruptible and the eternal, since in addition to measuring all things, it is a language of relationships and proportions. Metaphors most commonly used to explain its utility in cosmological study are "key," "guide," "motion toward," or "pathway." Terms like "order" (ordo), "reason" (ratio), and "number" (numerus) are sometimes used interchangeably,[8] for all equate ephemeral realities to the divine, preëxistent plan (forma) and offer the means of harmonizing the human mind with the Creator and the rest of creation. As pathway for exploring the harmonia mundi, number enables the Christian seeker of wisdom to appreciate created things with no sense of slighting God. For in discovering form, he exercises the highest of his God-created rights, the grace of participation in divine ratio. Number and its eternal language underlies not only such basic medieval concepts as macrocosm and microcosm, form and image, and the explaining through analogy of the relationships of the correspondent parts; it also correlates morality and mental states with external realities. Numbered analogies between the world at large and man in his corporateness (their corresponding 7s, their sharing of 4 elements, humors, conditions, etc.), and also analogies between man and the state, are commonplace.[9] But the doctrine of numbered correspondence goes beyond men and things or institutions. Even such basic moral concepts as St.

---

[5] In Somn, Scip., I.v.4. Or, as St. Augustine puts it, "The order and truth of numbers have noting to do with the bodily senses, but are unchangeable and true and common to all beings" (De Libero Arbitrio, II.viii.93 [p. 50]).

[6] De Libero Arbitrio, II.viii.80 (p. 54). Cf. Robert Grosseteste's discussion of the superior truth of mathematics beyond the inferiority of mutable natural things (Comm. post. analytics, 1.11).

[7] E.g., Plotinus writes, "Number exists before objects which are described by number. A variety of sense objects merely recalls to the soul the notion of number." See Christopher BUTLER, Number Symbolism (New York, 1970), p. xi.

[8] Numerous is indeed difficult to translate. F. J. THONNARD, De Musica (Paris, 1947), pp. 513-14, observes 4 ways in which the term is used: 1. the ordinary mathematical sense; 2. rhythm; 3. harmony among parts in movement or harmony among sensible, intellectual or moral activities; and 4. the unity of God, source of mathematical law, beauty, rhythm, and the sympathetic activities of nature and man. Cf. D. W. ROBERTSON, Jr., A Preface to Chaucer (Princeton, 1962), p. 114.

[9] For full discussion of the background of medieval theories of microcosmic and macrocosmic orrespondences, see Rudolf ALLERS, "Microcosmus: From Anaximandros to Paracelsus," Traditio, 2 (1944), 319-407. On the analogy between man and state see Ernst KANTOROWITZ, The King's Two Bodies (Princeton, 1957).

Augustine's definition of charity ("the *motion* of the soul towards the
enjoyment of God for His own sake, and the enjoyment of one's self and of
one's neighbor for the sake of God"),[10] originates in a fundamental number
concept in that the term *motion* implies not only direction (what medieval
writers were wont to call "entente"), but also both rhythm and measure.[11]
So too Boethius's notion of love as a knitting of chaste marriages and holy
bonds between God and creation, where the "nombres proporcionable"
draw all together into one participatory understanding.[12] Moreover, number
underlies medieval concepts of sin and mental sickness as well as their
antitheses. Writing in accordance with Latin Christendom's two greatest
numerologists (St. Augustine and Boethius), John Gower (ca. 1330-1408)
defines sin as "modor of divisioun" (that is, the fragmenting of one's sense
of being and the consequent loss of correspondence),[13] while Chaucer's
Parson equates one's psychic sense of Hell with disorder and lack of
number.[14] Atonement, that is, the return to a condition of oneness, comes
for both authors with the release from sin (division) or hellish alienation and
a return to participation in God's *ratio*. In short, numerology is the pulse of
the medieval synthesis, defining not only the bounds and correspondences of
nature, but ultimately, as we shall see further, a whole way of life.

The Middle Ages inherited the science of number, whether arithmetical, geometrical, harmonic, or moral, from rich and ancient traditions
stretching back through Platonism, Pythagorean lore, and Chaldean
astronomy. It provided a means of conjoining the apparently disparate.
Conversely, since the plan of Creation was rational and divine, it offered a
means of abstracting general principles from nature. In this respect
numerology differs from modern mathematics, for in addition to describing
analytically, it was often seen to have powers of its own derived from
Creation. Quite simply, things measured by the same numbers were held to
be in some way correspondent. Not only did such numbers explain
compatible forms in nature; they in turn acquired connotations from the
comparisons they purveyed. Their numerical tie was often said to have
meaning in and of itself; there was a reason behind the ratio, a reason
implicit in creation. Thus 7, for example, because of the 7 moving spheres,
the 7 day week, the four septad phases of the moon, the 7 ages of history,
and the 7 tones of the musical scale, all of which were evidently part of
God's plan, clearly was a measure of totality, particularly totality in a

---

[10] *De Doctrina Christiana*, III.x.16, trans. D. W. ROBERTSON, Jr. (Indianapolis 1958), p.
88.

[11] Macrobius, in fact, goes so far so to define "soul" as "a number moving itself" [*In
Somn. Scip.*, I.vi.6 (STAHL, p. 100)].

[12] *Consolatio*, III.m.9, 18-19, trans. Geoffrey CHAUCER, *The Works of Geffrey Chaucer*,
ed. F. N. ROBINSON (Cambridge, Mass., 1957), p. 350. All quotations from BOETHIUS's
Consolation will be from this translation and will be hereafter indicated by book, section, and
line number in Robinson's edition.

[13] *Confessio Amantis*, Prologue 1030. See lines 967-1052 for a more broad discussion on
the horrible effect of division on all aspects of society.

[14] *Parson's Tale*, 218-219, *Works of Geoffrey Chaucer*, p. 233.

mutable realm. For so had God used the number. Eight, on the other hand, since it was the first number beyond 7, must imply a return to unity, a new beginning, a sign of regeneration and rebirth as in Baptism (n.b., the octagonal font), the New Jerusalem (8th Age), Easter and Pentecost (*dies octavus*). (See Appendix II for a catalog of such connotations.)

Aristotle attributed this manner of bestowing meaning upon numbers to the Pythagoreans, who, he observed, not only strove to discover correspondences but supplied them on their own when nature was wanting so that their system might be complete. As he explains in the *Metaphysics*:

> The Pythagoreans were the first to pursue mathematical studies and to advance them. Having been nurtured in such studies they considered the first principles of mathematics to be the first principles of all things. Now in mathematics numbers are naturally first principles, and they considered that they discerned in number, rather than in fire, earth, and water, many similarities or analogies to existents that such and such a modification of number was justice, and such the soul and *nous*, another opportunity, and so on for most other things. They also saw melodic changes and ratios to be numerical. So, since in these and all other respects they discovered apparent correspondences between all nature and numbers, and numbers were first principles in all nature, they assumed that the elements of number were the elements in all existing things, and that the whole universe was a concord and a number. They made a practice of bringing together the correspondences they found between numbers and concords on the one hand and on the other the parts and attributes of the universe and the whole ordered world. They exhibited an eagerness to complete any gap there might be in their system. For example, since the decad seemed to be a perfect thing and to comprise within itself the whole nature of number, they asserted that the planets too were ten, but as only nine were visible they invented the counter-earth as a tenth.[15]

By the end of our period, neo-Aristotelians, armed with Latin translations of the *Metaphysics*, reasserted distinctions between the principles of numbers and things, thus dampening somewhat the ardor of the less literal-minded Platonists. Even so, despite its scorn, Aristotle's statement catches admirably the reasoning and enthusiasm of the cosmologists and their keen sense of number and order.

The centrality of number lore to medieval cosmology may best be remembered through specific examples, two of which may be mentioned here. In his *De Mundo*, Honorius of Autun measures distances between planets by intervals on the musical scale, confident that man as microcosm, whose number is 7 (3 parts soul and 4 parts elements which comprise the body) and who has 7 voices (the 7 tones on the musical scale), reproduces in facsimile the macrocosm's celestial music.[16] His confidence lies in his numbers which bear out the correspondences.

A fine graphic example of what we speak may be found in Pol de

---

[15] *Metaphysics* 985b-986a, trans. J. A. PHILIPS, *Pythagoras and the Early Pythagoreans* (Toronto, 1966), p. 78. Cf. *De Cælo*, 293a.

[16] *De Imagine Mundi Libri Tres*, II.59 and I.80-82 (*PL*, 172.154 and 140). Cf. ISIDORE, *Etymologiæ*, 3.23.2. The relating of the music of the spheres to the tones of the scale is a Pythagorean notion of course. Cf. ARISTOTLE's account, *De Cælo*, II.9.

Limbourg's correlation of the macrocosm with the human body in the Duc du Berry's *Très Riche Heures* (see pl. IV), with its 12 signs of the zodiac related to 12 parts of the body. The greater universe corresponds with man's mini-universe. Yet notice the prominence with which man is depicted, even though he is the microcosm. From mankind's perspective, his nature, replete with the necessary eternal numbers, must be the starting point of his quest for the universals. For as St. Anselm explains in the *Monologion*,

> The more earnestly the rational mind devotes itself to learning its own nature, the more effectively does it rise to the knowledge of that Being; and the more carelessly it contemplates itself, the farther does it descend from the contemplation of that Being.[17]

Pol portrays the central human figure as a twin, perhaps suggesting Adam and Eve, soul and body, virtue and effeminacy, or at any rate, as a duality one part of which the mansions influence. The side facing the viewer looks downward, or perhaps inward, in a stance of reflection. The artist utilizes the 4 corners of his world, that is to say, the page,[18] to delineate the 4 conditions (hot, cold, moist, dry) and 4 humors for each of the 4 seasons, thereby accounting for another correspondent, 12, which along with the heavenly mansions frame and at least partly govern man. The dual human figure is surrounded by 7 circles of clouds, whose numbered insubstantiality indicates the moving spheres. The mandorla around the fleeting spheres contains the mansions and indicates the 8th sphere of the fixed stars. Its substantial construction indicates its permanence, while its 360° circularity implies man's containment within the Universal One (8 being a return to 1). On the flat surface of a single page then, the artist has depicted the whole of the 4-square world with all its oppositions of macrocosm and microcosm symmetrically arranged and, though various, made equable through numbered correspondence. St. Augustine, commenting on the beauty possible when various meters are set harmoniously against each other, exclaims in *De Musica*: "For what can give the ear more pleasure than being both delighted by variety and uncheated of equality."[19] If we substitute eye for ear, which even Roger Bacon assures us we may do (for the eye has its music as well as the ear),[20] Augustine's eulogy provides fitting comment on Pol de Limbourg's picture. Its variety delights, but the highest pleasure it

---

[17] *Monologion* LXVI, *St. Anselm: Basic Writings*, tr. S. N. DEANE (La Salle, Ill., 1962), pp. 131-132.

[18] On the world as a book recall Hugh of St. Victor: "The world can be likened to books written by the hand of the Lord (that is, through the power and wisdom of the Lord), and each creature is like a word in those books, showing the power and wisdom of the Lord. The unwise looks only at its outward beauty and the comliness of the beautiful creation, and clings to it with love. But he who is wise sees through the beauty of the exterior and beholds the wisdom of the Lord." See Miloslav BOHATEE, *Illuminated Manuscripts* (Prague, 1970), p. 61. On the relation of "mansions" to parts of the human anatomy, see ROBERTUS ANGLICUS, *Com. in De Sphæra*, Lec. 6, *The Sphere of Sacrobosco*, ed. Lynn THORNDIKE (Chicago, 1949), p. 219.

[19] *De Musica* II.9.16, tr. Robert C. TALIAFERRO, *The Fathers of the Church*, ed. R. J. DEFERRARI *et al* (New York, 1947), IV, 225.

[20] "Whatever can be conformed to sound in similar movements and in corresponding formations, so that our delight may be made complete not only by hearing, but by seeing, belongs to music." *Opus Majus*, tr. BURKE, I, 260.

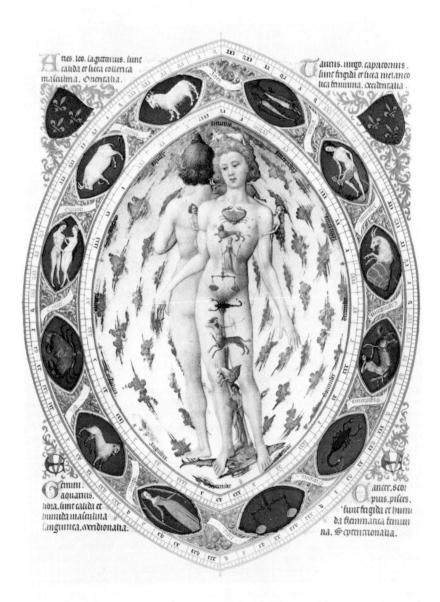

IV.   "Gemini" — Pol de Limbourg

affords lies in the mathematical equality of its parts. There one participates, as did Honorius in his healthful eulogy on the cosmos, in music fitting for both eye and the mind, for as Boethius points out, the ear is affected by sounds in quite the same way as the eye is by optical impressions.[21] The picture's meaning is its aesthetic unity.

II. — MATHEMATICS AS FOUNDATION OF THE ARTS

In his explanation of the intervals of the spheres Honorius is not concerned with scientific accuracy as we conceive of it. He is concerned with astronomy, but not astronomy as a separate science. Rather, he views it as an extension of numbering, which brings us to our second main point: for Honorius, all of the sciences are subdivisions of mathematics. His view is not unique; it reflects the most fundamental premise of the medieval curriculum. As Roger Bacon puts it a century later, mathematics is the "gate and key" of all the sciences.[22] He cites Boethius's prologue to *De Arithmetica* as his authority: "If an inquirer lacks the four parts of mathematics, he has very little ability to discover the truth."[23] The four parts of mathematics are, of course, what Boethius called the *Quadrivium*.[24] In explaining the mathematical foundations of all pursuits Bacon adheres to the ancient definitions: Arithmetic, the "mother and nurse" of all the arts, is the science of numbers absolute.[25] Bacon notes that it "teaches how all the proportions are investigated in the ratio of numbers."[26] It comes first in the *quadrivium*, since all the rest simply apply in different ways what arithmetic teaches.[27] Moreover, he says, according to Tully (who follows

---

[21] *De Musica*, I.32 (*PL*, 63.1194).

[22] *Opus Majus*, IV.1 (BURKE, I, 116).

[23] *Ibid.*, p. 117. BOETHIUS's *De Arithmetica* was the standard arithmetic in the schools of Western Europe until well beyond the Medieval period. Boethius is following NICOMACHUS, *Introductio Arithmetica*, I.iii.3-5, who in turn is following Plato, *Laws*, 13, and puts the matter this way: "Every diagram, system of numbers, every scheme of harmony, and every law of movement of the stars, ought to appear one to him who studies all things rightly; and what we say will properly appear if one studies all things looking to one principle, for there will be seen to be one bond for all things, and if any one attempts philosophy in any other way he must call on Fortune to assist him. For there is never a path without these." (Tr. Martin D'OOGE, *Introduction to Arithmetic* [Ann Arbor, 1938], p. 186. Cf. D'OOGE, p. 185, n.3.)

[24] Although the term "quadrivium" is Boethius's, the fourfold classification is ancient. Plato, Aristotle, Theophrastus, Nicomachus, Cicero, Macrobius, Boethius, Cassiodorus, and Martianus Capella all wrote on all four as being part of one greater mathematical science.

[25] NICOMACHUS, *Intro. Arith.*, I.v.3 and I.iii.1. Cf. *Opus Majus*, p. 198, where Bacon gives the credit to Cassiodorus, who in fact gets the idea from Boethius's translation of Nicomachus. Cf. HUGH of ST. VICTOR, *Didascalicon*, II.15.

[26] *Opus Majus*, p. 245.

[27] Again the idea goes back to Nicomachus, who eloquently explains arithmetic's preëminence "not solely because... it existed before all the others in the mind of the creating God like some universal and exemplary plan, relying upon which as a design and archetypal example the creator of the universe sets in order his material creations and makes them attain to their proper ends; but also because it is naturally prior in birth, in that it abolishes other sciences with itself, but is not abolished together with them." (*Intro. Arith.*, I.iv, tr. D'OOGE, p. 187.) Hugh of St. Victor (*Didascalicon* II.7) also treats the idea through etymology, deriving the term from *ares* (power) and *numerus*, to mean "the power of number," noting that "all things have been found in its likeness" (trans. TAYLOR, p. 67).

Plato's *Meno*), arithmetic is the science man learns most naturally, mathematical knowledge being an innate feature of man's understanding.[28] Geometry comes second. It is the science of quantity at rest, the application of arithmetic to surfaces and planes, angles and volume. The third science is astronomy, which explores quantity in motion and is the most elaborate of the sciences in the *quadrivium*. The last is music, the science of numbers in mutual relation; it is the most comprehensive of the sciences.[29] Bacon argues that even the *trivium* and theology as well rest upon mathematics. In fact, knowledge of numbers is that which sets men apart from brutes, "which know neither sacred things nor human."[30]

A glance at the *forma* of medieval university curricula confirms the emphasis Bacon puts upon the prominence of mathematics in the pursuit of knowledge. Although study in the arts in the later middle ages had become more varied than Martianus Capella's original outline of a sevenfold curriculum, the more numerous topics reflect subdivisions of the earlier scheme. One Oxford *forma* which lists 12 topics of study devotes 7 to aspects of the *quadrivium* (geometry, algorismus [algebra], meteorics, study of the spheres, arithmetic, computation, and study of heaven and earth),[31] while another from the early 14th century (Merton College) cites 9 items, 5 of which are devoted to mathematical subdivisions, including the study of gematria.[32] These curricula suggest that a gradual division was taking place between the purely descriptive and analytic side of mathematics (arithmetic, geometry, and algebra) and its metaphysical side (cosmology and gematria). Presumably, the division enabled a student to delve more deeply into all facets of this great and diverse subject. But in truth, the division promoted ultimately a means of sloughing off a murky area of study which was more akin to theology than pure mathematics. By the end of the medieval period, the "new math," freed of metaphysical speculation, became the most serious challenger of the hallowed theory of universals as it made possible more precise measurements and calculations, the results of which did not conform to symmetrical patterns.

Of what precisely did a medieval arithmetic consist? Nicomachus and Boethius (subsequent versions both in the Latin and Arab worlds were abridgments of one or the other)[33] begin with generalizations about the

---

[28] *Opus Majus*, p. 121. Bacon is alluding to Socrates' discussion with a peasant youth who is shown to know innately complex mathematical theorems. Tully's source is PLATO's *Meno*.

[29] Nicomachus gives the first clear statement of the classifications and definitions (*Intro. Arith.*, I.iii.1-7); unless otherwise noted I have followed his definitions here. The classification was standard, however. Cf. HUGH OF ST. VICTOR, *Didascalicon*, II.6 which follows Boethius's translation of Nicomachus (*De Arithmetica*, I.i.). On the comprehensiveness of music, see *Didascalicon*, II.12.

[30] *Opus Majus*, p. 243. Cf. BOETHIUS, *De Arithmetica*, I.i (*PL*, 63, 1082) and *Interpretatio Euclidis Geometriæ*, II (*PL*, 63, 1360).

[31] Hastings RASHDALL, *The Universities of Europe in the Middle Ages*, ed. F. M. POWICKE and A. B. EMDEN (Oxford, 1936), III, 480-481.

[32] *Ibid.*, p. 482. See Appendix for discussion of gematria.

[33] See Appendix for a survey of arithmetic sources.

importance of the language of numbers and its foundation of the sciences. Then after defining the categories of number study and various terms, both concentrate on proportions and sequences of numbers (e.g., squares and cubes, quadrangular, pentagular, and hexagonal numbers). Nicomachus divides numerologic analysis into 3 categories: study of limited multitude (i.e., 8 is multitude limited by 8 units); study of combinations of numbers (6 is a perfect number, 8 is 2 cubed, etc.); and study of the flow of quantity made up of unities (i.e., 8 holds the 4th position in the flow of even numbers, 2, 4, 6, 8, or the 4th position in the sequence of doubles 1, 2, 4, 8, etc.). Both Nichomachus and Boethius conclude by considering geometrical and musical harmonies as they relate to arithmetical harmonies.

Some of the arithmetic terms Nicomachus, Boethius, and their Pythagorean progenitors define must be understood before one can have any clear understanding of the relationship of arithmetic to philosophy and the rest of her entourage of arts. First is the Pythagorean distinction between elements of numbers and numbers themselves. This distinction reflects a principle typical of Platonic thought whereby complexity is reduced to simplicity. An *element* is the simplest factor beyond which there can be no further reduction. The Pythagoreans held that there were two elements, monad and dyad. How the monad is an element is self-evident: it is the basic unit out of which all other numbers are developed. The dyad's elemental nature is less obvious, for does it not consist of combined monads thus being no longer elemental? Nicomachus resolves the problem this way: although the dyad may be understood as a combination of two monads, nonetheless there is a quality of "otherness" about the dyad which the monad cannot possess. That is, the monad is *same*, while the dyad is *other than same*. Thus the dyad is elemental in its own right. All subsequent numbers, the flow from the monad through the dyad, consist of combinations of same and other and are thus not elemental. *One* (monad) is called "father of number." *Two* (dyad) is sometimes thought of as "mother of number." (Cf. male and female numbers discussed below.)

Closely related to the concept of elements is the notion of *real* and *unreal* numbers. The two elements of number, one and two, are classified as unreal numbers, 3 being the first real number. The reasoning here is mainly geometric, where 1 designates point, 2 designates line, 3 designates space, and 4 designates volume. In the world which our senses tell us is real, we perceive reality only as space and volume. That is, we cannot conceive of point or line except in the abstract (or unreal). This notion of 3 as the first real number is fundamental to the Christian concept of Trinity (eternity expressed or made real in temporal-spacial reality).[34] These first four

---

[34] E.g., St. BONAVENTURE, *Sententiæ*, dist. XXXI, art. iii, qu. 2. The notion is implicit in all arguments which see the 3rd Person as the bond or product of the first two Persons or of three containing one essence. Cf. St. AUGUSTINE, *De Trinitate, passim*; St. ANSELM, *Monologion*, xlix-lxiii and lxxviii-lxxix; ALANUS DE INSULIS, *Regulæ Cælestis Juris*, reg. i; PETER OF POICTIERS, *Sententiæ* (*PL*, 211.926); ALBERTUS MAGNUS, *De Cælo et mundi, ab initio*; Roger BACON, *Opus Majus* (BURKE, I, 245).

numbers (the parents of number and the first two real numbers) constitute the tetrad so important in Pythagorean arithmology.[35]

Another basic distinction the Pythagoreans made is between *odd* and *even* numbers. This distinction plays a crucial role in the discovery of ratios and proportions. In arithmology it provides the basis for *male* and *female* numbers. Male numbers are odd (i.e., when divided they have a middle part left over) and were considered strong since they had no even half (fractions don't count). Female numbers are even. They may be split into even or uneven factors and are thus called weak. If the unreal numbers *one* and *two* are called the parents of number, then *three* and *four* become the first real male and female numbers.

Marriage numbers, though not considered in the arithmetics of the time, were an important part of arithmology and take their meaning from combinations of male and female numbers. *Five* is the first marriage, number since it is a combination by addition of the female 2 and male 3. *Six* is the next, it being the product of 2x3. Since 5 is associated with Venus and the senses and is merely a sum, it implies worldliness and cupidinous marriages, while 6, being a product, is the fruitful marriage number. *Thirty* is also considered a marriage number, it being the product of the first two marriage numbers. Similarly 7 is sometimes considered a marriage number in that it is the combination of 3 and 4, these being the first male and female real numbers. As such it is a wordly marriage number, defining man's marriage of his soul (3) and body (4), for example. By the same logic, 12 is also a marriage number, it being the product of the first two male and female real numbers. Like 6, 12 denotes a more blessed and fruitful marriage than that produced by mere addition.

The terms *perfect, abundant*, and *deficient* were important in the arithmetics, however, and like marriage numbers, they take their meaning from their factors. A *perfect* number is equal to the sum of its factors (aliquot parts). Such numbers are rare. *Six* is the first, its parts being 1, 2, and 3, which totaled equal the number itself. *Twenty-eight* is next $(1 + 2 + 4 + 7 + 14 = 28)$, and so on.[36] An *abundant* number is one whose aliquot parts total more than the number itself (e.g., 12, whose parts total $1 + 2 + 3 + 4 + 6 = 16$); a deficient number is one whose parts total less than the number itself (e.g., 9, whose parts total $1 + 3 = 4$). This method of calculation was sometimes used to determine the spiritual character of a number, that is, whether it was given to excess or stinginess.[37] But such metaphysical speculation was for the most part

[35] On the importance of the tetrad and the tetrachtys as pyramid of justice see Christopher BUTLER, *Number Symbolism* (New York), 1970), pp. 8 ff.

[36] NICOMACHUS, *Intro. Arith.*, I.xvi, explains a foolproof method for calculating perfect numbers, whereby he adds 496 and 8,128 to the known list of perfect numbers.

[37] E.g., Nicomachus observes: "It comes about that even as fair and excellent things are few and easily enumerated, while ugly and evil ones are widespread, so also the superabundant and deficient numbers are found in great multitude and irregularly placed — for the method of

excluded from arithmetic texts which stuck rather closely to considerations of proportion, ratio, and factoring.

The geometries of the early medieval period were based on Boethius's redaction of Euclid. Boethius includes all the propositions of Euclid but eliminates most of the proofs. He calls his work a translation, though in fact it is an intelligent abridgment. It was all the West had until the 12th century, when Arab geometries which included the proofs were translated into Latin. Without the proofs Boethius's work was of limited value, though still important in defining terms such as point, line, plane, angles, spacial figures like triangle, square, etc., truncation, bisection, and so on. It also provided simple formulae for measuring area and volume. Boethius concludes his discussion with a short history of the science and its usefulness which he finds to be threefold: first, for practical matters such as mechanics; second, for matters of health such as medicine; and finally, for matters of the soul, such as philosophy.

Boethius's last point was often heeded by medieval theologians who used geometry in theological argument. For example, Duns Scotus compares the Trinity and the triangle to demonstrate that although only God knows all things through His essence, man's intellect can be moved by an object to know Him. Then, like Roger Bacon, he holds that knowledge of objects, e.g., a triangle, pertains to the theologian, for to know that the triangle's three angles are always equal to two right angles is "a kind of participation of God," since the figure "has such an order in the universe that it expresses more perfectly as it were the perfection of God."[38] He adds that this is, moreover, a more noble way of knowing triangles than simply thinking of 3 angles. Another favorite geometric figure useful to both philosopher and theologian was the circle, which we shall consider later in our discussion.

After the rediscovery of Euclid's proofs and with the revival of Roman methods of surveying, the subject of geometry was extended to include some elements of geography, though according to Hugh of St. Victor (*Didascalicon* II.9) geography had always been a part of geometry, the science having originated among the Egyptians who gave it its name ("earth-measurer") from their surveying of lands along the Nile. Hugh divides the study of geometry into three parts: planimetry (measurement of surfaces); altimetry (measurement of heights and depths); and cosmimetry (measurement of spheres).[39]

---

their discovery is irregular — but the perfect numbers are easily enumerated and arranged with suitable order; for only one is found among the units, 6, only one among the tens, 28, and a third in the rank of the hundreds, 496 alone, and a fourth within the limits of the thousands, 8125." (*Intro. Arith.*, I.xvi, trans. D'OOGE, p. 209.) The moral virtue of perfect numbers was a favorite topic with St. Augustine.

[38] *Concerning Human Knowledge*, trans. Allan WOLTER, in *Duns Scotus: Philosophical Writings* (Indianapolis, 1962), p. 138. Cf. Roger Bacon's discussion of geometry as tool of the Theologian in *Opus Majus* (Burke, I, 245).

[39] *Didascalicon*, II.13, trans. Jerome TAYLOR (New York, 1961), p. 70.

III. — Number and Concepts of Ethics and Mental Health

But let us return to Honorius and his beautiful analogy between the measurement of the spheres and the musical scale. In our discussion of medieval theories of correspondence and even in our survey of arithmetic and geometry texts, we have encountered a characteristic proclivity to extend number study into the pastures of ethics. When Honorius combines his knowledge of music and astronomy he is using his mind for its true "entente." In describing the *harmonia mundi* he binds his own mind into harmony with the thoughts of his betters who lived in former times and who made similar observations, and he binds his mind to that of the Creator whose numbers originally measured and gave form to the great plan. His numbering is both a form of imitation and meditation which enables him to achieve that rarified sense of oneness with God, the world, and men (both past and present) which Augustine called *caritas* and Boethius *unitas*. And such is usually the goal of medieval cosmology: study of the *universe* is a turning towards the One (*unus* and *versus*).

In making his assertions Honorius works within a long-established tradition which gives medieval man insights into the moral splendor of God's thought as well as the symmetrical workings of creation. Cosmic symmetries and motions teach men such valuable psychological concepts as "wholeness," "measure," "proportion," "harmony," "integrity," and "intention" (goal), all of which are Platonic in origin and essentially mathematical in their approach to ontology, and which constitute the basic vocabulary of medieval discussions of mental health. Plato's myth-making Timaeus had explained that God gave man vision in order that he might observe the circuits of intelligence in the heavens and adjust his own perturbed revolutions of thought to them. Hearing, too, like sight, was given to enable man to bring the revolutions of his soul into consonance with divine order by relating to celestial music. Though the orbits of man's thoughts were deranged at birth, "by learning to know the harmonies and revolutions of the world, he should bring the intelligent part, according to its pristine nature, into the likeness of that which intelligence discerns, and thereby win the fulfillment of the best life set by the gods."[40] Implicit in Plato's argument is a moral obligation to view creation from such a vantage point that the rhythms of creation might help man measure his own life. Science and morality are thus parts of one and the same discipline. Through number, ethics correspond with created nature.

---

[40] *Timæus*, 90d, trans. Francis M. Cornford (Indianapolis, 1959), p. 114. See also *Timæus*, 47c-e, pp. 45 ff. Plato's observations on planetary and spiritual motions did not go unappreciated in the later medieval period. Williams of Conches (12th century), and his *Commentary on Timæus*, writes of these passages: "God gave man eyes so that when man saw that there are two motions in the heavens and two in himself, and that the Divine Wisdom makes the erratic planets follow the rational motion of the firmament, man would subject the erratic movements of his flesh to the rational motion of his spirit, a matter for practical philosophy." (See J. Taylor, *Didascalicon*, p. 224, n. 22.)

Plato's paradigm on man's healthy reciprocity with nature's patterns was not wasted on Christian writers. Though at first reluctant to embrace pagan notions, Christian apologists, especially under the guidance of St. Augustine, were not long in discovering the usefulness (in fact, necessity) of Platonic arguments to support Christian theses. Indeed, before Christian times Greek methods of explicating the Old Testament had begun, and in a writer like Philo Judaeus, Greek and Hebraic attitudes towards numerology are inseparably fused. It is, moreover, in a Greek context that much of the New Testament was written, and, as Augustine makes clear in his 124 sermons on John, that gospel cannot be understood aright without grounding in the number tradition out of which it was composed.[41] In *De Doctrina Christiana* St. Augustine writes, "Ignorance of numbers.... causes many things expressed figuratively and mystically in the Scriptures to be misunderstood";[42] and in *De Civitate Dei*, "We must not despise the science of numbers, for in many passages of Holy Scripture it is bound to be of eminent service to the careful interpreter."[43] His biblical authority on behalf of numerological analysis is Wisdom 11.21: "Thou hast ordered all things in measure, and number, and weight" (Douai), a passage Augustine refers to more than twenty times in the course of his writings.[44] In response to the troubling question, "How could pagans have been so close to Truth without the assistance of divine illumination?" Augustine allows that not only did they benefit by study of the correspondent patterns of creation open to all observers, thereby arriving at a partial understanding of God's plan, but that Plato must have had at least indirect contact with the writings of Jeremiah and Moses.[45] Besides, "it is perfectly clear to the most stupid

---

[41] Cf. Augustine's glosses on the number and sizes of the vessels at the Marriage in Cana (tractate ix); on the meaning of the 46 years building the temple (tr. x); the meaning of the numbers surrounding the meeting with the Woman of Samaria at the well (tr. xv); the 5 porches around the pool at Bethesda at which the 38-year-old impotent man is healed (tr. xvii); the feeding of the 5000 (tr. xxiv & xxv); and the 153 fishes (tr. cxxii); etc.

[42] *De Doctrina Christiana*, II.16.25 (trans. ROBERTSON, p. 51). It is noteworthy that Roger Bacon, in his defense of the arts against the pejorative criticisms of theologians repeatedly cites *De Doctrina* and Augustine's defense of pagan learning, especially in his section on mathematics.

[43] *De Civitate Dei*, xi.30, trans. Marcus DODS, in *Nicene and Post-Nicene Fathers*, ed. Philip SCHAFF (Grand Rapids, 1956), II, 223.

[44] E.g., see CONFESSIONES, v.4.7; *De Civ. Dei*, xi.30 & xii.18; *De Trin.*, iii.9.16 & xi.11.18; *Enchiridion*, 29 & 118; *Contra Faustum Manichæan*, 21.6; *De Natura Boni*, 21; and *Ennarrationes in Psalmos*, 147.9. A second scriptural passage, "I and my heart have gone round to know and to consider and to search out wisdom and number" (Eccles. 7:26) also fascinated Augustine because of its yoking of wisdom with number as a means to an end in man's search for peace of mind. Cf. *De Libero Arbitrio*, ii.8.93-95 and *De Musica*, vi.4.7. Whether attempting to explore his personal journey to Christ, explain the nature of free will, discuss the magnitude of the soul or the order of the universe, define beauty and the ways in which men perceive Truth, or even in so practical a matter as his attempts to systematize scriptural explication theory, the vocabulary of number provided Augustine with a language for conceiving and understanding.

[45] *De Civ. Dei*, viii.11-12.

person that the science of numbers was not instituted by man but rather investigated and discovered.''[46]

It is not surprising then, to find Greek number theories in Christian writings with no sense of incongruity whatsoever. And they are there chiefly because of their ethical value. The symmetrical rhythm between healthy man and nature which Plato speaks of is emphasized repeatedly by St. Augustine in such treatises as *De Musica, De Ordine, De Liberto Arbitrio, De Quantitate Animæ*, and *De Trinitate*, and by Boethius in *De Consolatione Philosophiæ*. In the *Consolatio*, for example, Philosophy defines man's sense of freedom and happiness through a numerological perspective. In health, a man comprehends the motions of the heavens, seasons, indeed, all creation around him, "by nombres" (I.m.2, Chaucer's translation). The sane man is, in short, a mathematician (master of the *quadrivium*). When mentally disturbed, man's ability to number is lost, and he "waxeth withoute mesure" (I.m.2). Later in the argument, Philosophy explains the reciprocity of this process in greater detail:

> Ryght so as whan that cleernesse smyteth the eyen and moeveth hem to seen, or ryght so as voys or soun hurteleth to the eres and commoeveth hem to herkne; than is the strengethe of the thought imoeved and excited, and clepith forth to semblable moevyngis the speces that it halt withynne itself, and addeth tho speces to the notes and to the thinges withoute-forthe, and medleth the ymagis of thinges withoute-forth to the foormes ihidd withynne hymself.

(V.m.4, Chaucer's translation)

As in *Timæus*, species are related to universal notes, and images to forms, in which relationship lies man's health and happiness.

Aristotle complained that numerology reduces all to sameness.[47] But to the Platonists, this theological equatability was its main virtue and the justification of all the arts. The meaning behind all numerology, the reason for its being, is one and the same — God. We have already observed how the arithmetics defined the elements of number as "same" (*unitas*) and other (*alteritas*), sometimes referred to as monad and dyad. The link between numerology and theology lies in the equation of monad with God

---

[46] *De Doct. Christ.*, ii.38.26 (tr. Robt., p. 72).

[47] *Metaphysica*, 1093 a I. See Christopher Butler's discussion of Aritotle and the Pythagoreans in "Numerical Thought," *Silent Poetry*, ed. Alastair FOWLER (London, 1970), p. 10, and in *Number Symbolism, op. cit.*, pp. 1-7.

[48] *Theologumena Arithmeticæ*, ed. Ast, as cited by Frank Egleston ROBBINS, "The Philosophy of Nicomachus," *Introduction to Arithmetic*, tr. D'OOGE, p. 96. Cf. MACROBIUS, *In Somn. Scip.* V.vi.7-8. On the transmission of arithmological lore into 12th and 13th century Europe see Jerome TAYLOR's informative note 25, *The Didascalicon of Hugh of St. Victor* (New York, 1961), pp. 198-199; n. 29, p. 200; and esp. note 41, p. 202, where Professor Taylor cites THIERRY OF CHARTRES, *De sex dierum operibus* x1iii: "Just as all things derive their existence from the One, so from the One Equal to the One [the devine Mind or Wisdom] proceed the form, mode, and measure of each thing.... Therefore, as the One Equal to the One contains within himself and generates from himself the ideas of all things, so does he contain within himself and bring forth from himself the very forms of all things.... [together with] all proportions and inequalities. And all things resolve themselves into him."

and dyad with creation. In explaining the likeness, the *Theologumena Arithmeticæ* argues:

> [The monad] generates itself and is generated from itself, is self-ending, without beginning, without end, and appears to be the cause of enduring, as God in the realm of physical actualities is in such manner conceived as a preserving and guarding agent of nature.[48]

Just as God is the Creator of all nature (the ''other'' apart from His ''same''), so is the monad creator of all numbers of the dyad. Photius calls monad the σπεγματitus λογος.[49] All numbers share in each other through the monad. Without it they would have no being at all. Thus the numerological premise whereby God is the measure of all things in Augustine's definition of *caritas*; so, too, in Boethius's argument that God is ONE, determining the meaning of all created ratios. God is the number base of Creation. Through that number, geometry, music, and astronomy become things of man, and man attains his universality.

We see then that cosmology becomes the basis of the most subtle points in medieval ethics. Recall in the passage cited above that Boethius related man's ''freedom'' to his ability to number correctly. Augustine makes the same point: if man misnumbers, the only unfortunate consequence as far as man is concerned (there is no other consequence) is that he is bound to his error and his natural freedom is thus impinged. Augustine explains in *De Libero Arbitrio* that without the preëminent pattern of universals free choice would be meaningless. If wisdom were not manifest in the guise of numbers, man's choices would be blind and random. Even Augustine's notion of ''fate'' is thus tied up with number theory. A ''fated'' person is a weak person who has willfully given up his power of choice. A free man is a strong man who maintains his appreciation of order wholesomely.[50] That is, the fated man, or to put it another way, the sinful man, or, to use Boethius's idiom, the man in exile, is one whose number base is other than ONE. He is a man whose mental condition throws him out of kilter with the rest of the universe. The circuits are broken, he becomes a non-participant. ''I turned away from the One and melted away into the many,'' writes Augustine in his *Confessions*.[51] The consequence of breach of number is misery.

IV. — NUMBER AND THE UTILITY OF BEAUTY

Number is the surest pathway to Wisdom; indeed, Pythagoras is reported to have said that number *is* Wisdom.[52] Following Iamblichus, Pythagoras's biographer, St. Augustine likewise put number and wisdom in

---

[49] ROBBINS, ''The Philosophy of Nicomachus,'' p. 96.

[50] *De Civ. Dei*, v.9.

[51] *Confessiones*, II.1.

[52] IAMBLICHUS, *Life of Pythagoras*, xviii, trans. Thomas Taylor (London, 1926), p. 43.

the same class, calling both universal and explaining that one commonly manifests itself through the other.[53] Both are "identical" and "immutable," with rules that are "unchangeably present and common to all who see them.[54] But there is another characteristic of equal importance. Because the universe is well-numbered there is a way for man not only to know and participate in wisdom, but also to enjoy his own being as well. Number affords him both sentence and solace.

> The most pure and unadulterated character [writes Iamblichus] is that of the man who gives himself to the contemplation of the most beautiful things, and whom it is proper to call a philosopher.... The survey of all heaven, and of the stars that revolve in it, is indeed beautiful, when the order of them is considered. For they derive this beauty and order by the participation of the first and the intelligible essence. But the first essence is the nature of number and reasons.... which pervaded through all things, and according to which all these [celestial bodies] are elegantly arranged, and fitly adorned. And wisdom indeed, truly so called, is a certain science which is conversant with the first beautiful objects, and these divine, undecaying, and possessing an invariable sameness of subsistence; by the participation of which other things also may be called beautiful. The attention therefore to erudition is likewise beautiful, which Pythagoras extended, in order to effect the correction of mankind.[55]

Number defines a way of life and that way is intimately entwined with an elaborate theory of aesthetics.

St. Augustine followed the premises outlined by Iamblichus. He held that man is so created that he naturally desires beauty. If misdirected, this desire may bring man to grief, yet the desire is always present, a yearning (*cupiditas*) which keeps men vital. "As he gazes attentively at the whole creation," Augustine explains, "he who travels the road to wisdom perceives how delightfully wisdom reveals itself to him on the way, and meets him in all providence. The more beautiful is the road to the wisdom towards which he hastens, the more ardently he burns to complete the journey."[57] Boethius dramatically makes a similar point in the *Consolatio*. No reader can help but respond to the exuberance of Book III when the persona rediscovers his number base and bursts into praise of the Creator. His happiness is beautiful and beauty is his happiness.

Augustine emphasizes the pervasiveness of universal beauty surrounding man and explains the operation of the seed of desire implanted in man as it urges him to pursue beauty yet is trained to cooperate with reason.

> Wherever you turn, wisdom speaks to you through the imprint it has stamped upon its works. When you begin to slip towards outward things, wisdom calls you back, by means of their very forms so that when something delights you in body and entices you through bodily senses, you may see that it has number and may ask whence it comes. Thus you return to yourself: you know that you cannot approve or disapprove of what you touch

---

[53] E.g., *De Libero Arbitrio*, II.9.108; II.11.123; and II.11.127. Cf. IAMBLICHUS, *Life of Pythagoras*, xviii (Taylor, pp. 43-44).

[54] *De Libero Arbitrio*, II.10.3-II.11.127.

[55] *Life of Pythagoras*, xii (trans. TAYLOR, pp. 28-29).

[56] *De Libero Arbitrio*, II.17.174 (trans. BENJAMIN, p. 76).

with the bodily senses, unless you have within you certain laws of beauty to which you refer the beautiful objects that you perceive outside of you.[57]

The beauty of things in nature, even though mutable, has a peculiar importance for man. Their images possess unique value. "Although the terrestrial sphere is numbered among corruptible things it keeps as best it can the image of higher things and continually shows them to us as examples and signs."[58] Even the human body, a most corruptible and fragile vessel, instructs the soul and brings pleasure and insight, "for it has a beauty of its own and in this way sets its dignity off to fair advantage in the eyes of the soul."[59] "Look closely at the beauty of the graceful body and you will see that numbers are held in space. Then look closely at the beauty of motion in the body and you will see that numbers are involved in time."[60]

I have dwelt on Augustine's discussion of number's role in aesthetics and the influence of beauty on man's quest for stability because of its centrality in aesthetic and psychological theories of subsequent generations throughout the medieval period. The solace of beauty is inseparable from its instruction. As St. Bonaventure explains:

> Number is the outstanding exemplar in the mind of the Maker, and in things it is the outstanding trace leading to wisdom. Since this is most evident to and closest to God, it leads most directly to God.... It causes Him to be known in all corporeal and sensible things while we apprehend the rhythmical, delight in rhythmical proportions, and through laws of rhythmical proportions judge irrefragably.[61]

Apprehension, delight, and judgment — these constitute for Bonaventure, as they did for Augustine, the critical steps in aesthetic instruction. Like Augustine, he too insists upon number as the agency for aesthetic perception and participation: "Since.... all things are beautiful and in some way delightful, and beauty and delight do not exist apart from proportion, and proportion is primarily in number, it needs must be that all things are rhythmical (numerosa)."[62]

Bonaventure's qualifying clause that beauty and delight do not exist apart from proportion captures admirably the essence of medieval art theory. Proportion lies in the relating of the parts to the sequence and the whole. When Geoffrey of Vinsauf exhorts in his discussion of the poet's rhetoric,

---

[57] *De Libero Arbitrio*, II.16.163 (*ibid.*, p. 73). CHAUCER's *Book of the Duchess* offers a superb example of this aesthetic principle in action as the Black Knight learns the higher truth of measure and number through the beauty of the "goode faire White." For further discussion of the point see my "Theme and Number in CHAUCER's *Book of the Duchess*," *Silent Poetry*, ed. Alastair FOWLER (London, 1970), pp. 73-115.

[58] *De Libero Arbitrio*, III.9.100 (*op. cit.*, p. 109).

[59] *De Musica*, vi.4.7 (*op. cit.*, p. 332).

[60] *De Libero Arbitrio*, II.16.166 (*op. cit.*, p. 74). Roger Bacon picks up the point in *Opus Majus* (BURKE, p. 260) to explain that dancing is thus a category of music (i.e., number in motion).

[61] *Itinerarum Mentis ad Deum*, II.10, trans. George BOAS (Indianapolis, 1953), p. 70.

[62] *Ibid.* I have made a similar point, using these examples from Bonaventure in a somewhat different context, in "Numerology and Chaucer's *Troilus and Criseyde*," *Mosaic*, 5.4 (1972), 4-5.

"Let one and the same thing be covered with many forms. Be various and yet the same,"[63] his premise about art's relationship to Truth and delight is in tune with Augustine's notion that the "measured movements" of the Universal are perceived on earth through "a distinct variety of forms."[64] Hugh of St. Victor, in explicating Noah's Ark, may see fit to expound four levels of meaning, yet through proportion, they are all the same: "The form is one, though the matter is different."[65] The "artist," as writers like Augustine, Anselm, Hugh of St. Victor, and Bonaventure so often insist in their discussions of creative process, is a structurer. He is also an imitator of the idea held firm and well-shaped in his mind. Though he may work with mutable images, the one idea remains true and discernible through the numbers of his varied structures. In the discovery of that idea is the observer's delight.

The virtue of this view of creativity has not been well appreciated by modern man who has tended to scorn symmetry and the analogical perspective as arbitrary, impersonal, and even inhuman. Allegory, the most glorious of the numbering devices, becomes almost synonymous with "dreary." But so pejorative an approach to the medieval world misses its point altogether. Allegory and analogy were not for the Middle Ages a way of abstracting, but rather of internalizing, making personal, and thus humanizing all that was otherwise lost outside them. It was a process of mental incorporation. One should not be disgusted with a commentator like Pierre Bersuire (1290?-1362) who glosses a classical myth in more ways than an ordinary man might conceive. His point is not "what does the myth mean?" but rather what *can* it mean? One might do well to take delight in his ingenuity, if not applaud it.

The cosmologists admittedly allowed themselves less fancy than a commentator like Bersuire. Yet I suspect they would have been most reluctant to give up their stars for modern astronomy, for the losses of such a shift would outweigh the gain. They loved their metaphors, their plots and analogies, which made a comprehensive sense as opposed to an analytic sense. Their liberal arts not only orient, investigate, and explicate the universe *for man*, they also enable him to play. In reading their arguments, one is struck not only by the elaborateness and symmetry of their hypotheses, but also with the sophistication with which the hypotheses are ventured *as hypotheses*. The great medieval synthesis was very much an acknowledged construct of man's mind, and its principle explicators frequently emphasized, as does "Timaeus," Ptolemy, and Bacon, that they speak of hypotheses, not facts. When the sciences became separate and literal, much of their beauty was lost. Certainly the play was gone, and with

---

[63] *Poetria Nova*, 223-225, *Les Arts poétiques du XIIᵉ et du XIIIᵉ Siècle*, ed. Edmond FARAL (Paris, 1924), p. 204: repone/Pluribus in clausis unum; multiplice forma/Dissimuletur idem; varius sis et tamen idem.

[64] *De Libero Arbitrio*, II.xvi.171 (*op. cit.*, p. 76).

[65] *De Arca Nœ Morali*, I.11, *Hugh of St. Victor: Selected Spiritual Writings*, trans. by a religious of C.S.M.V. (London, 1962), p. 60.

that the fullness of mental engagement required to appreciate their domain was considerably diminished. With our lack of allegorical sense, our carefully indoctrinated inability to take delight in the play of ideas, and our contentment to see no ratio between what is inside ourselves and outside, we would appear the dreary ones.

V. — NUMBER AND CONCENTRIC TIME

A cosmology of concentric circles, 7 of which move and 3 of which are steadfast, combined with a Christian sense of linear time divided, according to St. Augustine,[66] into 7 ages with an 8th, a return to eternity beyond time, thus bringing the line full circle (linking alpha and omega), perpetrate for medieval man a time-sense different from and more complex than our own. Just as surely as the space around him was numbered and ordered, so too was time. For the sake of simplicity, let me suggest that the medieval Christian understood himself as living in three simultaneous time schemes, all of which required his attention. His problem was to coordinate the three in his mind. First, he understood time as we normally do, that is, as the chronology of an individual life through all its personal moments from birth to death. His perspective on personal time would, however, be more contained than ours, largely because of the numbered space around him. He would not be so aware of a flat span of senseless decades and centuries; rather he would have a keen sense of the cycle of a year, its numbered seasons and its feasts and parade of saints' days through the religious calendar. Because of the way the prayers and scriptural readings are laid out in the holy rites, he would also tend to view time in concourse with the events of Christ's life. If he were educated or inclined towards astrology, he might also have a sense of his life in conjunction with astronomical cycles and configurations which he might feel had some influence on his personal behavior. Individual events of his life he would date with reference to the reigning monarch or some memorable occurrence within or near his lifetime. But the main consideration which we should note is that for the most part this personal sense of time would be contained within the movements of an annual cycle which to him reflected God's plan. That is, his personal life is temporally contained and connected with the ordered world around it.

But in addition to this somewhat ritualized and contained personal sense of time, he would also see himself as part of a continuum of history. Here his perspective would be larger than that to which we are accustomed. Medieval man lives in the 6th Age, the age of the New Testament. It is the penultimate epoch during which the former 5 ages are rehearsed, reinterpreted, and perfected under the new dispensation in preparation for the 7th which will bring Apocalypse and Judgment. One would be reminded of this linear view of time through sermons and religious training. He would also

---

[66] E.g., *De Trin.*, IV.iv.7; *En narrationes in Psalmos*, vi; and *De Civ. Dei*, xi.31, xv.22, xvii.4.

V. "St. Michael et le Dragon" — Tapisserie de l'Apocalypse

VI.　　"Vision de la nouvelle Jérusalem" — Tapisserie de l'Apocalypse

encounter it, in more fathomable form, through the pageantry of the mystery plays on feast days, especially on Corpus Christi Day, when the whole drama of history would be unfolded before him. (I am thinking now of a man from England or the lowlands in the 13th-15th centuries.) The effect of these plays is remarkably personal, the only truly "living theater" the West has known. In such drama one participates, whether actor or audience, in the action of his own community, as people he knows begin with sunrise and continue until dark to re-enact the familiar roles of mankind from Creation to Judgment — all in the turning of a single day.[67] With such a view of history before him, he would think of himself not simply as, say, Hodge the Tinker of Bishop Burton, but would come to see that his life shared in that of Old Adam who lived in him by virtue of his very humanity. It also shared in that of the crude and selfish, yet laughable, Cain, and in Noah the ark builder with his fearful, sharptongued wife. And, hopefully, he would see his share in the Second Adam too. These figures would be for him more than mere roles in a play. They reflect the roles of the real life drama into which he has been cast. They typify those human plots which occur and recur daily throughout his life, roles through which he inevitably must define himself if he is to understand himself. Their plot is his plot; as far as he is concerned, their time is centered in him.

Ultimately, he must see himself as living within eternity. This time-sense is the most difficult of the three to remember and maintain. Augustine, Anselm, the Victorines, and the Franciscans all suggest that one's sense of immortality, so obscured by the Fall, is recovered by a journey inward, Eternity being discovered in the heart where the soul resides. With recovery of that center, one's triple time-sense is complete and his sense of Being focused within the concentricities of personal time, historical time, and eternity. The cycle of reference grows full.

One frequently encounters these three aspects of time simultaneously in medieval art, where contemporaries of the artist stand side by side with the ancients while a "time-line" separates, or better, relates them to the realm of eternity. Indeed, a reader unaware of multiple time-sense will find medieval art is confusing. Consider, for example, two 14th-century English tapestries from a series on the Apocalypse, now located in the Chateau du Roi René at Angers (Plate V). In the first, St. John stands at the left in his cubicle contemplating a plain upon which the Beast of the Apocalypse is being destroyed. John's cubicle represents the 4-square world of time and space, the realm of the individual moment. The scrim which forms the background for most of the scene marks the boundary of time and space, setting off the continuum of history which stretches out before him. Beyond the scrim is eternity, represented by a clear blue. In the complex moment of this scene the eternals are piercing the realm of time in the 7th age as viewed from the 6th, to bring all time to its conclusion. The tapestry presents all

---

[67] For a superb discussion of the mystery cycles, their meaning, presentation, and role in the life of a community, see V. A. KOLVE, *A Play Called Corpus Christi* (Stanford, 1966).

three time-senses converging in a vision such as man, fragmented in time, constantly strives for but seldom realizes. An angel holds a scroll from which he reads to John the Eternal Word. John uses his eyes, ears, and mind to try to comprehend, and, saint that he is, succeeds.

In the final tapestry of the series (Plate VI), Christ Himself (the Word) appears through the scrim and speaks directly to John who beholds the New Jerusalem as it will appear in the 8th Age. The vision is so transporting that John has actually stepped out of his cubicle onto the extended plane and looks upward to Christ his explicator. The water separating him from the Heavenly City reminds us that John is not himself in the eternal age when the ''sea shall be no more'' (Rev. 21:1). Yet through the convergence of time and eternity, he has his glimpse, at least.

This complex time-sense dominates much of medieval literature as well as art, especially dream vision literature and the drama, and accounts for much of what philologists at the beginning of the 20th century regarded as quaint anachronism. In the Towneley *Second Shepherd's Play*, for example, we begin in 14th-century northern England with English shepherds struggling against a miserable winter, then discover that we are participating in a second time scheme as well, namely the birth of Christ in our very midst. Ultimately, the players and audience share a glimpse of eternity as all sing with the angels. Time is reborn, perfected and made complete in our very presence. The play is designed to help the audience reclaim its own fullness of time.

Piers Plowman offers the most profound treatment of concentric time in Middle English literature. The persona, a restless wanderer named Will, sets out towards a goal whose definition keeps shifting, much to his consternation; yet it is a goal for which he senses a great need. The action all occurs on a middle ground, that is, on earth, the plane of time and space, where man must discover within himself the links between his existence and a greater reality. For about a third of the poem Will searches outside himself in a satirical version of 14th-century English society and mankind in general. Then, in the beginning of the middle third of the poem (Passus 8) he enters into his own mind to encounter such personifications as Thought and Imagination. Finally, in the latter part of the poem, after discovering Anima (Soul), who incorporates into one being the various aspects of self he had earlier explored, he has a transcendent vision which culminates in the Passion itself. In the climax of Will's search, time and the four directions converge on the center of mankind's circle, Christ's Crucifixion and Resurrection. While Will approaches from his 14th-century vantage point, he contemplates Abraham and Moses, rushing through time from the other direction. (They are presented as literally running.) They all meet in Christ, that redeeming human aspect of Trinity whereby eternity is realized in time and space.

Time and space are for the medieval metaphysician inseparable concepts. One cannot exist without the other.[68] To explore the soul and its motions the medieval philosopher frequently relies upon geometry and arithmetic, partly because of the peculiar nature of Soul as eternal entity. The figure most often used to explain the soul's paradoxical nature is the circle, since it is the only figure mysterious enough to encompass the soul's mysteries.[69] In *De Quantitate Animae*, 11.17-12.19, for example, St. Augustine expounds the perfection of the circle over other geometrical figures. Not only does it figure the shape of the soul; virtue is itself a roundness of life, completely in harmony with its parts as is a circle with its one undivided line and circumference of points all equidistant from its center. Boethius too uses the figure to explain one's sense of the soul's containment within a time world. Time is to eternity as "a cercle to the centre," Philosophia explains (*Consolatio* IV.pr.6.142-44, Chaucer's trans.). The metaphor suggests that Eternity resides within man at that point in his mental sphere where space ceases to exist and he slips through towards his "naturel entencioun." To help the lost Boethius find himself Philosophy uses her craft to weave "a manere wondirful cercle or envirounynge of the simplicite devyne" around his confused sense of being, thus containing the tangential vagrancies of his mind (III.pr.12). In doing so she not only helps him locate his center, but re-establishes for him a viable time-sense. He learns that the further his momentary residence is from the center of his circle, the weaker he becomes, the more slow and bound by external temporalities, the more fated. (Cf. Augustine's argument on "fatedness" as weakness, cited above.) The center is necessarily One. The ramifications of this Boethian kernel of wisdom reach far into all corners of medieval thought. Concepts like *place* or *steadfastness; home, feast, city*, and *New Jerusalem*; and *freedom, happiness*, and *rest*, are likely to be understood and explored through this fecund geometrical figure.

Considering the peculiar virtues of the circle, Roger Bacon concluded that the universe must be spherical. Moreover, since a circle can have only one center, he proved that there cannot be more universes than one.[70] His argument touches upon the great mystery of the circle. As long as there is space, there must be a center. The more precisely one defines that center the more closely one comes to infinity — the second and first dimensions beyond the third. Moreover, beyond the outer reaches of space is also infinity. The play between the infinite center and that infinite circumference

---

[68] E.g., St. AUGUSTINE, *De Civ. Dei*, xi.6, argues that time and space must have been created simultaneously, for one could not exist without the other. Cf. *De Civ. Dei*, xii.15, and *Confessiones*, xi 30-31.

[69] Their other favorite geometrical figure was the equilateral triangle which suggested to them unity in space (the first geometrical figure) and Trinity (see above, p. 57, and note 35). The triangle and circle share metaphysical qualities because of the idea of center, point, and 3 as the first real number. In seeking the center one moves from 3 (unity expressed) to one (point), one being the number base. Trinity is the spatial expression of that number base. Christ, the alpha and omega, completes the circle of time, thus providing the circumference to the circle; He is also the Creator and thus the center of the circle.

[70] *Opus Majus* IV, 4th distinction (BURKE, I, 176 and 185-86).

which includes all that is, was, and ever shall be, is the realm of time and space. In one's soul search, time can only be comprehended by turning simultaneously inward and outward until time and self become both circumscript and uncircumscript by center and circumference.[71]

But before quitting our discussion of time as a number concept, let me return briefly to our discussion of the finite continuum of history. Professor Grant wrote in his essay on St. Augustine of the Pauline doctrine on redeeming the time. It is indeed a central Christian teaching that the New Testament fulfills the Old and in its fulfillment explicates the blind patterns of former time. In his fulfillment and redeeming of time Christ makes all men equateable. Man living in this latter time reruns the lives of men in all previous ages, just as Christ lived as a second Adam, Noah, Abraham, David, and Daniel (those being the namesakes of the former epochs). The pathway to wisdom becomes "imitatio Christi": the world becomes a stage for both participation and parody of divine and human plots. Parody and participation through analogy are both forms of numbering and are as useful to the soul seeking orientation as the discovering and measuring the circuits of the heavens which in their harmonious patterns help man to discover harmony. It is on this principle that a work like the popular *Biblia Pauperum* was compiled. These blockprints are useful in exhibiting artistic utility of structural metaphors which convey meaning through number patterns. But they also demonstrate with remarkable clarity the idea of redeeming time by discovery of its true center, Christ the Creator and Savior. The beauty of the work lies not so much in skillful drawing of human figures, or in the use of color and line, but rather in the temporal and spacial proportions which become synonymous with the subject of the picture.

Although any of the prints in the various editions would demonstrate well the artist's thoughts on God's numbering of history as well as cosmos, let us consider the print of Christ and Longinus in the 40-leaf Blockbook (ca. 1440). (See Plate VII.)[72] The central panel portrays the blind Longinus piercing the crucified Christ's side, thus releasing the Eucharistic blood which trickles down to regenerate earth and the soldier's sight. Five soldiers stand on Christ's left, one of whom holds a pail while another, the most prominent of the five, points to the cross as if he has seen something he never saw before. Perhaps he represents Joseph of Arimathea, for in his hand he holds a walking stick which looks suspiciously like a cross and has turned his saddened face toward the man with the pail (grail?) as if to address him. On Christ's right Longinus kneels, gesturing towards his eyes with one hand and looking up to Christ's countenance which he now sees for the first time. Behind him stand two soldiers, there being 8 soldiers in all.

---

[71] See the last stanza of CHAUCER's *Troilus and Criseyde*, where Chaucer plays with the paradox. (Cf. DANTE, *Paradiso*, xiv, 28-30.) See "Number Symbolism in *Troilus and Criseyde*," 20-21.

[72] Facsimile editions have been made of the British Museum copy of the blockbook (London, 1859), in which our particular scene is plate 26, and of the Esztergom Cathedral copy (Corvina, 1967), in which our plate is numbered 21.

VII.   "Biblia Pauperum" Bib. Nat. MS. Ital. 115, f. 23r

The left panel (on Christ's right) shows Adam asleep in the Garden while Christ the Creator draws Eve from his side. In the background is a tree bearing 8 fruits. At first one might be dubious about the fruit being created for Adam; this division will lead to sin and the Fall for which Christ must eventually atone through His sacrifice. That is, the ultimate fruit of this action will be the Crucifixion (center panel). But the 8 fruits on the Tree of Life in the background remind us of the ultimate wisdom of Eve's creation, for in the 8th age Paradise will be restored and the fruits of time fulfilled. The 8 soldiers who witness the advent of the Eucharist in the center are likewise new fruit born from Christ's new tree of life, the Cross.

The panel on the right (Christ's left) depicts Moses striking water from the rock in the Desert of Sin (Deut. 22:51). Behind him, 5 men of authority look on. In the background stand 10 pine trees. Moses' act is juxtaposed to the centurion's. Both strike upon command of the surrounding multitude. Moses' act brings forth the Waters of Contradiction (Deut. 22:51). The consequence of his blind action is denial of entrance into the Promised Land. Longinus's act, on the other hand, brings forth the Eucharist which enables the faithful Christian to share in Paradise even though earthbound. The difference between the two actions is Christ's grace, which even Moses will share after Christ pierces Hell, a couple of pages later. The 5 men who surround Moses are probably meant to suggest the Old Law as do the 10 pines in the background (see Appendix 2 on 5 and 10 as signs of the Old Law). The trees are pine rather than deciduous to suggest the barrenness of the Law without Christ.[73]

Above the triptych David and Zacharias address the reader. David utters Psalm 68:21, a passage glossed as Christ's voice speaking through David to declare His forthcoming suffering and the reprobation of the Jews. Zacharias likewise speaks a mystery which he himself does not understand. Having declared a fountain which will flow at a time when prophets shall be confounded and say, "I am no prophet, I am a husbandman: for Adam is my example from my youth," he asserts, "And they shall say to him: What are these wounds in the midst of thy hands? and he shall say: With these I was wounded in the house of them that loved me" (Zach. 13:6). Like the words of David and the action of Moses in the Desert, the meaning of this ancient enigma is revealed in Christ's central panel. Until then, the words and acts were but empty parody.

Below the triptych Jeremias and Amos converse. Jeremias recalls how the Lord asked him what he saw and he replied, "I see a rod watching," whereupon the Lord replied, "Thou hast seen well: for I will watch over my word to perform it" (Jer. 1:12). His verse helps clarify the connection between Moses' rod, Longinus's spear, and the rod-like Eve (n.b., the

---

[73] The pine, because of its lack of fruit, is associated by St. Bernard (*PL*, CLXXXIII, 378-79) with the sterility of the old law, and in the *Romance of the Rose*, for example, it is the tree of the fleshly garden as opposed to the inner garden, or Shepherd's Park (tr. H. ROBBINS, p. 29; 434-35). Cf. HUGH OF ST. VICTOR, *De Fructibus Carnis et Spiritu* (*PL*, CLXXV).

common *virgo-virga* pun)[74] as she is drawn from Adam's side; but the true import of the rod metaphors lies only in the Cross of the center panel. Amos, the 4th corner figure, tells how it shall come to pass that the Lord shall let down his hook to draw up the fruit and darken the earth as if the sun had set at midday (Amos 8:9). Again, the enigma he speaks cannot be understood until the event of the central panel fulfills time and sense. The hook is the Cross.[75]

Without the center panel, the event which inaugurates the 6th Age, none of the earlier events can be truly understood. But through the triangulation of the triptych and the four scriptural prefigurations, all the events of the former times acquire full meaning. The panels are arranged like a cross with Christ's panel at the center. The arrangement and interlacing of ideas illustrates admirably this complex time process where we understand events through meaningful equations with that which is beyond equation. It is impressive that this single blockprint coordinates five of the first six ages (only the 2nd, Noah, is absent) and anticipates the 7th (Judgment) through rod and hook metaphors, and the 8th (New Jerusalem) through garden, fruit, husbandman, and "8" metaphors. Its graphic structure is such that even the eye tells us the center of time, as all angles, from Adam to our own post-Adventine perspective, point to Christ.

Cognizance of this analogic attitude toward history as well as cosmology is of greatest importance to a student of the Middle Ages. Little of medieval intellectual history can be understood without it. It means that people living in the 6th Age understood their lives (insofar as they considered history at all) in ways quite different from the modern perspective based on a simple chronological line. Their lives existed within concentric realities. It was not naive and myopic observation of external reality that convinced medieval cosmologists that earth must be the center of the universe. Their metaphysics demanded it. "Number teaches us," Hugh of St. Victor reminds us, "the nature of the going out and the return of the soul."[76] Indeed, it is not in fact earth that is center of their world, it is man's soul, that immortal point (thus necessarily an image of God, since "point" is beyond time and space) around which man in his temporal environment realizes his being.

---

[74] Aaron's rod which bloomed (Numbers 17:8) was commonly glossed as a figure for the Virgin whose bloom was Christ. See plate b (second plate) of the 40 Leaf Blockbook.

[75] The Cross is the supreme love-hook of Christ, the fisherman. (Cf. folk etymology of *amor* from *'amus* in Andreas CAPELLANUS, *De Amore*, I.3.) Recall the capturing of Leviathan by a hook (Cross) in the *Hortus deliciarum* illustration reproduced in Emile MALE, *The Gothic Image* (New York, 1958), p. 380.

[76] *Didascalicon*, II.4 (trans. J. TAYLOR, p. 64).

APPENDIX

The Noble Art of Glossing Numbers

By the 12th century the glossing of numbers, particularly numbers in the Holy Scriptures, had become an elaborate science. HUGH OF ST. VICTOR, *Exegetica de Scripturis et Scripturibus Sacris*, xv (*PL*, 175, 22-23), sets down nine guidelines for discovering numerological significance:

1. *Secundum ordinem positionis*, where numbers generally become more imperfect as they recede from unity. Two, which recedes from One, signifies sin which has deviated from the One Good.

2. *Secundum qualitatem compositionis*, where 2 can be divided and thus signifies corruptibility and transitoriness. *Three* can not be divided and thus designates the indissolvable and incorruptible.

3. *Secundum modum porrectionis*, were 7 after 6 equals rest after work; 8 beyond 7 equals eternity after mutability; 9 before 10 suggests defect among perfection; 11 beyond 10 denotes transgression outside of measure.

4. *Secundum formam dispositionis*, where 10, which has length, signifies rectitude in faith; 100, which expands in width, signifies amplitude of charity; 1000, which rises in height, signifies the altitude of hope.

5. *Secundum computationem*, where 10 signifies perfection, because by extension it is the end of computation.

6. *Secundum multiplicationem*, where 12 is sign of universality because composed of 3 & 4 by multiplication, where 4 is the corporeal, 3 the spiritual form.

7. *Secundum partium aggregationem*, where 6 is a perfect number, 12 abundant, etc.

8. *Secundum multitudinem partium*, where 2 signifies 2 unities, the love of God and neighbor; 3, that is, 3 unities, the Trinity; 4, that is 4 parts, the 4 seasons or 4 quarters of the world; 5, signifying 5 senses; and 7, the 7 sins.

9. *Secundum exaggerationem*, where the 7 penalties of Lev. 26 signify multiplicity of penalties.

The following index lists some of the more typical glosses bestowed on 1-12.

ONE   Monad: self-generating, self-generated; without beginning, without end (*Theo. Arith.*). Father of number: unity, both male and female, source of all numbers though not number itself (MACROBIUS, *In Somn. Scip.*, I.6). Unity of God repeatedly emphasized by the Church Fathers (e.g., Aug., *De Trin.*, IV.vii.11, *De Civ. Dei*, XI.10; BŒTHIUS, *Cons.*, III.pr. 9 & pr. 11-pr.12). Correlative metaphors: circle, Divine Simplicity, center, point, Wisdom, Truth, Order, fulfilled entente, goal, *summum bonum*, atonement, steadfastness, home, harmony, tranquility, peace of mind, virtue.

TWO   Dyad: other, the many, shadows as opposed to reality; corruptibility, mutability, division, disintegration, flux; divided mind, cupidity, selfpity; extension of point, motion. 2nd day of Creation not pronounced "good" by God; unclean number & breaker of unity (JEROME, *Adv. Jov.*, 1.16). Devil as duplicity (*Aug., De Civ. Dei*, XI.13-16). 20 (extension of 2) = unlucky number (*Adv. Jov.*, I.22), or "a twenty devil way." Sign of devils as opposed to simplicity of Christian. Correlative metaphors: duplicity, effeminacy, exile, isolation, alienation, illusion, Fortune. Can also have positive connotations, though more rarely: 2nd Person of Trinity; 2 New Commandments of love. Conjoiner, marriage bond as 2 made 1.

THREE   First real number. Expressive form of Unity. First figure in plane geometry; elemental form (Timæus's atoms). Completeness, all, or the whole. Like One and circle, a sign of perfection: Sum of monad and dyad, that is, of all its elements. (BACON, *Opus Majus*.) Number of Soul insofar as man in image of God (Trinity). (See AUG., *De Trinitate & Civ. Dei*, XI.24-28; ANSELM, *Monologion*; BONAVENTURE, *Itinerarum Mentis ad Deum*.) 3 = realized form of unity just as soul perceptible emanation of imperceptible God [PLOTINUS, *Enneads*, V.1.10. Cf. ALANUS DE INSULIS, *Regulæ de Sacra Theologia* (*PL*, 210, 623); PETER OF POICTIER, *Sententiæ* (*PL*, 211, 926).] Aquinas on substance, form, & Word, *Summa Theo.*, I.qu.45.art.7. See also I.qu.208 & qu. 290-91. 30 (extension of 3) = active life, marriage number, beginning of Christ's ministry, number of books in Bible (22 O.T. + 8 N.T., HUGH OF ST. VICTOR, *De Sacramentis*, prologue, ch. 7 & *De Arca Næ Morali*, I.14).

FOUR   Second real number (female). First figure in solid geometry (volume); first square number (Justice). Tetrad (sum of its integers = 10); forms base and sides of pyramid of Justice (tetrachtys). Body, carnality, earth: 4 elements, 4 humors, 4 conditions (hot, cold, moist, dry), 4 directions (see MACROBIUS, *In Somn. Scip.*, I.24-33, or HUGH OF ST. VICTOR, *De Arca Næ Morali*, I.16). Because of world's 4ness, then, 4 evangelists with 4 signs spreading the Good News (4 gospels) to all ends (4 quarters) of earth; 4 virtues (Justice, Prudence, Fortitude, Chastity); quadrivium; 4 branches of knowledge to assist soul (theoretical, practical, mechanical, logical). Correlative metaphors: earthliness, time, space, Fortune, mutability, time-weariness, contrariety; balanced opposition, harmony; 40 = period of exile or trial.

FIVE   Quintessence (PLUTARCH, *Moralia*, 389f-390). Created world, because of Euclid's 5 solid forms (Elements XIII), 5 zones of world, 5 species of living creatures (man, quadrupeds, fish, reptiles, birds) & 5 senses (HONORIUS, *De Imagine Mundi*, I.6). Thus, worldliness & animality: Philo says God began creating animals on 5th day since "there was no one thing so akin to another as the number 5 was to animals" (*De Mundi Opificio*, xv-xvi). Senses the most common gloss for biblical 5s. Also sign of Old Law (Pentateuch), spiritual blindness, rigidity (Cf. AUG., *On John*, tr. 24.6.1-14; *Glossa Ord.*, *PL*, 114.373; & *Catena Aurea*, trans. J.H.N. II, 536; III, 123-124; IV, 145; & IV, 309). In answer to 5s' worldliness & blindness Christ's 5 wounds, Mary's 5 sorrows & 5 joys. A love number: Venus & Mars (because of spheres), carnal marriage number (sum of first two number of dyad, 2 + 3), Solomon's star, & endless love knot. Circular number because of pentangle & arithmetic fact that in multiplication it repeats self in last digit. Pythagorean sign of Justice because of middle point in decad. (See "Numerology and Chaucer's *Troilus and Criseyde*," *Mosaic*, V (1972), 7-11.)

SIX   Perfect number (1 + 2 + 3 = 6). Completion of Creation on 6th day. Fruitful marriage number (2 × 3 = 6).

SEVEN   Totality, because of 7 moving spheres, 7 day week, & 7 ages of world. A uniquely strong number because it is indivisible and a factor of no other number in the decad. Sign of mutable world since no number so thoroughly measures the world: every physical object determined by 7 in that it has 3 dimensions (length, breadth, depth) & 4 boundaries (point, line, surface, volume); 7 motions, up, down, left, right, front, back, circular); 7 things seen (body, distance, shape, magnitude, color, motion, tranquility); 7 musical notes. Man reflects cosmic 7s: 4 (body) + 3 (soul); body has 7 visible parts (head, chest, belly, 2 arms, 2 legs) and 7 invisible parts (stomach, heart, liver, lungs, spleen, 2 kidneys); head (the most prominent part) has 7 orifices (2 eyes, 2 nostrils, 2 ears, mouth) and 7 voice changes (acute, grave, contracted, aspirated, tone, long & short sound) to accompany the 7 notes. Body secretes 7 fluids (tears, snot, saliva, sweat, 2 kinds of excrement & generative secretion). Children receive life in womb at 7 months; diseases & fevers reach climax on 7th day. Man's life measured by 7s: at 7 he gets teeth; 14, puberty; 21, beard; 28, fullness of manly strength; 35, season of marriage; 42, maturity of understanding; 49, most rapid improvement of intellect & reason; 56, reason & intellect perfected; 63, passions assume mildness; 70, desirable life comes to an end. (Cf. PHILO, *De Opificio Mundi*, 33-43 & MACROBIUS, *In Somn. Scip.*, I.6.) Hippocrates measures life by 7 (infancy, childhood, boyhood, youth, manhood, middle age, old age). Woman's menstrual cycle measured by 7s as is month. Augustine says 7 stands for all numbers together (*De Civ. Dei*, XI.31). Marks apprenticeship, steps to perfection, period of trial. 7 virtues & 7 vices equal all virtues and vices.

EIGHT   Eternity: sphere of fixed stars. Return to 1 or new beginning after 7. 8 survive deluge to begin again. Sign of circumcision as purification; sign of baptism. *Dies octavus* (8th day) = Easter or Pentecost (a week of weeks + *dies octavus*). 8th Age = New Jerusalem. As only cube in decad, sign of justice (MACROBIUS, *In Somn. Scip.*, I.v.17). Correlative metaphors: home, regeneration, redemption, felicity, harmony, transformation, new beginning.

NINE   An inbetween number. Defective if understood as short of 10. But also nearness to perfection: number of hierarchies of angels surrounding God's throne, obtaining their perfection in His ONE. Dante's number for Beatrice. Like 5, a potent number & circular because it reproduces itself in multiplication (e.g., 2 × 9 = 18, 1 + 8 = 9; 3 × 9 = 27, 2 + 7 = 9, 4 × 9 = 36, 3 + 6 = 9; 5 × 9 = 45, 4 + 5 = 9; etc.).

TEN   Unity, perfection, all-inclusiveness; one extended to include all numbers. 10 spheres. Old Law because of decalogue. Justice because of tetrachtys (Pythagorean pyramid of justice, $1 + 2 + 3 + 4$ forming equilateral triangle).

ELEVEN Sin: excess of 10, deficient of 12.

TWELVE Fullness, totality. 12 mansions, 12 months, 12 tribes of Israel, 12 apostles. Revelation: the spreading of Trinity to 4 corners of earth (AUG., *On John*, tr. 29; a very common gloss). Because of cosmic implications, sign of Apocalypse.

Glosses of this sort were particularly useful in scriptural exegesis, though they pertain to all the arts as well, since the basis of the glosses lies mainly in the number of Creation and, as Hugh of St. Victor points out, "the products of artificers, while not nature, imitate nature, and, in the design by which they imitate, they express the form of their exemplar, which is nature" (*Didascalicon*, I.4, trans. TAYLOR, p. 51).

In addition to numerical glossing based upon correspondences in nature, the 12th century witnessed the revival of gematric study. Gematria is the art of equating numbers with letters so that words might be expressed by numerical equivalents. Gematria had flourished among Greek and Hebrew scholars at the beginning of the Christian era simply because for a considerable period of time it had been the standard Greek method of arithmetical notation (See Louis Charles KARPINSKI, "Greek Arithmetic Notation," *Introduction to Arithmetic*, tr. D'Ooge (Ann Arbor, 1938), ch. 4). To the 24 letters of the Greek alphabet three were added (*digamma, koppa*, and *sampi* so that the 27 letters could provide signs for numbers up through the 3rd decimal place, whereafter accent marks were added to extend the notation system to higher numbers:

α	β	γ	δ	ϵ	ς	ζ	η	ϑ
1	2	3	4	5	6	7	8	9

ι	η	λ	μ	ν	ξ	o	π	φ
10	20	30	40	50	60	70	80	90

ρ	σ	τ	υ	ψ	χ	ψ	ω	λ
100	200	300	400	500	600	700	800	900

This system of notation prevailed in Greece from the time of Plato up into New Testament times and is reflected in New Testament writings and commentaries, especially in the Alexandria school. Gematria is stressed in the *Theologumena Arithmeticae*, a work once attributed to Iamblichus (probably a translation of a lost work by Nicomachus). As an example of its application in scriptural exegesis consider St. Augustine's explication of John 2:19-21 ["Destroy this temple, and in three days I will raise it up." Then said the Jews, forty and six years was this temple in building, and wilt thou rear it up in three days? But he spake of the temple of the body.] Augustine explains that 46 means ADAM, since by gematria a = 1, d = 4, a = 1, and m = 40, the sum being 46. The passage says, then, that the Jews will destroy the body (ADAM) by crucifying Christ (the 2nd Adam), but that Christ on the 3rd day will restore that temple through the Resurrection.

Gematria flourished along with Cabalistic studies into the 17th century. Knowledge of the art was spread throughout Europe by Franciscan preachers such as Jacobus de Fiore. A curriculum forma at Oxford in the 14th century, for example, indicates that 12 days were devoted to its study. Because of the occult nature of gematria, it is impossible to know with much certainty whether it was used for purposes other than scriptural explication, though instances of gematric poems do occur in Middle English (Cf. Rossell Hope ROBBINS, *Secular Lyrics of the XIVth and XVth Centuries* [Oxford, 1952], p. 80). A few gematric numbers were well known and crop up in literature as symbols, e.g., 18 or 888 as number of Christ [I (10) + η (8) + σ (200) α o (70) + u (400) + s (2) = 888].

The Contest of Apollo and Marsyas: Ideas About Music in the Middle Ages

BRUCE R. SMITH

In the ideal city there will be no plucking of many-stringed instruments and no piping on the aulos. On that rule Plato's spokesmen in the *Republic* are quick to agree. Of all the music instruments, Socrates at last exclaims, that leaves only the simple lyre and the cithara.

> "So our argument indicates," replies Glaucon.
> "We are not innovating, my friend, in preferring Apollo and the instruments of Apollo to Marsyas and his instruments."
> "No, by heavens!" Glaucon says, "I think not."
> "And by the dog," Socrates observes, "we have all unawares purged the city which a little while ago we said was luxurious."
> "In that we show our good sense."[1]

Plato's ideal city never existed, but the music which his spokesmen Socrates and Glaucon planned for it echoed for more than a thousand years. In the European Middle Ages as much as in the "classical" Renaissance, the liberal art of music was understood in accordance with ideas that Pythagoras, Plato, and other Greek philosophers originated. A Christian coloring, of course, was given to these ideas in late antiquity and the early Middle Ages. That failed to change their essential character and, if anything, made them more viable. At the same time, certain innovations during the Middle Ages set practical music onto a course of development that continues in our own time. Theorists were for a long time successful in accomodating these innovations to the inherited store of classical ideas about music; by the sixteenth century, however, musicians in several countries were calling attention to a glaring discrepancy between theory and practice. No lasting influence issued from their sometimes brilliant experiments in making modern music conform to the old ideas. The history of these ideas, the gradual dying away of the echoes of the music of Plato's ideal city, is the subject of this essay.[2]

---

[1] *Republic*, 399de [III.10]. The speeches directly quoted are from Paul SHOREY's translation, Loeb Classical Library (Cambridge: Havard Univ. Press, London: Heinemann, 1943), I, 249-251.

[2] As an exercise in the history of ideas, this essay takes for granted a great deal of scholarship in musicology, and it ignores a great many unsettled issues and technical problems. There has been room for only the most general remarks on the music itself: in particular, national differences have

I

Because they believe music possesses great educative power, Socrates and Glaucon carefully specify what kinds of music will be permitted in the Republic. As gymnastics train the body, so music trains the mind. Why music has such educative power Plato makes clear in the *Timæus*:

> .... music too, in so far as it uses audible sound, was bestowed for the sake of harmony. And harmony, which has motions akin to the revolutions of the Soul within us, was given by the Muses to him who makes intelligent use of the Muses, not as an aid to irrational pleasure, as is now supposed, but as an auxiliary to the inner revolution of the Soul, when it has lost its harmony, to assist in restoring it to order and concord with itself. And because of the unmodulated condition, deficient in grace, which exists in most of us,

---

not been emphasized, and musical forms that are not germane to the development of polyphony — troubador, trouvère, and Minnesang lyrics are a major instance — have had to be left out. For a total view of medieval music the pattern of thought laid out here needs to be supplemented with a music history of the period. Donald Jay GROUT's *A History of Western Music* (New York: Norton, 1960) is a particularly lucid introduction for a beginning reader unfamiliar with musical terminology. The standard history of medieval music, Gustave REESE's *Music in the Middle Ages* (New York: Norton, 1940), assumes more technical knowledge in the reader and patiently stops to consider scholarly problems whenever they arise. Granted the generalizations about *Zeitgeist* inevitable in a cultural history, Paul H. LANG's *Music in Western Civilization* (New York: Norton, 1941) succeeds admirably in discussing music in changing cultural contexts. The pattern of transformation traced in his first eight chapters is essentially that which informs this discussion; Reese's history has provided much helpful factual matter. I am also indebted to the *New Oxford History of Music*, ed. D. A. HUGHES and G. ABRAHAM, Vol. II, *Early Medieval Music up to 1300* (London: Oxford Univ. Press, 1954), and Vol. III, *Ars Nova and the Renaissance, 1300-1540* (London: Oxford Univ. Press, 1960).

No amount of reading can replace the experience of *hearing* medieval music, and the large number of recordings now available make that an easy matter. Each of the following groups has issued several outstanding recordings of medieval music: Deller Consort on The Bach Guild; Early Music Studio on Telefunken; Munich Capella Antiqua on Telefunken; New York Pro Musica on Decca; Purcell Consort and Musica Reservata on Argo, Philips, and Everest; Zurich Ancient Instrument Ensemble on Odyssey. Those currently available are listed under the "Collections" heading in the Schwann catalog. The 72 works included on the three-disc *Seraphim Guide to Renaissance Music* (Seramphim SIC-6052) make an attractive introduction in terms of both time-span (thirteenth to seventeenth centuries) and international variety. Printed commentary included with the album is minimal (the commentary with Telefunken albums is most extensive), but the performances by the Amsterdam Syntagma Musicum are superb.

Examples of medieval music transcribed into modern notation are most readily available in Vol. I of A. T. DAVISON and W. APEL, eds., *Historical Anthology of Music* (Cambridge: Harvard Univ. Press, 1946); in C. PARRISH, ed., *A Treasury of Early Music: An Anthology of Masterworks of the Middle Ages, the Renaissance, and the Baroque Era* (New York: Norton, 1958), available in paperback; and in C. PARRISH and J.F. OHL, eds., *Masterpieces of Music Before 1750* (New York: Norton, 1951). Later medieval examples of English provenance are collected in N. GREENBERG, ed., *An Anthology of English Medieval and Renaissance Vocal Music* (New York: Norton, 1970), also available in paperback. Of special interest are four volumes in the series *Anthology of Music: A Collection of Complete Musical Examples Illustrating the History of Music*, ed. K.G. FELLERER, which is being issued by the Arno Volk Verlag, Cologne. A. GENNRICH, ed., *Troubadors, Trouvères, Minnesang*, and *Meistergesang* (1961) and H. HUSMANN, ed., *Medieval Polyphony* (1962) have already appeared. Forthcoming are DREIMÜLLER, ed., *The Music of the Medieval Drama*, and STÄBLEIN, ed., *Songs of the Middle Ages*. All of the volumes in this series feature excellent introductions in English.

As an aid to reading and to listening, the articles in Willi APEL's *Harvard Dictionary of Music*, 2nd ed. (Cambridge: Belknap Press, 1969), provide clear and concise information.

VIII.   ''Flaying of Marsyas'' — Raphael (Stanza della Segnatura)

Rhythm also was bestowed upon us to be our helper by the same deities and for the same ends.[3]

To most twentieth-century thinkers such a formulation is no more than a clever metaphor: two musical concepts (harmony and rhythm) are being used to fuse a physical concept (revolutions in the universe) with a psychological concept (the soul of man). For us those are altogether different categories; for Plato they were conceptually alike. That mythic contest of Apollo and Marsyas to which Socrates referred above can perhaps explain. No full account of the myth from Plato's time or earlier exists today, but in the first century B.C., Diodorus Siculus tells the story this way in his *Bibliotheca Historia*, rendered into expansive late fifteenth-century English by John Skelton:

The coniecture that men haue of his [Marsyas'] mature reason and witte is for that he cowde with his mowthe make a mervelous sownde ensuying by immytacioun the armony of many whistels or recorders to-gedre blowyng at oones. And thus by his melodious sownde the bagpipe was first brought vp and envred among the people.... And when after theire long iourneyng, they [Marsyas and the goddess Cybele] were comme vnto Dionysius in the cittee of Nisa, they fownde there Apollo how he was hadde in grete auctoritie for thencheson [the reason] that men said there how he founde first the musicall experience of the melodious harpe; where Marsias and Apollo fell at a trauers and altercation bittwene theym-self, of theym ij which was the moost konnyng in swete armonye. For the triall wherof, thenhabitauntes of the said cittee were chosen for endifferent iuges. Apollo then occupied a syngle harpe, and Marsias vsed then an hornepipe so shrell and lowde which sownded among the people, that they all wondred therat, for they ne had sene any such enstrument tofore. And in this triall they estered in theire opynyon how in swetenes of his sowndye pipyng, Marcias farre passed Apollo. Theire arbitratours endifferently discussyng where eche of theym ij hym-self endevoired theire enstrumentes to preferre, Apollo arrected all his coraige melodiously *to syng* with his lusty harpe; and therin it was demed in theire supposell how he Marsias passyngly exeded. Therat Marsias havyng endignation, spake out alowde to all the audience, and openly shewed how Appollo asyet agaynst hym had not prevailed, and how/they ought by good advisement not to conceive the dulcoure [sweetness] of mannes voice, but to compare by theire endifferent assertions the artificiall experience of an enstrument, by which exquesite iudiciall the swetenes and armonye aswell of the hornepipe as of the harpe moche more endifferently shuld be tried; and ouer this he allegged for thenstrengthyng of his parte defensive, how it were agayne [against] all good equytie and right that ij artificiall experiences shuld be wayed ageyne oon allone. Then by repoort I vndrestonde that Apollo aunswered how he nomore employed nor fortherd his enstrument by his voice than Marsias did by his, in-so-moche as he also occupied his mowthe by enflative blastyng and lowyng in his pipe; by encheson [reason] wherof, it was lefull [lawful] for theym bothe the same to envre [do] orels [or else] neither of theym by mowthe, but by manuall craft to shew the solacious modulation and melodye of theire enstrumentes. When the arbitrers hadde wele apperceived that Apolloes request was moche more enstrengthed with reason endifferent, the discutions accomplished, they fynally concluded how Marsias was venquyssed and caste in his art. Apollo in this contravercye, of malice with the firy rancour enflamed. Marsias he so bitterly assawted that out of his skynne he fleed hym quyk.[4]

---

[3] *Timæus*, 47de, trans. R. G. BURY, Loeb Classical Library (London: Heinemann, New York: Putnam, 1929), p. 109.

[4] *Bibliotheca Historica*, III.58-59; italics are mine. Skelton's translation is edited by F. M. SALTER and H. L. R. EDWARDS, Early English Text Society, Nos. 233 and 239 (London: Oxford Univ. Press, 1956-57). Quotation is from this edition, I, 301-303. With variations in detail, accounts of the contest also appear in HYGINUS, *Fabula*, 165; APOLLODORUS, *Bibliotheca*, i.4.2.; and PLINY, *Natural History*, xvi.89.

Apollo wins the contest for two reasons: because of the superiority of his instrument (Marsyas cannot *pluck* his pipe "by manuall craft" when the contest comes to that) and because he *sings* as well as plays. Why these facts should be significant is explained by the nature of Greek music. Pythagoras (sixth century B.C.) had "discovered" music, so it was claimed, by mathematical calculation. Behind the heard consonances of music Pythagoras was sure there could be found "a certain instrumental assistance to the hearing, which should be firm and unerring, such as the sight obtains through the compass and the rule," as Iamblichus puts it in his fourth-century-A.D. biography of the philosopher.[5] One day the answer came,

---

[5] *Life of Pythagoras*, Chap. 26, trans. T. TAYLOR (London: Watkins, 1926), p. 62. Chapters 25 and 26 of Iamblichus's biography are devoted to Pythagoras's musical doctrine. Writing at the time he does, Iamblichus characteristically confounds Pythagoreanism with later Platonic doctrines. In Chapter 15, for example, he speaks of Pythagoras as using music as a "medicine" for the soul in much the same way that Plato describes the proper use of music in the *Timæus* (cf. passage quoted in text above) and in the *Republic*. Also Platonic is Iamblichus's testimony that Pythagoras "translated" unheard divine music into hearable mundane form; divine music has become a prescriptive model for earthly music: "Pythagoras, however, did not procure for himself a thing of this kind through instruments or the voice, but employing a certain ineffable divinity, and which it is difficult to apprehend, he extended his ears, and fixed his intellect in the sublime symphonies of the world, he alone hearing and understanding, as it appears, the universal harmony and consonance of the spheres, and the stars that are moved through them, and which produce a fuller and more intense melody than anything effected by mortal sounds. This melody also was the result of dissimilar and variously differing sounds, celerities, magnitudes, and intervals, arranged with reference to each other in a certain most musical ratio, and thus producing a most gentle, and at the same time variously beautiful motion and convolution. Being therefore irrigated as it were with this melody, having the reason of his intellect well arranged through it, and as I may say, exercised, he determined to exhibit certain images of these things to his disciples as much as possible, especially producing an imitation of them through instruments, and through the more voice alone." A specific connection between Pythagoras's discovery and Plato's theology is made by MACROBIUS in his *Commentary on the Dream of Scipio* (II.i-ii), written a little more than a century after Iamblichus's Greek account. Macrobius's fifth-century version became a major source for the Latin Middle Ages. Actual physical sounds, says Macrobius, are produced by the rotation of the heavenly spheres, and "Reason, which is present in the Divine," causes these sounds to be harmonious. "Pythagoras was the first of all the Greeks to lay hold of this truth." The circumstances under which Pythagoras supposedly made his discovery are the same in Macrobius as they are in Iamblichus, though the Latin writer says that the hammers Pythagoras heard were blacksmiths' and not brassworkers' (II.i). The cosmic numbers that Pythagoras disclosed, Macrobius concludes, prompted Plato to acknowledge a creator-god: "Now when Plato, guided by Pythagoras's revelation and drawing upon the godlike power of his own extraordinary genius, had recognized that no union could be lasting except one based on those numbers, he constructed his World-Soul by interweaving them, imitating the ineffable wisdom of the divine Creator" (II.ii; trans. W. H. STAHL [New York: Columbia Univ. Press, 1952], pp. 186-190). The circumstances of Pythagoras's discovery — especially his use of hammers, either a brassworker's or a blacksmith's — were widely disseminated in the Middle Ages and survived in Renaissance iconography. Genesis 4:20-22 gave a different account of the discovery of music, attributing it to Jubal: "And Adah bore Jabal: he was the father of such as dwell in tents, and of such as have cattle. And his brother's name was Jubal: he was the father of all such as handle the harp and organ. And Zillah, she also bore Tubal-cain, an instructor of every articifer in brass and iron: and the sister of Tubal-cain was Naamah." By a marvelous piece of medieval ingenuity, the conflicting pagan and Christian accounts of the origin of music were harmonized: Tubal-cain might easily be confused with his brother Jubal, and the importance of brassworkers' hammers in Pythagoras's discovery in fact encouraged just such a substitution. In his discussion of music in the encyclopedic *Etymologiæ* (sixth century) Isidore of Seville gives this felicitous error the force of authority. Isidore is

Iamblichus would have it, when Pythagoras was passing a brassworker's shop and heard familiar harmonic intervals in the striking of the hammers. The philosopher rushed inside. The difference in pitch, he discovered, had to do with the weight of the hammers. Back at home he suspended four strings from a peg in the wall, stretched them by tying hammers to the loose ends, and after experimenting with various weights found that he could reproduce the consonant intervals by plucking the strings. To Pythagoras's delight the weights necessary to produce these intervals turned out to be expressible in fixed ratios using only the numbers 1 to 4, i.e., octave = 1: 2, fifth = 3: 2, fourth = 4:3. It could be no accident that $1 + 2 + 3 + 4 =$ the sacred number 10. Given their concept of a totally interrelated cosmos, Pythagoras and his followers could seize on these numerical ratios as a revelation of universal order. This imaginative leap Aristotle treats succinctly in the chapter of the *Metaphysics* devoted to Pythagorean philosophy:

> .... since, then, all other things appeared in their nature to be likenesses of numbers, and numbers to be the first in the whole of nature, they came to the belief that the elements of numbers are the elements of all things and that the whole heaven is a harmony and a number.[6]

The ratios that Pythagoras discovered were at first descriptive; the particular musical intervals that he set out to express numerically were, after all, consonant only because men's ears had already subjectively judged them so. But once the ratios had been given cosmic application, they quickly became prescriptive. Music had now an objective model. As a stringed instrument, the lyre never lost its associations with Pythagoras's discovery and with the cosmic nature of music, and by Plato's time a distinction was commonplace between the native, Apollonian lyre and the Asian, Dionysian aulos.

But Marsyas had an even more obvious handicap: he could not sing and pipe at the same time. The sounds he produced simply failed to measure up to what the Greeks understood *mousike* to mean. At least up to the time of Aristotle (fourth century B.C.) poetry and music could be regarded as intimately related concerns. One possible way of dividing up things made by human craft is according to the medium that their maker uses. A painter, that is, "makes" with pigments; a sculptor, with stone; a choreographer, with

---

discussing the "inventors" of music: "Moyses dicit repertorem musicæ artis fuisse Tubal, qui fuit de stirpe Cain ante diluvium. Græci vero Pythagoram dicunt huius artis invenisse primordia ex malleorum sonitu et cordarum extensione percussa" (III.xvi, ed. W. M. LINDSAY [Oxford: Clarendon Press, 1911], Vol. I [unpaginated]). Martianus CAPELLA's De Nuptiis Philologiæ et Mercurii (fifth century) gave each of the seven liberal arts a personified feminine identity that remained familiar in visual inconography of the Middle Ages and Renaissance. Countless illustrators juxtaposed these seven ladies with their human "discoverers," and Lady Musica is usually depicted in the company of a human figure wielding hammers — a nicely ambiguous detail that manages to suggest both Pythagoras and Tubal-cain. For a good example see the frequently reproduced "Triumph of St. Thomas," a fourteenth-century fresco attributed to Andrea da Firenze in the church of Santa Maria Novella in Florence.

[6] *Metaphysics*, 986a, trans. H. G. APOSTLE (Bloomington and London: Indiana Univ. Press, 1966), p. 21. Book Alpha, chapter 5, contains Aristotle's account of Pythagorean doctrine, a major source in the absence of any genuine surviving Pythagorean texts.

rhythmic movement. An artificer of *mousike* "makes" with sound. Poetry and music share this medium. Plato and most medieval European commentators after him can thus describe music in terms of three elements: harmony, rhythm, and *words*. In his *Poetics* Aristotle concedes that there is a form of "imitation" that uses instrumental sound only, but he does not even have a name to give to the kind of poetry that is composed apart from harmonic intonation:

> Thus the arts of flute and lyre music, and any others of similar nature and effect such as the art of the panpipe, produce their imitation using melody and rhythm alone, while there is another which does so using speeches and verses alone, bare of music, and either mixing the verses with one another or employing just one certain kind — an art which is, as it appears, nameless up to the present time.[7]

As Plato's definition implies, words and music were united in two ways: in rhythm and in harmony. The quantitative character of Greek meant that spoken language, as much as the abstract sounds we limit music to today, was a species of quantitatively measurable sound. The rhythm of words could dictate the rhythm of their musical intonation. Harmony in Plato's definition refers not to simultaneous sounds but to sequential ones. Greek music, like most non-Western music even today, was basically monophonic ("one-sounded") and consisted of a single unaccompanied melodic line. The harmonic ratios that Pythagoras established governed how tones were sounded in sequence. Harmony defined as the consonance of several tones sounded simultaneously is, as we shall see, a different concept altogether.

The basis of ancient Greek monophony, like that of much other Eastern music, was most likely a repertory of recitation formulas and melodic motives that could be used over and over again, arranged in various combinations. *Ta'amin* technique in Jewish chant, *oktoechos* in Byzantine music, *maquam* in Arabic music, and *ragas* in Hindu music are all examples of this compositional technique. Choice of motives in such music is not arbitrary but is a function of the text, of the position of a phrase with respect to the whole composition, and of the circumstances of a particular performance. Two passages in Plato's *Laws* imply intimate connections in Greek music among melodic motives, kinds of text, and even the sex and social station of performers.[8] The various scale arrangements that lay behind these melodic motives were codified as "modes." Plato is not the only

---

[7] *Poetics*, 2.47, trans. G. F. ELSE (Ann Arbor: Univ. of Michigan Press, 1967), p. 16. It is important to note that Aristotle is tacitly acknowledging that both unverbal music and unsung poetry are in fact being cultivated, even though they do not fit the traditional classification. In this instance, as in others, Plato's pronouncements on art are affirmations of a traditional cultural order, pristine in the ancestral past, adulterated in the present.

[8] "Let us not hesitate, then, to mention the point wherein lies the difficulty of music…. The man who blunders in this art will do himself the greatest harm, by welcoming base morals; and, moreover, his blunder is very hard to discern, inasmuch as our poets are inferior as poets to the Muses themselves. For the Muses would never blunder so far as to assign a feminine tune and gesture to verses composed for men, or to fit the rhythms of captives and slaves to gestures framed for free men, or conversely, after constructing the rhythms and gestures of free men, to assign to the rhythms a tune or verses of an opposite style…. The poets rudely sunder rhythm and gesture from

writer to attribute spiritual powers (*ethos* is the technical term) to these modes, and Socrates and Glaucon rigorously exclude all but the most manly modes from the Republic.

Musicians, it seems, fare somewhat better in the ideal city than do other literary craftsmen, who, except for encomiasts, are summarily banished. Plato is lenient only because music, to a greater extent than other products of human craft is capable of realizing the rational, cognitive truth that he poses as the object of art. Like painting and fable-making, music for Plato is a species of imitation, as this exchange in the *Laws* makes clear:

Athenian Stranger:	We assert, do we not, that all music is representative and imitative?
Clinias of Crete:	Of course.
Athenian:	So whenever a man states that pleasure is the criterion of music, we shall decisively reject his statement; and we shall regard such music as the least important of all (if indeed any music is important) and prefer that which posseses similarity in its imitation of the beautiful.
Clinias:	Very true.
Athenian:	Thus those who are seeking the best singing and music must seek, as it appears, not that which is pleasant, but that which is correct; and the correctness of imitation consists, as we may say, in the reproduction of the original in its own proper quantity and quality.
Clinias:	Of course.[9]

The context of this exchange leaves no room for doubt that the "original" to be imitated is the number that harmonizes the cosmos.

Harmony, rhythm, and words — Marsyas's piping is mindless noise when judged with full awareness of what these terms imply. With no reference to cosmic harmony, with no embodiment of *logos*, his sounds

---

tune, putting tuneless words into metre, or leaving tune and rhythm without words, and using the bare sound of harp or flute, wherein it is almost impossible to understand what is intended by this wordless rhythm and harmony...." (*Laws*, II.69). N.B. also *Laws*, III.700, where, after enumerating "various classes and styles" of poetry, the Athenian remarks, "So these and other kinds being classified and fixed, it was forbidden to set on kind of words to a different class of tune.... but later on, with the passage of time, there arose as leaders of unmusical illegality poets, who, though by nature poetical, were ignorant of what was lawful and just in music; and they, being frenzied and unduly possessed by a spirit of pleasure, mixed dithyrambs, and imitated flute-tunes with harp-tunes, and blended every kind of music with every other...." Translation by R. G. Bury in The Loeb Classical Library (London: Heinemann, New York: Putnam, 1926), I, 145-147, 245-247. Both passages, it is interesting to note, state that current music violates Plato's prescriptions, particularly by appealing to the senses with "wordless rhythm and harmony."

[9] *Laws*, 668ab. Plato's ideas about music were important to all the Neo-Platonists. Music as an imitation of the beautiful accords well, for example, with Plotinus's consuming interest in how the soul can reascend the chain of being: "And harmonies unheard in sound create the harmonies we hear and wake the Soul to the consciousness of beauty, showing it the one essence in another kind: for the measures of our sensible music are not arbitrary but are determined by the Principle whose labour is to dominate Matter and bring pattern into being" (*Enneads*, I.xi.3, trans. S. MacKenna [third ed. rev., London: Faber, 1962], p. 59).

appeal only to the senses, not to the intellect and soul; Plato no doubt considered the ripping off of Marsyas's flesh an appropriate punishment.[10]

II

There are silences in the history of music between late Greek civilization and the early European Middle Ages. For a culture which has left so many monuments of the spoken arts, of oratory and drama, Rome has surprisingly left not a trace of its music. The music of early Christian Europe, however, both in theory and in practice, displays an obvious debt to Greece. Donald J. Grout provides this summary of the musical ideas inherited by the European Middle Ages:
(1) a conception of music as primarily pure, unencumbered melodic line;
(2) an idea of music and words as intimately linked, particularly in matters of rhythm and metre;
(3) a philosophy of music as interlocked into the system of nature;
(4) a mathematically determined acoustical theory;
(5) a system of scale-formation based on tetra-chords; and
(6) a musical terminology.
(1), (2), and (3) were common to all eastern nations; (4), (5), and (6) were specifically Greek.[11]

These inherited notions about music occupied a precise, well-defined relationship to the rest of human knowledge. Music was one of the seven liberal arts.[12] The Trivium (grammar, dialectic, rhetoric) and the Quad-

---

[10] Ficino and Pico later seized on this appropriateness of punishment; nor does it seem to have been lost on Raphael, who in the Stanza della Segnatura in the Vatican alters iconographic tradition to portray the crowning of Apollo and the flaying of Marsyas as simultaneous acts, not to mention making Marsyas an old man, with a likely allusion to St. Paul's "old man" of the flesh and "new man" of the spirit (Romans 6:6, Ephesians 4:22, Colossians 3:9). Cf. Edgar WIND, *Pagan Mysteries in the Renaissance* (New York: Norton, 1968), 171 ff. Fulgentius's interpretation of the Marsyas fable in his *Mythologiarum libri tres* (sixth century) is the prototype for most later medieval and Renaissance commentators. Citing the authority of "Orpheus" and Hermes Trismegistus, this first major post-classical mythographer notes that there are three kinds of music: *adomenon* (music of the human voice), *psallomenon* (music of the stringed cithara), and *aulumenon* (music of the tibia-pipe). In terms of their effects, these three kinds of music are arranged in a strict hierarchy, the voice being the most capable and the tibia the least. To conclude his explication of the "immer meaning" of this "mystical story," Fulgentius seizes on the fact that Marsyas discovered the pipe only after it had been cast off by Minerva (this detail is present in Diodorus's account). Now, since all who are learned in music know the respective limitations of the three instruments, the action of Minerva (*"id est sapientia"*) is manifestly an allegory of Reason's rejection of the paltry pipe in favor of the voice and cithara (*Mythologiarum libri tres*, III,ix [ed. R. HELM (Leipzig: Teubner, 1898), pp. 73-77]).

[11] GROUT, p. 19.

[12] A good account of the liberal arts in European tradition is to be found in Ernst Robert CURTIUS, *European Literature and the Latin Middle Ages*, trans. W. R. TRASK (New York and Evanston: Harper, 1963), pp. 36 ff. The place of the liberal arts in medieval philosophy was the subject of the fourth Congrès International de Philosophie Médiévale, held in Montreal in 1967. The papers delivered at this conference, many of them extremely valuable, are collected in *Arts Libéraux et Philosophie au Moyen Âge* (Montréal: Institut d'Études Médiévales; Paris, Vrin, 1969). Paul O. KRISTELLER's "The Modern System of the Arts," *Journal of the History of Ideas*,

rivium (arithmetic, music, geometry, and astronomy) had been introduced into the Greek curriculum by Pythagorean and Sophist teachers of the fifth century B.C. and by rhetoricians of the fourth century B.C.; Isocrates had conceived of them as *propædeutics* (''preparations'') to philosophy. With the disappearance in late antiquity of philosophy as a distinct discipline, the Trivium and Quadrivium became disciplines of speculation in their own right.

Martianus Capella's *De Nuptiis Philologiæ et Mercurii* (''the Marriage of Philology and Mercury,'' fifth century A.D.) laid out the seven arts as the Middle Ages knew them down to the twelfth century and beyond. The Quadrivium investigated what F. Joseph Smith has called ''the intellectual *content* of things; the Trivium, ''the logical, grammatical, and rhetorical expression of this metaphysical content.''[13] With the Trivium, D.W. Robertson has suggested, medieval men could read the ''allegory of words''; with the Quadrivium, ''the allegory of *things*,'' the ''book'' of created nature.[14] As a member of the Quadrivium, music for the Middle Ages was before anything else a mathematical discipline. Its particular concern was numbers in relation to each other. Despite this elaborate theoretical structure and these fine distinctions, it would be misleading to call the liberal arts a practical program for intellectual endeavor. Only the Trivium was ever really cultivated at Rome, and a mere handful of men — St. Augustine, Bœthius, Cassiodorus, Isidore of Seville (fourth to seventh century) — were almost entirely responsible for transmitting to the Middle Ages its inheritance of classical thought about music.

St. Augustine's *De Musica* is the earliest of the writings of these men. Cast as a dialogue between a learned Teacher and an eager Pupil, the *De Musica* proclaims even in its layout an unmistakable classical Greek heritage: Book I defines music as a liberal art; Books II, III, IV, and V discuss rhythm, poetic metre, and verse; Book VI, ''in which the mind is raised from the consideration of changeable numbers in inferior things to unchangeable numbers in unchangeable truth itself,'' concludes with an elaborate consideration of metaphysics and epistemology.[15] Augustine's definition of music is general enough for such breadth of vision: *Musica est scientia bene modulandi* (''Music is the science of modulating well''). Each

---

12 (1951) and 13 (1952), rpt. in *Renaissance Thought II* (New York: Harper Torchbooks, 1965), 163-227, outlines the slow progress by which music and the other fine arts finally became disentangled from the crafts and the sciences. Not before the eighteenth century are painting, sculpture, architecture, music, and poetry clearly set apart as ''aesthetic'' pursuits.

[13] ''A Medieval Philosophy of Number: Jacques de Liège and the *Speculum Musicæ*,'' in *Arts Liberaux*, pp. 1023 ff.

[14] D. W. ROBERTSON, *A Preface to Chaucer: Studies in Medieval Perspectives* (Princeton: Princeton Univ. Press, 1962), p. 297; on the notion of nature as a book, cf. Curtius, pp. 319 ff.

[15] Augustine's treatise is printed in J. P. MIGNE, ed., *Bibliotheca Patrum* (Paris, 1841), XVIII, 1081-1194. There is a complete English translation by R. C. TALIAFERRO in *The Fathers of the Church*, ed. R. J. DEFARRARI *et al*. (New York: Fathers of the Church, Inc., 1947), Vol. IV. My translations from the *De Musica* are based on Taliaferro's but depart from his rendering in several instances.

term in that definition, Augustine insists, has its importance. *Modulandi*, "a certain skill in moving," derives from *modus*, "measure," but has a more restrictive meaning: it is a particular kind of measure applied to movement in time. *Bene* limits the use to which modulation is put, the end that it serves:

> .... it is one thing to modulate, and another to modulate well. For modulation is thought to apply to any singer whatever as long as he does not err in the measurings [*in illis dimensionibus*] of voice and sounds; but good modulation [is thought] to have as its object [*pertinere*] the liberal art [*ad hanc liberalem disciplinam*] — that is, music. (I.iv.4)

Scientia, about which the Teacher and Pupil of the treatise carry on their lengthiest dialogue, clarifies further this distinction between modulation and *good* modulation. The *knowledge* of music to which *scientia* refers engages man's intellect and reason; the *practice* of music requires only the senses and memory. Later, Bœthius will insist on this same distinction between "true" musician and mere performer: "He however is a musician who on reflection has taken to himself the *science* of singing .... by the rule of contemplation [*imperio speculationis*]."[16]

Augustine's discussion of music as numerically ordered movement constantly plays on the pun of *ratio* (reason) and *ratio* (numerical proportion). Unlike many later medieval thinkers, Augustine *hears* music as well as speculates about it. In the *De Musica*, as in his other writings, Augustine's epistemology is a combination of sense perception and "illumination" from within.[17] To apprehend number man must hear it in time or see it in space; at the same time he has an innate "judging" capacity that predisposes him to enjoy equality and to prefer particular numerical ratios. Like the rest of creation, man participates in number; his every action is caught up in it:

> For whatever restrains us from walking with unequal steps or from striking at things in unequal intervals or from eating or drinking with uneven motions of the jaw and from scratching with unequal motions of the nails and, to be brief, from unequal motions in any application of ourselves to doing something with our bodily members — [whatever causes this] and tacitly demands a certain equality — that very thing is something — I don't know what — *judicial* that introduces God the builder of the animal, properly believed to be the author of all fittingness and agreement. (VI.viii.20)

But beyond the power of the senses to judge, man is imbued with more powerful, more lasting numbers that make possible an "appraisement" (the verb is *aestimare*) by reason, "a kind of judgment of the judicial numbers." These more powerful numbers that inform man's *ratio*, his appraising faculty, are the cosmic numbers that lead to God:

---

[16] *De Inst. Mus.*, I.33. The *De Institutione Musica* is printed along with the *De Institutione Arithmetica* in an edition edited by G. FRIEDLEIN (Leipzig: Teubner, 1867). Excerpts from the treatise are translated by Oliver Strunk in *Source Readings in Music History from Classical Antiquity through the Romantic Era* (New York: Norton, 1950), pp. 79-86.

[17] There is a concise consideration of Augustine's philosophy in David KNOWLES, *The Evolution of Medieval Thought* (New York: Random House, 1962), pp. 32 ff. Knowles discusses at length the importance of number in Augustine's Neo-Platonism.

> But what are the higher things if not those where the highest, unchangeable, undisturbed, and eternal equality resides? Where there is no time, because there is no change, and from where times are made and ordered and changed, imitating eternity as they do when the turn of the heavens comes back to the same state and the heavenly bodies to the same place and when days and months and years and centuries and other revolutions of the stars obey the laws of equality, unity, and order. So terrestrial things are subject to celestial, and their time-circuits join together in harmonious [*numerosa*] succession for a song of the universe [*quasi carmini universitatis*]. (VI.xi.29)

The music and verse of man-made poems imitate the numbers of this cosmic poem.

Augustine's vision is astonishingly broad and complete. We have numbers that are heard, we have numbers that are unheard, and we have a way to rise from one to the other. Bœthius's slightly later *De Institutione Musica* lacks this carefully articulated connection between sound and speculation — epistemology is not one of the treatise's concerns — but it is Bœthius who became the standard medieval authority. His treatise remained a textbook at Oxford into the eighteenth century. Accepting Plato's concept of music as a *speculum* of univeral order, Bœthius divides music into three kinds that reflect three aspects of that order. *Musica mundana* is the music of the spheres, the rhythm of the seasons, the harmonious combination of elements. *Musica humana* is the harmony of body and soul, the accord of rational and irrational within the soul and of the diverse elements within the body. Finally, *musica in instrumentis constituta* is the audible embodying (in the "instrument" of the human voice as well as in other instruments) of these ethereal harmonies. Recalling Plato's belief in the educative power of music, Bœthius declares that music is the only member of the Quadrivium that is related to morality as well as speculation. (See pp. 66-69 above.)

In the beginning the nature of early Christian *musica in instrumentis constituta* was, like its classical Greek prototype, intimately bound up with this store of theory. Most musicologists agree that Gregorian chant derives from the Eastern monophony of which classical Greek music was a type. Byzantine music, with its amalgamation of Greek theory and Near Eastern, particularly Hebrew, practice, was an important intervening influence.[18] One particular Syrian influence was of far-reaching significance. A shift from quantity to accent in determining poetic metre occurred in fourth-century Syrian verse and became standard in Greek and Latin poetry during the next century. Words and music were no longer, strictly speaking, both species of quantitatively measurable sound.

Chant as it was codified by Pope Gregory I (r. 590-604) betrays a combination of both systems of prosody. Its three kinds of melodic

---

[18] Greek was the language of all Christian liturgy until the end of the third century (the Kyrie still opens the Western mass), and Eastern influence continued during to reigns of popes of Syrian and Greek origin in the eighth century, ending only with the final division of the Church in 1050. A thorough and readable introduction to chant is Willi APEL, *Gregorian Chant* (Bloomington: Indiana Univ. Press, 1958).

formation suggest the old integrity of word and musical intonation: syllabic settings assign one tone to a syllable, the rhythm of the language determining the rhythm of the chant; melismatic settings make a single syllable the occasion for an elaborate, extended coloratura; and neumatic, or group-style, settings combine features of the other two by intoning one syllable over two, four, or more notes. The new accent, on the other hand, helps give shape to the melodic line of Gregorian chant, at least as it survives today: in most cases melody rises to a peak above adjacent tones whenever an accented syllable is intoned. Choice of syllabic melismatic, or neumatic setting is, as we would expect from other Eastern systems of melodic-formulaic composition, not a random matter. The place of the text in the liturgy, the degree of "liturgical solemnity" of the occasion, and the ability of performers (only trained singers performed the melismatic sections) were all considerations. St. Jerome (c. 340-420), for example, gives this explanation for the *jubilus*, a term that may refer to the melisma on Alleluia or to melismatic passages in general:

> By the term *jubilus* we understand that which neither in words nor syllables nor letters nor speech is it possible to express or comprehend how much man ought to praise God.[19]

Far from restraining creativity, as might first appear, Gregorian chant provided a matrix for invention that was doubtlessly appealing to medieval aesthetic sensibility. The fact that in the ninth century the liturgy was still to some extent fluid made it possible for composers to insert new texts into the received liturgy, carefully suiting them to their literary context. These amplifications might vary in length from a few words to lengthy sentences, even to entire poems, and they might assume one of several forms. In a *prosula* a new text was set syllabically to a pre-existing melisma. The melisma on *Alleluia* was particularly made the object of such amplification, and, given a syllabic text and perhaps expanded and embellished melodically, it became the basis for a *sequence*. In a *trope* new music as well as a new text were interpolated into the existing liturgy. In this twelfth-century composition by the Saxon Hermit St. Godric, for instance, a vernacular trope dramatizes the mercy-seeking of the *Kyrie* with an impassioned testimony spoken in the person of the composer's sister:

---

[19] Quoted in REESE, p. 63.

Distinctions among *prosulae*, sequences, and tropes were confused even by medieval writers themselves, and the term trope is sometimes used to designate any monophonic addition to the litrugy. The essential characteristic of all these additions is this: they "comment" on the existing liturgy. As Manfred Bukofzer suggests, this musical "commentary," like the glosses medieval writers produced for literary and philosophical texts, must have been a source of great artistic delight, with its appeal to *auctoritas* as the basis for new creation and with its accommodation of new material to old.[21] Tropes were never officially recognized as part of the liturgy, and after the objections of the Council of Trent, Pope Pius V abolished them with the exception of some few that are still in use today.

However different Christian chant may in fact have been from classical Greek monophony, early medieval theorists persist in describing contemporary practice in ancient Greek terms. To the anonymous writer of the tenth-century treatise *Alia Musica* the age is not "dark" but one of enlightened cultural continuity with Greece, at least in music. This theoretician's attempt to recover the Greek modes and to apply them to modern music gained wide currency and was continued in the eleventh century in the *Musica* of Hermannus Contractus. Several musicologists[22] have suggested that the eight Church Modes, or scale arrangements, were deduced from the vestiges of melodic formulas in Gregorian chant. Different formulas implied different underlying scales; the theorist's task was to

---

[20] A transcription of St. Godric's "Crist and Sainte Marie" is conveniently available in paperback in the Greenberg anthology. See note 1.

[21] "Speculative Thinking in Medieval Music," *Speculum, 17* (1942), 165-180. Bukofzer analyzes several examples.

[22] Among them Hans-Jörgen HOLMON, "Compositional Techniques and Concepts of Originality in Monophonic Church Music from the Ninth to the Thirteenth Century," in *Arts libéraux*, pp. 993 ff.; cf. also REESE, p. 153, and APEL, *Harvard Dictionary*, "Church Modes."

deduce them and to formulate them. Practice, not theory, came first. Ancient Greek theoreticians may have devised the original Greek modes from melodic formulas by a similar process. In any case, this bit of tenth-century classicism also entailed reviving the concept of *ethos*. Later commentators like Guido of Arezzo (eleventh century), Hermannus Contractus, and John Cotton (twelfth century) all attribute various moral effects to these eight Church Modes.

III

Creation of the Church Modes thus answered a felt need to reconcile contemporary music with classical Greek theory, and for most theorists that reconciliation was no doubt satisfactory. But by the tenth century innovations were already being made in European music that would make the task of reconciliation increasingly more difficult. More than a hundred years earlier the writer of an anonymous treatise called Musica Enchiriadis had described at length music that consists not of a single melodic line but of multiple lines sounded simultaneously. Greek music and Gregorian chant had been monophonic (''one-sounded''); the music that *Musica Enchiriadis* describes is polyphonic (''many-sounded''). Just how far-reaching in importance this appearance of polyphony is, the history of Western music up to our own day makes clear. Like classical Greek and other Near Eastern music, many non-Western musical systems of the world are monophonic; the focus of musical interest in such music is on pure melodic line, and the fine gradations of pitch, the subtleties of tone and rhythm that this interest produces are frequently lost on Western ears trained to hear and appreciate the sonority of many sounds at once. Western music since the Middle Ages has developed this dimension of polyphonic sonority all out of proportion to its importance in other musical systems of the world — and at the expense of other dimensions of music like rhythm and pitch.

The *Musica Enchiriadis* writer speaks of polyphony as already existing, and there are several earlier literary references,[23] though no complete manuscript of polyphony dates before the eleventh-century Winchester Troper. A coinage in Plato's *Laws*, heterophony (''other-sound''), has been adopted by modern musicologists to describe a kind of primitive variation in

---

[23] Including Bishop Aldhelm (seventh century) and John Scotus Erigena (ninth century). Early polyphony seems to have been associated particularly with Britain. A much-cited passage in GIRALDUS CAMBRENSIS's *Descriptio Cambriæ* (late twelfth or early thirteenth century) says that the people in Wales, unlike other peoples, are used to singing in different parts, not in unison; he believes that this practice originated with the Danes. There is indeed some documentary evidence for this assertion, and Icelandic *twiesongvar*, with its parallel thirds, is a modern survival of primitive organum. Whether or not the polyphony Giraldus mentions was really the staggered singing of one melodic line in round-fashion (as in the famous — and early — ''Sumer is icumen in''), there is no doubt about a British preference for euphonious thirds long before they were popular on the continent. Thirteenth-century English lyrics like ''Jesus Cristes Milde Moder'' and ''Edi Beo Thu Hevene Quene,'' both included in the Greenberg anthology, are composed in the so-called *gymel*-style that favors thirds and sixths.

parts that exists in Chinese, Japanese, Javanese, and African monophony and consists of occasional ornamentation and of modification in the same melody when sung simultaneously by several performers. It seems likely that heterophony had existed in Christian chant from the beginning and simply became more deliberate, calculated, and defined to produce the polyphony that the *Musica Enchiriadis* writer attempts to describe. A similar development from heterophony to polyphony has been observed in non-Western musical systems.[24]

Polyphony, in any case, first appears in Western music as a sounding of tones in a second melodic line in rhythmic sequence with an existing Gregorian melody. The second melodic line might be fixed at a constant interval above the original line; it might move in transverse motion to the original line, going down when the base line moves up; or it might "open out" into different intervals, as in this example that the *Musica Enchiriadis* writer gives, in which the two voices begin and end in unison but open out to move in parallel at a fixed interval in the middle:

Rex ce- li do-mi- ne ma- ris un- di-so -ne
Ty -ta-nis ni-ti- di squa- li-di-que so -li

Whatever the harmonic intervals, such sounding of multiple voices in parallel rhythm is known as *organum*. In general it was applied to sections of chant that were syllabic. Now, the interval into which the *Musica Enchiriadis* example opens is four tones removed from unison. This "fourth," along with the interval one tone wider, the "fifth," were especially favored by the composers of *organum*. To modern ears both intervals are apt to sound hollow. Why these intervals should have such central importance has been the object of much speculation then and now. Gustave Reese observes that the fourth or fifth acts as the most important determining interval in all primitive music that has a definite tonality system. The third, much more euphonious to modern Western ears, tends to make its appearance in primitive music, just as it did in medieval polyphony, somewhat later. There is an acoustical reason why this should be so, since, when a tone is sounded, the natural sequence of overtones its vibrations set up is octave, fifth, fourth, and third in that order. A variety of likely modern explanations have been proposed,[25] but the justification devised by a tenth-century commentator on the *Musica Enchiriadis* not only

---

[24] Arguments have, however, been made to the contrary. Unison singing, such theorists propose, is difficult to achieve. When more than one person sing together the "natural" thing is for each to set his own pitch and to feel his own rhythm. Cacophony may thus be the most primitive music and monophony an achieved sophistication.

[25] Summarized in REESE, pp. 250-251.

squares with the acoustical facts but also, once again, manages to reconcile contemporary practice with Pythagorean theory. This commentary, called *Scholia Enchiriadis*, is cast as a dialogue between a *Discipulus* wary of new-fangled polyphony and a *Magister* confident that he can provide a justification. Why are some sounds consonant and not others, the student wonders. By elaborate mathematical calculation the teacher "proves" why the fourth and fifth are consonant but the third, hopelessly dissonant. He concludes:

> Whatever is delightful in song is brought about by number through the proportioned dimensions of sounds; whatever is excellent in rhythms, or in songs, or in any rhythmic movements you will, is effected wholly by number. Sounds pass quickly away, but numbers, which are obscured by the corporeal element in sounds and movements, remain. As St. Augustine says [and he quotes this passage from the *De Ordine* (II.xiv-xv)]:

> Thus reason has perceived that numbers govern and make perfect all that is in rhythms ["numbers" in Latin] and in song itself; has examined them diligently; and has found them to be eternal and divine.... In this way, then, all things present themselves in the mathematical disciplines [i.e., also, arithmetic, geometry, astronomy] as harmonious, as having to do with the immortal numbers which are apprehended by reflection and study, those which are perceived by the senses being mere shadows and images.[26]

The *Musica Enchiriadis* commentator justifies the addition of other voices to chant as a kind of "ornamentation" — in effect, a "vertical" trope. As a modern scholar Jacques Handschin puts it, ".... polyphony did by superposition what the tropes did by interposition."[27] Just as "horizontal" tropes might vary in complexity, so could polyphonic embellishment be carried to various degrees of elaboration. One such means of elaborating a second voice was to free it rhythmically from the existing base chant. This rhythmic elaboration was particularly well suited to chant that was already melismatic. In *discant* writing composers allowed the second voice to play about the first voice rhythmically, to move in rhythmic counterpoint with it. A passage of such discant writing was called a *clausula*. In *organum* the voices move in strict rhythmic parallel; in a *clausula* their rhythmic relationship is more complicated. For example, a liturgical composer could take this piece of melismatic coloratura from plainchant:

Stretching out this melisma in time and assigning it to a lower voice, he could embellish it with the delicately articulated rhythm of a discant voice:

---

[26] Excerpts from the *Scholia Enchiriadis* are included in Strunk, pp. 126-138.

[27] Quoted in REESE, p. 264.

It is probably no happenstance that such architectonic refinement should flourish particularly in the twelfth and early thirteenth centuries, the time of the building of the great French cathedrals. During exactly that period *clausulae* and *organa* were the particular forte of the Cathedral School of Notre Dame in Paris; two of that school's composers, Leonin and Perotin, are known by name.

Addition of a *third* voice on top of an existing Gregorian melody naturally suggests itself, and this addition is precisely the step that composers took to create that most characteristic musical form of the thirteenth century, the motet. In *clausalae* the second voice had asserted its independence by assuming a rhythmic pattern of its own; in motets the second and third voice might assert their independence, from each other and from the base chant, by assuming not only independent rhythms but independent *texts* as well. In thirteenth-century motets, as in *clausulae*, a discrete and stratified sense of voices is a source of aesthetic delight. Not necessarily would the three voices be put together to sound harmoniously and rhythmically consonant at every point. Their predominant rhythmic modes might even be different. Harmony, rhythm, and words, we recall, are the three elements in the classical definition of music, and in all three ways the voice parts of a thirteenth-century motet assert their integrity. In the following example, the "Et Gaudebit" that we have already examined as an unadorned melisma and as the object of discant elaboration becomes the base melody, or *cantus firmus*, for a three-part motet. In this case the upper two texts are even in different languages, one in Latin, the other in the vernacular:

However chaotic polytextual motets like this one may first sound to an unprepared modern listener, they can assume a unity that, true to medieval sensibility, is all the more delightful because it must be sought after. To appreciate the rhythmic and harmonic complexities of motets like this one requires an ear at least as finely attuned as that required for appreciating Baroque polyphony, which is often more predictable harmonically. But the unity of motets like "El mois d'avril" — "O quam sancta" — "Et Gaudebit" goes beyond harmony and rhythm to *words*. The two upper texts have a literary appropriateness to one another that may not at first sight be apparent. The vernacular text is a celebration of the springtime joys of love and an earthly lady:

> In April when the winter was slowly retreating, when the birds were beginning to sing again, I rode through the woods one morning, came onto a path and, sunken deep in thought, rode on farther. Since my thoughts were of love, I no longer knew where I was riding (to), and when I came to myself and looked around, I rode into an orchard that was so tempting; there on the right the nightingales were singing and on the left the thrushes; no heart, however hard, could have failed to rejoice; the song sparrow and the lark sang so tenderly, the goldfinch joined in: Why should I tell you the names of all the songs? All of the magic of the birds was united around me. While I was so standing, I heard a maiden sing in full voice: "New love makes noble lovers handsome." The grace in her walk and her charm were so great that nature itself could not have imagined her, such beauty, such freshness and blossom-white complexion, her laughing green eyes, the blond and radiant hair that encircled her face, her red lips, the row of closely lying little teeth, her arched eyebrows so dark and well-formed. No mouth can describe, no heart can imagine her exceedingly great beauty. Love overwhelmed her; with a sigh she answered: "Beloved! I shall never forsake you, for I am true to you, my friend."

The Latin text celebrates the life-renewing joys of a higher kind of love and a yet nobler lady:

> O how holy, o how gracious shines the Mother of the Saviour! Highly praised, noble Virgin, Noah's arch, Jacob's ladder, treasure of the shy, court of the Redeemer, source of all sweetness, joy of the angels, while nursing the Son of God, the King omnipotent, hear, o salvation of the nations, the prayers of the entreating, hearken unto them, root of Jesse, noble Virgin, most worthy of honor, sole hope, help the miserable. You are the wonderful spring that stills the thirst of the soul. You will never leave your people to death. O soul! In your lowly position pray to the Virgin Mary that she be a true and active intercession for you with her high-born Son, the sole hope of the faithful, o Mother, rejoice in your Son; joyfully I rejoice in the Lord.[30]

The "multiple-sounding" of harmony and rhythm here coincides with that "multiple-seeming" of poetry that delights medieval sensibility.

Behind the aural surface of such music — which is likely to sound like verbal and harmonic chaos to ears used to eighteenth and nineteenth century music — are implicit principles of order that derive from all the inherited notions about music that we have surveyed. Repeated rhythmic

---

[28] Transcribed from HUSMANN, p. 28.

[29] Transcribed from Yvonne ROKSETH, ed., *Polyphonies du XIIIe Siècle* (Paris: Éditions de l'Oiseau Lyre, 1936), II, 83. The Early Music Studio perform this motet on Telefunken SATT 9504-A Ex.

[30] Translations are from the program notes to Telefunken SAWT 9504-A Ex.

patterns, for example, whether or not they always coincide in the same way
with repeated melodic motives, whether or not they are so prolonged in time
as to be difficult to hear, are as much a major structuring device as they
were in ancient Greek monophony. Apparent to the senses or not, the
presence of number still guarantees unity and coherence. Bukofzer makes a
useful distinction in medieval music between the "external perspective" of
a hearer who takes in the music through his senses and the "internal
perspective" of a participant who with his intellect can appreciate patterns
of order present in the music but practically unhearable.[31] *Musica in
instrumentis constituta* as an imitation of *musica mundana* means that
behind the surface taken in by the senses lies a numerically coherent
structure comprehensible to intellect alone.[32]

Rhythmic complexity in motets was such that by the middle of the
thirteenth century the notational system then in use and, even more
importantly, the rationale of rhythm that informed it were no longer
adequate to composers' practical needs. As in the extant fragments of Greek
music, the rhythm of early medieval music had for the most part been
dictated by the rhythm of the texts.

A notational system of fixed pitches was devised by Guido of Arezzo in
the eleventh century, but it was not until Franco of Cologne's *Ars Cantus
Mensurabilis* (c. 1280) that a system of fixed ratios between long notes and
short made possible an exact notation of time. Earlier in the thirteenth
century theorists had answered the new rhythmic problems posed by
polyphony with a "classical" scheme similar to the tenth century Church
Modes. Accent, as we have observed, had long since replaced quantity as
the basis of poetic metre, but these thirteenth-century theorists formulated
six "rhythmic modes" to correspond to six varieties of quantitative classical
metre. Trochaic (-◡) became (♩ ♪ | ♩ ♪ | ...), iambic (◡-) became
(♪♪ | ♪ ♩ | ..), dactylic (-◡◡) became(♩ |♪♪ |♩ |♪♩) etc.[33] Theoretical-
ly, a piece written in one rhythmic mode would repeat the respective
rhythmic pattern over and over, just as a poem written in a given metre
repeats the same metrical foot throughout. In practice modes were freely
mixed. However consciously "classical" their system may have been, the
thirteenth-century theorists took very telling liberties with the classical
metres, particularly the dactyl and the anapest, to render them all ternary. A
uniform time scheme based on three may have been as much an embodying
of cosmic number, a reflection of the Trinity, as it was an indication of
contemporary practice. There is some literary evidence for binary rhythms in

---

[31] *Studies in Medieval and Renaissance Music* (New York: Norton, 1950), p. 28. Bukofzer
applies such distinctions in close stylistic analysis of music selected to illustrate uses of pre-existing
melodic material.

[32] BUKOFZER, *Speculum*.

[33] For a complete table, cf. APEL, *Harvard Dictionary*, "Modes, Rhythmic."

dances and secular music, for example,[34] but only ternary rhythm was given official recognition.

The practical demands of the new complex polyphony were thus met and interpreted with as much theoretical ingenuity as chant, tropes, and *organum* had been before. To most thirteenth-century theoreticians contemporary European music was apparently still reconcilable with Greek ideas. But in at least two respects the new polyphony had radically altered the nature of music. The first of the changes concerns harmony. In monophony, as we have observed, harmony refers to the intervals separating tones sounded in sequence. The "harmony of the spheres" has to do with the ratios of their distances from one another; the harmony of earthly music imitates these ratios. With the universe as an objective model, such ratios, at least as Pythagoras formulated them, can be mathematically calculated. The *Scholia Enchiriadis* commentator makes an attempt to apply these same objective standards to polyphony, but the consonance or dissonance of tones sounded together is all too easily subject to the subjective appraisal of the ear. Harmony has acquired a new definition. That "dissonant" third that the *Scholia Enchiriadis* commentator had dismissed as theoretically unacceptable shows up with increasing insistence in the course of the thirteenth century. Walter Odington's *De Speculatione Musicæ* (c. 1300) makes the only possible compromise. If the third does not fit the Pythagorean ratios exactly, he says, it does come *close*. Be that as it may, human voices "lead them forth with subtlety into a sweet mixture."[35] The criterion of sweetness he has in mind is not mathematical.

The second and even more far-reaching change concerns rhythm. With the introduction Franco's *musica mensurata*, abstract sound is for the first time "officially" liberated from the text. *Musica mensurata* and the new, sonorous harmony appear at the same time, and Reese rightly interprets this circumstance as the culmination of a continuous process of change that began with *organum*.[36] The result is "a new way of weaving designs in time" that differs fundamentally from monophony.

It may be significant that the development of polyphony and the cultivation of the secular motet are datable to exactly the time when music was displaced as a speculative discipline in the new universities. The reappearance of philosophy, dormant as a discipline in its own right since late antiquity, forced a rearrangement in the divisions and relationships of intellectual activity. The Quadrivium survived in the curriculum of the new

---

[34] A retrospective passage in Walter Odington's *De Speculatione Musicæ* (c. 1300), for example, seems to imply as much; the texts of some twelfth century German *Minnelieder* and Spanish *Cántigas* call for binary metre, even though musical notation is sometimes lacking and indication of rhythm is lacking even in manuscripts that do notate pitch; there may well have been a distinction between "learned" and more popular music in regard to rhythm, with binary rhythm much more common in the latter.

[35] Quoted in REESE, p. 387.

[36] REESE, pp. 292-293.

universities, but only as a subdivision of one of the three philosophies.[37] The liberal art of music was not untouched by the European rediscovery of Aristotle that was such an important part of this intellectual ferment and change. Aristotle's practical and scientific interest in music had influenced the chief figure of Arabian musical science, Alpharabi (d. 950), and the Arabian's Aristotelian disquisition on music had an eager European translator and propagator in Domenicus Gundissalinus (fl. 1150). Alpharabi's division of music into *speculativa* and *activa* collapses Boethius's *musica mundana* and *musica humana* into one catch-all category; the Aristotelian's real interest is in the second half of his dichotomy. Vincent of Beauvais (d. 1264) and Roger Bacon (d. 1292), among others, found Alpharabi's ideas amenable.

The elaboration of Gregorian monophony, the development of *organum*, the rhythmic and tonal complexities of thirteenth-century polyphony — medieval theorists were on the whole successful in reconciling these modern practices with an inherited stock of Greek, and specifically Platonic, ideas about the nature of music. Most writers with Alpharabi's interests never really contradicted these ideas; they simply repeated a few clichés and went on to fill the bulk of their work with down-to-earth talk about practical music. What myopia in comparison with St. Augustine's perspective! The time had come for someone to see the difference.

One of many fourteenth-century writers on music with a practical bent was a Frenchman, Philippe de Vitry. Unlike many earlier theorists, he was a composer as well as a theoretician.[38] In two extant letters to him, his friend Petrarch calls him "the only poet among Frenchmen"[39] and "a very sharp and persistent inquisitor, a great thinker of our time."[40] About 1325 Philippe wrote a little treatise on notation which he called *Ars Nova* ("The New Art"). What was "new" about Philippe's notational refinements was the possibility of recording binary as well as ternary rhythms. An innocent enough proposal on the surface. Philippe had certainly not "invented" binary rhythm, as we have seen. One earlier commentator, Marchettus of Padua (fl. 1320), had even given binary rhythm a formal name, *tempus imperfectum*, to distinguish it from the standard ternary rhythm, *tempus perfectum*. "Perfect " and "imperfect" — the choice of terms is telling. Philippe seems not to have made an issue of what the acceptance of binary rhythm implied.

---

[37] Pearl KIBRE, "The *Quadrivium* in the Thirteenth-Century Universities," in *Arts Libéraux*, pp. 175 ff.

[38] A number of his works are extant. The Munich Capella Antiqua perform five of them on a recording that juxtaposes *ars antiqua* and *ars nova* motets (Telefunken S-9517).

[39] Quoted from manuscript sources in A. COVILLE, "Philippe de Vitri: Notes Biographiques," *Romania*, 57 (1933), 520-547. The standard edition of Petrarch's *Epistolæ de Rebus Familiaribus* (ed. Fracasetti [Florence, 1862]) for some reason omits this compliment from the text of letter IX.13. It is restored in Morris Bishop's translation of excerpts from the letter — a famous one, praising international travel — in *Letters from Petrarch* (Bloomington and London: Indiana Univ. Press, 1966).

[40] *Ep. de Reb. Fam.* XI.14.

That was done for him. About 1330 Jacob of Liége set out in his *Speculum Musicæ* to attack *ars nova* by setting down the theoretical assumptions and practical methods of "the old music" (*ars antiqua*) in an unfavorable comparison with the new. The first six books of his treatise deal with *cantus planus*, not just "plain-chant" but the whole theory of music as "numbered sound"; his last book deals with *musica mensurata* and contains his principal critique of the new techniques. The confrontation Jacob sets up is one of an old man versus a new generation:

> Long ago venerable men (among them Tubal Cain, before the flood) wrote reasonably on plainsong; since that time many more.... have done the same.... and many others.... have written on mensurable music. Now in our day have come new and more recent authors, writing on mensurable music, little revering their ancestors, the ancient doctors; nay, rather changing their sound doctrine in many respects, corrupting, reproving, annulling it, they protest against it in word and deed when the civil and mannerly thing to do would be to imitate the ancients of what they said well and, in doubtful matters, to defend and expound them. Considering these things in the modern manner of singing and still more in the modern writings, I was grieved.... I am alone, while those whom I attack in this last satiric and controversial work are many.... I still belong to the ancient company which some of the moderns call rude. I am old; they are young and vigorous. Those whom I defend are dead; those whom I attack are living. They rejoice in having found new conclusions about music; in this I am content to defend the ancient ones, which I deem reasonable.[41]

Reason, indeed, is the key to Jacob's defense, and the confrontation goes far beyond a misunderstanding between two generations: it is a conflict between ancients and moderns, between music as a speculative science and music as a practical art, between the music of Plato's ideal city and the ear-pleasing music of fourteenth-century Europe. The tone of Jacob's treatise combines touching personal involvement and cool philosophical assurance:

> Some moderns regard those singers as rude, idiotic, undiscerning, foolish, and ignorant who do not know the new art of who follow the old art , not the new, in singing, and in consequence they regard the old art as rude and, as it were, irrational, the new as subtle and rational. It may be asked, what is the source of this subtlety in the moderns and this rudeness in the ancients? For if subtlety comes from a greater and more penetrating intellect, who are to be reputed the subtler: those who discovered the principles of this art and found out what things are contrary to them but have scrupulously followed these principles, or those who protest their intention of following them but do not and seem rather to combat them?.... What is the value of subtlety which is contrary to the principles of science? Are not the subtlety and difficulty involved in the many diverse imperfections in notes, times, modes, and measures which they have contrived, incompatible with a science which is based on perfection? Is it great subtlety to abound in imperfections and to dismiss perfections? Should the ancients be called rude for using perfections, the moderns subtle for using imperfections?.... the art of Bœthius and Bœthius himself should not on that account be reputed rude and irrational. For he laid the foundations of the art and furnished the principles from which others, following him, have drawn good and useful conclusions, consonant with the art and not contrary to or incompatible with those principles.

---

[41] Books VI and VII of Jacob's treatise are printed in Charles Edmond Henri Cousemaker, ed., *Scriptorum de Musica Medii Aevi* (1864-76, reissued Milan, 1931), II. Excerpts from Book VII are translated in Strunk, pp. 180-190, from which the quotations are taken.

Jacob could not be more clear in stating what *ars nova* is a break away from. It abnegates reason, the principles of musical science, and the moral principles of Bœthius's speculative music. Even the character of Bœthius himself seems not to have been free from abuse!

Jacob's *Speculum* lives up to its name in focusing all its arguments and observations into one coherent image, in mirroring a unified "world picture." A modern student of Jacob, F. Joseph Smith, has called the treatise "the high point of medieval number theory." *Ars nova*, he maintains, was a challenge not just to ternary musical theory but to the very metaphysical ideas that made such a numerological theory possible.

> Jacobus stands as the champion not just of rational trinary musical consonance but of a whole rational world view, basically theological and metaphysical, which was already crumbling away at the time of the writing of the *Speculum*. Jacobus had attempted to shore up the shaky edifice of the medieval hierarchy of being by painting its intellectual picture, by "mirroring" all reality in his compilation, written thus in *speculum* or mirror style.... In a real sense, the Ars nova was the practical deathblow to the Age of (medieval) Reason.[42]

Innovations after the generation of Philippe de Vitry display marks of "liberation" from the old theoretical structures: a new "lyricism" in melodic line, as well as full, sonorous harmonies, point toward modern conceptions of music. Not that "liberation" was an instantaneous affair. The elegant virelais, ballades, and rondeaux of Guillaume de Machaut, the most celebrated *ars nova* composer and a contemporary of Chaucer, still show a stratified sense of voice parts, and for ears used to hearing eighteenth — and nineteenth-century music Machaut's harmonies still sound "exotic" if not downright dissonant. Isorhythms in *ars nova* polyphony — repeated rhythmic patterns too prolonged to be heard — are but one vestige of the unheard music of *ars antiqua*. On the other hand, form in *ars nova* has become a matter not so much of text as of musical exigencies. At least one theorist, Aegidius of Murino (fl. c. 1400), says that in writing a motet the music should be written first and the words added later. Just one line from a polyphonic composition by Machaut, in this instance a polytextual "triple ballade," will illustrate not only harmonic euphony but also a canonic

⁴² Sᴍɪᴛʜ, *Arts libéraux*, p. 1038.
⁴³ Transcribed from F. D. Hᴀʀʀɪsᴏɴ, ed., *Polyphonic Music of the Fourteenth Century* (Monaco: Éditions de l'Oiseau Lyre, 1956-67), III, 114-15. A rendition of this ballade is included on New York Pro Musica, *Ah! Sweet Lady* (Decca DL 79431).

echoing of melody and rhythm among the parts that makes for a tightly woven, smoothly wrought surface:

Discussing similarities in style between one art form and another is beset with difficulties, not the least of which is trying to find a critical vocabulary adequate to more than one form. There is a striking connection to be observed, however, between *ars nova* music and the "realistic," subjectively observed nature, of late medieval visual art. D.W. Robertson's *Preface to Chaucer* articulately analyzes a parallel progress from "Romanesque" to "Gothic" to "Renaissance" in literature. The sharp theoretical conflict between *ars nova* and *ars antiqua*, at least as Jacob of Liége sees it, makes it possible to pinpoint this stylistic shift in music with even more exactness than in literature and the visual arts. However we choose to define the change — whether from objectivity to subjectivity, from Platonic mimesis of idea to Aristotelian mimesis of experienced nature, or, as Jacob would have it, from perfection to imperfection — the practical results are present in the music for us to listen to.

Particularly is this true in music of the fifteenth century. One of the most influential figures of the century is British. In his chordal-sounding polyphony John Dunstable (c. 1370-1453) abandons multiple texts, redefines the relationship among the parts to do without a *cantus firmus*, liturgical or otherwise, and carefully plans an harmonic framework made up of "blocks" of sound. Just how different fifteenth-century polyphony is from the plainchant that was the classical heritage of medieval music can nowhere be seen more strikingly than in Dunstable's treatment of the plainchant ninth-century hymn "Ave Maris Stella." Dunstable first states the hymn one time through in its original monophonic form, then subjects it to a three-part harmonization. To emphasize the chordal quality of this harmonization the three voice-parts are collapsed onto one staff in this transcription:

Looking back near the end of the fifteenth century, Johannes Tinctoris could say, "At this time, consequently, the possibilities of our music have been so marvelously increased that there appears to be *a new art*, if I may so call it, whose fount and origin is held to be among the English, of whom

---

[44] Transcribed from M. BUKOFZER, ed., *Complete Works* (London: Stainer and Bell, 1953), p. 9. This and three other compositions by Dunstable are recorded by the Purcell Consort and Musica Reservata on *Music of the Early Renaissance* (Turnabout TV 34058S).

John Dunstable stood forth as chief.''[45] In describing "the new art," with all its marvelous possibilities, Tinctoris maintains that, with all due respect to "the ancient musicians.... including even Boethius,....

> concords of sounds and melodies, from whose sweetness, as Lactantius says [*Divinarum institutionum*, VI.xxi], the pleasure of the ear is derived, are produced, then, not by heavenly bodies, but by earthly instruments....[46]

Even so thorough-going a Neo-Platonist as Marsilio Ficino, who along with the innovating composer Heinrich Isaac enjoyed the patronage of Lorenzo de' Medici, gives prominence to faculties of "imagination" and "heart," in addition to intellect, in describing effects of music on the soul:

> Since song and sound come from the thought of the mind, from the impulse of the imagination, and from the passion of the heart and, together with the broken and formed air, move the air-like spirit of the listener, which is the bond of Soul and body, it easily moves the imagination, affects the heart, and penetrates the innermost sanctuary of the mind.[47]

V

The European Middle Ages had inherited from classical civilization a musical tradition uniform in theory and practice; the Middle Ages passed on to the Renaissance a tradition with a fundamental incongruity. On the one hand the Renaissance inherited a highly developed body of speculative thought about music; on the other hand it inherited a tradition of *musica activa* that had less and less to do with this body of theory. Two groups attacked the problem head-on and attempted to restore European music to classical Greek models. The first, a Florentine circle who styled themselves "the Camerata," met in the third quarter of the sixteenth century to experiment with musical declamation of poetic drama, ostensibly on the Greek model. Greek tragedy, they knew, had been musically declaimed. The Camerata's experiments in reviving this ancient practice by matching musical rhythm to the rhythm of spoken language produced *recitar cantando* (modern "recitative") and, ultimately, opera. Ottavio Rinuccini and Jacopo Peri's *Euridice* (1600), the earliest opera that survives entire, is cast in recitative throughout but already shows a tendency toward lyric *arioso* passages that later in the seventeenth century blossomed into the arias that characterize modern opera. Recitative became subordinated to the function of connecting these musical show-pieces.[48] In France, a second group,

---

[45] Quoted in Friedrich BLUME, *Renaissance and Baroque Music*, trans. M. D. H. NORTON (New York: Norton, 1967).

[46] From the dedication to the *Liber de Arte Contrapuncti* (1477). Excerpts are translated in STRUNK, pp. 197-199, from which this quotation is taken.

[47] Quoted in Paul O. KRISTELLER, *The Philosophy of Marsilio Ficino*, trans. V. Conant (New York: Columbia Univ. Press, 1943), p. 307. The New York Pro Musica perform some of Isaac's compositions on *Music for the Court of Lorenzo the Magnificent* (Decca 79413), as do the Munich Capella Antiqua on Telefunken S-9544.

[48] D. J. GROUT's *A Short History of Opera*, 2 vols. (New York: Norton, 1947), includes an excellent introduction to the neoclassical origins of opera.

poet-musicians of Antoine de Baïf's Academy, attempted to revive Greek lyrics by writing French texts in classical quantitative metres, then setting the texts to music by carefully matching note values to the artificial syllable values. The result was *vers et musique mesurés*.[49]

Sir Philip Sidney's English exercises in quantitative classical metres are part of this same neoclassical movement, though no extant musical settings of Sidney's verse can be claimed as his own. Early in the seventeenth century Thomas Campion set himself apart from other writers of airs by insisting that his songs be sung only by solo voice with lute accompaniment and not in the polyphonic vocal settings that most other composers of airs had published along with their solo versions. One song from Campion's first collection, "Come, let us sound with melody," is written in Sapphics with a perfectly metred musical setting, making it the only perfect example of *musique mesuré* in English. Campion's insistence on lute accompaniment may in itself be a conscious neoclassical remembrance of Apollo's lyre.[50]

If imitation by successors is any criterion, *recitar cantando* and *vers et musique mesurés* were experiments that failed. Main currents in Western music were inalterably in the direction of abstract instrumental music and fuller polyphony. By the middle of the seventeenth century speculative music exists only as a pœtic subject,[51] sometimes (as in Dryden's St. Cecilia's Day odes) brilliantly treated, but hardly the "science" that Plato, Augustine, and Bœthius had in mind.

Marsyas won the contest after all.

---

[49] Chapter III of Frances A. YATES's *The French Academies of the Sixteenth Century* (London: The Warburg Institute, 1947) gives a superb account of these neoclassical experiments in France.

[50] Several kinds of evidence point to an association between Renaissance stringed instruments and the ancient lyre. In a study of paintings, manuscript illuminations, sculpture, and original instruments Emmanuel WINTERNITZ, "The Survival of the Kithara and the Evolution of the English Cittern: A Study in Morphology," *JWCI*, **24** (1961), 222-229, discovered nonfunctional survivals of the ancient kithara in depictions of medieval and Renaissance string instruments. The reason for these survivals, he maintains, was an "archeological interest" in ancient instruments, not only in the 1400s and 1500s but in Carolingian times as well, both ages of "classicism". A letter from Ficino to Paulus Middelburgensis indicates that in late fifteenth-century Florence, at least, performance of songs with a stringed lyre was quite consciously "antique": "Our century, like a golden age, restored to light the liberal arts that were nearly extinct: grammar, poetry, rhetoric, painting, sculpture, architecture, music, the ancient performance of songs with the Orphic lyre, and all that in Florence." Quoted in KRISTELLER, *Ficino*, p. 22.

[51] John HOLLANDER's *The Untuning of the Sky: Ideas of Music in English Poetry, 1500-1700* (Princeton: Princeton Univ. Press, 1961) surveys this tradition.

The Meaning of Space in Fourteenth-Century Tuscan painting*

Changes in artistic representations of space provide a valuable vantage point for assessing the radical revolution in referential vocabulary that occurred in Tuscan Painting ca. 1280-1350. Giotto, the founder of the Florentine school of painting, is the first Italian artist to make space an essential part of his pictorial vocabulary.[1] A comparison of Giotto's *Ognissanti Madonna* (Florence, Uffizi; c. 1300-1310) with Cimabue's *Santa Trinita Madonna* (Florence, Uffizi; c. 1285-12900) reveals the new role space plays in Giotto's art: Cimabue's irrational, heavenly space is decidedly unrealistic, while Giotto's consistently believable depth is measured out by three-dimensional figures who not only occupy space, but which have mass and are subject to the laws of gravity which govern our everyday existence.[2]

The illusionistic vaulted chambers on the triumphal arch of the Arena Chapel in Padua (1303-1305) especially reveal Giotto's ability to create the illusion of space through purely architectural forms.[3] These chambers convincingly suggest carefully-defined rooms which continue the observer's space. The autoptical space which these chambers communicate succeeds partly because Giotto implies for the observer a particular vantage point in the middle of the nave, and paints the chapels so that one seems to see what would be visible were there actual chapels at these points. One implication of this adjustment of perspective is that the frame very naturally cuts off

---

* This essay originated as a lecture presented at the University of Rochester on February 26, 1971, and I have maintained the original structure for this published version. My intent was to present to a somewhat general audience some new ideas about early Trecento art. I wish to extend special thanks to Professors Bruce Cole and Marvin Eisenberg.

[1] For further discussion see M. BUNIM, *Space in Medieval Painting and the Forerunners of Perspective*, New York, 1940; J. WHITE, *The Birth and Rebirth of Pictorial Space*, London, 1957; and E. PANOFSKY, *Renaissance and Renascences in Western Art*, New York, 1969, pp. 114-161. I am especially indebted to E. BORSOOK, *The Mural Painters of Tuscany*, London, 1960.

[2] E.g., D. WILKINS, "On the Original Appearance of Giotto's *Ognissanti Madonna*," *Art Quarterly*, 33 (1970), 1-15; see especially fig. 4.

[3] J. STUBBLEBINE (ed.), *Giotto: The Arena Chapel Frescoes* (New York, 1969), pp. 182-202, figs. 3, 70, 71.

what would normally be invisible: the innermost walls of the two chambers and portions of the rear walls and vaults. By this device of truncation Giotto suggests that space extends behind the frame.

Giotto also uses truncation in purely figural scenes, such as the *Betrayal of Christ*.[4] Here figures on the right are cut off to heighten the effect of a large and pressing crowd, while on the left the apostles are fleeing; only St. Peter is still fully visible. Another apostle has lost his cloak to a sinister figure seen from the rear while yet a third casts a furtive glance over his shoulder as he disappears behind the frame. What Giotto allows us to see is only one small part of an obviously more extensive drama.

The scene of the *Expulsion of Joachim from the Temple* offers a cogent example of Giotto's attitude toward pictorial space. Placement of the temple on an oblique angle gives a powerful three-dimensional effect, but the blunted front corner reveals the artist's reluctance to pierce the picture plane.[5] He maintains intact this traditional barrier between viewer and object viewed. To rupture the barrier by extending the temple platform into our space would have been a radical step; it occurs only when painters experiment with heightened pictorial space to achieve deception. Despite Giotto's hesitation here, he does use this device elsewhere in the Arena Chapel, for example, where he represents the four prophets who surround the Madonna and Child in the western half of the blue, star-bedecked vault.[6] These figures appear in tondi which are enframed with decorative bands. The gold background behind the figures is symbolic of the heavenly realm and implies that the natural sky is punctured to allow us a glimpse into some higher level of existence. The four prophet's scrolls, however, seem to flutter out into the space over our heads, and one even hits against the decorative frame and adjusts its course accordingly, furthering the illusion that the frame is a palpable opening. These scrolls destroy the neat boundary between the space of life and the space of art.

The Arena Chapel frescoes reveal Giotto's interest in pictorial space and his successful development of complex spatial effects. Moreover, we can trace the involvement of his pupils in this investigation, as they develop their own increasingly complex conceptions. Maso di Banco's frescoes in the St. Sylvester Chapel of the Bardi and Bardi di Vernio families (Florence, Santa Croce; c. 1336-1339) exemplify the trend. Maso's masterpiece, *St. Sylvester Muzzling the Dragon and Resurrecting Two Pagan Magicians* (Pl.

---

[4] See STUBBLEBINE, fig. 41, for a rare uncropped reproduction of this scene; cf. figs. 7, 8, 12, 17, 19, 25, 27, 29, 30, 34, 37, 50, and 52.

[5] WHITE, *Birth and Rebirth*, p. 60; STUBBLEBINE, fig. 7.

[6] See G. PREVITALI, *Giotto e la sua bottega* (Milan, 1967), Pl. XLVII, figs. 457, 458, 460.

[7] Two examples survive in Santa Croce, closing the entrances to the St. Louis of Toulouse Chapel in the north transept and the Rinuccini Chapel in the sacristy. See also J. GARDNER, "The decoration of the Baroncelli Chapel in Santa Croce," *Zeitschrift für Kunstgeschichte, 34* (1971), 94.

IX. ''Miracle of St. Silvester''. — Maso di Banco

X.   ''Prophet: Miracle of St. Silvester'' — Maso di Banco

ix), is astonishingly deep by Trecento standards, with a vista of carefully-staggered ruins receding so succesfully into the distance that the traditional blue fresco background actually suggests the vastness of sky overhead. The construction of a convincing landscape is aided by the more literal scale of relationships between figures and architecture. In *St. Sylvester's Journey to Rome* Maso's careful truncation of the horses by the two sides of the awkwardly narrow lunette format suggests that we are glimpsing only the central figures of an impressive procession. In the *Resurrection and Last Judgment of a Member of the Bardi di Vernio Family* the donor is truncated by the sculpted tomb in such a way that we seem to be witnessing his resurrection on the day of judgment; for the fourteenth-century observer who had known the man depicted so vividly portrayed here, the effect must have been arresting.

The two prophets in tondi above this tomb (e.g., Pl. X) may be compared to those represented by Giotto on the vault of the Arena Chapel previously discussed. Here the extension into the viewer's space is more pronounced, for haloes in addition to scrolls overlap the frame and in one case even a hand projects toward us. The illusion that the circular frame is an opening is heightened by the fact that for it is represented as a three-dimensional window with a lamb painted as it would appear to an observer standing at the threshold of the chapel. This viewing point is precisely where the traditional wrought iron gate would have blocked the entrance. The left prophet seems to lean forward out of the opening, and, in an optical adjustment unusual in Trecento art,[8] his neck and face are slightly foreshortened to coincide with the perspective of one almost directly below.

Similar spatial experiments can be noted in the works of Taddeo Gaddi, whom Cennino Cennini reported was Giotto's godson and his assistant for twenty-four years.[9] In the inner bay of the Baroncelli Chapel (Florence, Santa Croce; 1330's?), for example, Taddeo painted the *Virtues* (in the vault) as full-length figures enclosed in carefully-defined cylinders of space which are adjusted to the observer's viewpoint at the threshold of the chapel.[10] Yet he ruptures the picture plane in his figure of *David with the Head of Goliath* in the same chapel,[11] for David's arm and the severed head seem to extend in front of the illusionistic tabernacle which encloses the figure

---

[8] This technique does not become commonplace until the early Quattrocento; e.g., the figure of God the Father above Donatello's *St. George Niche* (Florence, or San Michele; c. 1417) and the Christ in Masaccio's *Crucifixion* from the *Pisa Polyptych* (Naples, Capodimonte; doc. 1426).

[9] Cennino CENNINI, *The Craftsman's Handbook*, trans. D. THOMPSON, Jr. (New Haven, 1933), p. 2.

[10] The same level of illusionism may be noted in the virtues and personifications of the window splay. For interesting recent comments on Baroncelli Chapel and a useful diagram, see J. GARDNER. I cannot, however, agree with his conclusion that Giotto is responsible for the design of the program.

[11] B. BERENSON, *Italian Pictures of the Renaissance: Florentine School* (London, 1963), 1, Pl. 22.

and whose outer surfaces define the picture plane. On the wall to the left of the entrance, Taddeo has painted two niches containing casually-placed liturgical objects which are based on functional niches common in Trecento chapels.[12] These niches are calculated to fool the observer, at least momentarily, and Taddeo's obvious delight in this artistic conceit is engaging. Although acclaimed as marking the beginning of still-life painting,[13] it seems evident that the main function of these niches is primarily illusionistic, and the still-life subject is only an accidental byproduct of that intention. Taddeo, in other words, chose this genre and subject because they offered an appropriate vehicle for his desire to embrace a wider conception of reality.

An illusionistic arched corbel table which Taddeo painted above the entrance to the chapel reveals yet another application of new spatial concepts. While the architectural membering used in Santa Croce to unify a wall of diverse openings is no new idea, it is especially successful because it parallels a real corbel table used for a catwalk along the clerestory walls and across the east wall above the choir.[14]

Taddeo is also the author of what must be the most audacious illusionism of the whole century: the *Last Supper* frescoed on the end wall of the refectory of Santa Croce (Pl.XI).[15] This is the earliest surviving example of the use of this subject in a refectory. But the unique spatial conception of Taddeo's design is neither rivaled nor repeated by any later example. The traditional flat bands which function to unify the decorative scheme and to establish the plane of the wall in the upper area are painted in the lower section as if they were three-dimensional architectural supports which pass *behind* the figures and tables. This thrusts the *Last Supper* forward in front of the bands, so that the table and figures dramatically share the viewer's space.

The evidence indicates that beginning with Giotto and continuing with his pupils, there was a continuous experimentation with the role illusionism

---

[12] Similar but larger examples, to the best of my knowledge still unpublished, were discovered in the high altar chapel of Santa Croce when the flood of 1966 prompted the removal of the choir stalls.

[13] C. DE TOLNAY, "Les origines de la nature morte moderne," *La Revue des Arts, 2* (1952), 151-152, and "Postilla sulle origini della natura morta moderna," *Rivista d'arte,* (1961-1962), 3-10. See also C. STERLING, *Still Life Painting from Antiquity to the Present Time* (New York, 1959), pp. 17-21. I do not share with these authors the belief that Taddeo's illusionistic niches were inspired by ancient Roman examples.

[14] BERENSON, Pl. 118. Perhaps the earliest appearance of this motif is in Cimabue's frescoes in the choir and transepts of San Francesco at Assisi (1290's?). It reappears as a unifying device in the St. Francis Cycle in the nave; see A. SMART, *The Assisi Problem and the Art of Giotto* (Oxford, 1971), pp. 11-12. In my forthcoming monograph on Maso di Banco I present evidence to suggest that an illusionistic arched corbel table might also have been used along the side aisle walls of Santa Croce as a unifying device.

[15] F. Bologna has suggested that Ghiberti's mention of Taddeo as "dotissimo maestro" might be a reference to his special mathematical and perspective skill (*Novità su Giotto* [Turin, 1969], pp. 90-91).

XI.   "Last Supper" — Taddeo Gaddi

could play in enhancing realistic effects in painting. It is worth noting that all the works discussed above are executed in fresco with its monumental scale which, when an artist in painting figures that are near life-size, makes the possibility of deception seem more reasonable. It seems undeniable that an especially intimate relationship must develop between an artist and those figures he creates whose scale is equivalent to his own.

One might offer yet another possible reason for the development of illusionism in fresco painting. In panel painting the artist works on an enframed wooden surface of limited physical depth. When the panel is put into position on the altar of a chapel it is not flush with the wall, but set out from it, so that its actual depth is always apparent. In fresco painting the surface on which the artist paints is more than just that; it already has an existence of its own as a space-defining element. The artist who must always work *in situ* would be constantly reminded of this spacial limitation, one is led to believe that this would encourage experiment with illusion. An artist might be inspired either to deny the flatness by seeming to puncture it, thus creating a new space, or to use the flatness as a positive pictorial factor, as a foil against which forms may be projected. Taddeo does the latter in his *Last Supper*, where the illusionistic three-dimensional bands suggest the actual thickness of the wall and the figures are thrust into our environment.

In Siena, the other great center of Tuscan painting in the early fourteenth century, there is a development similar to that of Florence in that there is a move from simple experiments to more complex solutions. Duccio, the great founder of the Sienese school in this period, creates architectural and landscape spaces in the narrative scenes of the *Maestà* (1308-1311) that have a more independent existence than do those of Giotto in the Arena Chapel. Such scenes as the *Entry into Jerusalem* and the *Temptation of Christ on the Temple* (Siena, Museo dell'Opera del Duomo) and *Christ Healing the Blind Man* (London, National Gallery)[16] reflect close observation of reality. Duccio's brilliant palette, crowded compositions, and his lack of interest in consistent spatial or scale relationships have so attracted the modern critics' attention that the revolutionary nature of these scenes has remained obscure; but to see them against a background of their immediate predecessors, the narrative scenes of Guido da Siena and his school,[17] is to begin to understand the impact they must have had in contemporary Siena.

And the revolution caught on. Duccio's pupils and followers expand the investigation of space which he instigated as much as did Giotto's in Florence. Simone Martini develops consistency of perspective in the predella of the *St. Louis of Toulouse* (Naples, Capodimonte; c. 1317),[18] and

---

[16] J. WHITE, *Art and Architecture* (London, 1966), Pls. 67A, 67B; *National Gallery Catalogues: Earlier Italian Schools: Plates* (London, 1953), 1, Pl. 136. White has pointed out that Duccio also truncates architure to heighten realism (*Art and Architecture*, p. 154).

[17] E.g., J. STUBBLEBINE, *Guido da Siena* (Princeton, 1964), figs. 3-6, 12-13.

[18] *Art and Architecture*, p. 235, and frontispiece.

his acute observation of real places is apparent in the narrative scenes of the *Beato Agostino Novella Altarpiece* (Siena, Sant'Agostino; c. 1335-1336).[19] The Lorenzetti use Duccio's compositional patterns, but they create more realistic effects of space in, for example, the Franciscan scenes in San Francisco, Siena, by Ambrogio (c. 1329-1331) and Pietro's *Carmelite Altarpiece Predella* (Siena, Pinacoteca; d. 1329).[20] The climax of the Sienese interest in space is Ambrogio's *Good and Bad Government* in the Palazzo Publico, Siena (doc. 1338-1339), where he paints a panoramic portrait city-scape and landscape of Siena and its *contado*.[21]

The *Annunciation* in the center pinnacle of Pietro Lorenzetti's *Pieve Polyptych* (Arezzo, Pieve; commissioned 1320) reveals a kind of spatial experimentation possible only in panel painting. Large panels such as this one involved a complex wooden structure and framing which was planned by the painter and constructed before the painting began. Here Pietro takes advantage of the three-dimensionality of the double-arched frame by painting within the openings two rooms which are carefully related to their enframement through matching capitals and consoles and heightens the illusion by establishing a continuous spatial relationship between forms that actually exist in three dimensions and their painted image. Pietro has here transformed an essentially abstract, decorative frame into a positive aid in the creation of space in a manner comparable to Taddeo's achievement in the *Last Supper*. In both cases a traditional decorative motif has been transformed to perform a completely new function, spatially-profound. Pietro continues the same idea on a larger scale in his *Birth of the Virgin* (Siena, Museo dell'Opera del Duomo; d. 1342),[22] where the space of the scenes is so completely unified to the abstract triptych form that it seems as if the frame has resulted from the interior space, rather than from the actual, opposite evolution of technique.

The Sienese artists were as interested in heightening effects of space as were the painters of Florence. Their experiments, however, are almost exclusively performed in panel painting, [which is the traditionally popular medium in Siena.] But the delimitations of the panel differ from the fresco and this may explain why the puncturing of the picture plane by forms thrust out into our space, as in the fresco paintings in Florence, is not found among the Sienese painters.

The phenomenon of increased spatial realism has been established. But what does it mean? It is, of course, only one part of a broader revolution which encompasses all aspects of art and is found in the literature of the period as well as the visual arts. It must be related to the complex interaction of many factors — historical, political, social, economic, religious, to

---

[19] G. PACCAGNINI, *Simone Martini* (London, 1957), Pls. XVII-XX.

[20] G. ROWLEY, *Ambrogio Lorenzetti* (Princeton, 1958), p. 2, figs. 104, 112; and E. DEWALD, *Pietro Lorenzetti* (Cambridge, Mass., 1930), Pls. 10, 11, 13.

[21] ROWLEY, figs. 153-160.

[22] *Art and Architecture*, Pl. 113A.

mention only the obvious. For purposes of understanding the new attitudes toward space, however, one factor looms beyond all others: the Franciscan religious revolution of the thirteenth century.

St. Francis's attitude toward the traditional religious stories is crucial here, for he made a distinct effort to humanize these remote and miraculous happenings so that would be more accessible to people of his own time. As Professor Jeffrey has suggested elsewhere in this volume, the writings of the early Franciscans, such as the *Meditations on the Life of Christ*, a devotional handbook written in the late thirteenth century by a Franciscan friar living in Tuscany,[23] best reveal the saint's intent. The devotee is exhorted to recreate the religious events in his mind and the author helps make them palpable by his intimate details, personal style, and evocative suggestions. In discussing the Nativity, for example, he says:

> .... kneel and adore your Lord God, and then His mother, and reverently greet the saintly old Joseph. Kiss the beautiful little feet of the infant Jesus who lies in the manger and beg His mother to offer to let you hold Him a while. Pick Him up and hold Him in your arms. Gaze on His face with devotion and reverently kiss Him and delight in Him.... Then return Him to the mother and watch her attentively as she cares for Him assiduously and wisely, nursing Him and rendering all services, and remain to help her if you can. (38-39)

Even more vivid is his description of the tortures of Christ:

> But in what battle is He tormented? You will hear (and see). One of them seizes Him (this sweet, mild, and pious Jesus), another binds Him, another attacks Him, another scolds Him, another pushes Him, another blasphemes Him, another spits on Him, another beats Him, another walks around Him, another questions Him, another looks for false witnesses against Him, another accompanies the one that searches, another gives false testimony against Him, another accuses Him, another mocks Him, another blindfolds Him, another strikes His face, another goads Him, another leads Him to the column, another strips Him, another beats Him while He is being led, another screams, another begins furiously to torment Him, another binds Him to the column, another assaults Him, another scourges Him, another robes Him in purple to abuse Him, another places the crown of thorns, another gives Him the reed to hold, another madly takes it away to strike His thorn-covered head, another kneels mockingly, another salutes Him as King. (318)

The author of the *Meditations* even encourages the olfactory sense of the reader:

> He is pushed and anguished, afflicted and pulled, and exhausted, and scourged, and soaked, and completely sated by infamy; He is not given rest, not once, and Hardly could His spirit rest until He reached the place of Calvary — a most ugly and evil-smelling place; and all these things were done with great noise and furor. (319)

Widespread attempts by Franciscan preachers and authors to translate these the events of biblical narrative into vital personal experience by such concrete and vivid descriptions must be intimately connected with the

---

[23] *Meditations on the Life of Christ*, trans. I. RAGUSA, ed. I. RAGUSA and R. GREEN (Princeton, 1961), pp. xxi-xxii, n. 2. Cf. the chapter by JEFFREY, pp. 148-9.

growing valuation of the depiction of natural reality in painting during this period.

It can be demonstrated, in fact, that Trecento artists are not interested in exploring realism in art purely for its own sake, but that the motivation for the growing naturalism of this period, of which space is just one aspect, must be directly related to the artists' concern with narrative.[24] The Tuscan painter of the Trecento is still very much a storyteller; he is not yet involved with the theoretical bases for art which become so important in the fifteenth century. That the search for greater realism is directly tied to the artists' desire to make their stories more believable and forceful receives support from the fact that the exploration of pictorial space is directly related to particular narrative problems. Deep landscape, for example, appears in Trecento art only when the story's plot calls for it: Simone Martini's *Portrait of Guidoriccio da Fogliano* (Siena, Palazzo Pubblico; 1328), where the portraits of the towns he recaptured in the background are essential to the meaning of the image; Ambrogio Lorenzetti's *Good and Bad Government* (Siena, Palazzo Pubblico; doc. 1338-1339), where the application of the allegory to the local government is directly expressed by the depiction of Siena and its contado; and Ambrogio's *St. Nicolas of Bari and the Miracle of the Grain* (Florence, Uffizi; c. 1331), where the ships from which St. Nicolas requests the grain are described in the legend as imperial galleys bringing wheat from Alexandria.[25] Maso di Banco's *St. Sylvester Muzzling the Dragon* (Pl. 1) is another of the rare examples: here the silent landscape expresses the devastation wrought by the dragon and, thereby, the power of Sylvester who brings his reign of terror to an end. Contrast this with the Quattrocento, when the development of the theory of scientific perspective, as promoted by Alberti's *Della pittura* (c. 1435), led to the representation of deep and carefully-structured spaces which are irrelevant to the meaning of the narrative.[26]

Further support for the theory that narrative plays a central role in the realistic revolution of Giotto and his pupils may be illustrated in the use of blacks and orientals in the paintings.[27] The presence of exotic peoples in Italy is well-documented,[28] but their appearance in art has never been convincingly explained. Olschki concluded that it merely meant that realism

[24] John Larner cites an important reference from the fourteenth century where a Sienese account book records not only payment to an artist for a painting of St. Savino, but also an entry of payment to "Cecco, master of Grammar, who translated the story of Sant Savino into the bulgar tongue, so that it might be portrayed on panel." (*Culture and Society in Italy, 1290-1420* [New York, 1971], p. 297; this reference was kindly drawn to my attention by Bonnie Apgar Bennett.)

[25] *Art and Architecture*, pp. 235-236, Pl. 102A; ROWLEY, figs. 157, 159; and fig. 92.

[26] L. B. ALBERTI, *On Painting*, trans. J. SPENCER (New Haven, 1956).

[27] For some typical examples see WHITE, *Birth and Rebirth*, figs. 33b, 39a, 39b, 45b, and 46b.

[28] I. ORIGO, "The Domestic Enemy: The Eastern Slaves in Tuscany in the Fourteenth and Fifteenth Centuries," *Speculum, 30* (1955), 321-366 (with a lengthy bibliography).

was extending to the accessories, while Kühnel, in a peculiarly twentieth-century interpretation, judged it to depend "chiefly on the chromatic interrelationships in the work and the free play of the artist's imagination unfettered by any symbolic content." Yet to the contrary, these figures appear only when they have a specific narrative function. In Giotto's *Mocking of Christ* (Padua, Arena Chapel; 1303-1305) the central black figure signals that these men are non-Christians, while in Giotto's *St. Francis' Trial by Fire before the Sultan* (Florence, Santa Croce, Bardi Chapel, c. 1315-20) the carefully-observed blacks and orientals convincingly set the locale in a foreign, heathen land.[30] The same explanation is evident for the Tartars who appear in Ambrogio Lorenzetti's *Martyrdom of the First Franciscans* (Siena, San Francisco; late 1320's).[31] In this case the heathen setting is also indicated by the use of classical sculptural models for the statues of vices which decorate the architecture.

Taddeo Gaddi's *Annunciation to the Shepherds* (Baroncelli Chapel)[32] offers another example of the important role narrative played for the Trecento artist. This earliest known example of a night scene in painting since antiquity may be the result of Taddeo's careful observation of natural phenomenon. But Taddeo's angel, whose glowing form lightens the darkness around the shepherd, clearly arises from the dramatic and historical sense of the narrative: "And there were in the same country shepherds abiding in the field, keeping watch over their flock by night. And, lo, the angel of the Lord came upon them, and the glory of the Lord shone round about them" (Luke 2:8-9). Taddeo uses this striking pictorial device of the glowing form only where it is appropriate to the narrative. (Cf. *St. Francis' Appearance in the Fiery Chariot at Riva-Torto* [Florence, Accademia; c.1330].)[34]

The brilliant and dramatic spatial effect of Taddeo Gaddi's *Last Supper* in the refectory at Santa Croce (Pl. XI) is generalized from scriptural narrative. The illusion that the table and its thirteen occupants exist within the real space of the refectory would have been all the more forceful when this room was used as a confraternal dining hall, filled with tables and men

---

[29] L. OLSCHKI, "Asiatic Exoticism in Italian Art of the Early Renaissance," *Art Bulletin*, 26 (1944), 95-106; E. KÜHNEL, "Exoticism," *Encyclopedia of World Art*, 5, col. 295.

[30] STUBBLEBINE, *Giotto*, fig. 44; PREVITALI, fig. 373, Pl. XC. One possible reason for this iconographic use of Africans may relate to an association with Jer. 13:23, "Can the Ethiopian change his skin, or the leopard his spots? Then may also you do good who are accustomed to do evil." The gloss on this passage by RABANUS MAURUS's *Allegoria in Sacram Scripturam*, (ed. J. P. MIGNE, *PL*, Paris, 1878, CXII, col. 918), is "Ethiopes sunt peccatores".

[31] ROWLEY, Pls. 111-117.

[32] P. DONATI, *Taddeo Gaddi* ("I diamanti dell'arte,'', no. 12), Florence, 1966, Pl. 18.

[33] I find the light source to be the angel, not the window as is suggested by GARDNER, p. 96.

[34] DONATI, Pl. 37. For the textual source see G. KAFTAL, *St. Francis in Italian Painting* ("Ethical and Religious Classics of East and West," no. 4), London, 1950, p. 52. Alastair Smart points to yet another example of this in Taddeo's *Stigmatization* in the Refectory at Santa Croce; see Smart, p. 205, for the notice and the textual source.

eating in silence as they listened to inspirational readings or sermons. The idea of suggesting in this way that Christ and the apostles were effectively fellow diners with the friars was, I would suggest, conceived by Taddeo when he received the commission to paint the *Last Supper* on the end wall of the refectory. The result is an innovation in the use of space in fourteenth-century Tuscan painting consistent with innovations in the narrative and spirituality of its subject matter of the kind earnestly advocated by the Franciscans in their revolution.[35]

---

[35] What was the future of these early Trecento spatial innovations? To take Taddeo's *Last Supper* as an example, its composition in space has no progeny, in spite of the continued popularity of this theme as a refectory decoration. The *Last Supper* of c. 1360 painted by Orcagna followers in the refectory of Santo Spirito, where the figures and table appear to be enclosed in a neat space box recessed into the wall, becomes the traditional type (R. OFFNER, *A critical and Historical Corpus of Florentine Painting*, sec. IV, 1 (New York, 1962), pp. 65-71, Pls. V¹-V²⁸). The second half of the Trecento has little of the exciting experimentation of the first half of that century and, in general, reveals a retreat from realism. The reasons for this are still a matter of controversy, but Millard Meiss's idea, now more than twenty years old, that the trauma of famine, financial disaster, and plague were partially responsible must be at least partly true (*Painting in Florence and Siena after the Black Death*, Princeton, 1951). It is also worth noting that by 1350 all the painters we have discussed, with the exception of Taddeo Gaddi, were dead.

Taddeo's motif of thrusting figures forward into the observer's space does appear again, but not until the early Quattrocento in Masaccio's *Trinity* (Florence, Santa Maria Novella; c. 1425; Berenson, Pl. 585). Here Brunelleschian pilasters establish the plane of the wall and function to exclude the contemporary Florentine donors from the timeless space of the central group. It is tempting to postulate some connection between Taddeo and Masaccio, for the latter was the Renaissance artist who best understood what Giotto and his immediate followers had accomplished. (On this see the interesting article by M. BOSKOVITS, "Giotto Born Again," *Zeitschrift für Kunstgeschichte*, 29 [1966], 51-66.) This theory finds some support in the fact that this illusionistic device does not fit the Brunelleschian perspective scheme which controls the rest of this fresco, for the space occupied by the donors is not a part of the measurable construction. In any case, Taddeo's construction preceded Masaccio's by almost a century, whether the latter knew it or not.

II

CULTURAL TRANSLATION

Indeed, in every creature there is a refulgence of the divine exemplar, but mixed with darkness: hence it resembles some kind of opacity combined with light. But it is still a way, leading to the exemplar.

St. BONAVENTURE, *In Hexaemeron*, 12.14-15.

The Practical Transmission of Medieval Culture[1]

ROBERT S. LOPEZ

Let us begin at the bottom. Unquestionably the elementary vehicle for cultural diffusion is language, the first treasure of the common man. As the prince of Italian philologists, Dante Aligheri, observed, "only to men was given speech, because to them alone was it necessary, not to the angels, nor to inferior animals."[2] These statements open his treatise in defense of the Italian vernacular, and the defense, as is proper, is not in Italian but in Latin. We also should acknowledge the special merits of official Latin: even in the most unhappy centuries of the early Middle Ages it allowed cultured individuals, whether clergymen or laymen, officials or scholars, Romanic or Germanic, to understand each other. Latin became debased, it is true, at least until the scholars assembled by Charlemagne revived its classical forms with the aid of ancient manuscripts and of the oral tradition of the British Isles; but they froze it, so that it could better serve the understanding of sacred Scripture, the public administration of a polyglot Empire and the diffusion of culture.

There can be no sustained dialogue among interlocutors who have not at their disposal a common language. Latin was like a fence that kept together the peoples of the West but isolated them from those of the East. Without allowing himself to be impressed by its revival in the Carolingian era, the Byzantine Emperor Michael III called it a "barbaric and Scythian" language; Pope Nicholas I replied that Latin was one of the languages of God, and that an Emperor who wanted to be called Roman and did not understand the Roman language was ridiculous.[3] One could also add, with the knowledge of hindsight, that the finicky Greek language of Byzantium was incapable of doing for the Hellenic *koinè* what the debased Latin did for the Romano-Germanic community: Byzantine Greek did not superimpose itself everywhere on the vulgar languages as Latin did. The same Michael

---

[1] This paper was first published as *Discorso inaugurale* (keynote speech) in the eleventh *Settimane di Studio del Centro italiano di studi sull'alto medioevo (Centers and Routes of Cultural Diffusion in the Early Middle Ages)*, Spóleto, 1963, and is published here in slightly abridged form. It was translated for this volume by John F. D'AMICO, University of Rochester.

[2] *De Vulgari Eloquentia*, I, 2.

[3] *Monumenta Germaniæ Historica, Epistolæ*, VI (*Karolini Aevi*), 459.

III who abandoned Latin to the barbarians of the West sent Cyril and Methodius to teach religion to the Eastern barbarians, but not the Greek language.

Let us proceed to the vernacular languages. I would like to propose a question to which my inexpert curiosity has not found a satisfactory answer. It is a question from a historian, for use by other historians; philologists should forgive me if I do not succeed in explaining it save in a 'barbaric and Scythian' form. How does one explain the parallelism of the principal structural modifications undergone by all or almost all the European vernacular languages? Whether one deals with medieval and modern Greek, with the Romance languages, with the Germanic languages, or even with Bulgarian, the declensions disappear or are simplified. The simple or inflected forms of conjugations give place to compound forms relying on auxiliary verbs. Definite and indefinite articles take their place before the noun.[4]

We may limit ourselves to one example, which seems to me typical: the future tense. In the classical languages. Greek and Latin, the future tense was formed by means of inflection: γράφω γράφω; *scribo, scribam*. On the other hand, in *Urgermanische*, the hypothetical proto-Germanic, there was no future tense; a most natural thing according to some philologists, such as Otto Jespersen, because to think of the future tense is for refined and sophisticated peoples. Now, in the Middle Ages, all the languages, both those which had the future tense and those which did not have it, began to experiment with a new form; the future tense formed by means of the auxiliary verb. The Germanic languages tried different devices: "to want to write," "to be able to write," "to have to write." Today, English still wavers between "to want" and "to have to," "will" and "shall," without counting circumlocutions like "I am going to write" (analogous to the French *je vais écrire*) and "I am to write" or "I have to write;" this last form is acceptable even in Italian. The Dane "wants" to write. The German, having grasped the idea of the future tense, throws himself into it with so much enthusiasm that "he becomes to write" (*Ich werde schreiben*); it is true that in common use he continues to use the present with the meaning of the future as the Russians also do.

The axuiliaries "to want" and "to come" are also found in the periphery of the Romance languages: Rumanian and Rheto-Roman. But the other Romance languages adopted temporarily the most common and the

---

[4] Not for the philologists, who do not need it, but for the outsider to the field who might wish an elementary orientation, I indicate some books which have aided me: E. AUERBACH, *Literary Language and its Public in Late Antiquity and in the Middle Ages* (New York, 1965); Ch. BALLY, *Linguistique générale et linguistique française* (sec. ed., Bern, 1944); L. BLOOMFIELD, *Language* (New York, 1933); O. JESPERSEN, *Language: Its Nature, Development and Origin* (London, 1922); E. SAPIR, *Language: An Introduction to the Study of Speech* (New York, 1921); A. SCHIAFFINI, *Momenti di storia della lingua italiana* (sec. ed., Rome, 1953); W. VON WARTBURG, *Problèmes et méthodes de la linguistique* (Paris, 1946).

most pliable of all auxiliary verbs, "to have." The same verb that before a participle indicates a form of the past (*habeo scriptum*, in Italian *ho scritto*, I wrote) after an infinitive indicates the future (*scribere habeo, scriverò*, that is "I have to write"). But as far as the future tense is concerned, it is merely a passing stage; the auxiliary, reabsorbed into the principal verb, becomes a new verb, a new form of inflection; *scribere habeo* gives *scriverò, j'écrirai*, and so forth. In modern Greek, on the other hand, "to have" is not ambidexterous; if the perfect tense is obtained with it, $\dot{\epsilon}\chi\omega\ \gamma\rho\alpha\mu\mu\dot{\epsilon}\nu o$, the future tense adopts the auxiliary "to will (or want)" as in the Germanic languages, $\vartheta'\dot{\alpha}\ \gamma\rho\dot{\alpha}\varphi\omega$ or $\vartheta\dot{\alpha}\ \gamma\rho\alpha\psi\omega$.

To these phenomena, the philologists have given various explanations, which, it seems to me, can be reduced to only one: the development of languages resembles that of all other living things. The future tense obtained with the inflection and the future tense composed of the auxiliary verb are said to be two successive ages in the life of one language: the first, synthetic, and the second analytic.[5] But this explanation, let it be said with all the respect due to our eminent colleagues, leaves the historian as tantalized as before. At the beginning of the early Middle Ages, Greek, Latin, and Germanic, even if stemming from the same Indo-European tree, were not in the same phase of development, did not have the same age. Greek already had the future tense, Germanic did not. Latin had been refined by Vergil and regimented by Quintilian; Germanic had not received a literary baptism before Ulfilas. It is in the Middle Ages that Greek, Latin and Germanic fell into step, remaining involved in what many years ago a philologist at Yale, Edward Sapir, called a linguistic "current," the analytical current. This common current ought then to have an historical cause, a common meaning.

Would it be proper, in this instance, to relate linguistic phenomena to "cultural diffusions?" This is merely a question: I neither know how to answer nor whether it is for me to propose an answer. Yet my mind runs to an historical process, noticeable in many other fields: in the course of the early Middle Ages the Latins, Germans and Byzantines had shortened the distance that separated them and almost met on a level which for the Germans represented a painstaking ascent, for the Latins a terrible fall, for the Greeks a partial decline. The analytical current might perhaps be related to this new level of engagement; the particulars of this relationship I leave to specialists in language.

---

[5] Actually Bally, p. 16, attributes to the Romance form of the future another explanation, which seems to me more persuasive and more consonant with the cultural development of the barbaric age; the new future is a more "expressive" form than the old one; on this point see also my longer comments in *The Birth of Europe* (New York, 1967), pp. 207 ff. On the other hand Bloomfield, p. 415, seems little convinced by the explanation of the form of the future as a contracted derivation from the infinitive combined with the auxiliary *habeo*, and he adds the comment: "The fusion of two words into only one is extremely rare.... a similar development ought to be produced in conditions quite uncommon." But what were those uncommon conditions? The question is nowhere answered.

Let us move up a step. After speech, there is nothing better than writing for the spreading of culture. Even before Byzantine Europe, Catholic Europe found, for the art of writing, as in its utilization of official Latin, a superior vehicle. In the West, the experiments and the pluralism of "national" scripts of the early medieval centuries blossomed between the end of the eighth and the beginning of the ninth century into a uniform writing, that Caroline minuscule which even today is the base of our manner of writing and printing. Triumphant in a few years in the whole of the Carolingian Empire, it soon asserted itself even into Southern Italy and the Catholic lands of the North, supplanting "national scripts" and runes. In contrast, Byzantium, which had maintained internally its own political and calligraphic unity, in the ninth century had not yet arrived at a definitive form for the new Greek minuscule, and it did not teach to the catechumenes of the Slavic language its own alphabet, but Glagolitic writing. This last in its turn remained in use only in Croatia, while other Slavic lands adopted later the more evolved characters of the so-called Cyrillic writing.

We Westerners should not jump to arrogant conclusions like those of Michael III. If Carolingian Latin and Caroline minuscule had an easier and more complete victory than Greek and the minuscule of Photius, Cyril and Methodius, it is not because these men were more 'barbaric' and Scythian than Alcuin, Theodulf or Paul the Deacon, but on the contrary because Western culture was a greenhouse flower, a patrimony reserved for the few and therefore easily watched over. How many spoke and wrote good Latin? I think of a Lombard document of 767 in which one Gaidualdo, who called himself "royal physician" at Pistoia, merely affixed to the charter the sign of the cross in lieu of a signature, and the scribe who wrote it down commented: *Cartulam fieri rogavit, et ei omnia relecta ut sunt complacuit*.[6] ("He asked that the charter be drawn up, and when everything was read to him, he was pleased.") We must admit that if the doctor did not know how to write, the scribe was somewhat weak in grammar! It is true that the charter was prior to the Carolingian revival, and that Italy would soon distinguish herself due to the culture of some of her laymen; but as late as the tenth century, there were in Salerno many intelligent yet illiterate physicians.[7] The recommendations of the Council of Tours, which in 813 counseled the clergy to preach in the rustic Romance or Germanic language if they wanted to be understood by the faithful, and the bilingual Strasbourg Oaths some thirty years later leave us no illusion as to the efficacy of restored Latin as an instrument of cultural dissemination among the masses. Nor will anyone give too much credit to the Caroline minuscule who remembers the observations of Ganshof on the extremely limited use of writing in the administration of the Carolingian empire. It would be

---

[6] L. SCHIAPARELLI, *Codice Diplomatico Longobarda*, II, 212. On the other hand, a good number of moneyers of the same epoch seemed to have known how to write, see LOPEZ, "An Aristocracy of Money in the Early Middle Ages," *Speculum*, XXVIII (1953), 34 ff.

[7] See, for instance, P. KRISTELLER, "The School of Salerno," *Bulletin of the History of Medecine*, XVII (1945), pp. 138-194.

worthwhile to count, in the small but not insignificant number of extant charters, the witnesses or parties who signed them and those who did not. This would give us an approximate idea of the comparative size of what we may call "the aristocracy of the pen," no doubt a less numerous elite than the aristocracy of the sword.[8]

Obviously the broadest channels for the diffusion of early medieval culture were not written and Latin but oral and vernacular. It is difficult, however, to reconstruct what went through those channels; we often read too much in what we suppose to be the influence of lost sources on famous works of later ages. There may be much more to be learned from humbler testimonies which most historians tend to neglect: folk tales and legends, tools and techniques, housing and recipes. History, as Gian Piero Bognetti used to say, is made not only in the drawing room but in the kitchen as well. How much we wish he were among us, to trace back to the Burgundian invasions, as he alone could do, the progress of certain gastronomic specialties! And we should not omit the contributions of musicologists. If it is true, as we are told, that popular songs served the propaganda of Arius and the counteroffensive of Ambrose; if the Carolingian empire may be defined, as it has been, "a civilization based on liturgy;" if the twin evolution of Ambrosian and Gregorian chant is a main stream of early medieval history and the emergency of sequences and tropes an essential element in the cultural revolution of the tenth century, then the contribution of musicologists must not be overlooked.

As for the historians of art, they certainly have their reasons to look at cathedrals and castles rather than at houses and huts. This is why domestic art, or, if you will, "non-art," is mainly the business of ethnologists, geographers, or — wherever archaeology stoops to postclassical times — archaeologists. So be it, but let us listen to them, for they have much to teach us. Such investigations as those that have brought to light the log huts of Biskupin and Gdansk in Poland and the oval fenced lodgings of Trelleborg and Firkat in Denmark have put at our disposal precious datable documents of early medieval culture. Still it remains for us to extend the research and coordinate it, so that we may delimit the zones where one or another type of housing predominates and follow its influence and diffusion.[9]

---

[8] F. L. GANSHOF, "Charlemagne et l'usage de l'écrit en matière administrative," *Moyen Age*, XLVII (1951), pp. 1-25; see also A. DUMAS, "La parole et l'écriture dans les capitulaires carolingiens," *Mélanges Louis Halphen* (Paris, 1951). For the early centuries, the relations between pluralism in scripts and general culture have been described by Cencetti and discussed by Pratesi and by Campana during the IX Settimana di Spoleto; one would like to hope that the problem will be examined with equal thoroughness for later centuries in the course of another Settimana.

[9] The thoughtful volume of G. KUBLER, *The Shape of Time, Remarks on the History of Things* (New Haven, 1962), invites us to an all-embracing conception of history of art; "from this point of view, the totality of things done by man coincides with the history of art.... the sole tokens of

It may be much harder to identify in time and in space the different types of domestic construction of stone and brick. Comparative studies, if I am not mistaken, are not very numerous; archaeological probings are scanty; forms have a singular tendency to repeat themselves unchanged, so much so that one can speak with De Negri of "prehistoric survivals in rustic architecture" or of "continuing Romanesque architecture."[10] However, other documents aid us: coins, miniatures, written texts like that of the *Memoratorium* of the Comacini Masters (early Italian architects), where Bognetti glimpsed a first distinction between a proto-Romanesque style in stone and in tile — *opus romanense* — and a Nordic style in wood and straw — *opus gallicum*. A layman is led to seek in the taste and in the proportions, materials and forms of this *opus gallicum* a forerunner of that which the Germans will call, in the thirteenth century, *opus francigenum* and which we will call the Gothic style. But here I stop before I am stoned by the experts.[11]

Historians feel less far from home ground when using epic and narrative poetry as source material; but how much should they trust it? If we ask medieval scholars we receive contradictory responses. In the sixth century, Jordanes spoke with contempt of the "primitive chants" of his Ostrogothic country-men, and he adds "We do not find written anywhere the fables that tell of the Goths reduced to servitude in Britain.... Rather than giving credence to the stories of the old women, we must believe what we read." In the ninth century, Areta of Caesarea treats even worse oral Byzantine traditions: "These accursed Paphlagonians," he says, "have fabricated I know not what songs on the adventures of famous heroes, and go and tell them from house to house to beg for money." But Snorri Sturluson, the foremost Icelandic historian of the thirteenth century, holds in far greater esteem the songs which transmit to him an echo of things happening three hundred years before: "With King Harald Fairhair," he says, "there were skaldic poets whose poems were well known, and we prefer the testimony which is found in these poems delivered before the leaders and their sons.... It is true that the poets were accustomed to praise the personage for whom they sang, but no one would have dared to attribute to the leader exploits that all the listeners, and the leader himself, would

---

continual history accessible to our sense are the desirable things made by man." (p. 1). More particularly for Denmark see the book of my former student Sidney COHEN, "Viking Fortresses of the Trelleborg Type" (with ample bibliography); for Poland, W. HENSEL and A. GIEYSZTOR, *Archeological Research in Poland* (Warsaw, 1958) and the collection of studies *L'Artisanat et la vie urbaine en Pologne médiévale*, which forms the third volume of *Ergon* (Warsaw, 1962).

[10] T. O. DE NEGRI, "Porte rustiche," *Bollettino Ligustico per la Storia e la Cultura Regionale*, II (1950), 81 ff., and other studies in the same review. Italy possesses now an excellent survey in *Ricerche sulle dimore rurali in Italia*, directed by R. BIASUTTI (Bologna and later Florence, 1938 ff., 22 volumes published up to 1962); but the survey is not aimed at historians. The latter should find more useful the essays collected in *Les constructions civiles d'intérêt public dans les villes d'Europe au Moyen Âge et sous l'Ancien Régime* (Pro Civitate, Bruxelles, 1969).

[11] G. P. BOGNETTI, G. CHIERICI, A. DE CAPITANI D'ARZAGO, *Santa Maria di Castelseprio* (Milan, 1948), pp. 286 ff.; and see *The Birth of Europe*, pp. 191 ff.

have known as lies." Snorri approves of the historical writings of his predecessor, Arni Frodi, and plunders them without scruple, but declares that he prefers poems, "when they are composed correctly and understood with intelligence."[12]

If the value of epic poems as documents of events earlier than their actual composition is dubious (and cannot in any case be great), we can still use them as mirrors of mental attitudes and cultural diffusion at the time when they were drawn up. Thus, for instance, the Eddic poems bear witness to the lingering influence of older and foreign traditions on the cultural formation of Scandinavia: most of the legends they pick up are not of native origin, but must be regarded as adaptations of earlier Frankish, Burgundian or Saxon themes. The enduring fascination of pre-imperial exploits in imperial Germany is shown by the fact that the most celebrated sovereigns in its epic poems are neither emperors nor orthodox Christians, but three kings of the age of migrations: Ermanric, Attila and Theodoric, that is, two pagans and one arian, or more specifically, two Goths and one Hun. If I am not mistaken, none of the Christian emperors who ruled Germany from Otto I to Frederick Barbarossa attained epic stature in his country, and even Barbarossa had to wait a long time and to be sometimes confused with Frederick II. Charlemagne made it more promptly, though there were poets who represented him as a greedy old dotard, but his great deeds were dimmed by the magnified image of an ultimately unsuccessful frontiersman. Roland stole the show.[13]

Roland's popularity seems to indicate, among other things, that for a long time after Charlemagne's death people expected very little from the central government but pinned their hopes on the defenders of the border zones. There is a striking parallel here between the epics of the West and those of the East. Not without some apprehension, because the historical background is still the object of heated scholarly debate, I would like to recall the basic similarity between the two marquesses or frontier generals who lived in flesh and blood in the late eighth century and became posthumously the top heroes respectively of the Latin and the Greek worlds. Digenis "the marquess" (Akritas), who died in 788, is described as the son of a Byzantine noblewoman and of a converted Emir, an incomparable warrior but not devoid of a certain refinement and intellectual sophistication. His image dimmed that of the great Isaurian and Macedonian emperors, fascinated the Byzantine world and still survives in the "Akritic" ballads of modern Greece. His legend had a Russian version, and, blended with that of

---

[12] See for example R. Menendez PIDAL, "Los Godos y el origen de la epopeya española," *I Goti in Occidente* (Spoleto, 1956); G. COHEN, preface to H. GRÉGOIRE, *Digenis Akritas* (New York, 1942); J. GLÉNISSON, *Iniciaçao aos estudos históricos* (San Paulo, Brazil, 1961), pp. 86 ff.

[13] We find ourselves here on the outskirts of folklore, a field of study which in Italy has a great tradition going back to Pitrè, supported by the prestige of Benedetto Croce, but insufficiently exploited for the study of medieval history. One can follow its development in a good volume by G. COCCHIARA, *Storia del folklore in Europa* (Turin, 1952).

an Arab hero, his contemporary, was incorporated into Islamic literature. This, incidentally, goes to show that the differences of language, literature and religion between Byzantium and Baghdad could be overcome by the similarity of cultural levels. Roland, who died in 778, was more simple-minded. He did not enter into the Islamic epic tradition, because Paris and Cordova were not at the same cultural level. But he charmed France, crossed the English Channel with the minstrel Taillefer who followed William the Conqueror, and won over all of Catholic Europe. Paradoxically, the great warrior became the protector of peace in the Rolands of stone of the German markets.[14]

In regard to the diffusion of epic traditions as well as to that of literacy, an economic and social historian would like to attempt a quantitative calculation, however rough and incomplete it might be. Almost always, students of medieval literature concentrate their attention on masterpieces, not on popular works which may have been more read; and from their point of view, they are not wrong. But whoever wants to draw near to the sentiments of the masses will have to take into consideration the fact that only one manuscript of *Beowulf* and one of the *Cantar del Cid* are known. Only one manuscript, which disappeared a few years after the burning of Moscow, transmitted to us the text of the Russian epic poem the *Sayings of Igor*; and there are those who doubt its authenticity. (If it is not authentic, however, it still is a good poem!) On the other hand, we have very numerous copies of the *Chanson de Roland* besides the manuscript recognized by the scholars as more authoritative than the others. Leaving aside the high literary value of the work, the plurality of copies is an indication of its importance for the spread of culture. But even if all the ancient manuscripts of the chanson de geste were put together, we would still be very far from the abundance of hagiographic production. Many thousand lives of saints, written between the sixth and the tenth centuries, are collected in the Latin volumes of the Bollandist Fathers. This was an imposing production for the quantity, if not for the quality; so much so that it mitigates somewhat what I said at the beginning concerning the small role of writing in the culture of the early Middle Ages.

For centuries, in contrast with the illiteracy prevalent in the lay world, the clergy almost single-handedly maintained as best they could the tradition of reading and writing. Let us acknowledge our debt: without the Church, we would hardly know more about the early Middle Ages than about prehistoric times. But, at the same time, let us remember that our information is almost hopelessly biased. Granted that the church and religion had crucial importance, they must have been less dominant than the

---

[14] It would be impossible and probably useless to cite the immense bibliography of these noted questions; let us limit ourselves in recalling the bold work of H. GRÉGOIRE, "The Historical Element in Western and Eastern Epics," *Byzantion*, XVI (1942-43). Most particularly on the parallelism between Digenis and Roland see R.S. LOPEZ, "Marquis et monostratèges," *Mélanges offerts à René Crozet* (Poitiers, 1966), pp. 77 ff.

ecclesiastic quasi-monopoly of media leads us to believe. Were we to rely only on church-inspired sources in our interpretation of early medieval culture and its diffusion, we might be not much better off than we would if, today, we had nothing else to read about contemporary culture than the *Osservatore Romano* or the *Brooklyn Tablet*.

On the historical worth of medieval hagiographic literature let us defer to the judgment of an unimpeachable observer, Bollandist Father Hyppolite Delehaye. "The elaboration of legends," he wrote in 1927, "may be numbered among the great unconscious forces of nature. The popular soul cannot be vividly impressed by a great event or by a powerful personality without its sentiments finding expression in stories where its fantasy is given free reign.... Legend is a homage of the Christian people to its protectors. One cannot neglect it. But it is not necessary to take it for history. It is a confusion that the zeal for the glory of the saints does not require, and that presents serious inconveniences."[15] Once that is said, the fact remains that a great countryman of Father Delahaye, Henri Pirenne, has taught us to discover grains of truth concealed among the lines of the most incredible legends. Like epics, hagiography is a very bad chronicle of the past, but a precious mirror for its own present.

This analogy cannot astonish us: epic poetry and hagiography are the product of the same mentality. "Epic heroes are saints; saints are epic heroes."[16] My friend and teacher, Robert Reynolds, communicated to me another proof not long ago. In the daring research on the sources of *Beowulf* which he conducted for years with his students, Reynolds had been intrigued by the name of a sword, *Naegling*, used by the hero in his fight against the dragon. Etymologically, *Naegling* means, "daughter of the nail." What could a nail ever serve against the tough monster who wants to devour Beowulf? Reynolds noted that in the cathedral of Exeter there are relics which had been given to the Anglo-Saxon king Athelstan by his son-in-law Hugh the Great (the father of Hugh Capet), who had inherited them from the direct decendants of Charlemagne, who in his turn had received them as gifts from the Caliph Harun al-Rashid. Among these relics there was a nail from the true cross. Such a nail, enclosed in a sword, would have made it invincible. *Beowulf*, according to Reynolds, is substantially a poem of the tenth century; the epic theme is enriched by a hagiographic fringe; the word *Naegling* takes us back to Athelstan and Athelstan to Harun al-Rashid.[17]

---

[15] H. DELEHAYE, *Les Légendes hagiographiques* (third ed. Brussels, 1927), preface, pp. xiv-xv.

[16] This citation also is taken from the preface of G. COHEN to H. GRÉGOIRE, *op. cit.*; but much more incisive and less hazy than Cohen is E. DELARUELLE, *La pietà popolare nel secolo XI*, in *Relazioni del X Congresso internazionale di scienze storiche*, III (Florence, 1955), with bibliography.

[17] Professor Reynolds was still alive when the following words were added with his consent: "I wish to thank Robert Reynolds for letting me use his article, *Two Naeglings?*, still unpublished as is his *Argonautica and Beowulf*. They hold many surprises for students of the Anglo-Saxon Epic."

Not all roads lead to Baghdad. I underlined once before, in another essay, that we should not see in every object of foreign provenance a proof of economic and cultural relations with a far off land. If we did not know their story, the relics of Exeter might lead us to imagine commercial exchanges between Exeter and Baghdad in the tenth century, whereas their arrival in the West is connected with diplomatic courtesies between Charlemagne and Harun in the ninth century. In the same article, I underlined that sometimes the very rarity of a foreign object gives it an importance out of proportion to its value as an indicator of cross-cultural contact. A letter written in 906 to the Caliph al-Muktafi by an Italian princess on woven byssus (byssus is extracted from a mollusk) seemed so extraordinary that one Arab writer after another spoke of it; Chinese ambassadors to the court of Baghdad talked about it to their emperor, and finally a mention of the letter was included in the official annals of the T'ang dynasty in China. Not all roads lead to Peking (or to Ch'ang An, the Chinese capital in the early Middle Ages), or better yet, the best known roads do not necessarily carry much traffic. From the point of view of cultural diffusion, it is much more important to follow the course of the silkworm, that humble little animal which in the course of the early Middle Ages crawled from China to the Byzantium of Justinian and then, in the tenth century, to Italy and to Spain.[18]

Here I have now arrived at the little field that, although reserved for an expert of the caliber of Fernand Vercauteren, can give me a chance to offer a few remarks based on personal research: the diffusion of culture by means of the merchants. To make a smooth transition, I will point out first of all a possible direction of research through hagiographical sources; the history of the theft of relics. This history, according to the *Dictionnaire d'archéologie chrétienne*, "would merit a comprehensive work that has been begun but not finished."[19]

Stealing relics has always been a profitable operation, for all of its dangers. We may pass over the story of the Trojan horse which the Trojans sought to appropriate, with consequences we all know. We can barely mention the Theodosian Code, that prescribes "Let no one abduct, let no one sell a martyr," and the skepticism of St. Augustine concerning certain monks who sold abusively "limbs of martyrs, supposing that they really deal with martyrs." All that is pre-medieval, (the early Middle Ages invented nothing), but they were particularly industrious in this field.[20]

---

[18] R. S. LOPEZ, *East and West in the Early Middle Ages: Economic Relations*, in *Relazioni del X Congresso* cit., III, 127 ff.; ID., "China Silk in Europe in the Yüan Period," *Journal of the American Oriental Society* LXXXII (1952), 72-73.

[19] H. LECLERCQ, "Reliques et reliquaires," in *Dictionnaire* cit, pp. 2312 ff.; the author of the unfinished work will be A. Budinsky, but I do not know whether he has ever published the first pages. The whole problem of thefts of relics will be investigated in the dissertation of my student, Patrick Geary.

[20] Cod. Theod., IX, 17; St. AUGUSTINE, *De Opera Monachorum*, 28.

The culminating age for the theft of relics (or "translations" as it was said with a pious euphemism) coincides exactly with the first phase of the economic and commercial revival between the beginning of the ninth and that of the twelfth century. I am not aware that this coincidence has been noted before now, and I wonder if it is proper for me to study it under the aspect of "the diffusion of culture." For example, the two most sensational translations, that of the body of St. Mark from Alexandria in Egypt to Venice and that of St. Nicholas of Mira from Asia Minor to Bari, would seem to underline the passage from the maritime primacy of the Moslems and of the Greeks to the Italian maritime cities. It is to be noted that in 1087 the Catholic Church instituted the feast of the translation of St. Nicholas. The Greek Church, victim of the translation, naturally did not celebrate it, but the Russian Church inscribed it on its calendar, seemingly because a group of Russian Varangian merchants who had settled in Bari were infected with the enthusiasm of the populace and communicated it to their countrymen in Russia.[21]

Let me now pause a minute to consider two humbler "translations" which were similarly connected with the development of commercial exchanges. I have selected two saints so obscure that even the Bollandists doubt their authenticity: St. Appian of Comacchio, who perhaps is only a duplicate of the African bishop of the same name buried in St. Pietro in Ciel d'Oro in Pavia, and St. Sanctin of Meaux or of Verdun, who perhaps was not really bishop of either city. No matter; both saints performed their miracles, and the miracles are recounted by two anonymous writers who reflect the savory rusticity of early medieval Europe.

St. Appian (ninth century) is the saint of salt traders. From Byzantine Comacchio salt collected in lagoons was exported toward Lombard Pavia and Cremona up the Po and the Ticino: at the time of King Luitprand it was shipped on the dromonds of Comacchio, at the time of Louis the Pious, on Cremonese and Pavian barges. The anonymous writer tells us that at first St. Appian had been buried in a chest in front of a rural church of the diocese of Comacchio. The place was little frequented, and a little girl — I quote the hagiographer verbatim — "sat on the chest to satisfy a necessity of human nature, but.... all of a sudden the little body of the little girl was invaded by so much pain.... that the poor little thing could no longer move." The bishop, after the unconsciously sacrilegious little girl had been cured, had a chapel built to protect the relic; but even this was not enough. "A long time having passed," the hagiographer resumes, "some citizens of Pavia, who were coming to Comacchio to buy salt, entered stealthily and secretly at night into the chapel and took the body of blessed Appian; having put it cheerfully into their boat, they returned to their house.... but when they arrived at the lagoon, the aforesaid Confessor.... refused to deprive the land

---

[21] G. Vernadsky, *Kievan Russia* (New Haven, 1948), pp. 345-346, and the sources cited therein.

of Comacchio of his patronage.... He had his sacred body weigh down on the sacrilegious hulk so much so that it could not move from the place where it had taken root.... The oarsmen, tired by excessive exertions.... understood that they had perpetrated a monstrous crime.... Finally, terrified and confused, they decided to change course.... in such a manner, that not one of them.... touched the oars, but all, raising their hands and eyes to Heaven, prayed to God that he might lead the ship wherever the will of the Confessor would have allowed. The ship was thus led to the river, in front of the Basilica of St. Mauro. Then, the people took the body and placed it in that church."[22]

St. Sanctin (fourth century, but the translation is of the tenth) is, I regret to say, the saint of slave merchants. It is well known that the merchants of Verdun, according to Luitprand of Cremona, exported eunuchs to Moslem Spain "with immense profit." Charles Verlinden, the noted historian of medieval slave merchants, relying on Ibn Hawqal, sees them as all Jews; but the hagiographer whom I am about to cite (in part from second hand, because the full text was not accessible to me) presents them to us as devoted if not really scrupulous Christians. "Behold the merchants of Verdun," he writes, "they appeared all of a sudden in great pomp, on their return from Spain.... [They were] most honorable men and, as far as one can gather, full of riches, with loaded horses, mules and asses that transported copious riches...." Is it to be wondered at if, in a year of great famine which forced many citizens of Meaux to emigrate in search of food, one of the four priests who remained to guard the relics of St. Sanctin was tempted by what he could gather? "The merchants of Verdun," he confessed later to a Verdunese colleague, "invited me to dinner. There was a lot of idle takl; I said that the body of St. Sanctin was under my custody. They begged me to give it to them, with so much insistence that in the end I promised to do what they asked. They gave me a not small sum of money; I divided it with the other three priests.... We opened the reliquary, entrusted the sacred bones to the merchants, and they transported them in great haste to Verdun."[23]

Note the difference in the moral of the two tales, both of which refer to contacts between various peoples (in the first case Lombards and Byzantines; in the second, French and Arabs). At Comacchio, where short-dis-

---

[22] *Acta Sanctorum*, March 4; and see G. ROMANO, "Il Codice Diplomatico di San Pietro in Ciel d'Oro," *Bollettino della Società Pavese di Storia Patria* VI (1906), 302. On the commerce of salt at Comacchio see the old study of L. M. HARTMANN, *Analekten zur Wirtschaftsgeschichte Italiens im frühen Mittelalter* (Gotha, 1904), which remains fundamental, although other scholars have reexamined briefly that subject.

[23] The second citation comes from *Acta Sanctorum*, but the first from a manuscript of the municipal library of Verdun, which I know only through the interesting article of Y. DOLLINGER-LEONARD, "De la cité romaine à la ville médiévale dans la région de la Moselle et la Haute Meuse," in *Studien zu den Anfängen des europäischen Städtewesens (Reichenau Vorträge*, 1955-56, IV, Lindau and Constance, 1958). See also Ch. VERLINDEN, *L'Esclavage dans l'Europe médiévale* (Bruges, 1955), I, pp. 221 ff.

tance trade was carried on with cheap merchandise, we witness a theft attempted, unsuccessful and barely forgiven; at Meaux, where long-distance trade is carried on with rich merchandise, we witness a corruption attempted, successful and celebrated. Must we conclude that the justice of the hagiographers was not equal for all?

I am afraid so. But if we follow the history of the two items of the commerce we may reach a more comforting moral. Salt, which is humble but valuable, remains equally indispensable in the fourth and in the tenth centuries. Venice, which owed its first fortunes to it, does not abandon it even when her ships are full of riches from the East. Slaves, which were indispensable in the fourth century, will become hard to obtain in the tenth century; the traffic did not quite die out, but it changed character. What had been a profitable and easily available "merchandise" became an article of luxury, and, as such, an object of dangerous contraband.

We have thus broached a very important chapter in the history of the common man: the decline of slavery in Western Europe in the early Middle Ages. Let us recall briefly its principal stages. In the sixth century, St. Gregory the Great, though recommending that slaves be treated humanely, considered mass emancipation a dangerous utopia: it would undermine the economic stability of any ecclesiastical institution that might free its slaves without restrictions. In the eighth century, Charlemagne waged a continuous fight against the slave trade, and a pope, though declaring himself powerless to forbid Tuscan families from selling their children in time of famine, deplored the custom. In the tenth century, a linguistic shift singled out by Verlinden indicated that slavery was becoming exceptional for the natives of Catholic Europe. The word *servus* designated by now a serf, and slaves were only the *Sclavi* (Slavs), that is, pagans beyond the Catholic frontier. Nevertheless, the *Doomsday Book* shows that in England, then on the periphery of the civilized countries, real and true slaves still were far from rare in 1086. Toward the end of the eleventh century, when finally slavery had become unusual even in England, Catholic Europe had completed what seems to us moderns one of the best diffusions of culture. It compensates in some manner for other cultural inferiorities of the Romano-Germanic world as compared to the East; for the Byzantine and Islamic worlds, though ameliorating the conditions of the slaves, continued to rely upon the institution of slavery throughout the Middle Ages.

Was this progress primarily related to a change of conscience or to changed economic conditions? The researches of the latest fifty years oblige us now to reply in agreement with Lefebvre des Noëttes and with Marc Bloch, that the decisive factor did not lie in ethics but in economics. No doubt Stoic and evangelical moral philosophy created a favorable moral climate, but the Stoics did not presume to shatter the chains imposed by the arbitrary will of the Gods, and the reign of Christianity was not proposed as feasible in the City of Man. To teach Catholic Europe how to do without slaves, it was necessary that lack of labor, which had become critical by the early Middle Ages, oblige the Westerners to introduce new labor-saving techniques. Only then did the slaves become useless, or indeed unprofitable, and economic change at long last lent strength to ethical change. Byzantium, which was no less Christian than the West, but less hard hit by the demographic crisis, was not as receptive to technical change; therefore, at Byzantium, slavery remained.

The drive for technological progress was consistent all over Catholic Europe; but that does not mean that it was uniformly distributed or equally efficient. Cultural diffusion in the early Middle Ages was slow and spotty in every field; we can hardly share the enthusiasm of certain historians of technology who come across two or three examples of a new device and jump to the conclusion that the device became prevalent in a few years or in a couple of centuries. Just as handwriting, an invention of the fourth millennium B.C., was still a rare technique a thousand years ago, so the progress of other, less obviously useful innovations was braked by lack of information, of money, of mental flexibility, of initiative. Let us take one of the best known and most seminal examples, the water mill. Probably a Hellenistic invention, it is mentioned for the first time some twenty years before Christ, in what had been the residence of King Mithridates. A few decades later a Greek poet, in an epigram that is perhaps the Muse's earliest tribute to industrial art, congratulated all girls: no longer have they to rise early for the grind, since the water nymphs take care of it. More imaginatively, Irish poetry ascribes to King Cormac of the Long Beard (third century) the merit of having "brought in from overseas a builder of mills" — this in order to spare exertions for a slave girl whom he has seduced and made pregnant. We should not believe a word of it: in the third century slave girls are expendable, slaves in general cost too little and mills cost too much to be built anywhere but in very large cities, where the number of consumers makes speedy grinding desirable.[24]

At any rate, the practicality of the water mill hinged on more things than the cost of labor and the cost of the "machine." Whoever wanted to build one needed on the one hand a flow of running water, on the other a supply of grain to be ground, both of them in sufficient abundance to offset the expenses of the first installation and of maintenance. At Constantinople water is scanty; in the tenth century, when the slaves became too costly to be assigned to unskilled work, they were replaced not by a new machine but by putting beasts to the grind. Indeed, the donkey, which turns the

---

[24] The study of M. BLOCH, "Avènement et conquêtes du moulin à eau," *Annales d'Histoire Économique et Sociale*, VII (1935), remains unsurpassed; among the more recent studies see B. GILLE, "Le moulin à eau, une révolution technique médiévale," *Techniques et Civilization*, III (1954), and above all A. M. BAUTIER, "Les plus anciennes mentions de moulins hydrauliques industriels et de moulins a vent," *Bulletin Philologique et Historique du Comité des Travaux Historiques et Scientifiques*, 1960, II. On the legend of Cormac see J. VENDRYES, *Choix d'études linguistiques* (Paris, 1952), pp. 277 ff., where he reprinted an article originally published in *Revue Archéologique*, XIV, 1921.

grindstone, was still in use in the beginning of our century in the dry (and conservative) climate of some Sardinian village. In the larger part of the West, however, running water was easily available; and every village could supply grain enough for a water mill, provided the local lord built it and obliged the entire community to bring him their grist and pay him the tax for grinding. Thus the progress of feudalism, an instrument of servitude, favored the progress of the water mill, an instrument of liberty. In newly feudalized England there were in 1086 approximately five thousand mills, almost all of them actioned by water; that is, roughly, one mill for every four thousand inhabitants. That helps explain why slavery in that country soon became a thing of the past.

Further progress was around the corner: the wind mill, which was more easily built than the water mill and needed no water supply, took its place at the side of the older "machine." One wishes its history were better known; here is research that remains to be done. There certainly were wind mills in early medieval Iran, especially in its arid, wind-swept eastern regions; just how and when they appeared in Europe has not been fully explained. We find them in England and France shortly after the First Crusade; but their design is different from that of Iranian mills, and the suggestion that returning crusaders imported them from the Islamic world is hardly credible. The islands of Greece and the sea coast of Portugal are even today dotted with wind mills, and it seems more likely that the "machine" came to the West through the Mediterranean; but the whole story has not yet been told.[25]

Naturally, mills of the two types were not the only cases of social betterment, nor the only manifestation of the diffusion of technical culture. The technical progress of the early Middle Ages was made up of hundreds of mechanical and mental instruments that obscure men have adopted and spread taking them up again from antiquity, importing them from the East and (more rarely) from the North, or developing them little by little in the local Latin and barbarian experiences. Some inventions, like the Latin sail, perfected methods of hauling, the breeding of more vigorous mules and

---

[25] The fundamental essay on the wind mill goes back to the same epoch as that of Bloch on the water mill but is not as brilliant: H. T. HORWITZ, "Ueber des Aufkommen, die erste Entwicklung, und die Verbreitung von Windradern," *Technik Geschichte*, XXII (1933). An altogether more stimulating article is that of J. C. BAROJA, "Disertacion sobre los molinos de viento," *Revista de dialectologia y tradiciones populares*, VIII (1952); but neither he nor more general studies such as B. GILLE, "Les développements technologiques en Europe de 1100 à 1400," *Journal of World History*, III (1956) and Lynn WHITE, *Medieval Technology and Social Change* (New York, 1962) have offered decisive arguments regarding the connection between the types that may be called fundamental (Persian, Mediterranean and Norman) and the entire process of cultural diffusion (one center of diffusion or three independent centers?). As a matter of fact, early medieval techniques were the subject of the eithteenth Settimana of Spoleto, and I returned to the topic of both mechanical and mental techniques in the *Discorso Inaugurale* of that session and in the discussion that followed. The transactions of the Settimana were published in 1971 under the title *Artigianato e tecnica nella società dell' alto medievo occidentale*.

horses, gave an impulse to communications, and in this way fabricated other diffusions of culture. Other innovations, like the better qualities of cereals, of vegetables and citrus fruits, and the experiments of crop rotation made less precarious the survival of the populace and prepared new workmen for economic and intellectual rebirth. Still others, like the new tempers of iron, the production of paper, and, towards the end of the early Middle Ages, the pedal loom and the spinning wheel enriched the industrial equipment. And perhaps more important than all were the invisible innovations, those mental ones, from the first and modest attempts to use the so-called Arabic numerals to the early evolution of commercial contracts unknown to the Graeco-Roman world.[26]

In most of the cases, we are dealing with phenomena poorly known in their origins, diffusion and range; if I wanted to summarize only that little that I know, neither the time nor the reader's patience would be sufficient. I will limit myself therefore — to conclude with greater security than when I began — to an innovation that I studied with a certain intensity, and that brings me back to the studies of my early youth; the contract of commendation (*commenda*), known also under the names of partnership (*colleganza*), of *entica* and of still others.

We are in the field of mental techniques, and what techniques! Unknown to classical Roman and Justinian law, but already mature at Venice before the end of the early Middle Ages, the *commenda* was the backbone of medieval maritime commerce, just as the joint-stock company is the backbone of the modern industrial and banking organizations. Although a summary description of the contract will prove superfluous to one who knows it and insufficient to the one who might not know it, it seems to me suitable to recall in a few words the principal characteristics of its simpler form, the Genoese unilateral *commenda*. In this, a lender of capital entrusted to a merchant, for a round trip sea voyage, a sum in money or in merchandise. The merchant used the sum in his tradings in his own name and without involving the name and the patrimonial responsability of the lender of capital. On the return, the *commenda* was liquidated. The capital was returned to the lender with a part of the profit, usually three

---

[26] Some general sources on the history of techniques are: A. C. CROMBIE, *Medieval and Early Modern Science* (indispensable for the relations between pure science and applied science: sec. ed. New York, 1959); U. FORTI, *Storia della tecnica dal medioevo al Rinascimento* (Florence, 1957; rather elementary, well illustrated); S. LILLIE, *Storia della tecnica* (Turin, 1951; Marxist summary, but imaginative); C. J. SINGER and others, *A History of Technology*, II (Oxford, 1956; monumental but very unequal and, all in all, not very successful); A. UCCELLI and others, *Storia della tecnica dal medio evo aigiorni nostri* (Milan, 1945; good compilation); Lynn WHITE, *op. cit.* (interesting, sometimes a little too enthusiastic). See besides various chapters of the first three volumes of the *Cambridge Economic History* (1941-63), specifically those of Parain on agricultural technology, of De Roover in Commercial and banking technics, of Nef on mining and metallurgic techniques. Very short illusions to the development of techniques is found in my *The Birth of Europe* and in G. WIET, Ph. WOLFF and V. ELISSÈEFF, *Histoire du développement scientifique et culturel de l'humanité*, II, the latest publication for UNESCO.

fourths; the travelling merchant kept for himself the rest of the profit. If there was a loss, the lender sustained all the loss of the capital (but not beyond the sum invested by him); the merchant lost his time and his work. The advantages of a contract so well defined and flexible were maximum division and limitation of risks; maximum opportunities for profits for both parties, whatever the wealth or the poverty of each of them outside the specific contractural connections might be; maximum autonomy for both the lender as well as for the merchant; brevity and renewability of the obligation; the unobjectionability for the point of view of the canons against usury.

The first medieval documents that I happen to have read and studied (in a time so distant that it is almost confused with the early Middle Ages) were contracts of *commenda*. At that time, there were still alive the heroes of the great battles fought concerning the origins of the *commenda*: by irregular loan or by participation? by deposit or by leasing of service or by partnership? and finally, derivation more or less indirect from Roman, Byzantine, Islamic, Germanic, Neo-Babylonian contracts, or a new creation? The epic generation had already one foot in the grave when a talented youth, Guido Astuti, proposed a solution that received the greatest consensus even if it did not gather all the votes: the *commenda*, according to him, derived from Graeco-Roman maritime loan through the Byzantine *chreokoinonia*, mentioned in two obscure passages of the *Rhodion Nomos* (and, one can add, in a passage of the *Ecologes*).[27]

Some years ago I began to read lives of Byzantine saints (in Byzantium as in the West, the hagiographic sources are among the juiciest and among the least exploited), to see if the hypothesis of Astuti, based on texts of the eighth and ninth centuries, could find some confirmation in the seventh century. It was a pleasant surprise to read in the Life of St. Spiridone of Trimitunte (in the island of Cyprus) a passage that seemed to anticipate the formula of the oldest known *commenda* and Venetian partnership, save that the name of the contract *collegantia* at Venice, was still *daneion*, that is loan, in the Cypriot text of the seventh century. Here is a translation of the most important parallel phrases:

Life of St. Spiridone: "A captain of Trimitunte.... asked that I give him as *daneion* a little sum of money, to invest as *entica* in his ship and put it to work."

Venetian collegantia of 1075: "I received as a *colleganza* twenty Venetian pounds.... invested in a ship.... and promised to put it to work as best I can."[28]

---

[27] G. ASTUTI, *Origine e svolgimento storico commenda fino al secolo* XIII (Turin, 1933); my opinions on the contract in its western forms are summed up in N. S. and I. W. RAYMOND, *Medieval Trade in the Mediterranean World* (New York, 1955); pp. 174 ff., with bibliography, and in my *The Commercial Revolution of the Middle Ages* (Englewood Cliffs, 1971) pp. 73-79.

[28] R. S. LOPEZ, "The Role of Trade in the Economic Readjustment of Byzantium in the Seventh Century," *Dumbarton Oaks Paper*, XIII, 80 ff., and the cited sources.

The similarities between the two texts is certainly not decisive, but it can be considered a good one remembering that a life of a saint in Greek is one thing, and a notarial deed in Latin another. It therefore seemed to me that the connection between the *commenda* or *colleganza* of the Graeco-Roman maritime loan, with the two intermediate moments of the *daneion* of Cyprus and of the *chreokoinonia* of the *Rhodios Nomos*, could be considered as almost proven. But one of my students, Abraham Udovitch, who, unlike his professor, knows Arabic and Hebrew, made me change my mind.

We will not linger with him on a contract of medieval Hebrew law, the *isga*, which though having many points in common with the *commenda* differs from it in others; but the Arab *girad* (known also under the name of *mugarada* or *mudaraba*) has all the earmarks of being the real progenitor of the *commenda*. In the detailed description that the great jurist of the eighth century, Malik ibn Anas, gives of it, the *girad* presents us with a lender of capital who uses it in his own name in his dealings. Upon the return, the *girad* is liquidated. Risks and profits are divided as in the *commenda*. The sole difference is that according to Malik ibn Anas, the sum invested ought to consist of liquid capital and not merchandise. And since the *girad* appears in the juridical texts of the eighth century and in oral traditions which go back to the seventh century, but it is never named in the Koran, it seems to Udovitch (and also to me) that one must be dealing with a pre-Islamic institution, used in the customary law of the caravans. This is not at all to exclude a connection of this law with the Babylonian *tapputum* which other scholars already considered analogous to the *commenda*; but on this it would be necessary to consult the specialists in another language.[29]

With or without Babylonia, I would be ready to conclude that the *commenda* of Catholic Europe is the child of a mixed marriage. The father is the Moslem *girad*, born on the ships of the desert, the camels. The mother is the Byzantine *chreokoinonia*, derived from the Graeco-Roman maritime loan but impregnated by Arab influences. It would be difficult to discover a better example of the diffusion of culture in the Middle Ages.

---

[29] A. UDOVITCH, "At the Origins of the Western Commenda: Islam, Israel Byzantium?" *Speculum*, XXXVII (1962), pp. 198-207. We await now, with impatience, the collection of documents of the *Geniza* of Old Cairo, promised by S. Goitein, which will cast new light in the argument; for now, Udovitch had to use exclusively juridical texts. A few other documents are cited in registers by H. N. IDRIS, "Commerce Maritime et Kirad en Berberie Orientale," *Journal of the Social and Economic History of the Orient*, IV (1961), but the registers are too short and imprecise to recognize the nature of the contracts.

Franciscan Spirituality and the Growth of Vernacular Culture

DAVID L. JEFFREY

Even medievalists, when they think of St. Francis and the early Franciscan movement, too readily find themselves doing so in quasi-romantic terms. This Don Quixote of the hagiographers, preaching to birds, converting wolves, or rolling naked on a fiery hearth before the Egyptian prostitute might farily enough tempt almost anyone to such placable imagination. Yet, when the same medievalists turn to fraternal phenomena of the later thirteenth and the fourteenth centuries, whether in the troubles at Paris, in the stinging assaults by Fitzralph and William of St. Amour, or in the literary castigations of Jean de Meun and Geoffrey Chaucer, any lingering romanticism is stunningly obliterated by a chorus of proclamations that the friars had somehow, in the briefest interlude between hagiography and reality, become a public nuisance on almost every front from ecclesiology to politics. Yet the interlude involves less a transition in time than in topical judgment, and some of its significant cultural phenomena are critical for our appreciation of the emergent role of Franciscan spirituality, a great motive force in the transmission of late medieval popular culture.

Perhaps the most striking feature of late medieval cultural development, wheter in science or in the arts, is the transformation of a culture whose heralded virtues had hitherto been courtly, ideal, and intellectual, by cultural forces and motive directions which were dominantly "vulgar", material, and emotional. Whether in the poetry of Boccaccio, the painting of Giotto, or in the juvanescent development of parliamentary representation, one sees, in the vulgar sense, the elevation in almost every cultural arena of lowly vocabulary and forms. That the Franciscan and the other fraternal groups had something to do with this we in part already realize. But their key contributions deserve a general appreciation, both in terms of the larger social context of the Franciscan movement, and in terms of the particular focus and direction which their spiritual commitments afforded significant cultural developments.

* By permission of the author and *Annales canadiennes d'Histoire*. This essay is a revision of one which appears in Vol IX, 1, (1976), pp. 1-18 of that journal as "Franciscan Spirituality and the Elevation of Popular Culture."

When a student of cultural history looks at such an influential phenomenon as Franciscan spirituality, one of the basic chicken and egg questions which confronts him is an impossible speculation about whether the Franciscans produced the cultural influence and transformation he identifies, or, alternately, whether those tendencies simply found, by other accidents, a natural expression in the Franciscan movement. The available evidence suggests, in this case, that both answers have truth; while social contexts help to account for the Franciscan role as a vehicle for many ideas and innovations not properly their own, their own spiritual and aesthetic value structures served to build an ongoing vocabulary and rationale without which numerous changes could not have been so rapidly effected.

Consider, for example, the social context of Franciscan spirituality. In large part, this context is the economic pluralism which, in southern France and northern Italy, both favored the development of art and literature and nourished political and ecclesiastical rebellion. Wealth, practical independence from the central power of the French kings, a broadly based merchant trade, the cultural vivacity of Latin community life — all of these had fostered a degree of "individualism" and consequently a tendency toward fragmentation or differentiation unmatched in northern feudal Europe. Predictably, such an environment was admirably suited for the growth of heresies of all kinds.

At first the heresies were largely non-doctrinal — that is, they were expressions of anticlericalism and spiritual zealotism by striking individuals like Eon d'Etoile or groups as diverse as the Cathars and Patarines.[1] Although a real divergence of doctrinal positions did develop — a fact often confused, even by the Inquisition, through lumping all heretic groups as "Albigensian", — most of these groups, powerful enough for a brief period to overshadow the Church from Padova to the Loire, would have liked to have been able to live a life of poverty and the *vita apostolica* under the aegis of a more sympathetic ecclesiastical authority.[2] But, as we realize, for the most part it did not work out that way.

---

[1] For accounts of these groups, see PETER THE VENERABLE, *Patrologia Latina*, 189:719, 850; St. BERNARD OF CLAIRVAUX, *PL*, 182:434 ff. Initially the heresies were primarily manifestations of anticlericalism and zealotism, and were largely "non-doctrinal;" see Georges BOURGIN, ed., *Guibert de Nogent, histoire de sa vie* (Paris: A. Picard, 1907), bk. 3. Pierre BELPERRON (*La Croisade contre les Albigeois et l'union de Languedoc à la France* [Paris: Plon, 1945], pp. 61-63) observes the various distinctions relevant to the period. He divides the Albigeois into their constituents, principally Cathars and Vaudois, plus the many associated groups. See also Christine THOUZELLIER, *Catharisme et Valdëisme en Languedoc à la fin du XIIIe et au début du XIIIe siècle...* (Paris: Presses Universitaires de France, 1966).

[2] The Third Council of the Lateran in 1179 condemned many heresies but not the Vaudois; see Jean JALLA, *Histoire des Vaudois des Alpes et de leurs colonies* (Paris: Pignerol, 1904), pp. 13 ff. The Vaudois, however, were often subjected to severe scrutiny. Lucie VARGA, "Peire Cardinal était-il hérétique?" *Revue d'histoire des religions*, 117 (1938):213, has noted their attempt to return to a "primitive" catholicism. Cf. S. R. MAITLAND, *Facts and Documents Illustrative of the History, Doctrine, and Rites of the Ancient Albigenses and Waldenses* (London, 1832), pp. 342 ff.

Among the heretical groups, the Waldensians, or Vaudois, are particularly interesting in relation to the more durable Franciscans. There are many parallels: Peter Waldo, the founder, came from the same merchant middle class as Francesco Bernardone; he was converted to "holy poverty" (1173) by the same biblical passage as St. Francis; and his followers, the Poor Men of Lyons and Lombardy, responded to popular culture in much the same fashion as the Franciscans.[3] The Waldensians, or Poor Men of Lyons, laid a heavy emphasis on the Holy Scriptures. God's word was regarded by them as more authoritative than human glossing. In order to spread their belief as well as the Scripture itself, Waldo's early followers turned to a vehicle which seemed to lend itself well to the problems of transmitting scriptural and doctrinal instruction to unlettered people — popular song, vernacular verse. The idea was hardly original: Waldo himself had first been moved to repentance by the vernacular song of a *jongleur* (who sang at a market fair the life of St. Alexis). Nor was this model isolated. While in the past it has been argued that monastic poetry gave rise to popular poetry, by the late twelfth and early thirteenth centuries we can show that the tide was really flowing the other way,[4] and the surviving poetry of the Waldensians highlights their characteristic motivations: penitence, praise, and narrative instruction. It is the last point which is here most interesting. Reinerius Saccho tells us that out of the six causes to which he ascribed heresy, four were directly involved with the *learning* of the heretics.

> They teach and learn without books.... night and day.... To those who would excuse themselves, as not being able to learn, they say 'learn only one word every day, and in a year's time you will know 300, and you will get on.'

The result was that Saccho had "seen and heard a certain lay countryman who repeated the book of Job word for word, and many who knew perfectly the whole New Testament."[5] Saccho goes so far as to say that the

---

[3] Ronald A. KNOX, *Enthusiasm* (New York: Oxford University Press, 1950), p. 104, writes: "It is permissible to suggest that if St. Francis had lived a century earlier there would have been no Waldensians," to which Bernard MARTHALER replied in "Forerunners of the Franciscans: the Waldenses," *Franciscan Studies* 18 (1958): 133-42, that "if it weren't for Peter Waldo there would have been no Franciscans." I agree with Felix M. Bak, whose article takes its title from Marthaler's conclusion, "If it weren't for Peter Waldo, there would have been no Franciscans," (*Franciscan Studies* 25 [1965]: 4-16) that both statements are logically indefensible; however, the striking similarity of the two groups bespeaks a response to common cultural stimuli which leads to their methodological similarity. The fact of their historical relationship is sufficiently established in these articles.

[4] M. A. Bayle (*La Poésie provençale* [Aix, 1876], p. 194) presented the view that monastic poetry led to popular poetry, while C. C. Fauriel (*History of Provençal Poetry* [New York, 1860], pp. 162-63) had indicated that, in the late twelfth and thirteenth centuries, the Church had to make use of the vernacular to compete with a vernacular tradition already well geared to meet popular demand. But it is Fauriel's evaluation which has been upheld by modern scholarship: see, for example, Ernst HIRSCH, *Beitrage zur Sprachgeschichte der wurttembergischen Waldenser* (Stuttgart: W. Kohlhammer, 1962).

[5] Quoted in MAITLAND, *Facts and Documents*, pp. 400 ff. See the edition of Saccho's work by A. DONDAINE, in *Le Liber de Duobus Principiis suivi d'un Fragment de Rituel Cathare* (Rome: Istituto Storico Domenicano, 1939), pp. 65-78.

"learning" of such people was very often superior to that of noblemen and the clergy.

A few years later, St. Francis was born and raised in Assisi, a town which in 1203 had chosen an "Albigensian" for *podestà* — something suspicious enough to later be held against Francis by some papal advisors.[6] And while the Franciscan movement is not to be confused with that of the Waldensians, it is undeniable that many of their basic objectives were identical. Like the Poor Men of Lyons, St. Francis demanded absolute poverty; like them, his group was an apostolic and penitential order, wandering preachers and singers — the *ioculatores Dei* who sang men into the Kingdom of Heaven.[7] And we know that in the years of the most severe persecution of heretical and unorthodox groups many of the repatriating "fraternities" as well as individual heretics, mystics and vagrant clerks, did attach themselves to the Franciscans, and some of these were *jongleurs* in their own right.[8] One of St. Francis' followers, Brother Pacifico, in the world a composer of wanton songs, had been crowned *rex versum* by the emperor before joining the Order.[9] As for St. Francis himself, we learn from his early biographers that he first learned to write poetry in Provençal, and that for many years whenever he composed songs it was in the tongue of Languedoc, and not in Latin or even his own native Umbrian. Later he did write in Umbrian dialect the earliest surviving lyric in that vernacular, the "Canticle of the Sun."[10] And with the injunction of Francis to transform popular song to sacred melody, in Umbria and elsewhere in Italy lay brotherhoods of *Laudesi* soon sprang up, giving employment to *jongleurs* and poets who, often "with more devotion than art, framed rude songs or dramatic pieces on the chief events of the Gospel story,"[11] the Passion, the miracles of the Virgin, the joys of Paradise. These pieces, often just old melodies with new words, would be sung by friars to attract crowds for a sermon, by the fraternal groups in session, and ultimately for the entertainment and devotion of middle class households.

---

[6] Johannes JORGENSON, *St. Francis of Assisi* (New York: Longman's, Green, 1912; rpt. 1955), p. 81.

[7] See the original account in St. FRANCIS OF ASSISI, *Speculum Perfectionis*, ed. Paul SABATIER (Paris: Fischbacher, 1898), p. 210.

[8] When Pope Innocent III gave his approbation to the Franciscans, he clearly saw them as a tool for the reclamation of heretic groups. See Herbert GRUNDMANN, *Religiose Bewegungen im Mittelalter* (Berlin: Verlag der Emil Ebering, 1935), pp. 59 ff., 70-100, 156, etc. In 1216, at the height of antiheretical activity, St. Francis persuaded Honorarius II to grant the Portiuncula Indulgence, which also benefited former heretics wishing to escape reprisal. See Raphæl M. HUBER, *The Portiuncula Indulgence*, Franciscan Studies 19 (New York: Wagner, 1938).

[9] Paul SABATIER, *Life of St. Francis*, trans. Louise Seymour HOUGHTON (New York: Scribner's, 1894), p. 210. See also Umberto COSMO, "Frate Pacifico: Rex Versuum," *Giornate storico della letteratura italiana* 38 (Turin, 1901).

[10] J. R. H. MOORMAN, *The Sources for the Life of St. Francis* (Manchester: University of Manchester Press, 1940), p. 17.

[11] F. J. E. RABY, *A History of Christian-Latin Poetry, from the Beginnings to the close of the Middle Ages*, 2nd ed. (Oxford: Clarendon Press, 1953), p. 430.

The Franciscans seemed to carry with them everywhere a passionate determination to harness popular culture as medium, and to elevate it as value. Even if we stay only with examples from literature for a moment, we can find a large number of luminous exemplars of this instinct: in the field of vernacular verse these extend from Germany and Hungary, with Franciscan Berthold von Regensburg by 1250 actively seeking out vernacular composers for spiritual songs, asking that the songs be short (lyric) and accessible to learning by a child,[12] to England as late as 1316, where we have another interesting model in Franciscan Richard Ledrede's famous *Red Book of Ossory*.[13] In this latter collection, lines of the original songs are preserved as rubrics to the spiritual ones (here in Latin), acting as keys to their melodies. But the instinct for preserving the secular songs is persistent, and results in a healthy admixture in many a medieval manuscript, including the major manuscripts of Middle English and Anglo-Norman lyric verse, for example, of which the vast majority are of Franciscan provenance.[14] Even in a poet like Jacopone da Todi, who writes in two 'modes', both latinate and vernacular, the affection for that which is vulgar, material and emotional is fundamentally characteristic. It shapes both style and content. In Franciscan artifice, the ordinary, physical, common culture becomes graphically portrayed as never before in Christian art.

The justification for this emphasis on the tangible rises, however, not only from the middle class roots of the poets, or from the Franciscans' desire to speak in the language of the common culture to which they ministered, but from the spiritual principles which defined the Franciscans' origin and calling. The two most important of these principles are those of identification and redemption, which can be but briefly outlined here as they pertain to the issue of cultural transmission.

The most striking illustration of Francis' conviction that the Christian was called to a life of identification with Christ is not his detailed imitation of the *vita apostolica* and the poverty of Christ, but the *Stigmata*, the referential marks of identification which Francis received on Monte Verna. But for Francis, this symbol of his identification with Christ's Passion was merely the visible acknowledgement of his response, already made, to a previous identification — that which God had made with the world in sending Christ. That Christ was also a man was the ground of man's identification — the referral for understanding in this sense was also man-ward. In Christ's becoming man, what happened was not so much that

---

[12] *Berthold von Regensburg: Vollständige Ausgabe seiner Predigten*, ed. Franz PFEIFFER, 2 vols. (1862-80; rpt. Berlin: De Gruyter, 1965), 1:405-6.

[13] See the discussion of the *Red Book* in Rossell H. ROBBINS, ed., *Secular Lyrics of the XIVth and XVth Centuries*, 2nd ed. (Oxford: Clarendon Press, 1955), p. xxxv, but especially Edmund Colledge, O.S.A., *The Latin Poems of Richard Ledrede, O.F.M.* (Toronto: Pontifical Institute of Medieval Studies, 1974).

[14] See chapter five, "*Ioculatores Dei* in England," in my *The Early English Lyric and Franciscan Spirituality* (Lincoln: University of Nebraska Press, 1975).

poor men, donkeys, cows, straw, shepherds and carpenters were "elevated", as that they all were golrified — recognized as worthy of the Son of
God, and therefore truly Worthy. When Francis runs to embrace the leper's
sores, when he preaches to the birds, or gives his last rags to a beggar, he is
at one level merely acknowledging an identification — a glorification —
which God has already made with humble folk and humble things.

Apart from the *Fioretti* and the *Speculum Perfectionis*, the book which
makes this double action of the referential principle of identification most
clear is perhaps the *Meditations on the Life of Christ*.[15] An extremely
popular medieval book, it was translated into Middle English — seven times
— and into other European vernaculars many more times during the first
hundred years after its writing. In this book the humanizing tendency which
is manifest in a simple desire for contact with the life of the Lord extends
itself to an intimate affection for the ordinary life surrounding Him. Besides
cows, sheep and chickens, the Franciscan author, John of the Cabbages, will
refer to such items as a stone column to which Christ was fastened before
his trial (averring that it was preserved to his day, as he knew "from a
brother of ours, who saw it" [*Med.* 326]). Again, he describes the table of
the Last Supper, which he says he saw and measured at the Lateran Church
in Rome (*Med.* 277). One Middle English translator faithfully transcribes
the description of the table and the seating arrangements so as to indicate
how it was physically possible for them all to eat from one dish on the night
of the betrayal. Other examples abound, and in illustrated versions of the
manuscripts the drawings are characteristically concerned with tangible,
common physical details and are rendered with a very high degree of
verisimilitude. (From them, for example, one can learn a considerable
amount about medieval tools and tool skills.) In the *Meditations*, as
elsewhere in Franciscan popular literature, and explicitly in the Christology
of its theologians,[16] such a full identification with the human life of Christ
intimates a higher valuation, or indeed glorification, of simple mankind and
the human environment.

Yet the theological connection between identification and redemption is
straightforward, and really a matter of emphasis within the same development. The atonement is typically seen by the Franciscans as redemptive, but
with a special emphasis on the Incarnation which made it possible. That is,
in Franciscan theology and spirituality there is taken up a twelfth century
idea, formulated by St. Anselm, in which the Fall of man, and man's fallen

---

[15] *Meditations on the Life of Christ: An Illustrated Manuscript of the Fourteenth Century*,
ed. and trans. Isa RAGUSA and Rosalie B. GREEN (Princeton: Princeton University Press, 1961).
    [16] *Meditations*, pp. 262-3. See for example D. J. UNGER, "Robert Grosseteste.... on the
Reasons for the Incarnation," *Franciscan Studies* 16 (1956): 1-37. Also St. BONAVENTURE, in
Tractatus de preparatione ad missam, 1:10 (Quaracchi, 8.1026); *Feria sexta et Parasc.*, Sermo
I (9.259b); and *Dom. II pro Pascha*, Sermo I (9.295a), etc. Also see Jean BONNEFOY, "La
Question hypothétique: Utrum si Adam non pecassett.... au XIIIᵉ siècle," *Revista espanola de
teologia* 14 (1954): 327-68, esp. 334-35.

condition, is almost to be praised. "Cur deus homo," they asked, "si Adam non pecasset?"[17] If Adam and Eve hadn't sinned, there would have been no need for the greatest of human glories, the Virgin birth. Christ's human nature, necessarily central if his sacrifice for men is to be substitutionary, becomes dramatically intrinsic to the life of Francis and the spiritual style of his followers because, in an immediate sense, Christ's merely taking on human conditions redeems time, flesh, and the world all by itself — glorifying them, rather than merely transcending them somehow. Franciscan theologians were sensitive, for example, to the model offered not only in the Incarnation (where the light comes down into the world, rather than mankind ascending from the world into the light, as from Plato's cave), but also in the Apocalypse, when Paradise is not a separate plane beyond this one, but rather a condition, when this world is fully transformed by a descent of the Heavenly Kingdom into our time and space (Revelation 21:1-3, 10; cf. John 1:9). Part of man's stewardship in the world is thus to honor the garden — even the fallen garden — and to participate in its redemption by the Incarnation.

It is in this connection that we must understand that most important modifications of the neo-Platonic traditions of twelfth-century theology which is to be found in Franciscan thought. In detailing how his four lights to knowledge are to be related to the light of Sacred Scripture, Bonaventure significantly considers first that one which is most basic and literal, the illumination of sense perception. This process, he says, concerns itself exclusively with the cognition of sensible objects, and occurs in three phases: "cognoscendi *medium*, cognoscendi *exercitium*, cognoscendi *oblectamentum*."[18] Here the consistent triune pattern unfolds again. If we

---

[17] St. ANSELM, *Cur Deus Homo*; a modern translation is in *Trinity, Incarnation and Redemption; Theological Treatises*, ed. J. HOPKINS and H. RICHARDSON (New York: Harper Torch Books, 1970).

[18] *Reductione artium ad theologiam*, ed. and trans. Emma Thérèse HEALY, 2nd ed. (St. Bonaventure, New York: Franciscan Institute, 1955), p. 48. The entire passage is as follows.

"Videamus igitur, qualiter aliæ illuminationes cognitionum reducie habent ad lumen sacræ Scripturæ. Et primo videamus in illuminatione cognitionis *sensitivæ*, quæ tota versatur circa cognitionem sensibilium, ubi tria est considerare: cognoscendi *medium*, cognoscendi *exercitium*, cognoscendi *oblectamentum*. — Si consideremus *medium* cognoscendi, intuebimur ibi Verbum æternaliter generatum et ex tempore incarnatum. Nullum enim sensibile movet potentiam cognitivam, nisi mediante similitudine, quæ egreditur ab obiecto, sicut proles a parente; et hoc generaliter, realiter, vel exemplariter est necesse in omni sensu. Illa autem similitudo non facit completionem in actu sentiendi, nisi uniatum cum organo et virtute; et cum unitur, nova fit perceptio, et per illam perceptionem fit reductio ad obiectum mediante similitudine illa. Et licet non semper obiectum sentiatur, semper tamen, quantum est de segignit similitudinem, cum est in sua completione. — Per hunc etiam modum intellige, quod a summa mente, quæ cognoscibilis est interioribus sensibus mentis nostræ, æternaliter emanavit similitudo, imago et proles; et ille postmodum, cum *venit plenitudo temporis*, unitus est menti et carni et hominis formam accepit, quod nunquam fuerat prius; et per illum omnes mentes nostræ reducuntur ad Deum, quæ illam similitudinem Patris per fidem in corde suscipiunt."

"Let us see, therefore, how the other illuminations of knowledge are to be reduced to the light of Sacred Scripture. First of all, let us consider the illumination of *sense* perception,

consider the *medium* of perception, he says, we shall see therein the word
begotten from all eternity and articulated — made flesh, in time — because
of generic, specific, or symbolical likeness to the Creator. Words inhere in
the Word: in language and in vision the processes of creativity are analogous
to the formulations of the Creator. When the contact between organ or
faculty and object is established, there results a new percept, an expressed
image by means of which the mind reverts to the object. The exercise of
sense perception reveals, accordingly, the pattern of human life. But in the
delight, as we have already observed, is opened the union of the soul with
God.

> Indeed, every sense seeks its proper sensible with longing, finds it with delight, and seeks
> it again without ceasing, because 'the eye is not filled with seeing, neither is the ear filled
> with hearing' [Eccl. 1:8]. In the same way, our spiritual senses must seek longingly, find
> joyfully, and seek again without ceasing the beautiful, the harmonious, the fragrant, the
> sweet, or the delightful to the touch. Behold how the Divine Wisdom lies hidden in sense
> perception, and how wonderful is the contemplation of the five spiritual senses in the
> light of their conformity to the senses of the body.[19]

The potential for sense perception expressed here is remarkable. It says that
the spiritual senses not only may, but *must* "seek longingly, find joyfully"
the divine wisdom hidden in it. Sense perception begins in delight and ends
in transcendent delight, as language and desire retranslate, in tangible
expression, the metaphor of the body. Bonaventure concludes by calling on
all works of art and artifice — not only music and poetry, but such diverse
human enterprises as medicine, navigation, pharmacy and drama — to
illustrate the necessary harmony of creation and creativity.

It is at this point that one begins to see how, among the friars, the
Franciscans stand most to the center of this spiritual and ultimately cultural
tradition. Albert the Great, a Dominican, also had very pragmatic interests
in the natural world — for example, his extensive experimental interest in

---

which is concerned exclusively with the cognition of sensible objects, a process in which
three phases are to be considered: namely, the *medium* of perception, the *exercise* of
perception, and the *delight* of perception. If we consider the *medium* of perception, we
shall see therein the Word begotten from all eternity and made man in time. Indeed, a
sensible object can make an impression upon a cognitive faculty only through the medium
of a likeness which proceeds from the object as an offspring from its parent, and in every
sensation, this likeness must be present either generically, specifically, or symbolically.
That likeness, however, results in actual sensation only if it is brought into contact with
the organ and the faculty, and once that contact is established, there results a new
percept, an expressed image by means of which the mind reverts to the object. And even
though the object is not always present to the senses, still, the fact remains that
perception in its finished form begets an image. In like manner, know that from the mind
of the Most High, Who is knowable by the interior senses of the mind, from all eternity
there emanated a Likeness, an Image, and an Offspring; and afterwards, when "the
fulness of time had come" He was united to a mind and body and assumed the form of
man which He had never been before, and through Him all our minds, which bear the
likeness of the Father through faith in our hearts, are brought back to God." (*Reductione
artium*, pp. 48-51.)

[19] *Ibid.*, p. 51.

the physiology of human sex[20] —, but when he came to theology or even sociology, was less interested in sense experience than in logic: "God is he who is proved to be, more than he who is experienced."[21] A Jacopone da Todi or St. Francis, in many ways more broadly influential in medieval culture, were less scientific in the modern sense of the term, but far more generally celebratory of ordinary physical nature and common sociology, and this spilled over into a variety of "popular media."

> Terra, erbe con lor coluri
> arbori, e frutti con sapuri
> bestie, miei serviduri
> tutte en mia bavolcari.
>
> Acque, fiumi, lachi e mare,
> pescetegli en lor notare,
> aere, venti, uncel volare
> tutti me fo iollarià.[22]

Trees, plants, fruits, beasts of the field, rivers, lakes and sea, barnyards, little birds flying, and fishes — all are a source of his particular joy, and Jacopone celebrates them. For a Franciscan philosopher like Bonaventure, redemptive grace is not compartmentalized, but flows through the realms of nature and human art as well as Scripture. Following this spiritual emphasis, one may readily distinguish between the aesthetic of the Dominicans, for example, reflected in Aquinas, and that of the Franciscans, represented by Bonaventure. The experience of the beautiful for St. Bonaventure embraces not only the sense of touch, smell, and taste, but all of the senses which can stimulate enjoyment in the individual without any immediate consideration of the role of their object.[23] Enjoyment derived from the senses is the primary Franciscan aesthetic experience.[24] In the system of Aquinas the aesthetic impression rests on an intellectual act, and consequently the object of the aesthetic becomes "the form of the thing as the end."[25] Or, to point up the contrast in another way, whereas Aquinas finds sublimity in the loft, the noble, and the grand, Grosseteste finds it in the smallest fleck of dust,

---

[20] His treatise is entitled *Quæstiones super de animalibus*, ed. Ephren PHILTHAUT, O.P. (Munster in Westphalia: Aschendorff, 1955), and is discussed extensively by J. R. Shaw in a subsequent chapter of this volume.

[21] From M. M. GORCE, *L'essor de la pensée au Moyen Âge. Albert le Grand — Thomas d'Aquin* (Paris: Letouzey et Ané, 1933), p. 128; translation mine.

[22] *Lauda* 59, in *Jacopone da Todi: Laudi*, ed. Franca AGENO (Florence: F. Le Monnier, 1953), p. 235. This is a modernized edition.

[23] E. J. M. SPARGO, *The Category of the Aesthetic in the Philosophy of St. Bonaventure* (St. Bonaventure, New York: Franciscan Institute, 1953), pp. 14 ff.

[24] See the article by E. LUTZ, "Die Asthetik Bonaventuras nach den Quellen dargestellt," Festgabe Baeumker, *Beitrage zur Geschichte der Philosophie des Mittelalters*, Supplement (Munster in Westphalen: Aschendorff, 1913), 1:202 ff., which does more than Spargo's chapter to relate the Bonaventuran aesthetic to Augustinian and Neo-platonic models.

[25] SPARGO, *The Aesthetic*, p. 15. See also Harry B. GUTMAN, "The Rebirth of the Fine Arts and Franciscan Thought," *Franciscan Studies* 25 (1945):225, and Clement M. O'DON-NELL, *The Psychology of St. Bonaventure and St. Thomas Aquinas* (Washington: Catholic University of America Press, 1937), p. 100.

whirling in the sunlight.[26] Those perspectives on late medieval art which concentrate largely on its traditional theological verities (e.g. "word as sign") are incomplete without an appreciation of the double action of reference in the sense-oriented Franciscan aesthetic tradition, and may fail to see how fully incarnational is its new sense of reference.

There is a natural correspondence between Franciscan spirituality and its aesthetic, and its interest in education, in the "science of ordinary things" at a number of levels. One of the first things Friar Agnellus did after establishing some of the first Franciscans in Oxford was to have a school built in the friary, and to seek out Grosseteste to lecture to the friars.[27] Grosseteste, typically enough for him, lectured on many subjects other than theology, including mechanical physics, practical science, and optics, and it was Grosseteste who supported the Franciscans in their campaign for vernacular instruction at every level.[28] The explorer of the manuscripts of English mendicants will find that theological material, handbooks of pastoralia, dramatic texts, or collections of songs and short poems are regularly transcribed all together, and even with cookery books, or with treatises on astronomy and animal husbandry. In fact, manuscripts of fraternal provenance in the thirteenth and fourteenth centuries offer the most amazing hodepodge of diverse learning imaginable. A friars' handbook, such as Franciscan William Herebert's collection (MS. Philipps 8336), MS. Harley 2253, MS. Cambridge University Library Cg.I.1, or Cotton Julius D. VII, can contain, besides theological treatises and homiletic and vernacular lyrics in English or Anglo-Norman, many other kinds of items. MS. Philipps 8336 (now Additional MS 46919) includes works so diverse as a treatise for learning French, "L'art de Venerie," a dialogue between a hunter and chevalier on the art of hunting, a cookery book, a treatise on falconry, and a series of proverbs. Cambridge University Library MS. C.g.I.1 includes the following: poetry (mostly in Anglo-Norman) on subjects such as the signs of judgment, the Passion, penitence, and the Virgin, as well as metrical homilies; an extract from Aristotle used to fill a column; Latin pieces, including treatises entitled "De recepcione medicinarum," "De tonitruo experimenta" (prognostications); a prose treatise in Anglo-Norman on physiognomy; the Proverbs of Hending (in English); the childhood of Christ (in Anglo-Norman); a treatise on the military "feoda" of England and "cantreda" of Ireland; an Anglo-Norman "Compendium historiarum Biblie;" and a prognostication on the nature of man (apocalyptic psychology). MS. Cotton Julius D. VII contains a treatise on astronomy, ecclesiastical computation and the calendar by Friar Johannis de Wallingford, English chronicles and lists of English kings, "Versus rhythmici, de mensibus anni," a calendar and "tabula literarum dominicalium," a

---

[26] In Hexaëmeron, 7.4.5. See also chapter two of The Early English Lyric.

[27] A. G. LITTLE, ed., De adventu fratrum minorum in Angliam (Manchester: University of Manchester Press, 1951), pp. 48 ff. (Collatio XI).

[28] See Margaret SCHLAUCH, English Medieval Literature and its Social Foundations (Warszawa: Panstwowe Wydawnictwo Naukowe, 1956), p. 157.

description of the climates of the world, the chronicle of Johannis de Wallingford, notes on the kings and bishops of England, a chronicle of English history to the reign of Henry III, arithmetical questions, another treatise on the calendar, a poem on the corrupt state of the Church, and a marvellous "Figura rudis et descriptio elephantis invecti in Angliam,"[29] a drawing ascribed to Matthew Paris. Everything from calendars to elephants nestles with theology and spiritual songs. Yet it is from the point of view of the science of ordinary things that we should perceive the enormous interest and involvement of the Franciscans in science, from Grosseteste's work on optics down through the early fifteenth century.

When Roger Bacon left his teacher Grosseteste to go to Paris, for example, he cast about for a teacher whose studies he could respect and himself pursue. The man he found was Peter de Maricourt, a man whom Bacon found personally unambitious and modest, but of such genius that for Bacon there could be no other tutor. Yet notice how he defines de Maricourt's qualifications:

> .... He knows everything relating to the art of war, to the making of weapons and the chase; he has looked closely into agriculture, land mensuration, and practical arming work; he has even taken note of the remedies, lot casting, songs and charms used by the old women, wizards and magicians, and of the illusions and ingenious devices of minstrels.... It is impossible that philosophy should be carried to its perfection or handled with utility or certainty without his aid.[30]

Peter de Maricourt may or may not have been himself a Franciscan, but his tutelage was certainly congruent with Bacon's own decision to join the Order.

It is among the Franciscans, as Lynn White has observed, "that the scientific expression of the new attitude toward nature is most clearly

---

[29] Lists of the complete contents of the manuscripts may be found in the appropriate library catalogues. For MS. Phillipps 8336 (British Library Addit. MS. 46919), see *Catalogue of Additional Manuscripts in the British Museum*; for Cambridge University Library MS. Gg. I.1, see *Catalogue of the Manuscripts Preserved in the Library of the University of Cambridge*; for MS. Cotton Julius D.VII (British Library), see *Catalogue of the Cottonian Manuscripts in the British Museum*.

[30] Fr. ROGERI BACON, *Opus Tertium*, in *Opera Quædum Hactenus Inedita*, ed. J. S. BREWER, Rerum Britannicarum Medii Ævi Scriptores (London: Longman, Green, Longman, and Roberts, 1859), pp. 46-47 (cap. 13), translation mine. The original passage contains a fuller description of the wide range of Master Peter's learning:

> "Et ideo quod alii cæcutientes nituntur videre, ut vespertilio lucem solis in crepusculo, ipse in pleno fulgore contemplatur, propter hoc quod est dominus experimentorum; et ideo scit naturalia per experientiam, et medicinalia, et alkimistica, et omnia tam cœlestia quam inferiora; immo verecundatur si aliquis laicus, vel vetula, vel miles, vel rusticus de rure sciat quæ ipse ignorat. Unde omnia opera fundentia metalla, et quæ operantur auro, et argento, et cæteris metallis, et omnibus mineralibus, ipse rimatus est; et omnia quæ ad militiam, et ad arma, et ad venationes ipse novit; omnis quæ ad agriculturam, et ad mensuras terrarum et rarum et rusticorum, examinavit; etiam experimenta vetularum et sortilegia, et carmina earum et omnium magicorum consideravit; et similiter omnium joculatorum illusiones et ingenia; ut nihil quod sciri debeat lateat ipsum, et quatenus omnia falsa et magica sciat reprobare. Et ideo sine eo impossibile est quod compleatur philosophia, nec tractetur utiliter nec certitudinaliter."

seen."[31] For Bacon, as for most Franciscan thinkers, it is by knowledge of created things that we reach a knowledge of the Creator (*Opus Majus*, II). But also, typically, "the *utility* of knowledge" is the constant theme of the works he addressed to the Pope.[32] Conversely, in the middle of a biblical commentary or theological treatise, a Friar like Thomas Docking can at any minute give over pages to some phenomenon from physical science, a problem in animal husbandry or the wool trade, or even turn to extensive analysis of the role of theatre and the lyric arts in his own time.[33]

The Franciscans had a major role, through their interest in chronicling, in making available to modern historians information which otherwise might well have gone unvalued or even unnoticed. The point is not so much that many Franciscans were distinguished historians, as that their historical interest attached itself particularly to ordinary life. In Thomas of Eccleston, Jordan of Giano, Salimbene de Adam, the author of the *Chronica Tribulationum*, in Arnold of Sarano, in Bartholomew of Pisa, John of Winterthur and the author of the *Lanercost Chronicle*, we see a vital and distinct tradition of medieval chronicling. Unlike the Dominicans, who had a more traditional interest in universal histories,[34] the Franciscans focus in detail on popular, vernacular culture, with great attention to things as mundane (and practical) as the practices of wine-making in different districts of France, a ranking of the best in white and red, and a selection of the appropriate local drinking songs.[35] Chronicles like these are typically less histories of an order or province or any particular country, than popular histories of an individual writer's life and times. As such, they are invaluable documents in the cultural history of the Middle Ages.

There are a number of other areas in which to trace the influence of Franciscan spirituality on the elevation and transmission of popular culture, as on the development of the epistemological principles which undergird it. An example which deserves much more study, from the poems of Francis to the works of Duns Scotus, is culture's most basic medium, language itself, particularly in its written form. Every student of the Middle Ages is aware that during the early years of Franciscan spirituality several European vernaculars emerged in forms of communication hitherto reserved only for Latin. While one must allow, as Professor Lopez suggests, that there were a variety of forces operating to bring about the replacement of Latin by vernacular language, it is nevertheless completely in character with

---

[31] Lynn WHITE, Jr., "Natural Science and Naturalistic Art in the Middle Ages," *The American Historical Review*, 52 (1947): 433. This article documents the effect of the movement toward naturalistic description in medieval sciences, with illuminating connections to developments in a number of the disciplines of medieval inquiry. Especially valuable is his discussion of the impact of these changes on manuscript painting and marginal illustration (pp. 424-28).

[32] A. G. LITTLE, *Franciscan Papers, Lists, and Documents* (Manchester: University of Manchester Press, 1943), p. 80.

[33] See LITTLE, *Franciscan Papers*, pp. 98-121.

[34] *Ibid.*, p. 36.

[35] *Ibid.*, p. 31.

Franciscan spirituality, given the objectives already discussed, that the first vernacular poems preserved in a number of Italian dialects should be Franciscan, that the first lyric poetry in English should date from 1225-30, immediately after the Franciscans arrive, and that an astonishing four-fifths of extant manuscripts of this poetry from 1225 to 1350 should be of Franciscan provenance.[36]

Most students of the Middle Ages will be familiar with Dante's great argument for vernacular language in his *De Vulgari Eloquentia*. Fewer may remember that his initial interest in the subject came about through his Franciscan education, that he was in fact taught writing at one time by a Franciscan, the minor poet Miro da Colle, and that though he was to criticize the vernacular extravagance of some Franciscans such as the popular preacher Remigio Girolani, his first invitation to vernacular usage came from this quarter.[37] Nor was he the only great poet in the developing Italian language to be educated by the Franciscans. Besides Franciscan friars such as Guittone d'Arezzo and Jacopone da Todi, Francesco Petrarca was a Franciscan tertiary, and so was Michelangelo.[38]

Further, it may have taken until Chaucer's time for English to really become dominant in courtly cultural usage in that country, but when the change finally occurred it owed greatly to over one hundred years of building pressure brought about by the influence of the friars on the enormous expansion of vernacular preaching, as well as on the other popular culture in English. Owst, in his book on medieval preaching, argues convincingly what dialectologists have since accepted,[39] that homiletical manuscripts and collections of pastoralia are to be credited with the preservation and emergence into literary recognition and tradition of numerous English dialects.[40] It is to such preaching collections, including the Franciscan *Gesta Romanorum* and the *Contes Moralisés* of Franciscan Friar Nicole de Bozon, that we owe the transmission and thus the preservation of scores of popular fables and vernacular exempla.

---

[36] See chapter six of *The Early English Lyric*.

[37] T. C. CHUBB, *Dante and His World* (Boston, Toronto: Little, Brown, 1966), pp. 224-27.

[38] See B. J. MUSSER, *Franciscan Poets*, Essay Index Reprint Series (1933; rpt. Freeport, New York: Books for Librairies Press, 1967), pp. 73, 80.

[39] See especially W. Nelson FRANCIS, "Graphemic Analysis of Late Middle English Manuscripts," *Speculum* 37 (1962): 32-47. See also M. L. SAMUELS, "Some Applications of Middle English Dialectology," *English Studies* 44 (1963): 81-94; two articles by Angus McINTOSH, "The Analysis of Written Middle English," *Transactions of the Philological Society* 1956 (1957): 25-55, and "A New Approach to Middle English Dialectology," *English Studies* 44 (1963): 1-11; Samuel MOORE, *Historical Outlines of English Sounds and Inflections*, rev. by Albert H. Marckwardt (Ann Arbor, Michigan: Wahr, 1957).

[40] G. R. OWST, *Literature and Pulpit in Medieval England*, 2nd ed. (New York: Barnes and Noble, 1961), p. 6; cf. pp. 3-8, 571-72, 590-91. "The first point to be made in estimating the literary contribution of our preaching is its early influence upon the development of the language. It is surely no extravagance to speak of the activities of the Mendicants in this respect.... In no other way, so it seems, could a language otherwise virtually abondoned to the common uses of common folk have been preserved for any future cultural revival" (pp. 3-4).

It would be highly inappropriate to separate poetry, preaching, chronicling, and science in our consideration of the Franciscan educational enterprise, since all of these are seen by the Franciscans, in terms of their commitments, as consonant media, and are seen by them, in the same terms, in their social context. And each of these activities, from poetry to the science of ordinary things, has a social function which is intimate to their theology and spirituality.

Culturally what is happening in all of these spheres is really an interdisciplinary change in *style* which both expresses and is brought about by a new spiritual and aesthetic valuation of popular cultural concerns. The present introductory essay can not provide an extensive ''stylistic'' analysis, even for the few disciplines we have mentioned. Yet even in these limited examples one can observe that the characteristic influence of Franciscan spirituality, even more so than with the Dominicans, moves away from theoretical, ideal or purely theological structures toward more practical, tangible, and homely considerations. This can be seen in what they do with chronicling, science, poetry or preaching. The Franciscans are consistently interested in a basic vocabulary in which the spiritual ideal can be referred for understanding to the tangible world.

This is not to say that the effect of their influence is to deny beauty of ''form'' or intellectual precision to the study of the natural world. In fact, precisely the reverse is true. The dominating influence of Franciscan spirituality on the ''great style change'' in graphic and plastic arts of the thirteenth century has already been observed by art historians such as Emile Mâle, Raimond van Marle, Milliard Meiss, and others.[41] Here the influence of the *Meditations on the Life of Christ* is of fundamental importance to a study of the transmission of these ideas in popular culture, but it is only the best known of a number of direct influences on that transformation of the thirteenth century pictorial style that made of late medieval art one of the most sublime achievements in western sculpture, illustration and painting. To move from stylized and Byzantine representations of the crucifixion to the crucifix which Donatello made for the Franciscans at Santa Croce is to leap from a world where Christ is identified with princes to one where He is given the forearms and calloused hands of a carpenter, the feet and legs, as Brunellesci observed (with distaste) of a ''contadino''. Yet it is to trace at the same time stunning and irrefragable advances in technique and in composition, in the achievement of formal beauty. And this movement in art is one to which Franciscans everywhere in Europe are accessory, from Assisi to the confraternity workshops of the Low Countries and France.

What informs stylistic change throughout Franciscan contribution to late medieval culture is the two principles so colourfully emphasized in their

---

[41] Émile MALE, *Art et Artistes du Moyen Âge* (Paris: Flammarin, 1968), pp. 22-30; Raimond VAN MARLE, *The Development of the Italian Schools of Painting* (The Hague: Nijhoff, 1923-38), 1:258 ff.; Millard MEISS, *Giotto and Assisi* (New York: New York University Press, 1960). Cf. n. 31.

spirituality: identification and redemption. It is, in fact, the joint articulation of these principles, as a translation of the traditional idea of reference for understanding, which places the Franciscan movement at the centre of popular cultural transmission in the period. Both of these conjoint spiritual principles have very tangible and practical illustrations in the activity of the Fransciscans and their confreres, and they may be illustrated most simply with two models from the literature of popular culture.

The first of these is the emergence of medieval vernacular drama. Whether in Italy, Holland, France, England, Czechoslovakia, or Hungary, the Franciscans' spirituality is the dominating influence. Partly this is because of the *Meditations on the Life of Christ*, which lies behind nearly all medieval cycle drama, from the first Italian plays to French *Mystères* to the *Ludus Coventriae* (which is heavily dependent on borrowings from this book).[42] But in instance after instance it is Franciscans who are identified with medieval drama. The two surviving manuscripts of medieval shepherds plays from Hungary are of Franciscan authorship and provenance.[43] The only surviving Czechoslovakian cycle is of Franciscan authorship and provenance.[44] In Holland there is a definite relationship between confraternities in the Franciscan spiritual tradition and the authorship and production of medieval plays.[45] In Italy and in France this is also true, although more work needs to be done on the provenance of French drama particularly.[46] In England the only religious group specifically identified in connection with medieval drama is the Grey Friars.[47] Such attributions occur, among other places, in their recorded performances at Coventry, and in the Franciscan provenance of a major dramatic text, the famous Digby Manuscript (133), in which, incidentally, the plays are bound up with Franciscan scientific

---

[42] Part of the *Ludus Coventriae* depends, line for line, on Nicholas LOVE's 1400 translation of the *Meditations* (*Ludus Coventriae*, ed. K. S. BLOCK, EETS ES 120 [Oxford, 1922], pp. xxiii-xxiv, lviii ff.); the peculiarly Franciscan interpolation of Scripture which has the Resurrected Christ appear first to the Virgin closely corresponds to the *Meditations* (see text of the play, BLOCK's edition, p. 321); the play also relies on the "Four Daughters of God" tradition in the context of the *Meditations*.

[43] Lajos PASZTOR, "Two Franciscan Christmas High Masses Containing Hungarian Shepherd's Plays," *Archivum Franciscanum Historicum*, 43 (1950): 411-32.

[44] The unedited passion play of Skofja Loka is discussed by Filip KALAN, "Le Jeu de la Passion a Skofja Loka," *Le Livre Slovene*, 3 (1966): 24-34.

[45] For medieval Netherlandish drama, see my article (and notes), "Bosch's 'Haywain': Communion, Community, and the Theater of the World," *Viator*, 4 (1973): 311-31.

[46] For medieval Italian drama see Arnaldo Fortini, *La Lauda in Assisi e le origini del teatro italiano* (Assisi: Edizione Assisi, 1961); see also Emile Roy, *Le Mystère de la Passion en France du XIVe aux XVIe siècle* (Dijon, 1903-4), pp. 467 ff.; Vincenzo de Bartholomaeis, *Laude drammatiche e rappresentatione sacre* (Florence, 1943), vol. 1; *Le Origini della poesia drammatica italiana* (Bologna, 1924).

[47] See BLOCK, *Ludus Coventriæ*, p. xxxix, who quotes Thomas SHARP's *Dissertation on the Coventry Mysteries* (London, 1825), p. 12; also see E. K. CHAMBERS, *The Medieval Stage*, II, 358; William HONE, *Ancient Mysteries Described* (London, 1823), p. 204; Lawrence CRADDOCK, "Franciscan Influences on Early English Drama," *Franciscan Studies* 10 (1950): 388. See my essay "Franciscan Spirituality and Early English Drama," *Mosaic* 9 (1975), 17-46.

treatises, some of which are in the same hand.[48] Also, in the extant attacks
made upon vernacular drama by the Wycliffites, the specific target is the
Grey Friars, or, as in one instance, a lost saint's play on St. Francis.[49]
Students of the York cycle will remember that the only named person whose
directive commentary on the performance of those plays survives, William
Melton, was a noted Franciscan preacher who is described in connection
with the York plays as "sacrae pagine professor."[50]

"Identification" provides the first motive for all this Franciscan
involvement in medieval theatre. From the time (1221) when Francis
obtained papal permission for the first vernacular nativity play in Italian
literary history down to the revival of the Corpus Christi cycle in the Marian
restoration by the London Grey Friars in 1556,[51] the Franciscans valued
dramatic art for its participatory identification of the Incarnation and the
history of salvation with ordinary, common cultural experience. Bonaventure, in his *De reductione artium ad theologiam*, had heralded the role of all
arts (including what we should call practical crafts) as illuminating "the
eternal generation and Incarnation of the Word, the pattern of human life,
and the union of the soul with God." But of all the arts, he continued, "it is
dramatic art, or the art of putting on plays, which embraces every form of
entertainment, whether song, music, fiction or pantomine," which best
fulfils these goals of art: "*theatrica autem est unica*."[52] Dramatic art, by
definition, exists through identification. Medieval drama, accordingly,
informs and expresses the world of a popular culture thoroughly imbued
with a sense of its identification with the Kingdom of Heaven.

The last cultural model I would offer is the medieval vernacular lyric.
Since, as Bonaventure observes, it is related by Franciscan aesthetics and
spirituality to the social context and spiritual function of dramatic art, it too
has much to do with identification. But if the drama must readily illustrate
identification as the motif of the spirituality in question, the vernacular lyric
illustrates the motive of redemption as well — not only in the usual

---

[48] The two plays found in the Digby MS, *The Conversion of St. Paul* and *Mary Magdalene*,
are available in *The Digby Plays*, ed. F.J. FURNIVALL, EETS (Oxford, 1896). See my essay,
"English Saints' Plays,"in *Medieval Drama*, Stratford-upon-Avon Studies 16 (London:
Edward Arnold, 1973), pp. 69-90.

[49] Two surviving treatises, apparently by Wyclifites, illustrate thirteenth century criticism of
the friars. The first, *A Tretise of Miraclis Pleyinge*, is edited by Thomas WRIGHT and J. O.
HALLIWELL, *Reliquæ Antiquæ* (London, 1841), II, 42-57. The second, *On the Minorite Friars*, is
edited in *Monumenta Franciscana* (Rolls Series, 1858), I, 606 ff., by J. S. BREWER.

[50] Quoted in *Monumenta Franciscana*, II, xxviii. See also A. G. LITTLE, *The Grey Friars in
Oxford* (Oxford, 1891), p. 259; an extract from the city records of York by Francis DRAKE,
Eboracum, in the *History And Antiquities of the City of York* (London, 1736), II, App., xxix; Leo
SPITZER, "Pageant-Latin *Pagina*," *American Journal of Philology*, 64 (1943): 327-30.

[51] St. Bonaventure records St. Francis' first request for a play in *Legenda Maiora* (Quaracchi,
8.535). During the Marian restoration, on Corpus Christi Day, 1556, the Grey Friars of London
performed the old play of the Passion (CRADDOCK, "Franciscan Influences," p. 391).

[52] *Reductione artium*, p. 40.

theological sense, but in the redemption and elevation of popular culture through a beautiful literary expression. The following Middle English poem is from MS. Harley 2253:

> Wynter wakeneþ al my care,
> nou þis leues waxeþ bare;
> ofte y sike ant mourne sare
>   when hit comeþ in my poht
>   of þis worldes ioie hou hit geþ al to noht.
> Nou hit is ant nou hit nys,
> also hit ner nere ywys.
> pat moni mon seiþ soþ hit ys:
>   al goþ bote Godes wille,
>   alle we shule deye þah vs like ylle.
> Al þat grein me graueþ grene,   [All that seed I buried green,
> nou hit faleweþ al bydene;   Now it decays too quickly]
> Iesu, help þat hit be sene,
>
>   and shild vs from helle,
>   for y not whider y shal ne hou longe her duelle.[53]

This poem — in its haunting tone, deft strokes of vernal imagery, and semi-alliterative whispering cadence — is a beautiful example of the style change in Franciscan spirituality transforming an old form. The metaphor is natural, the vocabulary rural and agricultural (as well as biblical), and the form is a fascinating hybrid of popular and courtly styles. But the principles of identification and redemption are also at work together here in beautiful ways. The difficult first two lines of the last stanza, which have caused modern glossators real problems, have been confusing in large part because they occur in a strong colloquial formulation, and, in or out of the poem's rich dialect, are a particularly rural expression, to be found in agricultural treatises. But this is marvellous. In the capturing of a plowman's vernacular phrasing, the persona of the poem is identified not only with the almost archetypal figure of the Plowman, but with local, rural plowmen. The two lines, at the emotional and personal climax of the poem, refer of course to John 12:24, 25, but do so in the particular language of particular men in the particular community where the seed is sown, the word spoken.

The manuscripts of the Middle English lyrics represent, in their recipes, proverbial literature and quasi-scientific lore as well as in their poetry, the sort of vernacular tradition which was increasingly gearing itself to an emergent middle class. Their expression of style change, as an elevation of popular culture in the arts, is consistent here with the impact of fraternal and confraternal groups in extending the arts throughout middle class European culture in the fourteenth and fifteenth centuries. Illustrated Books of Hours, lyric manuscripts, and panel painting were soon to follow, born of the same tradition of cultural transmission and transformation. The influence of Franciscan spirituality on the elevation of common life seems to have

---

[53] Edited by G. L. BROOK, in *The Harley Lyrics* (Manchester: University of Manchester Press, 1964), no. 17.

offered a basic encouragement to changes in style in every area from poetry to politics as well as to the extension of education from Grosseteste's Oxford to the middle class household. And in a perspective which found everything in creation made to praise the Creator, particular nature became naturally elevated in such a way that the effect of the ''style change'' which springs to life in the spirituality of the Franciscan movement was to preserve and transmit in every sphere the science of ordinary things.

The *Societas Riccardorum* and Economic Change

RICHARD W. KAEUPER

Among the Exchequer Accounts Various preserved in the Public Record Office, London, there is a package of letters written on heavy paper and bound up in brown wrapping and twine.[2] On the top page some modern archivist has written "Italian" in a bold hand, almost as if in surprise; and on a letter from this set which has somehow strayed from its fellows, "diplomatic" is written in a similarly modern hand.[3] The first archival notation is correct, for the letters are in fact written in a late thirteenth and early fourteenth century Tuscan version of Italian, but the second note reveals a natural error. In fact the letters do not represent diplomatic exchanges at all, but rather commercial correspondence, the business letters of merchant-bankers. They are in the English archives because of basic commercial developments in late thirteenth century Europe.

Historians as a breed may suffer from a surfeit of revolutions, but we ought to recognize that distinguished economic historians of the Middle Ages speak legitimately of a commercial revolution in their era. Our particular set of letters found their way into the English archives because of this revolution. Some scholars would, in fact, date the changes exactly in the period when the letters were written, and it does seem that the changes were most pronounced then, the pace of development most swift.[4] But other medievalists quite justifiably argue that the changes had been coming for some time and that the development evident at the end of the thirteenth century was a culmination of the economic progress of High Medieval Europe. The changes have been in preparation at least across the twelfth and thirteenth centuries.[5] Perhaps the age in which the letters were written could

---

[1] This essay is largely based on several chapters from my monograph, *Bankers to the Crown, the Riccardi of Lucca and Edward I* (Princeton University Press, 1973). Complete documentation on the Riccardi will be found there. All manuscript references are to documents in the Public Record Office, London (PRO).

[2] PRO, E 101/601/5. There are about twenty letters or fragments of letters.

[3] PRO, S C 1, 58 no. 20. There is another fragment of a letter in S C 1, 58 no. 15.

[4] Raymond DE ROOVER, *Money, Banking and Credit in Mediaeval Bruges* (1948), p. 11.

[5] R. S. LOPEZ, *Cambridge Economic History of Europe*, 2, 335. Cf. his *The Commercial Revolution of the Middle Ages, 950-1350* (1971), Howard L. ADELSON, *Medieval Commerce* (1962), Chapter 6.

best be thought of as the cresting of a wave of economic growth and prosperity. Broad generalizations always shelter half-truths, but somewhere around the turn of the fourteenth century the commercial prosperity and expansion of Medieval Europe came to a peak and then began to subside, giving way to stagnation and depression.[6]

More specifically we should note the role of the Italians in the medieval commercial revolution. "Italy was to the medieval economic progress," Lopez suggests, "what England was to that of the 18th and 19th centuries. It was the cradle and pathfinder of the commercial revolution."[7] It is well known that in economic and urban development Northern Italy was the most advanced region of medieval Europe, the low countries taking second place. From sometime in the late eleventh century an important axis of trade connected these precocious areas. The Italians took the lead and in fact crossed the Alps in such numbers and in so many capacities that the movement has been termed an "Italian diaspora."[8]

But instead of going directly to the far Northern markets, they traveled only as far as the famous fairs of Champagne,[9] the great cycle of six fairs held just outside the gates of four towns in the county of Champagne (Troyes, Provins, Barsur-Aube, Lagny). These fairs were the nerve centers of long distance trade in the twelfth century. Here the Northern merchants met the Italians, buying and selling wool and woolen cloth above all. The Italians were also developing highly sophisticated commercial techniques, creating the economic expertise which would eventually change the fairs drastically. The timing of the development of these techniques is currently in dispute;[10] the late thirteenth century result is not. Although many examples of advances in bookkeeping, communication, and transportation could be cited, perhaps one of the most important commercial developments came in the area of contract or partnership.[11] Older forms of partnership such as the

---

[6] A heated controversy has developed over the nature of the late Medieval economy. For the majority view, emphasizing stagnation and depression see especially Michael POSTAN, *Cambridge Economic History of Europe*, 2, Chapter IV, "The Trade of Medieval Europe: the North," Section III, "The Age of Contraction," and also R. S. LOPEZ in the same volume, Chapter V, "The Trade of Medieval Europe: the South," Section II, Part 3, "Depression and Recovery." Cf. his *Commercial Revolution*, pp. 162-167.

[7] R. S. LOPEZ, "Hard Times and Investment in Culture," *The Renaissance: Six Essays* (Harper Torchbook edition, 1962) p. 31.

[8] R. S. LOPEZ, *Cambridge Economic History of Europe*, 2, 316-317.

[9] For recent studies of the fairs see O. VERLINDEN, *Cambridge Economic History of Europe*, 3, Chapter III, "Markets and Fairs"; Robert-Henri BAUTIER, "Les foires de Champagne: recherches sur une évolution historique," *Bulletin de la Société Jean Bodin*, V, *La Foire* (1953); R. D. FACE, "Techniques of Business in the Trade Between the Fairs of Champagne and the South of Europe in the Twelfth and Thirteenth Centuries," *Economic History Review*, series 2, no. 10 (1957-58); Rosalind Kent BERLOW, "The Development of Business Techniques Used at the Fairs of Champagne from the End of the Twelfth Century to the Middle of the Thirteenth Century," *Studies in Medieval and Renaissance History*, 8 (1971).

[10] See the articles by R. D. FACE and Rosalind Kent BERLOW cited in the previous note.

[11] R. S. LOPEZ, Cambridge Economic History of Europe, 2, 323ff.; Raymond DE ROOVER, *Money, Banking and Credit*, pp. 12-13.

commenda gave way to the *compagnia* or *societas*. The *commenda* were a very limited kind of contract which linked a supplier of capital with a supplier of managerial skill; i.e. one man provided the money and the other took to the road as travelling merchant. The contract was severely limited in time (often to one voyage) and in liability (each partner being liable only for the amount of money involved in the contract). The new *compagnia* was more lasting and more sophisticated in that it associated several (usually many) merchants in a partnership lasting for years at a time. These partners who agreed to act together over a span of years were all active, i.e. they all contributed capital and managerial skill, receiving in return a share of profit proportional to their investment. In case of failure liability was unlimited, but if a partnership prospered the terms of agreement were extended or redrawn. By midthirteenth century the famous Italian companies, the merchant-banking *societates* which lasted for decades or even for several generations began to appear.[12]

They created a new pattern of commercial activity. The old travelling merchant, the caravan merchant who constantly wandered out from his home town with goods, began to be replaced; roving caravan trade (a pattern as old as history) was superseded by the great companies which established branches in the important trade centers. The *societates* planted their partners or factors all over Europe, carried on trade, and effected credit transfers through this network of branch offices.[13]

Clearly with this kind of organization the Italians did not need to limit themselves to the Champagne fairs, but could go directly after the business they wanted. They penetrated France, England, and the Low Countries and established agents there. They became leading wool merchants; they sold luxury goods in London, Paris, and Bruges. The Champagne fairs were gradually transformed into the center of the European money market. No longer essentially markets where goods were bought and sold, they developed instead as centers where merchants settled accounts and balanced their books on sales that took place elsewhere.[14]

Most of our evidence on these companies, certainly most case histories, date only from the fourteenth century. But there is a surprising amount of previously untapped material in the English archives on one particular firm in the last quarter of the thirteenth century. The company is that of the

---

[12] Raymond de Roover provides a convenient list of these companies in *Cambridge Economic History of Europe*, 3, 75-76. Armando SAPORI's *Le Marchand Italien au Moyen-Âge* is a useful introduction to the Italian merchant-bankers. It has recently been translated into English by Patricia Ann Kennen.

[13] See the discussions by Raymond DE ROOVER, in *Money, Banking, and Credit*, pp. 11-13, and *Cambridge Economic History of Europe*, 3, 42-43, 49, 70-74.

[14] In addition to the sources cited in the preceeding note, see O. VERLINDEN, *Cambridge Economic History of Europe*, 2, 132-133; E. B. and M. M. FRYDE, *ibid.*, Chapter VII, "Public Credit with Special Reference to North-Western Europe," Section III.

Riccardi of Lucca, the *Societas Riccardorum de Luka*.[15] The letters mentioned at the beginning are theirs and form only a small part of the evidence from which their history can be reconstructed. Since they were bankers to Edward I from 1272-1294 they figure prominently in the miles of parchment, crowded with highly abbreviated Latin and old French, on which the details of royal finance are recorded. It would be a fairly safe wager that in any royal financial document from this period, selected at random, the Riccardi of Lucca will appear. Their activity as crown financiers means that the Riccardi are as much a part of the history of the English state as of the thirteenth century economy. Although our concern here is with the merchants as a *societas*, it is their involvement with government which provides evidence of their activities.

The Riccardi, then, were one of the earliest of the companies coming into North-western Europe for which we can construct anything like a clear picture. This makes the company especially interesting, but it also means that the evidence will be more spotty than would be the case for a firm of the next century. In asking several basic questions about them, we must realize that the answers cannot be as complete as we wish.

First we need to ask questions of size. How large was the company? How many branches? How many men? Over how large an area of Europe did they operate? International is an imprecise word to use in a period before there were nations, but the anachronism may be pardoned in emphasizing that the Riccardi were an international firm. The main office was naturally located in Lucca, and there were branches at the Roman curia, the Champagne fair towns, Nîmes, Bordeaux, Paris, Flanders, London, York, and Dublin. In fact there were likely more branches than surviving evidence shows, but it is clear that these merchants operated throughout a business network stretching from Tuscany to Ireland.

It was no small feat to coordinate rational business activity across more than a thousand miles of bad roads, swift streams, mountain passes and competing political jurisdictions. The Riccardi did so above all through a constant stream of business letters. They had their own couriers: we read of Stephano, Rubino, and Bocco carrying letters, and there were probably others. We can picture these men carrying bulky pouches stuffed with rolls of account, letters of exchange, copies of epistles to important clients, and the company letters themselves. If we figuratively open one of these pouches and read a paragraph of one of the business letters almost at random, the strongly international nature of the firm is emphasized:[16]

> We tell you that, as you know, our men in Champagne have loaned to the
> Bonsignori of Siena a great amount of money, and they have told them to pay it back to

---

[15] See KAEUPER, *Bankers to the Crown*, E. B. Fryde, *Cambridge Economic History of Europe*, 3, Chapter VII, Section IV; Emilio RE, "La Compagnia dei Riccardi in Inghilterra e il suo fallimento alla fine del secolo decimoterzo," *Archivio della Societa Romana de Storia Patria*, 37 (1914).

[16] PRO, E 101/601/5 p. 5, letter of 5 December, 1297.

our men over there [in England] and in Ireland. Therefore, until now we have not known, nor have been paid back, either all or in part, nor how much you have gotten back. Therefore we ask you to let us know both how much you have received, and when, both you and the men in Ireland.

And just as you should let us know, so you should also tell our men in France, because the companions of the Bonsignori, when our men in France ask them for that money, make excuses and say that they do not know if that money has been paid there or in Ireland, nor how much has been paid. Therefore do not fail to send word both to us and to them, so that if that money has not been paid we can recover it.... Speak of this with their companions over there and have them and their companions in Ireland write to their companions in France.

Here, in one transaction, we can see the networks of two firms stretching from Lucca and Siena across France and England to Ireland.

In another paragraph we might find something more personal. When the London partners fired an unreliable agent the home office in Lucca agreed so heartily that they devoted nearly a page of one letter to raking the man over the coals. Here is merely a sample:[17]

Now it seems to us that he is so wicked and dangereous because of his wicked and lying tongue that you should warn your friends at court that he is not to be believed in anything he may say, as he is a drunkard, a liar, and wicked without any principles.

Ghirardo Chimbardi who was assigned to a branch in Ireland showed the reaction we might expect from an Italian posted to Ireland. Not only did he complain, his father in Lucca plagued the leading partners, as they wrote to London,

blaming us harshly and crying sorrowfully because of the fact that his son went to Ireland at the service of the company more than thirteen years ago; and he has spent no more than five months together with his wife since that time, so that he can very reasonably, and with many reasons, grieve much because of his assignment, and blame us."[18]

How many men would these operations from Tuscany to Ireland involve? The evidence in the English archives sheds only a little light on the continental branches, but it seems there might be no more than a dozen partners or agents in England at any time who were important enough to appear in government documents, with perhaps another three or four in Ireland. A list of about seventy-five names can be compiled for the entire period 1272-1294, but is probably not exhaustive. In any given period it would be unlikely that total Riccardi personnel in the British archives numbered more than thirty men. Surprisingly, this ranks the company as a large firm. In 1336 the Peruzzi, second largest company of the day, employed no more than ninety factors scattered throughout fifteen branches.[19] In 1466 the Medici branch in Bruges had a staff of seven, including

---

[17] PRO, E 101/601/5 46d., undated letter.
[18] PRO, E 101/601/5 p. 39d., letter of 3 November, 1301.
[19] Raymond DE ROOVER, *The Rise and Decline of the Medici Bank* (1963), p. 3. He mentions here and on p. 5 that the Medici never attained the size of the giant companies of the fourteenth century. The Accaiuoli company, third largest in fourteenth century Florence, had fifteen branches and employed forty-one factors, with two each in London and Bruges and one in Paris. See DE ROOVER, *Money, Banking and Credit*, p. 39.

two office boys.[20] Both in geographical area and number of personnel the scope of Riccardi activity is impressive.

This raises a second question: how strong was the company? What resources did the Riccardi command? As a standard for comparison we might take the famous Medici once again. Their main house and seven out of eight branches in 1458 had capital of about 30,000 florins.[21] We cannot say what capital the Riccardi commanded, but there is indirect evidence of their resources in the boast made in one letter that at the height of their power they could borrow 100,000 or even 200,000 *livres tournois* at the Champagne fairs.[22] This means a sum of approximately 160,000 to 320,000 florins. Should this claim be dismissed as mere exaggeration? The letter is internal company correspondence, not a letter for the eyes of some bishop, earl, or the king; the Riccardi had little reason to stretch the truth with each other. Moreover, the claim seems plausible when we note that the Peruzzi in the early fourteenth century had a capital of more than 100,000 florins. More important, other evidence indicates that the Riccardi actually operated on this scale. Over a twenty-two year period they lent the English crown an average of more than £14,000 a year,[23] a sum equivalent to 112,000 florins. In times of intense borrowing the sum was much higher, as for example in the king's stay in Gascony, 1286-1289, when they lent at least £103,733.[24] During the entire time they acted as crown financiers they were also money lenders to all ranks of society, sometimes investing as much as £2500 a year in private loans (roughly 20,000 florins).[24] These sums take on more meaning when compared to the range of incomes in thirteenth century England. While an earl or a rich bishop might enjoy a landed annual income of some £2000, a skilled workman would earn less than £8 a year if he worked every week at 3s. per week; for a common workman the figure is about £2, working six-day weeks all year, at $1\frac{1}{2}$d. a day.[25]

The sizeable scale of Riccardi financial operations raises a related question. How was it possible for them to operate on so grand a scale? Of course it is important to remember at once that they were crown financiers and that the crown turned over basic sources of royal revenue to them. The resources of the English king quickly become involved in the question of their capital. On their loans to the government they were also apparently collecting interest rates which would make modern bankers weep with envy; as much as 33-$\frac{1}{3}$% seems to have been paid on the king's outstanding

---

[20] Raymond DE ROOVER, *The Medici Bank, Its Organization, Management, Operations and Decline* (1948), p. 23.

[21] R. S. LOPEZ, in *The Renaissance: Six Essays*, pp. 40-41.

[22] PRO, E 101/601/5 p. 25, letter of 10 October, 1295.

[23] See the analysis in KAEUPER, *Bankers to the Crown*, Chapter II, Section 4.

[24] Based on recognizances for debt in the King's Remembrancer's Memoranda Rolls (PRO, E 159 series) and the Lord Treasurer's Remembrancer's Memoranda Rolls (PRO, E 368 series). There were additional private loans for which no recognizances were made.

[25] See KAEUPER, *Bankers to the Crown*, preface, and sources cited there.

balance after periodic accountings.[26] But royal resources and interest hardly give the entire answer. The crown wanted the Riccardi as financiers because they had significant resources beyond what it entrusted to them; had the Riccardi not possessed sizeable resources of their own there would have been little point in making them crown bankers.

One additional source of funds came from their position as papal bankers. The centralizing papacy had developed its power to tax clergymen throughout Christendom, especially for the purposes of crusade. In the England of Edward I the money for the Holy Land was promised to the king whenever he would go on crusade, but the act of taking the cross and actually freeing himself for the venture were quite different matters. While Edward assured the pope of his good intentions, and prudently prohibited the export of the money from England, it had to be held in safe-keeping; naturally the pope turned to the Italian merchant-bankers who were also his financiers and deposited the money with them. The Riccardi were not the only papal bankers in England and the money had to be divided among them all, but their share was at times as high as £13,000.[27] The usefulness of this amount of ready cash need not be emphasized.

Nor can we forget that the Riccardi were merchants as well as financiers. They were primarily wool merchants and our evidence at least suggests that they may have been the greatest wool merchants in England, exporting more of the prized English wool to continental looms than any other single company. The religious houses were especially prominent customers, and often contracted with the Italians to sell their wool for several years in advance in return for the cash they needed so badly.[28]

Their activities both as merchants and as bankers, then, help to explain their economic strength. But what do we know of the Riccardi as men? This third basic question is the most difficult. If we ask whether they drank French wine and loved their wives our sources, needless to say, fail. Only rarely do we learn something of the merchants' personal lives, such as Matteo Rosciompelli's fondness for hunting which led to his temporary arrest for taking hares in the king's warren.[29] In fact, one is not always even certain of the merchants' names, for we have many of these Italian names

---

[26] For the Riccardi accounts see *Calendar of Patent Rolls, 1272-1281*, pp. 131-132, PRO, E 101/126/1, E 372/124 m. 1d., E 372/134 m. 3, E 372/125 m. 1, E 372/133 m. 32d., E 372/134 m. 3, E 372/143 m. 35d., E 372/143 m. 35d. The question of interest is discussed in KAEUPER, *Bankers to the Crown*, Chapter II, Section 3.

[27] See the work of W. E. LUNT, *Financial Relations of the Papacy with England to 1327* (1939), Appendix VI, and *English Historical Review*, 32 (1917), p. 87.

[28] KAEUPER, *Bankers to the Crown*, Chapter I, Section 2. For background on the wool trade in general see Eileen POWER, *The Wool Trade in Medieval English History* (1941); R. J. WHITWELL, "English Monasteries and the Wool Trade in the 13th Century," *Viertiljahrschift für Sozial- und Wirtschaftsgeschichte*, 2 (1904); Eleanora CARUS-WILSON, *Cambridge Economic History of Europe*, 2, Chapter VI, "The Woolen Industry."

[29] *Calendar of Close Rolls 1279-1288*, p. 445.

only in the Latin or French forms given in the accounts and writs penned by English clerks, or in the translations of documents printed by modern scholars. The result can be awful. Matteo Rosciompelli once appears as Matthew Rogyumpel, and a much more important figure, Orlandino da Poggio, becomes Rouland de Podio, and the like. Certainly their personal appearance remains unknown. The name Orlandino da Poggio suggests to me a man tall, thin, and imperious; my wife insists he was short, fat, bald, and swarthy.

But in more important ways we know fairly well what sort and condition of men we are considering. In the final analysis, whether they drank French wine and loved their wives was much more important to them than to us. Above all we can see in them that worldly wise quality which seems so widespread by the end of the century. At a time when they were in severe trouble the Lucca partners wrote to London that the bishop of Durham (who was auditing their accounts with the crown) owed them 800 marks, "if you think you should mention it to him."[30] There can be no question of their shrewdness or toughness. The London Riccardi once accused the Lucca partners of giving way to the fault of sentiment and personal feeling. They responded:[31]

> About the special consideration (*sofferenza*) which you say we have given to Ranuccio Ronsini.... for which you blame us greatly, we tell you that what we have done we have not done out of love for him or because he is related to any one of us, or because of any request he might have made to us. Whatever we have allowed we have done for our benefit and not for his.

Perhaps this quality appears with special clarity in their dealings with John Pecham, the reform Archbishop of Canterbury. A Franciscan, "whose vows of poverty were not the most convenient preparation for the costliness of the archiepiscopal state,"[32] Pecham borrowed 4000 marks from the Riccardi, but was unable to repay the loan on time. The merchants obtained a papal bull threatening the archbishop with excommunication, leading him to complain that he was being harassed by the saracenic cruelty of men aided by the devil.[33]

As this incident would lead us to believe, the piety of the Riccardi was of a fairly conventional sort and came mixed with a strong dash of pure acquisitiveness. The point had not yet been reached when a company could begin its books with the invocation "In the name of God and profit." That

---

[30] PRO, E 101/601/5 p. 26d., letter of 10 October, 1295.

[31] PRO, E 101/601/5 p. 5d., letter of 5 December, 1297.

[32] Dorothy SUTCLIFFE, "The Financial Condition of the See of Canterbury, 1279-1292," *Speculum*, 10 (1935).

[33] See the *Register Epistolarum* of Peckham, cited by SUTCLIFFE, in *Speculum*, 10 (1935). The practice of securing bulls of excommunication against defaulting ecclesiastics was not uncommon. See Adolf GOTTLOB, "Kuriale Prälatenanleihen im 13. Jahrhundert," *Vierteljahrschrift für Sozial- und Wirtschaftsgeschichte*, I (1903).

was to come in the fourteenth century.[34] But the juxtaposition of religion and business in the Riccardi letters is jarring enough. At a time when the company was on the brink of disaster they wrote, "May God in his mercy not look at our sins, but rather may He look at the good that our ancestors have done, and grant grace to those who hurt us so that they may see the right way."[35] Such solemnities suitable for any sermon, however, often give way to another level of expression: "Let us hope in God and in the Virgin that shortly we will be in the position to give back to everyone in the same way as they have dealt with us. For the time being it is more suitable if we keep our mouths shut."[36] Or again: "Now may God through his mercy no longer look at our sins and may He have it in His heart and will that those who have to pay up the company, pay up."[37] When English officials apparently began to hint that a price would have to be paid for the return of their confiscated business records, the Riccardi decided they could not spend a large sum; they would hope in God, await grace from the pope, and meanwhile bribe with smaller sums "those people to whom a payment is useful."[38] Despite the divine majesty and papal grace, a few well-placed gifts would help.

The question we would most like to ask of the Riccardi cannot be answered in any detail. Their attitude towards the ecclesiastical prohibition of usury and the suspicion churchmen traditionally felt for the world of commerce never appears in the letters. The merchants were clearly collecting interest on loans and were surely intelligent enough to know that despite all subterfuges and claims only for licit "damages," the intent to commit usury, however subtle the evasion, was sinful in the law of the Church and in the eyes of God.[39] Whatever agonizing introspection such knowledge produced was never, of course, discussed in business letters.

If we can empathize with these merchants it would come largely at the time of their precipitous fall. To ask why so strong a company buckled and collapsed is to pose our final question about the Riccardi company. At the beginning of this century an Italian scholar, Emilio Re, outlined one of the only explanations of Riccardi failure ever to be offered, in one of the few studies of the Riccardi ever written.[40] Re explained the company failure by a simple, cumulative series of misfortunes which gradually overtook them. Ruin began in 1291 when Philip the Fair arrested the Italians in France and

---

[34] See Raymond DE ROOVER, "The Story of the Alberti Company of Florence, 1302-1348, as Revealed in Its Account Books," *Business History Review*, 32 (1958), 46.

[35] PRO, E 101/601/5 p. 17, undated letter.

[36] PRO, E 101/601/5 p. 18, undated letter.

[37] PRO, E 101/601/5 p. 11, letter probably written in 1300.

[38] PRO, E 101/601/5 p. 40, letter of 3 November, 1301.

[39] There is a large literature on the subject. See especially John T. NOONAN, *The Scholastic Analysis of Usury* (1952), and T. P. MCLAUGHLIN, "The Teachings of the Canonists on Usury (XII, XIII and XIV Centuries)," *Medieval Studies*, 1 (1939).

[40] RE, "La Compagnia dei Riccardi," *Archivio della Società Romana de Storia Patria*, 37 (1914).

extorted large fines from them, including the Riccardi. At the same time Edward I finally convinced the pope that he was a crusader and was given the sexennial crusade tax imposed on the clergy at the second council of Lyons; it was the fruit of eight years of patient negotiations at the curia. According to Re this hurt the Riccardi in that the money deposited with them was recalled and turned over to the English king. Other papal taxes deposited with Italians, those designated for the aid of Charles of Valois in Sicily, were similarly recalled about the same time and the result was again damaging to the Riccardi. In 1294 their troubles were multiplied when Edward I and Philip the Fair went to war over Gascony, a dress rehearsal for the Hundred Years War fought by their descendants. The war measures of both kings hurt the Riccardi: Edward I seized the wool of all foreign merchants; Philip arrested the Riccardi in France as agents of his enemy. Soon there was a classic "run on the bank" as depositors withdrew their money from the Riccardi in fear. Internal dissention completed the ruin as quarrels racked a failing company. The collapse in 1301 was a foregone conclusion, the result of a long, unmitigated slide to disaster which had begun a decade earlier.

Although Re's account is clearly argued and might seem credible, it can be shown that such an analysis is essentially wrong. The Riccardi retained their full financial strength up to 1294; they weathered the storms of 1291-1294 well — so well, in fact, that (to note only one piece of evidence) they could lend nearly £17,000 to Edward's ambassadors in France in early 1294.[41] Far from appearing as a company in the last stages of decline, they functioned normally as king's bankers and great merchants in these years.

Why, then, should the king break with them, as he did in the summer of 1294? Why were the Riccardi deprived of the royal revenues in their charge and then arrested, ending a relationship that had worked splendidly for more than two decades? If we look at official documents, we read again and again that the merchants were overwhelmingly in debt to the crown, owing so much that the king could take everything they had as partial payment. But in checking the specific list of charges drawn up against them[42] one quickly discovers that the list is false, the kind of phony list that might be drawn up against any fallen royal official. Reading the Riccardi business letters then takes on a special importance. The letters were written in precisely this period of crisis, 1295-1303; perhaps they might contain colorful denunciations of "the English Justinian," or some interesting charges against the king of legend whose tomb bore the stern warning, *pactum serva*. Was he in fact a perfidious monarch who used the Riccardi for twenty-two years and then ruined them as an alternative to paying his

---

[41] PRO, S C 8 file 260 no. 12970. There is other evidence to substantiate this conclusion, such as the loan of £10,000 for expenses of the royal household between 1 August and 18 November, 1293, PRO, E 372/139 m. 6, C 81/7 no. 597, *Calendar of Patent Rolls 1292-1301*, p. 59.

[42] PRO, E 372/143, E 372/129 m. 5d., E 368/70 m. 26, E 159/68 m. 83d.

debts? The Riccardi letters can be searched in vain for such sentiments. The merchants write of Edward in terms of lavish respect:[43]

> He must be quite willing to have us return to prosperity and honor, so that we might be able to serve him as we used to; for even if he looks to all the merchants in the world we are certain that he will not find there merchants who will serve him with as great a faith or love, or as willingly as we have served him, and will serve him even more so, if God puts us in the condition of being able to do so.

In another letter the Riccardi in Lucca exhort their London partners to handle affairs there wisely, adding ''and may God…. give you the grace to do so that it may be to the honor of Milord the king, to whom God grant life and wealth, and to our safety, and also so that we may return to our former state and serve the king and the other lords as we formerly did.''

Even more puzzling, not only did the merchants readily acknowledge their debt to the king, when they gave an estimate of how to repay it, the total was twice as large as the official charge. Their total obligation entered on the pipe roll was less than £30,000; the Riccardi estimated their indebtedness at about £60,000.[44] The problem of interpretation seems formidable. How can we explain the apparently severe losses in 1291-1294, the normal operations of the company in these years, the 1294 arrest, and the merchants' estimate of their indebtedness?

A solution to the puzzle can be found if we reconsider one assumption. It has been assumed that when the pope granted Edward this tax, directed the Riccardi to collect it and deliver it to the king, that this was done.[45] What would be the result if the Riccardi collected the money but simply kept it for Edward, as they and their fellow-countrymen had previously kept it for the pope? The Riccardi as papal and royal bankers often handled papal transfers for Edward; as crown financiers they had collected royal revenues for two decades as repayment for past loans and as a cushion against future demands. The proceeds of the crusade tax amounted to the enormous sum of 100,000 marks, or £66,666. If the Riccardi did keep this money for Edward they would surely have invested it, perhaps sending much of the sum to the continent. They could not have anticipated the Anglo-French war of 1294; it caught them by surprise even as it caught Edward by surprise. For the Riccardi it was a disaster. Edward naturally wanted massive loans for his war chest, expecting the Riccardi to repeat their financing of his three earlier campaigns in Wales. But the war had split apart their two main areas of activity, preventing the old flow of business activity and credit across the Channel. Riccardi resources may well have been tied up in long range projects on both sides of the channel. When the king called for his 100,000 marks and more, his financiers were relatively helpless.

---

[43] PRO, E 101/601/5 p. 27, letter of 10 October, 1295.

[44] PRO, E 101/601/5 p. 26d., letter of 10 October 1295.

[45] William Lunt thought that the Riccardi had paid the money to Edward, but with the painstaking accuracy characteristic of his work confessed in a footnote that ''payment is not well attested in royal documents.'' *Financial Relations*, p. 341 and note.

Such a hypothesis fits all the evidence. If the Riccardi had just added £66,666 to their resources they could have easily handled the losses of 1291-1294; but after Edward's demand for the money in 1294, they would owe him whatever they could not repay, leading to their estimate of about £60,000. This debt would not appear in exchequer records, for the money had never come within exchequer jurisdiction and accounting. We can picture Edward exploding in rage upon learning that in a major crisis his bankers were crippled. It is not surprising that he arrested the merchants and drew up a bogus list of charges against them; it is perhaps surprising that he did not send their bodies to the Tower and their heads to London bridge. Actually, the conditions of their arrest seem to have been mild, for although their goods and the debts owed them were taken by the crown, they were apparently not personally molested.

Yet there is still poignancy in the Riccardi fall, as the wheel of fortune turned past their days of international business, the financing of armies and courts, and they fell headlong into bankruptcy and disgrace. By 1301 their seven-year struggle for survival was over and the firm was bankrupt. The date is not without its symbolic value. The fourteenth century would bring a long list of failures of the great *societates*, as on a wider scale it would bring plague and economic stagnation. If the Riccardi serve in one sense as exemplars of economic change in the High Middle Ages, of commercial expertise and relatively sophisticated credit, in another sense they show the fragility of thirteenth century credit structures and point toward the closing of the age of medieval commercial revolution.

III

TURNING TO ANALYSIS

I am moved with spiritual sweetness towards the Creator and Ruler of this world, because I follow him with greater veneration and reverence when I behold the magnitude, beauty and permanence of His creation.

VINCENT OF BEAUVAIS,
prol. 6, *Speculum Majus*

Nature is not confused and without system, and so far as human knowledge has progressed, it should be given a hearing. Only when it fails utterly should there be a recourse to God.

ADELARD OF BATH,
Quaestiones Naturales, ch. 4

Albertus Magnus and the Rise of an Empirical Approach in Medieval Philosophy and Science

JAMES R. SHAW

I

Insofar as it is possible to generalize meaningfully about such things, it is true that at the beginning of the thirteenth century Plato was the establishment philosopher, but at the end of the same century he was not so firmly established. At the end of the century, though Aristotle was not yet recognized as a Christian, he was not completely ostracized from the Church, and he was certainly at home in the Continental universities. This radical change was due, in part, to the efforts of Albertus Magnus.[1]

When Albert began his commentaries on Aristotle (sometime in the 1240s) Aristotle had already been the subject of several ecclesiastical condemnations, not only papal, but also provincial and episcopal. Of course, the logical works of Aristotle were not the subject of the condemnations. The ecclesiastical authorities had long since learned to live with the parts of the *Organon* which had been known to the early Middle Ages. The *Categories* especially were used in the early cathedral schools, but the *Categories* can easily be read — and were so read — in the light of the more favored Platonic and Neoplatonic philosophy. One can still read the *Categories* as a rather analytical elaboration of the Platonic theory of Ideas.

It was this theory of ideas which from the beginning of Christianity had favorably disposed educated pagan converts to Plato. Since they only had a bit of the Platonic corpus they could not know that the theory, especially as interpreted by some Neoplatonists, plays a very small part in Plato's own thought. Nevertheless, some of the most influential Church fathers read Plato, particularly in the *Timæus*, as promoting a belief in subsistent ideas which the Fathers saw as eternal exemplars of things existing in the mind of

[1] My interest in the scientific work of Albertus Magnus is largely due to the lectures of William A. Wallace, O. P., now of the Department of Philosophy, Catholic University of America. Discussions with him, carried on intermittently over the past ten years, have been of great help, and I am happy to acknowledge this assistance and inspiration.

God. Accompanying the belief in the reality of these eternal exemplars was
the corresponding view that this world was but a shadow of the Real world.
Platonism was also compatible with the Fathers' interpretation of Christianity. Thus the eternal χώρα of the *Timæus* was thought to be the created
chaos of *Genesis* out of which God the Father had made the world. Other
dialogues known either completely or in part in the early Middle Ages, such
as the *Phædo*, *Meno*, and *Alcibiades* I, show the influences of Pythagorean
mystical beliefs, and were easily appropriated to the Christianity of many
early Church Fathers. Doctrines such as the complete separation of soul and
body, the definition of man as a soul who uses a body, the need for
purification, the eternity of the soul, were associated with Platonic
philosophy and made possible the very early baptism of Plato into the faith.
As Plato's philosophical views were honored, so his rather meager scientific
views came to be accepted by churchmen. The views expounded in the
Timæus about the macrocosm and the microcosm, i.e., about the universe
and about man, were carefully repeated and finely elaborated upon in the
hexameral literature. These treatises or homilies were commentaries on the
two accounts of creation found in the Scripture. The scientific education of
many people in the early Middle Ages was founded on this hexameral
literature, and while the intelligentsia concentrated on many of the physical
details, several of the major themes were generally adopted. In addition to
the Platonic views already mentioned, another belief that emerges very
clearly in the hexameral literature is the belief in the geometrical or
mathematical construction of the macrocosm and the microcosm. Though
for many this came down to an interest in what we might be tempted to call
mystical numerology, for others, such as early astronomers or astrologers, it
meant that a paradigm for true science was a kind of geometry of celestial
spaces.[2] In this kind of science empirical observations played little if any
part. Such non-empirical science was easily compatible with what they knew
of Plato and the little Aristotle that they possessed.

When an integral Aristotelian corpus began to be translated in Latin,
however, it was seen that many of the major Platonic doctrines were
repudiated by Aristotle. When, for example, the biological works were
made available in the mid-thirteenth century, the schoolmen were startled to
see someone who claimed, as Aristotle does in the *Generation of Animals*
(760b27), that "credence must be given to observation rather than to theory,
and to theory only insofar as it agrees with what is observed," or that his
own earlier astronomy (which was largely an *a priori* construction) was a
"conjecture" (*Parts of Animals* [645a5]) and not based on observed facts.
Though many of the schoolmen were startled, others were shocked and there
began the long series of ecclesiastical condemnations of Aristotle referred to

---

[2] For discussion of the mathematical basis of the arts and the origins of metaphysical
vagaries, see PECK, "Number as Cosmic Language," *passim*; on the Euclidian basis of the
systems of Ptolemy and his commentators, see ABRAMS, "The Development of Medieval
Astronomy," pp. 190-91.

at the beginning of this study. This is something pointed out by all the histories of medieval philosophy and science. What is not generally pointed out is that most of the early condemnations, such as those of 1210, 1215, and 1231, were aimed specifically at the books of so-called natural philosophy and that the books of Aristotle with a specifically biological content were sometimes mentioned by name.[3] It is in these books that we find the strongest statements of Aristotle's demand for empirical observations in the natural sciences, as well as the complete absence of any sort of mathematical or deductivist explanations. This is an absence which is especially noticeable when one looks at other — earlier — works of Aristotle as well as the Platonism that they knew. Though these two views, '1) the stress on the need for empirical observations in the biological sciences and (2) the implied rejection of mathematical accounts in biological investigations, were certainly not the sole reason for the many condemnations of Aristotle's works in the natural sciences, these views were inimical to the house-Platonism of the time, and yet constitute an approach which is quite typical of much of the writing of Albert the Great on the natural sciences.

II

Albert's exact date of birth is unknown, but he died in 1280 when he was more than eighty years old. Though there is uncertainty about the date of his birth and his family background, quite a bit is known about his later life and travels, since Albert himself — unlike most other scholastics — records many autobiographical details in his voluminous writings. From his birthplace in a small town on the Danube, Lauingen, between Regensberg and Ulm, he traveled to Padua for his university education. There he studied the usual arts curriculum, as well as medicine. It was not until he was over thirty years old that he joined the Dominican Order and was sent back to his native country to study in the houses of the Order there. This education consisted almost entirely of the study of Scriptures and the more famous commentaries on them. Soon after he completed his own education he became a lector himself and began a long career in his Order as an educator and administrator. Though he spent a considerable amount of the rest of his life in Germany, his duties involved much traveling, almost always on foot. These journeys were the opportunity for many observations which he minutely recorded in one work or another.[4] In 1243 he walked to Paris from Cologne, a distance of over 300 miles, the first of many times. At the

---

[3] For the role which the condemnations of Aristotle played in the development of medieval science, see Edward GRANT, *Physical Science in the Middle Ages* (New York: 1971). In addition to the condemnations mentioned in the text of this paper, and that of 1277 discussed by Grant, there were many other local and provincial condemnations which were important.

[4] The work *On Animals* provides many examples of the records he made on his journeys. Cf. *De Animalibus Libri XXVI*, Edited by Hermann STADLER in 2 vols (Munich; 1916-1921), pp. 1519 (eels are found in many of the rivers of Germany but not in the Danube), 1584, 1594, *et passim*.

University of Paris he took an advanced degree in theology and taught there
for a short while. It was here that he first met up with something like an
integral Aristotle. For, despite the many prohibitions, the Dominican library
at Paris had a comparatively good collection of Aristotelian works. Albert,
as he tells us explicitly in the beginning of his commentary on the *Physics*,
decided that he would read and write commentaries on the entire Aristotelian
corpus, because he said that it is important to make Aristotle's works
"intelligible to the Latins."[5] The entire project took Albert about twenty
years and is an amazing achievement. It seems even more amazing when
one realizes that the commentaries on Aristotle form only seventeen of the
forty volumes in the Cologne critical edition of Albert's own work, that the
actual writing had to be squeezed into a very busy schedule, and that there
was great opposition to the entire project. There was some temporary
opposition from within his own Order, and the early chronicles contain
stories of the devil appearing to his fellow Dominicans and warning them of
the dangerous project Brother Albert was about. However, the external
opposition from the secular clergy and the Franciscans proved more
continuous. Albert was aware of the opposition to his project and apparently
thought that those opposed to it should at least read his work before they
condemned it. If they did not do that much, he cared little for their
opinions.[6]

The commentaries themselves were by Albert's own design intended to
be paraphrases with brief explanatory notes. However, many of the
explanatory notes are not very brief and Albert adds what he calls
'digressions'. A single digression in the work *On Animals* is over three
hundred pages long in the edition which was published in 1920.

The work *On Animals* was probably written over a four-year period and
the actual writing of it did not begin until around 1258. There is absolutely
no doubt about its authenticity and since the autograph still exists it provides
a unique opportunity for examining Albert at work. The Stadler edition of it
which was published 1917-1920 runs to 1598 pages of text. It was, of
course, intended to be a commentary on Aristotle's biological treatises. The
text shows that Albert had access to the translation of these works which
was prepared by a friend and fellow Dominican, William of Moerbeke,
sometime in the middle 1260s. Another earlier edition, that of Michael Scot,
was also used by Albert, as was a Greek text. This work is the first of its
kind, and remained a reputable, acknowledged authority for almost five
hundred years. Like all pioneers, Albert left a trail of mistakes behind him;
but in the period between Aristotle and the sixteenth century there is no

---

[5] "Nostra intentio est omnes dictas partes facere Latinis intelligibiles," Comm. on the
Physics, Bk. I, Treatise 1, Chap. 1.

[6] "Si autem non legens et comparans reprehenderit, tunc constat ex odio eum
reprehendere vel ex ignorantia: et ego talium hominum parum curo reprehensiones." *On
Animals*, p. 1598.

other work which even comes close to Albert's in its attempts to provide a descriptive and experimental approach to biological phenomena.

Of course, one has to be very careful when one sees in Albert (or any other medieval author, for that matter) references to "experience" and "experiment" as well as claims about having observed some particular phenomena. In Albert's case some of the repeated statements about the need for observation should, I think, be thought of as part of his polemic against those (e.g., the "Plato" whom Albert knew) who denied the essential role of observations. Nevertheless, it is quite easy to make a case for the claim that Albert's general approach is empirical in a sense of that word which is contemporary.

To support this claim I would like to mention three aspects of Albert's writings: (1) his theoretical defense of an empirical approach against those who claimed that the divine will was a sufficient explanation of natural events; (2) his repeated references to empirical criteria in his own works on natural science; (3) his comments on sexual anatomy.

One of the strongest criticisms of an observational approach to nature was the claim that such an approach led to a denial of divine causality. In Albert's work *On the Causes and Properties of the Elements and of the Planets*, Albert raises this question in the beginning. Albert says that some men attribute the Biblical flood to God's will; he answers that he too believes that ultimately God was the cause of the flood. However, this does not mean that to attribute it to God's causality explains the phenomenon. God acts through natural causes, and it is important to seek out the *natural* causes of *natural* phenomena. And the way to do this is to make observations of particular phenomena. He ends the discussion of the question with the following comment: "It is not enough to know in terms of universals, but we seek to know each object's own peculiar characteristics, for this is the best and perfect kind of science."[7] Though Albert thought that one must deal with the general principles of natural sciences, he stresses the necessity for including the details.[8] This demand for concrete, specific, detailed, accurate knowledge of discrete particulars is a complete about-face from the contemporary interpretations of Plato and from much that is also in Aristotle's earlier works. It amounts to a rejection — at least for the natural sciences — of any practical interest in the subsistent ideas of Plato.

In addition to this theoretical defense of the need for observation in the natural sciences, the work *On Animals* contains many references to empirical criteria to justify a claim. This can be made clear by examining Albert's attitude to some of the ancient authorities and by noticing the

---

[7] As translated and quoted by Lynn THORNDIKE, *A History of Magic and the Experimental Sciences* (New York: 1923), II, 535.

[8] "... quia omnis physica consideratio de communibus ad particularia descendit, ideo primo in communi de avium dicendum est natura, et postea secundum ordinem alfabeti Latini nominatim aves secundum suas species et modos exprimantur." *Ibid.*, p. 1430.

phrases he uses to describe animals and their behavior. Though Albert used Pliny as a source for his work, he is doubtful of Pliny's accuracy and even observes that Pliny says many things which are quite false.[9] Others come in for equally strong condemnation.[10] Even Aristotle is occasionally questioned,[11] though always diffidently.

The usual grounds on which Albert corrects some authority, and the customary verification of some claim is that he has "tested" it. "Expertus sum" or some variation on it appears over and over, especially toward the end of the work *On Animals*.[12] Sometimes he says that he has tested it by observing some particular animal behavior,[13] other times that he not only tested it himself but showed it to his associates,[14] or that he has observed it many times.[15] He many times indicates that he has himself not observed some phenomena, but is relying on the reports of others. Among those who make reports he attempts to distinguish between those who are believable and those who are not. Thus he says an associate who is trustworthy (unus de nostris sociis fide dignus) told him that large lizards, as large as the shinbone of a man, can be observed in Spain.[16] Other times he says that a common belief is not proved,[17] or something just has not been proved,[18] or that it has not been proved "per experimentum."[19] Occasionally he simply reports ("dicitur") some claim without commenting,[20] or simply comments that he is uncertain ("an verum sit ignoratur").[21]

Not only does Albert use expressions indicating that he has "tested" the truth of certain claims through observations, he also reports some crude experiments which he conducted in order to verify or falsify certain empirical claims. The kind of experiments were, of course, simple and crude by our standards. Thus he says that he and his associates discovered that if cicadas have their heads cut off, they will continue to make their distinctive noise. ("Experti sumus ego et mei socii quod capite amputando aliquando diu cantat in pectore sonans sicut fecit antea.")[22] He dismissed the view that ostriches eat iron, and suggests a possible source for this

---

[9] "Plinius enim iste multa dicit falsissima et ideo in talibus non sunt curanda dicta ipsius," p. 1440. Also p. 1437.

[10] Cf., e.g., *On Animals*, pp. 1448, 1596 (lines 32 and 33), and 1525 where he says, "Haec sunt quœ de cetorum natura nos experti sumum, et œ quœ scribunt antiqui prœterimus quia non concordant cum expertis."

[11] *Ibid.*, pp. 51 and 1436.

[12] *Ibid.*, p. 1575.

[13] *Ibid.*, p. 1586.

[14] *Ibid.*, "hoc sœpius aspeximus," and 1594, "multotiens experti sumus."

[15] *Ibid.*, p. 1569

[16] *Ibid.*, p. 1583.

[17] *Ibid.*, p. 1511.

[18] *Ibid.*, p. 1587.

[19] *Ibid.*, pp. 1377, 1586, 1587.

[20] *Ibid.*, p. 1435.

[21] *Ibid.*, p. 1585.

[22] *Ibid.*, p. 1510.

erroneous belief, when he reports his own attempts to feed different bits of things to these birds. ("De hac ave dicitur quod ferrum comedat et digerat: sed ego non sum hoc expertus quia ferrum sæpius a me pluribus strutionibus obiectum comedere noluerunt. Sed ossa magna ad breves partes truncata et arida et lapides avide comederunt.")[23] He talks about the dissection which he and his associates have done on bees and grasshoppers,[24] and the behavior of scorpions which he submerged in olive oil.[25] Though these are not experiments devised to test a sophisticated modern hypothesis, they are controlled attempts to empirically verify or falsify some observational claim. Thus, in addition to Albert's theoretical defense of the need for observation of particulars (against those who claimed that such interests were irreligious and inclined one to deny Divine causality) Albert's own practice of making many empirical observations shows, at the very least, his commitment to an empirical approach.[26]

This commitment can be made even more apparent by paying close attention to what Albert has to say about sexual anatomy and physiology. There are, of course, many mistakes in Albert's treatment of these topics. However, I think we should remind ourselves that of all areas of human structure and function, the sexual seems to be most incapable of throwing off mistaken and often quite superstitious beliefs. Even our own day (which is supposed to be one of sexual enlightenment) holds onto some absurd beliefs. Thus as recently as 1969, the coaches of the Superbowl warned the players not to have intercourse the night before the game since intercourse debilitates the body. And William Ogle, M.D., in what is an extremely well done and accurate commentary on Aristotle's *Parts of Animals*, notes that some Negroes have bones in their penises. If supposedly educated people in the 20th Century hold such beliefs, we cannot expect a 13th-Century Dominican priest to be entirely free of error on these matters. That he is comparatively free of the kind of errors that can be found, for example, in his early contemporary Constantine the African, is, I believe, a tribute to Albert's reliance on observation.[27]

Albert's major comments on sexual anatomy and physiology are in Books 1, 15 and 22 of his work on animals; there are also many other references to sexual structure and function in the other twenty-three books of this work. The sections in Books 1 and 15 are attempted periphrastic restatements of Aristotle's views in the *Parts of Animals* and the *Generation of Animals* with the frequent digressions spoken of earlier. By Book 22,

---

[23] *Ibid.*, pp. 389 and 390.

[24] *Ibid.*, p. 1596.

[25] The kinds of examples I have cited to show Albert's commitment could easily be multiplied: how he captured a vulture (p. 1513), how a little dog he once had had eyes of different colors. *Quæstiones Super De Animalibus*. Ephrem FILTHAUT, O.P., ed. (Westphalia: Aschendorff, 1955), p. 99. There are many others.

[26] Cf. Paul DELANY, "Constantinus Africanus' *De Coitu*: A Translation," *Chaucer Review*, IV (1969), 55-65.

[27] Avicenna is referred to as an authority more than anyone else, except Aristotle.

Albert has long since given up the paraphrasing-with-additions and presents a synthetic treatment of various topics with occasional references to authorities, both ancient and modern, especially to Avicenna.[28]

Albert's treatment differs from his chief ancient authority, namely Aristotle, by the addition of empirical observations not found in Aristotle, by stressing homologies — that is, the parallels — between male and female structures and functions and by adding a "psychology of sexual arousal" not found in Aristotle. Albert differs from his early contemporary, Constantine the African, in several ways: Albert has much more detailed and accurate description of anatomy; Albert's treatment of physiology is not nearly so dependent on the four-humor theory and Galenic physiology; Albert devotes about equal space to his description of male and female — whereas in Constantine's treatise, references to the female are quite incidental; finally, Albert leaves out all mention of Constantine's dubious pharmaceutical remedies for impotence and for prolonging intercourse. I think that this omission is significant and an indication of Albert's more empirical approach, since Albert quotes Constantine by name and explicitly refers to the work *On Intercourse*. Albert also refers to the problems of sterility and impotence. He apparently even repeated a putative test for sterility which Aristotle mentions in the *Generation of Animals* (747a5). Albert claims[29] that the sperm of a fertile male will briefly float on the surface of water and then gradually sink to the bottom in sort of viscous globs. On the other hand, the sperm of an infertile man — especially an older male — lacks the viscous, globular texture and will therefore be diffused on the surface of the water. This "test" — which, given certain qualification, happens to be the case — shows that Albert was interested in problems of sterility and the several passages where he discusses them provided the opportunity to analyze Constantine's views. However, he never mentions them; and in one place, where he refers to pharmaceutical preparations connected with sterility, he says, "All these kinds of things seem absurd to us,"[30] though Albert does say that he must study the causes of sterility since "medicine must cure them."[31] Having noticed these passages from Albert, it seems at least probable that he left out the preparations mentioned by Constantine because he thought that they, too, were "absurd". It is well known that Albert and other 13th-century

---

[28] *On Animals*, pp. 1349-1350. One of Constantine's preparations which Albert leaves unmentioned is: A lotion which helps intercourse: 6 drams scammony; I dram euphorbea; Grind separately — drams white beeswax, add the other ingredients, cook breefly, shake well and set aside. When needed, put it on a cloth and place on the penis — when the warmth takes effect the penis becomes erect and potent. If you want to quench it, anoint the member with water in which celery has been cooked. Cf. DELANEY, *op. cit.*, p. 65.

[29] *Ibid.*, p. 1134. I have translated the Latin word "sperma" as sperm and this can be very misleading. Albert knew absolutely nothing of sperm as germ cells. In some passages what he means is merely "ejaculate"; in other passages he means "a seed"; in still others he means "a fluid which is emitted by both male and female."

[30] *Ibid.*, p. 749: "Hæc autem omnia nobis absurda esse videntur."

[31] *Ibid.*, p. 730: "rectificare per medicinam."

scholastics generally did not mention by name their immediate predecessors and contemporaries when they were in serious disagreement with them. Of course, it is not too difficult to show that Albert's work, from a scientific standpoint, is quite superior to that of Constantine, even though Constantine's works were required texts in the medical curriculum until long after Albert's time.

However, I think that Albert's work compares favorably with Aristotle's. Though Albert did not do the extensive dissections that Aristotle did, when the opportunity presents itself, he adds observations of his own and points out homologies that Aristotle either denied or did not mention. From a technical viewpoint, Albert is wrong about some of his homologies, but he is convinced that there are structural parallels between the male and female sexual organs. An indication of Albert's conviction about the homologies between male and female is that he uses one word for penis and clitoris (usually *virga*). He several times refers to various homologies such as when he talks about the vagina as a sort of invaginated scrotum,[32] and about the two testicles in the male and two testicles in the female.[33] These parallels are not stressed in Aristotle, who says, in the *History of Animals* (493a25), that the vagina is proper only to the female and the penis is proper only to the male, and the "privy parts of the female" (to use the rather Victorian phrase at 493b2 in the Oxford English Aristotle) are the opposite of the male's. In another place[34] Albert notes carefully what the differences are between the structures which he parallels in these passages. For example, he says that the testicles of the male are exterior to the body and larger than those of the female which are interior.

Albert also sees a parallel in the physiology of intercourse. Albert apparently thought that Aristotle's explanation of engorgement is too simple, and Albert speaks of a special substance, *ventositas*, which he sometimes refers to as a gas and other times as a liquid. He thinks of it as a special modification of body heat, which modification is only found in the genital region.[35] By means of this ventosity, the heat "enlarges the genital organs (of both sexes); and since there is some difference between the sexes, the male organs swell out and harden while the female organs open up and become engorged, though less so than the male organs."[36] I should point out that his reference to "some difference" occurs after he has stressed that the differences between the sexes are mainly differences of shapes of the breasts and genital organs. Albert thinks of the differences between the sexes as "modal" and not "real".[37]

---

[32] *Ibid.*, p. 1012: "diminuta et retenta intus."

[33] *Ibid.* The testicles of the female were the ovaries.

[34] *Ibid.*, p. 160.

[35] *Ibid.*, p. 1350.

[36] "... membra genitalia extendit: et cum sint disparis sexus, viri membra tumescunt et rigescunt, ferminœ autem aperiuntur et intumescunt, sed minus quam genitalia viri." *Ibid.*

[37] Cf. the *Quæstiones Super De Animalibus*, p. 261 in the edition referred to in note 26. This earlier work is a more "scholastic" treatment of some general problems raised by Aristotle's biological works. In the passage cited Albert replies negatively to the view that male and female are specifically different, though he refers to no empirical observations.

Another interesting difference between the Aristotelian text and Albert's commentary are the additional comments he makes to verify some things Aristotle has said by referring to some observation or "experiment" Albert has made. I have already referred to Albert's description of the action of male sperm in a container of water. Albert similarly elaborates when he says that not only is the hymen broken during the first intercourse, it can also be broken by sticking one's finger through it.[38] He adds to Aristotle's account of the ejaculation of sperm that one can produce a substance in both the male and female, which is intermediate between sperm and sweat, by slight sexual stimulation.[39] He says that this substance is not an ejaculation but is produced in a man, for example, by the touch of a woman with whom he would like to have intercourse. According to Albert, one can also show that women have sperm. He says that the way to do this is by moving rapidly the end of the clitoris with the hand. Albert adds that thus she will feel the delight of intercourse and have an orgasm.[40] Parenthetically, mention should be made of the fact that in Book 22, after Albert has given up paraphrasing Aristotle, he says that "Generation among men is through intercourse in which there is a mixture of the powers of the two sexes; from the male sperm which acts as the mover and from the female sperm or rather the female clear fluid as well as the menstrual blood which is the material."[41] This passage seems to indicate that though Albert has apparently adhered to the male and female sperm view of Aristotle as well as assigning to each a different kind of causality, he believes that the two are by no means the same liquid.

Albert does not offer a "proof" that males have sperm, but he does say that the way we know that the source of the male sperm is in the testicles is that during coitus at the time of orgasm, the testicles are drawn up and hug the pecten or pubic bone so that the sperm may be expelled. This localization of the sperm apparently was a problem for Albert. In the same section as the above comment, he says that one should not be surprised if a bull is fertile right after castration: it may be the case that sperm is already in the canals of the penis itself.[42]

I think that all of these comments — and others could be cited to the same purpose — show that Albert was committed to serious, scientific observation of things some might think are not the proper business of a 13th-century friar. As mentioned before, there were those who thought that the study of Aristotle and the adoption of an empirical outlook would lead to irreligion. Some apparently found in Albert's work the incarnation of their

---

[38] *On Animals*, p. 164.

[39] *Ibid.*, p. 166.

[40] *Ibid.*, p. 1013.

[41] *Ibid.*, p. 1349: "Generatio igitur hominis universaliter est per coitum in quo virtutes sexuum permiscentur, et ex spermate viri quod est sicut operator et factor, et ex spermate sive gutta muliebri et sanguine menstruo quæ sunt materia."

[42] *Ibid.*, p. 996.

worst fears. The Franciscan, Roger Bacon, thought that Albert's reputation for learning had seduced the Latins and that Albert's learning was a disgrace. However, Albert's championing of Aristotle's later empirical approach caught on in some quarters. But lest these pages lead the reader to believe that Albert's empirical approach should have been in the eyes of his ecclesiastical colleagues entirely unobjectionable, let me close with one of his own summaries:

> So far we have spoken of the act of generation among animals in general. However in man, since his nature is nobler, the act of intercourse is more complex. One important difference is that humans enjoy sex more than other animals. In the human animal at the time for intercourse consciousness of a sexual form exists: thus in the male with the image of a lovable woman before the eyes of his heart, and in the female with the image of a desired man before the eyes of her heart, there arises a fierce longing for intercourse. These interior images are like the first movers toward those things which lead up to intercourse.

There follows a short passage in which Albert explains briefly how body heat is changed into the "ventosity" mentioned above, and his text continues

> .... and when the ventosity is firm and plentiful the penis becomes almost bone-like; the penis becomes so hard that sometimes the canals through which the sperm should be ejaculated is closed off with ventosity and the sperm cannot shoot out until a moment later when the ventosity is given off.[43]

How Albertus got his information we can only guess. But his observations clearly manifest a growing interest in the empirical.

---

[43] *Ibid.*, p. 1350: "Licet autem hœc communiter de generatione animalium dicta sint, in homine tamen maxime sunt cuius natura dignior est, complexio nobilior: et ideo coitus est cum maiore quam in aliis animalibus delectatione: et agit in coitu hominis forma sexus apprehensa, ita quod ymago mulieris amabilis agit in viro præ oculis cordis posita et ymago apprehensa viri desiderati agit in muliere coitus concupiscentiam, et est hæc quasi primum præcipiens in hiis quæ ad coitum faciunt:.... Et quando ventositas est sicca et multa, fit virga viri quasi ossea, ita quod aliquando ventositate opilantur meatus per quos eici debebat sperma, et non exit nisi quando aliquantulum ventositas remissa fuerit."

The Development of Medieval Astronomy

JOHN W. ABRAMS

In his monumental study of the history of cosmological doctrine, Pierre Duhem suggests that medieval astronomy defines itself through a debate between "physiciens et astronomes" — physicists and astronomers — or, to simplify, between Aristotelians and Platonists.[1] Although Duhem had relatively little interest in the theological overtones of Platonic metaphysics which so infiltrates medieval cosmology, the dichotomy he sets out provides a useful and accurate approach to medieval astronomy. The problem as seen by the astronomers was to represent mathematically the observed celestial motions of both the fixed stars and the seven wandering stars or planets (Moon, Mercury, Venus, Sun, Mars, Jupiter, and Saturn) so that their future positions could be predicted. The problem as seen by the physicists was to depict the physical reality as well. In the extreme the two problems may be separable: in the historic case they were not. Europe in the 12th Century received both traditions in a form which few were able to understand and, partly because of incompleteness of transmission, none could unravel. Yet astronomy and astronomical knowledge were very important to the Middle Ages. "Astronomy is the law of the stars," writes Hugh of St. Victor, and "investigates the regions, orbits, courses, risings, and settings of stars, and why each bears the name assigned it."[2] Or in the words of Robertus Anglicus, it is "the noblest science.... as it were, a road leading to God." As a subdivision of mathematics astronomy was the science of quantity in motion, offering important evidences to the rational soul of the most sublime rhythms of God's great plan. Moreover, it dealt with a pragmatic concern which greatly disturbed the High Middle Ages, namely, the ordinary calendar which was clearly going astray.

---

[1] Pierre DUHEM, *Le Système du Monde* (Paris, 1914) II, 59.

[2] *The Didascalicon of Hugh of St. Victor: A Medieval Guide to the Arts*, trans. Jerome TAYLOR (New York, 1961), p. 68. Hugh defines astrology as "discourse concerning the stars" and observes that although it properly treats of "the temper or 'complexion' of physical things, like health, illness, storm, calm, productivity, and unproductivity, which vary with the mutual alignments of the astral bodies," so much superstition and chance is involved that it has become mainly the art of bogus "mathematicians." The quotation from Robertus Anglicus comes from his commentary on Sacrobosco's *The Sphere*, trans. Lynn THORNDIKE (Chicago, 1949), p. 199.

I. — ASTRONOMY IN ANTIQUITY

To set in perspective the scope of astronomy in the later Middle Ages, one must understand something of the heritage of the discipline, for to medieval man it was an ancient as well as a pragmatic science; and rightly so, for unlike the other arts, even the practical side of astronomy requires centuries of calculations beyond the observations of a single lifetime. At least as far back as the empires of the Tigris-Euphrates, men had observed the heavens. Chaldean astronomers mapped the sky and named permanent stellar configurations or constellations. They identified the nightly motion of the stars as being regular about a pole (the North Celestial Pole) with an equatorial circle which cut the horizon in the east and west points. They appreciated that the sun (and planets) moved within a belt (the zodiac) inclined some 23° to the celestial equator, and they used a co-ordinate system for the sphere of the heavens similar to our present terrestrial latitude and longitude. Positions of celestial objects were given relative to the 12 zodiacal constellations, each of which covered 30°. They constructed tables, which facilitated calculation of planetary positions, based on an elaborate empirical system with no theoretical physical assumptions other than that the future reflected the past. They could calculate and predict eclipses which required detailed knowledge of both solar and lunar motions. They formulated a calendar based on the moon and reconciled it with the solar calendar of the seasons. The Jews used such a lunar calendar to calculate Passover, and in Christian times, Easter was calculated by the same basic calendar.

Unlike the Chaldeans, the pre-Socratic Ionian Greeks initially did not concentrate on tables, but expounded non-mythological physical explanations of the cosmos. From Pythagoras and his followers stemmed ideas of perfection of form in the heavens, characterized by the circle (without beginning or end), and perfection of motion, characterized by uniformity of circular motion. They probably put forth two physical models for stars and planets, one geocentric and the other not. Both models were known in the early Middle Ages through Pliny, Cicero, and Martianus Capella.

The trouble with the Pythagorean systems was that they could not closely represent the well-known non-uniformities of planetary motion. Aware of the problem, Plato put forth his call to "save the phenomenon"[4]

---

[3] See T.L. HEATH, *Aristarchos of Samos* (Oxford, 1913), p. 49, and D. R. DICKS, *Early Greek Astronomy to Aristotle* (London, 1970), p. 69. The order of spheres in the geocentric system would have been (numbering from center outward): Earth, Moon, Mercury, Venus, Sun, Mars, Jupiter, Saturn, fixed stars. The non-geocentric scheme, sometimes attributed to Philolaus, began with central fire, then Mercury and Venus. Earth formed the third sphere with the moon rotating around it; opposite Earth, beyond the central fire and thus unseen, was possibly a "counter-earth." The Sun formed the 4th circle, then Mars, Jupiter, and Saturn, with the fixed stars at the outer edge.

[4] An account of Plato's decision is given by SIMPLICIUS, *In Aristotelis physicorum libros quatuor priores commentaria* 2, ed. Diels (Berlin, 1882), pp. 291-92, quoted in P. DUHEM, *To Save the Phenomena*, trans. Edmund DOLAND and Chaninah MASCHLER (Chicago, 1969), p. 5. Duhem's work was originally published in 1908 in French.

and saw it taken up by his elder contemporary, the astronomer Eudoxus. By this call, Plato and his followers meant exactly what they said, "save the appearances," and no more. They held that a complete knowledge of reality was unattainable from the appearances and that mathematical theory, which is in truth what they were seeking, was the suitable path towards whatever possible useful knowledge.

The system ultimately proposed by Eudoxus was geocentric. The regular daily or diurnal motion of stars from east to west was reproduced by suggesting that the stars were on the surface of an earth-centered sphere which rotated about an axis between the North and South Celestial Poles. Since the 7 wanderers (Sun, Moon, Mercury, Venus, Mars, Jupiter and Saturn) possess additional motion with respect to the stars, they called for additional spheres. The motions of Sun and Moon which progress always easterly on apparently circular paths inclined to the celestial equator were expressed by combined rotation of three spheres. Those of the other planets which at times may move either easterly or westerly amongst the stars were expressed by the resultant effect of four spheres. Altogether there were some twenty-seven geocentric spheres in the system.

When the Sun and Moon were found to move with different speeds at different times, two additional spheres had to be added by Callipus (ca. 340 B.C.) to account for this new anomaly in motion. Yet for the Platonists there was no need to consider the actual physical nature of the spheres. Their calculations dealt with appearances only and needed only to fit the evidences. Hipparchus (161-127 B.C.), for example, initially explained the change in apparent speed of the sun by considering it to move uniformly on a circle (as befitted a celestial object) but employed an eccentric circle rather than a geocentric one. The geometer Apollonius (ca. 262 B.C.), however, demonstrated that the resultant motion could be equally well represented by simultaneous motion on two circles, a geocentric deferent and an epicycle. This demonstration fostered the mathematical view that the circles and spheres need only be fictions, and, indeed, with no grounds for choice, it was hard to impute reality to either alternative.

Plato's approach to the heavens was mathematical; Aristotle's was physical, but the Eudoxian system proved equally adaptable to his physics. Below the sphere of the moon was, for Aristotle, the place of change, generation, and corruption. The four elements (earth, water, air, fire) sought their natural places about the earth as center. Each had its own sphere with the heavens above the sphere of fire. Beyond fire came the planetary spheres. At and above the sphere of the moon was perfection, the realm of the element aether which exhibited no change and of which the heavenly bodies were constituted. These features of Aristotle's scheme were widely circulated in the Middle Ages through encyclopedic compendia such as Vincent of Beauvais's *Speculum Naturale*, Brunetto Latini's *Trésor*, the *Speculum Astronomiæ* (variously attributed to Roger Bacon and Albertus Magnus), or the popular *Secreta Secretorum*, and through commentaries on his *De Cælo et Mundi*. But his model was more complex still. To the system of Callipus, Aristotle added further spheres to "unroll or react on the others in such a way as to replace the first sphere of the next lower planet in the same position as if the spheres assigned to the respective planets above it did not exist, for only in this way is it possible for a combined system to produce the motion of the planets."[5] He thus increased the number of spheres to fifty-five.

As an integral part of his philosophic system, Aristotle had propounded laws of motion for terrestrial as well as celestial bodies. Celestial bodies naturally moved in uniform, circular paths about the coincident center of the earth and cosmos. Clearly, Aristotle was interested in more than mathematical fictions. He discussed the shape of the earth, the stars, and the planets, choosing spheres on observational and logical grounds. He was aware that the observed diurnal motion of the stars could be equally well explained mathematically by a rotation of the earth, but opted for a fixed stationary earth as the immobile center in accord with his theory of natural place of the elements. To a "pure" mathematician such matters would have been of no concern, but Aristotle's interests were those of the physicist. His decision, however, set up one of the major obstacles to reconciling the debate.

Two further ancient systems entered the source stream of medieval astronomy before Ptolemy, those of Heraclides of Pontus (4th cent. B.C.) and Aristarchus of Samos (ca. 280 B.C.). Heraclides, known in the Middle Ages through Chalcidius, Vitruvius, and Martianus Capella, had the planets Mercury and Venus circling the Sun rather than Earth, although the remainder of his scheme was geocentric. Aristarchus developed an heliocentric system which received little acceptance, probably for physical reasons, although the system was also said to have been impious.

II. — PTOLEMY

Up to this point, our knowledge of ancient astronomers comes largely from indirect narrative accounts. Ptolemy (d. after 161 A.D.) introduces quite another situation. Practical mathematics had early been developed both in Egypt and the Tigris-Euphrates region. The abstraction of geometric problems, however, to an ideal form in which universally applicable conclusions could be deduced from a set of obvious truths (axioms) was a Greek contribution. From the time of Thales (b. 624 B.C.) a cumulative body of geometric knowledge was amassed. Advances in this science of quantity at rest made possible advances in the sister quantitative science, astronomy. Euclid (ca. 323-285 B.C.) collected the geometric propositions and proofs into the books of "Elements." Ptolemy adopted the form and content of Euclid and applied them to the accumulated astronomical knowledge in an extension of the system of Hipparchus. His principal work,

---

[5] *Metaphysics*, trans. T. L. HEATH, *Greek Astronomy* (London, 1932), p. 66.

Mathematical Compositions, better known as the *Almagest* (an adaptation of its Arabic name), contains the first mathematical system capable of calculating planetary, including solar and lunar, positions, for which we have a continuous record up to the present.[6] Greek science, including Aristotle, Euclid, and Ptolemy, reached a temporary culmination in the Eastern Empire after Ptolemy, but because of hostile religious pressures the available texts were carried further east to centers in Asia like Harran, from there to pass into Arabic, sometimes through Syriac.[7] In the hands of Islamic, Indian, and Hebrew scholars, astronomy underwent minor extensions and mathematical modifications to simplify calculation. In fact, its direct Western reappearance in the 12th century was preceded by earlier translations of arabic commentaries and Euclid. Not until 1160 was the *Almagest* itself translated from Greek into Latin.

The *Almagest* marks a high point of ancient astronomy. It is the only astronomical system known to the Middle Ages which could quantitatively save the appearances. Moreover, as it came on the scene without an immediate history but with considerable authority, it interacted powerfully with contemporary local thought. After an initial short statement of Aristotelian philosophy, Ptolemy proceeds to a series of statements (e.g., the earth is spherical, immovable at the center of the universe, and of negligible size with respect to the sphere of the stars). Each statement is elaborated and justified on both physical and philosophical (Aristotelian) grounds. Ptolemy makes full use of Euclid in setting up tables of the ratio of chord to arc in any circle, a necessary preliminary to calculation. Whereas these tables might have been used without a full mathematical comprehension of how they were calculated, this section and the bulk of the remaining ten books could not be followed in any detail by one without a good working facility in Euclidean geometry, and Euclid's proofs were not known in the west until the 12th century.

The *Almagest* is among other things a technical treatise on how to calculate future and past positions of the planets, sun, and moon. Book II contains descriptions of the lengths of day at various parallels of latitude. It relates latitude to the meridian altitude of the sun which is reflected by the length of the shadow of the gnomon or pole in a sundial. It also contains tables for star altitudes. The calculations had a theoretical basis. The daily apparent motion of the stars was taken as uniform in a circle about earth as center. This explanation proved inadequate for the sun, moon, and planets whose motion had to be resolvable into component circular motions. To preserve Aristotelian celestial physics these circular motions should all have been geocentric. But this in fact would not save the appearances. Ptolemy seems to have remained as close to Aristotle as he could, though some of

---

[6] See PTOLEMY, *The Almagest*, trans. R. C. Taliaferro, in Great Books of the Western World, ed. R. M. Hutchins (Chicago, 1952), XVI. See also PTOLÉMÉE DE PELUSE, *Composition Mathématique*, Greek text with French translation by M. Halma (Paris, 1927).

[7] DeLacy O'LEARY, *How Greek Science Passed to the Arabs* (London, 1949).

Aristotle's laws had to be relaxed. Uniform motion about a center was preserved, as were the Hipparchian epicycles and eccentrics, but for the planets, except in the case of the sun, the center of uniform motion was neither the center of the circle nor was it earth or any other body, but another point, the equant. Even more complicated combinations were required to save the appearances of the moon and Mercury.[8]

A further complication was employed by Ptolemy to explain why the motions of the moon and planets amongst the stars were not exactly along the sun's path (the ecliptic). This north-south variation in celestial latitude was accommodated by placing eccentric circles, or deferents, in planes slightly inclined to the ecliptic, but maintaining epicycles in the ecliptic plan. Double inclination was thus introduced.

Ptolemy, following Hipparchus, recognized that the intersections of the ecliptic and the celestial equator were not fixed with respect to the stars. These points (the equinoxes) manifested a slow eastward motion (precession) which he took to be constant at 1° per century. The year of the seasons is the time elapsed from the passage of the sun at one equinox until its return to the same equinox. This important interval is the length of the average year of the solar calendar. Non-uniformity of the sun's motion is reflected by the fact that the time of passage from the vernal to the autumnal equinox is greater than half the year.

Any description of the *Almagest* must emphasize its mathematical character. Written to enable astronomers to calculate, it was not primarily designed to describe the physical reality of the universe. Since it could only be read understandingly by one well-versed in mathematics, its informed audience was limited in antiquity as well as in the Middle Ages. In order to assign values to such quantities as the radii of circles, or more properly to the ratio of the radii, Ptolemy employed observations of the planets extending back over a period of more than 400 years. He made good use of Hipparchus whose star catalog he extended. Presumably he also used Babylonian observations, particularly of eclipses. But although he offered a few physical explanations, particularly in Books I and II, his work is essentially a mathematical *tour de force*. Ptolemy was aware, for example, that either an epicycle or an eccentric could yield the same position for a celestial object. He did express preferences by choosing to use one epicycle and one eccentric rather than the equivalent two epicycles. He nevertheless left the door open for the system to be considered only as a computing device and not necessarily as a model of physical reality. It was so regarded by many through the medieval period.

More difficult to assess is the light in which Ptolemy himself viewed the *Almagest*. In another work, *Hypotheses of the Planets*, Ptolemy

---

[8] An excellent description of the Ptolemaic system appears in BENJAMIN and TOOMER, *Campanus of Novara and Medieval Planetary Theory* (Madison, 1971), p. 39. Other useful accounts are D. J. PRICE, *The Equatorie of the Planetis* (Cambridge, 1955), ch. 7, and R. SMALL, *An Account of the Astronomical Discoveries of Kepler* (Madison, 1963), p. 32.

describes what he clearly understands to be the physical system of the world.[9] The stars are located on a hollow spherical shell centered on Earth within which a series of eccentric hollow spheres mark the planetary deferents. Rolling within the eccentric spheres are smaller ones corresponding to planetary epicycles. The planets themselves are located on epicyclic spheres. No account is taken of the anomalies of motion for which the equant was introduced, nor is it clear that the observed vagaries of Mercury or the Moon could be accommodated. Although the *Hypotheses* as such was not known directly in the Middle Ages, its contents were discussed by Greek commentators and the physical picture it contains was transmitted in works of Islamic astronomers, particularly Ibn-al-Haitham (Alhazen). Whereas the system of the *Almagest* may be regarded as solely a computing device, that of the *Hypotheses* can only be taken as a physical system. Ptolemy may have meant the *Hypotheses* as real, or he may have written the work for those who required a physical picture. We cannot answer, but we can see both physical and mathematical strains coming from Ptolemy himself.

Still another aspect of Ptolemaic thought can be seen in a third work, the *Tetrabiblos* (or *Quadripartium*), sometimes called the "Bible of Astrology."[10] The *Tetrabiblos* assigns various significances to the relative positions of the planets to one another and to their locations among the zodiacal constellations. This is a magical rather than a scientific work, making such connections as: Mars is red; red is the color of blood; blood is associated with war; therefore, Mars is associated with war. The *Tetrabiblos* reminds us that the legacy of the magicians was important in the motivations to calculate accurate astronomical tables and that these tables were frequently used by astrologers.

III. — THE PTOLEMAIC TRADITION

In the indirect transmission of Greek science to the Medieval West some works and commentaries came from Byzantium where they had been preserved, but the main path was through Islamic astronomers. Although Islam was not in itself particularly disposed to scientific study of the world, the religion called for accurate time keeping, and the affluence attained by the Caliphs made it possible for them to act as patrons to astronomy. So the Greek works were early made available. Al-Hajjaj (ca. 786-833) translated both Euclid's *Elements* and the *Almagest*, the latter from a Syriac version.[11]

---

[9] PTOLEMY, *Opera Astronomica Minora*, ed. HEIBERG (Leipzig, 1907), esp. pp. 111-45; see also Bernard GOLDSTEIN, *The Arabic Version of Ptolemy's Planetary Hypotheses* (Philadelphia, 1967).

[10] PTOLEMY, *Tetrabiblos*, ed. and trans. F. E. ROBBINS (London, 1940). Ptolemy was also author of an authoritative work on geography, another on the astrolabe, and a set of Handy Tables which could be used to calculate planetary positions by those unable to follow the *Almagest*. The Handy Tables are also attributed to Theon of Alexandria. See O. NEUGEBAUER, "The Transmission of Planetary Theories in Ancient and Medieval Astronomy," *Scripta Mathematica*, XXII (1956), 190.

[11] G. SARTON, *Introduction to the History of Science* (Baltimore, 1927), I, 562.

With appropriate mathematical background, astronomers and astrologers of
Islam were not only able to understand Ptolemy, but to build on him even as
early as the 9th century.

In the West, Greek science remained essentially confined to the Greek
world, gradually losing its creative character by the 6th century. Although
Rome had extended its hegemony over Greece by the beginning of the
Christian era, its genius lay in organization, not science, and its cultural
emphasis turned to rhetoric rather than mathematics or science. The Latin
scientific works tended towards encyclopediae rather than treatises or even
commentaries. Astronomy might be discussed and described, but subser-
viently to other disciplines. For example, Martianus Capella (ca. 470)
outlined the partial heliocentric theory of Heraclides in his *Marriage of
Philology and Mercury and of the Seven Liberal Arts*, but the geometrical
depth of Capella, a standard source for the Early Middle Ages, was
insufficient to understand fully Euclid or Ptolemy. Boethius (c. 480-524),
whose works were highly influential throughout the medieval period, was
author of an astronomy now lost and a redaction of Euclid, but one which
omitted many proofs while presenting the theorems. The earliest known full
translation of Euclid into Latin is that of Adelard of Bath (c. 1120), made
from the Arabic; another translation from the Arabic by Gerard of Cremona
(1147-1187), perhaps the greatest of the translators, soon followed.

But even if adequate mathematical background had been available to
sustain transmission and improvement of the *Almagest*, interest in physical
science during the early Middle Ages was not sufficient. There were periods
of outright hostility to science by many of the Church Fathers whose views
were often staunchly antiempiricist, literally insisting on such biblical
concepts as the "waters above the earth," a flat earth, and Heaven in the
sky. At dawn the sun entered one of the "two doors of Heaven" and at
sunset left by the other. Some features of the mystical side of Neoplatonism
led both Christian and non-Christian away from a rigorous empirical
approach, though the argument from design at least directed people to look
at the world around them. (In fact, during the High Middle Ages, the
leading empiricists, with the exception of Ockham, were Christian
platonists.) But the main disruption came from the breakdown of the Roman
Empire with its relative political chaos and disbanding of the ancient
schools.

We have no clear picture of internal transmission of astronomical
knowledge in the West. Chalcidius's Latin translation of part of Plato's
Timæus contained virtually the whole of direct knowledge of Plato for the
West until the 12th century. Its pre-Ptolemaic astronomy meagerly
augmented their astronomical knowledge. At its best the *Timæus* is unclear
on the subject; nor is it in the tradition of Platonistic mathematical
astronomers. It contains references to oblique circles and spiral paths that
may be interpreted to mean qualitative knowledge of planetary motions, but
it is no practical guide. The fact that this popular book is cosmological

rather than astronomical pointedly suggests the medieval preference for cosmology over practical science.

In the elucidation of such priorities, St. Augustine, a dominant influence even in astronomy, remains for the historian of that science an enigma. He states, "It is not necessary to probe into the nature of things referring to the physicists, nor need we be in alarm lest the Christian should be ignorant of the force and number of the elements, the motion, and order of eclipses.... and a thousand other things which those philosophers either have found out, or think they have found out."[12] Augustine does, however, show knowledge of the motions of heavenly bodies, and although there is little encouragement to others to extend this scientific knowledge, his readers must have absorbed some of his learning. But his emphasis was not astronomical. In speaking of retrograde and direct motions of planets he speculates about their cause: it may be due to the sun or something "more hidden" (De Genesi ad litteram, II.16). In De Doctrina Christiana, while making allowances for the usefulness of study of most of the arts (even Egyptian gold could help clothe the Israelites), he is most cautious of all when he comes to astronomy, largely because of its proneness to abuse by astrologers:

> The stars, of which Scripture mentions only a few, are known through description rather than narration. Although the course of the moon, which is relevant to the celebration of the anniversary of the Passion of Our Lord, is known to many, there are only a few who know well the rising or setting or other movements of the rest of the stars without error. Knowledge of this kind in itself, although it is not allied with any superstition, is of very little use in the treatment of the Divine Scriptures and even impedes it through fruitless study; and since it is associated with the most pernicious error of vain prediction it is more appropriate and virtuous to condemn it.[13]

Despite these judgments, it has been suggested that the entire works of Augustine have not been adequately studied from the point of view of the historian of science.[14] Perhaps when this is done we may better see his astronomical legacy; but we may be certain it was not in the physical tradition.

Isidore of Seville's De Natura Rerum, dedicated to Sisebut, King of the Visigoths (late 6th cent.), was another influential source of ancient astronomical knowledge. We find in Isidore a more hearty endorsement of the science than in Augustine's works. For Isidore, astronomy, though a legitimate study for a Christian, was still mainly descriptive; he did not go into the mathematical problems of table calculation. In fact, he extended the world system to include the Biblical "waters" above the earth and an outermost Heaven for the "blessed."[15]

---

[12] De Enchiridion, Works of St. Augustine, ed. Marcus DODS (Edinburgh, 1871-76), IX, 180-81.

[13] De Doctrina Christiana, II.xxix.46, trans. D. W. ROBERTSON, Jr. (Indianapolis, 1958), pp. 65-66.

[14] SARTON, Introduction, I, 383.

[15] Etymologiæ, XIII.5 ("De Partibus Cæli"). See A. C. CROMBIE's discussion, Medieval and Early Modern Science (New York, 1959), I, 12.

More significant to our survey of the history of astronomy is the writing of the Venerable Bede (c. 673-735), one of the great masters of chronology in the Middle Ages.[16] Much of his work had as its immediate object the reckoning of the year. But Bede also had a real curiosity about things of this world. His *De Natura Rerum* improves greatly on the astronomical information given in Isidore, mainly because of his familiarity with Pliny; he also wrote on tides and chronology. Indeed, his position marks a turning point not only in the revival of astronomy as an ancient science, but ultimately in advancing it as well. For as A. C. Crombie observes, "From the time when Bede wrote on arithmetic and on the calendar, scholars had been interested in measurement."[17] It is a small beginning, but with the development of increasingly sophisticated clocks and other measuring devices, a new attitude was being born.

Time reckoning had become a major problem for the medieval Christian church. The discrepancy between the tropical year (365.2422 days) and the Julian calendar (365.25 days) began to manifest itself in a gradual shift of dates for the equinoctal periods. Holy Days of the Church were linked to the calendar by the Council of Nice, which had calculated that Easter fell on the first Sunday after the first full moon after the vernal equinox. Without correct constants, existing calculations were separating farther and farther from the observable phenomena. Happily, a theoretical substructure for the calculation of constants, no longer available to the West, was about to appear from a most unexpected source — from the Infidels themselves. Islam also needed accurate time calculation and geographic surveillance. The direction to Mecca, the Qibla, needed to be known for prayer and the hours for prayer were set in the Koran by astronomical criteria. Not only did Islam, through patronage of the Caliphs, have a headstart in time calculation; it had one other major advantage as well. In its transmission eastward from Byzantium, Greek astronomy had passed through Iran and on to India. In its return voyage to Islam it had picked up mathematical sophistication in algebra and trigonometry and the rudimentary Hindi-Arabic numerals which facilitated calculation.[18] Islamic astronomers employed improved instruments to make observations of stellar positions, planetary movements, and eclipses which were utilized in the production of tables similar to those of Ptolemy, but more convenient to use.

In the 11th and 12th centuries the Christian West rapidly took full advantage of Islamic advances. Armed with Adelard of Bath's translation of

---

[16] See the discussion of his *de Tempore Ratione* by R. L. Poole in "The Beginning of the Year in the Middle Ages," *Proceedings of the British Academy*, X (1921), 113-37, esp. 120ff.

[17] *Robert Grosseteste and the Origins of Experimental Science: 1100-1700* (Oxford, 1953), p. 19. Crombie repeatedly hearkens back to Bede in his explorations of the beginnings of technology which are soon to set the West apart from and advance them beyond scientific exploration of the Greeks. (Cf. pp. 11 and 16.)

[18] Full advantage was not taken of the Hindu-Arabic numerals, however. Most Arabic tables used an alphabetic sexagesimal system, as did Ptolemy. See Neugebauer, "Transmission," p. 172.

Euclid from Arabic sources and the knowledge that there was more to be had where that came from they welcomed the new lore with gusto. It was a period of great technological advancement accompanied by a sense that "natural causes" were indeed worthy of study.[19] To cope with the problem of measuring liturgical hours (1/12 the interval between sunrise and sunset), elaborate clocks were developed. One type, the astronomical clock, indicated time by representation of the configuration of the heavens rather than by shadow line or symbolic dial. Such a clock is really a model of the Universe. Islamic water clocks, improved by an escapement developed in China where there was also a well-established astronomical tradition, were also built. Such clocks (introduced as early as the 10th century) could be set by taking nightly observations of the polestar.[20] Gerard of Cremona (1114-87) translated a book on the motion of the spheres by the 9th century Egyptian (?) Jew Mashallah (Messahala), along with an Islamic work on the astrolabe, a device which greatly facilitated astronomical calculation.

The Arabic tradition which began to open its pages to Western Europe was rich in major scholars. Besides Messahala, three in particular (all likewise of the 9th century) were translated into Latin and exerted significant influence. Thabit-ibn-Qurra, through solar observations, believed that he found changes in rate of precession that indicated an oscillation, called trepidation, rather than a complete motion of the equinox along the equator.[21] Trepidation called for the introduction of a 9th sphere and remained a controversial possibility until after the time of Copernicus. Al-Farghane (Alfraganus) wrote an encyclopedic compendium which gave a complete description of stellar motions more or less after Ptolemy, and which did not accept trepidation but extended precession to planets as well as stars. His work was translated by John of Spain and again by Gerard of Cremona and was a major source of Dante's considerable astronomical knowledge. Finally, al-Battani (Albategnius), perhaps the greatest of the Arab astronomers, wrote an influential treatise which included a new set of tables. His treatise was translated into Latin by Robert of Chester and also by Plato of Tivoli.

Another influential Arab astronomer, al-Zargali (Arzachal, c. 1080), is said to have compiled the famous Toledan Tables.[22] These tables incorporated the trepidation of Thabit, but otherwise were devolved mainly from works of al-Khwarismi, al-Battani, and the Handy Tables of Ptolemy or

---

[19] Much work has recently been done on these aspects of medieval technological history. Besides A. C. CROMBIE, *Robert Grosseteste and the Origins of Experimental Science* and Marshall CLAGETT, *Mechanics of the Middle Ages*, see Lynn WHITE, Jr., "Technology and Invention in the Middle Ages," *Speculum*, XV (1940), 141-59, and, in a more entertaining vein, WHITE's "The Legacy of the Middle Ages in the American Wild West," *Speculum*, LX(1965), 191-202.

[20] NEEDHAM, WANG LIN, and PRICE, *Heavenly Clockwork* (Cambridge, 1960). See especially plate xix, facing p. 192.

[21] F. J. CARMODY, *The Astronomical Works of Thabit-ibn-Qurra* (Berkeley, 1960).

[22] G. J. TOOMER, "A Survey of Toledan Tables," *Osiris*, XV (1958), 5.

Theon. They crossed the Pyrenees about the middle of the 12th century. Tables are prepared for a particular geographical locale; they can, however, be translated to another locale, requisite knowledge for such an adjustment being far less than that needed to prepare a new set, a task so momentous that no novel set of tables appeared between Ptolemy and Copernicus. Numerous adaptations of the Toledan Tables were to appear, beginning with that by Raymond of Marseilles for his place of origin in about 1140. Tables for London appeared in 1149, prepared by Robert of Chester who used the older tables of al-Battani along with the Toledan ones. About 1272 the Alfonsine Tables were prepared, again in Toledo, by two Jewish astronomers under the King's order.[23] Jewish tradition in astronomy is strong, and many translations into and out of Hebrew were made about this time. Isaac ibn Sid (c. 1263), one of the two authors of the Alfonsine Tables, also wrote on astronomical instruments and invented new ones. Indeed, new and more accurate instruments continued to appear in the later Middle Ages which, in turn, fostered more critical examination both of tables and their theoretical bases.[24]

The Alfonsine Tables differed from the Toledan by the inclusion of both precession and trepidation. They reached Paris by the end of the century and probably because of greater accuracy slowly supplanted the Toledan Tables. They, or their adaptations, remained standard until the 16th century. This is not to say that other tables were not prepared, but they contained no real theoretical astronomical advance, although the mathematical introductions did show improvement in method. Neither East nor West realized a new astronomy before Copernicus.

There was, however, lively discussion on the physical aspect of astronomy. An influential approach was offered by Ibn-al-Haitham (Alhazen), better known for his work on optics. His *Epitome of Astronomy* was translated by order of Alfonso the Wise into Latin from a Spanish version of an Arabic text, also well known in a Hebrew version.[25] His system reflected that of the *Hypotheses of Ptolemy*, some version of which may have served as inspiration, although his orientation may have come from a work of Thabit which has not come down to us.[26] The material, hollow, transparent orbs of this system apparently satisfied those who demanded a mechanical model for a Ptolemaic system and, somewhat embellished, served to preserve the Ptolemaic system under the attack it was about to suffer with the resurgence of Aristotelian physics. We must recollect that, although the *Almagest* in derivative form was the base of all satisfactory methods of

---

[23] D. J. PRICE, *The Equatorie of the Planetis*, p. 80. See also RICO Y SINOBAS, *Libros del Saber de Astronomica del Rey D. Alfonso X de Castilla* (Madrid, 1863-67), V.

[24] B. GOLDSTEIN, "Theory and Observation in Medieval Astronomy," *Isis*, LXIII (1972), 39-47.

[25] M. STEINSCHNEIDER, "Notice sur un ouvrage astronomique inédit d'Ibn Haïtham," *Bulletino di bibliografia e di storia delle scienze matematiche e fisiche*, XIV (1883), 733-36.

[26] P. DUHEM, *To Save the Phenomena*, pp. 26-27.

calculation until the 16th or 17th centuries, it was utterly unacceptable to one whose primary goal was an Aristotelian physical picture.

One direct attack on Ptolemy was made by al-Bitruji (Alpetragius, latter 12th Cent.). His only known work, *The Principles of Astronomy*,[27] translated into Latin by Michael Scot in 1217, enunciates a system conforming to Aristotelian physics in an attempt to refute the physical implications of the *Almagest*. Because of its explicitness, the system of al-Bitruji was of continuing influence up into the 16th century. Al-Bitruji returned to the only devices which could conform with Aristotle, namely, homocentric spheres centered on the coincident center of Earth and Universe. He referred directly to Aristotle in expounding his physical principles. While praising Ptolemy for his accomplishments, he nevertheless apologetically criticized his defections from Aristotle. Yet al-Bitruji's respect for Ptolemy was underlined by the fact that he employed Ptolemaic parameters in his system. His scheme has been called a return to Eudoxus, but recent analysis of extant Arabic and Hebrew versions indicates that the author was probably unaware of the Eudoxian system.[28] The differences are marked. Al-Bitruji introduced polar epicycles in which each pole of the sphere carrying the celestial object moved in a small circle about the corresponding pole of the diurnal motion. Similar motions in minor circles can be found in earlier Islamic writers, but for other reasons. Thabit had used them to explain trepidation.[29]

Al-Bitruji also entered the precession-trepidation argument; he argued for a variable precession in which equinoxes always move in the same direction but at variable rates, clearly aware at the same time that for computational purposes his system could not produce tables with the accuracy of those produced by Ptolemaic devices. Nevertheless, he was confident that he was on the right track. The resurgent Spanish Aristotelians and their successors agreed with him; astronomers did not. Al-Bitruji considered the speed of celestial motion to be that seen by an observer on the fixed earth. Thus the stars in their diurnal westward motion was taken to be the most rapid and the moon the least. Early astronomers, who measured the speed with respect to the stars, used the reverse order. Assignment of the greatest speed to the more distant spheres is compatible with assignment of the location of the cause of motion to the outermost regions, the speed diminishing with distance from the outer cause. Thus the Prime Mover for al-Bitruji was a further sphere beyond that of the stars.[30]

---

[27] B. GOLDSTEIN, *Al-Bitruji: On Principles of Astronomy* (New Haven, 1971).

[28] Compare DREYER, *Planetary Systems*, p. 265; M. DELAMBE, *Histoire de l'astronomie du Moyen âge* (Paris, 1819); and F. J. CARMODY, *Al-Bitruji: De Motibus Celorum* (Berkeley, 1952). But see also GOLDSTEIN, *Al-Bitruji*, p. ix.

[29] CARMODY, *Thabit*, p. 86.

[30] DREYER, *Planetary Systems*, p. 265.

Another critic of the theory of epicycles was Ibn-Bajja (Avempace: d. 1138-39). His criticism was expanded by Ibn-Rushd (Averroes: 1126-1198) to a full-fledged attack on the methods of the astronomers. Ibn-Rushd argued that there was a logical fallacy in assuming truth in the Ptolemaic devices on grounds that their results agreed with observation. The same results might follow from other devices as well.[31] But astronomers in the Platonic tradition and that of the *Almagest* were not targets for this criticism, since they did not argue for the reality of their devices. In the course of his criticism Ibn-Rushd called for an astronomy with foundations in the principles of physics, insisting that "in our time astronomy is non-existent; what we have is something that fits calculation but does not agree with what is."[32]

Indeed, the struggle between "physiciens et astronomes" remained the stumbling block of medieval astronomy. Moses Maimonides (1135-1204), in his *Guide for the Perplexed*, demonstrated clearly the incompatibility of Aristotle and the *Almagest*. Preferring Ptolemy, he appreciated his use of mathematical devices, yet found himself perplexed by the need to picture a mechanism for the observed motions. He found his resignation in the Bible: "The Heavens are the heavens of the Lord, but the earth hath He given to the sons of man" (Ps. 114:16). Man might understand earthly physics; he could not resolve the dilemmas in the heavens.[33] Yet the stumbling block was there — as it had been from the beginning — and would, in its resolution, lead to an entirely new "art."

IV. — ASTRONOMY IN THE HIGH HIDDLE AGES

In its revival of astronomy through translations from the Arabic, Western Europe received a divided tradition. From one perspective they seem to advance the new astronomy very little. But how could the science as they received it have been advanced? Theirs is a holding action while a new beginning, originating in epistemology, optics, and motion theory rather than "astronomy" is puzzled out. Johannes de Sacrobosco (John of Holywood: mid-13th cent.) offers a good example of the initially assimilative response to the new translations. His textbook, *De Sphæra*, remained in use until the 17th century.[34] *The Sphere* was written at just the right time to make a combination of and compromise between the old literary astronomy of the Early Middle Ages and the new "scientific" astronomy of the

---

[31] AVERROES, *De Caelo* 2.35. A partial translation is given in DUHEM, *To Save the Phenomena*, p. 30. The point was picked up and developed by the Oxford empiricists; e.g., GROSSETESTE, *Commentary on Aristotle's Posterior Analytics* ii, 5, f. 30rb as cited by CROMBIE, *Robert Grosseteste*, p. 81.

[32] AVERROES, *Metaphysica* 1.12, *summa secundae*, cap. 4 comm. 45, quoted in DUHEM, *ibid.*, p. 31.

[33] *Guide for the Perplexed*, trans. PINES (Chicago, 1963), esp. pp. 325-26.

[34] Lynn THORNDIKE, *The Sphere of Sacrobosco and Its Commentators* (Chicago, 1949), contains texts and translations.

12th-century translators. John's sources (Macrobius, Ptolemy, and Alfraganus) have been welded with remarkable skill.[35] Less than one-twentieth the size of the *Almagest*, it contains no diagrams, virtually no calculations, and no star catalog. (Calendar reckoning is treated in a separate *Computus*.) The treatise is concerned primarily with naming the auxiliary circles used to describe motions in the heavens and with relating the earthly climes to latitude and the length of day in a similar manner to Ptolemy. Space devoted to eccentrics, epicycles, and equants is limited and while there is a slight introduction to the Aristotelian idea of natural places, there is no accompanying philosophical treatment or justification. It is clear, however, that Sacrobosco feels he is describing a real world. Precession is mentioned with the Ptolemaic figure of one degree in one hundred years; trepidation is not discussed, nor is the starless sphere, put in by some to act as the *primum mobile*.

The *Sphere* was popular, accruing commentaries by Michael Scot (ca. 1127-1235), Robertus Anglicus (ca. 1271), and others.[36] It was followed by similar works from the hands of Robert Grosseteste (1173-1253), John Pecham (d. 1292), Bernardus de Trilia (ca. 1240-92), and others, which, although somewhat longer, appear to have leaned on it. (They used other sources as well; e.g., Grosseteste mentions trepidation.) These works served as non-technical texts for an introduction to astronomy. Sacrobosco's *Sphere* was a required part of the curriculum of the universities of Paris, Vienna, Bourges, Oxford, Bologna, and so on,[37] and may be taken as an indication of the level of astronomical knowledge required of the educated.

Yet more was going on than the compilation of divergent arguments. Whether due to the influence of Aristotle or not, we discover in the 13th century the explicit re-emergence of a fundamental preliminary to science, namely, a formal expression of the necessity for a theory to conform to the evidence of the senses. In antiquity Parmenides had examined paradoxes arising from the incompatabilities between logical analysis of motion and observed phenomenon. He and the mainstream of astronomical tradition had chosen to follow logic, the path of reason.[38] In the 13th century, the shift was towards experimental science. Bernard of Verdun, in his *Tractatus Optimus super totam Astrologium*, insists that a theory which cannot give results in agreement with observation is, practically speaking, false. Even as derivative a work as Sacrobosco's *Sphere* shows evidence of the new

---

[35] See THORNDIKE's excellent discussion of Sacrobosco's knowledgeability and skill in composition, *The Sphere*, pp. 14-21.

[36] See Thorndike for texts and translations. These commentaries were usually done for specific needs of specific groups. For example, Pecham's treatise was most likely composed for convent schools of his Franciscan Order; Bernardus de Trilia's, for the Dominicans in his native town of Nimes; Robert Anglicus's for lecture purposes at Paris or Montpelier, and so on. (See THORNDIKE, pp. 24-25.) The commentaries often contain lore of a nonscientific kind which may be of particular interest to the historian of the period.

[37] THORNDIKE, pp. 42-43.

[38] KIRK and RAVEN, *The Pre-Socratic Philosophers* (Cambridge, 1966), pp. 263ff.

priorities. Sacrobosco's empirical proofs that the universe is not flat and that the earth is round are many and convincing.[39] If the earth were flat and the heavens flat above it the sun would appear small when it arose, then be large when directly over head simply because it would be closer. In fact, he explains, the sun seems larger at sunrise and sunset, but that is because the vapor in the air scatters the rays and gives the impression of magnification. (He cites as a parallel example a penny dropped in water which appears larger because of like diffusion of rays.) Moreover, if the earth were flat, a star would appear above the horizon at the same time at all points of the flat earthy plane. In fact, a star rises earlier for Orientals than for Westerners, this being due to the bulge of the sphere. Similarly, for people living in a northern region, the polestar is high in the heavens, while the farther one journeys south the lower it seems to reside, this fact also being explained by the earth's roundness which intervenes. But his most elaborate proof, one not found in his sources, is a full-fledged experiment:

> Let a signal be set up on the seacoast and a ship leave port and sail away so far that the eye of a person standing at the foot of the mast can no longer discern the signal. Yet if the ship is stopped, the eye of the same person, if he has climbed to the top of the mast, will see the signal clearly. Yet the eye of a person at the bottom of the mast ought to see the signal better than he who is at the top, as is shown by drawing straight lines from both to the signal. And there is no other explanation of this than the bulge of the water. For all other impediments are excluded, such as clouds and rising vapors.[40]

Even contingencies are accounted for. The reason the earth's surface appears flat to human eyes is due to its great size relative to the eye of the beholder.

By the end of the 13th century an empirical school of thought was strong, especially at Oxford and Paris. Instead of compendia which characterized works of the early part of the century, we get treatises on precise problems, treatises which challenge the ancients (including Aristotle) and go beyond them. Robert Grosseteste, for example, writes on comets (*De Cometis*), rainbows (*De Iride*), and the nature of stars (*De Generatione Stellarum*). A. C. Crombie cites numerous examples in which Grosseteste criticizes his sources when evidence to the contrary is at hand. For example, the learned Bishop objects to the theory that the tail of a comet is caused by reflection of the sun's radiation falling on a planet on grounds that reflected rays would not be visible unless they were associated with a transparent medium of a terrestrial nature, and also because "the tail of the comet is not always extended in the opposite direction to the sun, whereas all reflected rays go in the opposite direction to the incident rays at equal angles."[41] And

---

[39] THORNDIKE, *The Sphere*, 120-121. Some of Sacrobosco's proofs occur in Alfraganus, but Socrobosco displays them more prominently and adds others.

[40] *Ibid.*, p. 121. Some manuscripts of *De Sphaera* add a further proof based on the roundness of the earth's shadow cast on the moon during an eclipse. Sacrobosco is not entirely original with his "ship-at-sea" proof. It is an old chestnut. (Cf. PLINY, *Naturalis Historia*, II, 65, where the example occurs amidst a plethora of "proofs" of the earth's roundness.) What is new is Sacrobosco's detailed method of proof.

[41] *Robert Grosseteste*, pp. 87-89. Grosseteste, of course, considered study of comets as a subdivision of meteorology.

so on (he disputes four theories in all). That Grosseteste's conclusion is inaccurate is not very important. What matters is that he is developing a new method of analysis. That he had no access to the right facts (e.g., comets' tails do always project away from the sun) is less important than his awareness that facts are to be sought and industriously used to establish accurate middle terms so that valid conclusions might be drawn which conform through validated experiment with external reality. Pre-eminently, he was a methodologist.

These early empiricists often exhibit a strange blend of acceptance and challenge as they rely on tradition when they have no better proof, yet still sense the need for a valid method. It is worth examining in detail the views of one like Roger Bacon (1212?-1292), Grosseteste's student. Well-versed in mathematics, Bacon is able to comprehend with sophisticated understanding the various sources he works with. Although he is sometimes referred to as the father of experimental science for the strong emphasis he placed on the value of observation and experiment controlled by logical methods of analysis and verification, his argument on behalf of astronomy still tends to be encyclopedic rather than analytic; he applies his interest in physics to other areas where he has more certain data.[42] For astronomy, he turns more often than in other sciences to tradition, though his sources are many — Aristotle, Ptolemy, Hali Rodohan (an 11th-century Egyptian doctor and commentator on Ptolemy), Averroes, Avicenna, Albumazar, Alfraganus, Arzachel, and Messahala, as well as theologians, historians, and mathematicians who occasionally comment on astrology.

It is important for our purposes to note what Bacon considers the scope of astronomy to be. It is first of all, as it had been for Ptolemy and the Platonists, a subdivision of mathematics. As the science of "quantity in motion" it explores all that pertains to celestial bodies — the measurement of the spheres and their heavenly residents, their magnitude, height, and number, as well as their chronological regulation. Bacon proves by Euclidian geometry that the earth must be a sphere, and notes from his sources (Alfraganus, Ptolemy, and Avicenna) that its diameter is 6500 miles.[43] He is convinced that the heavens do influence Earth and its creatures and offers an elaborate "ray" theory to explain how it works. (A ray striking on the perpendicular is more intense than one striking on an oblique angle.) The chief cause of differences between people, climates, and

---

[42] Bacon's plea on behalf of descriptive mathematics and inductive analysis through observation and experimentation may be found in the 6th book of *Opus Majus*. This work is readily available in Robert Belle BURKE's translation, *The Opus Majus of Roger Bacon*, 2 volumes (Philadelphia, 1928). *Opus Majus* is not a scientific treatise but rather a defense of the arts. Bacon's principal astronomical works on the motions of celestial bodies were part of the *Opus Minus* which has not survived. In a miscellany, the *Communia Naturalis*, he poses the problem of incompatibility between Aristotle's physical theory and observed motions. There he stresses physical theory, though in his last work, *Opus Tertiam*, he rejects the argument of al-Bitruji, perhaps with some reluctance.

[43] *Opus Majus* (BURKE, I, 176, 185-86, and 247 ff.).

places cannot be found in earth or in men, he explains, but rather in the heavens, as all scientists agree:

> whence.... on every point of the earth there is incident the vertex of a pyramid full of force from the whole heavens. These virtues are different in nature, and the pyramids likewise, because they have different bases owing to the differences in their horizons, since every point of the earth is the center of its own horizon. Therefore of necessity a great difference in all things arises from this cause, no matter how close they are, like twins in the same womb; and such is the case in all things, just as we see that from two points very close to each other on the earth plants spring differing according to species. On this principle the astronomer rests the foundations of his judgment, and rightly so, because the complete diversity in things is thus discovered to be due to the heavens. Wherefore the skillful astronomer is able not only in the things of nature, but also in human affairs, to consider many things regarding the present and the future and the past, and therefore at least as regards kingdoms and states is he able to judge by means of the heavenly bodies and of the secondary members of the same, which are renewed by the special forces of the heavens, such as comets and the like, because it is an easier judgment in regard to a community than in regard to an individual.[44]

A curious application of geometry. Yet through the intensive interest in light, refraction, and optics which so characterizes the writings of Grosseteste, Bacon, Bernard, and William of Ockham, tools for new astronomy emerge. For the experiments with lenses ultimately lead to the telescope.

Because of the influences of the heavens on earth of which Bacon speaks, astronomy as a science includes more than mere measuring of activities in the heavens. It includes study of places on earth and the peoples and creatures abiding in those places. That is, for Bacon, what we call geography and meteorology are subdivisions of astronomy. The reason is obvious — since the stars affect the character of locations on earth, study of people, places, and the weather lies within astronomy's domain. Much of his information, such as the three great divisions of the habitable world or the seven known climates and their conditions, he takes from Ptolemy. Other matters he gleans from Aristotle and Pliny. "It is the function of astrology and astronomy," he insists, "to give explanation and full certitude in regard to places in the world."[45] Thus portions of his discussion dealing with Tartars and Troglydites from Ethiopia remind one more of *Mandeville's Travels* than a modern astronomy book.

The third main area included within astronomical study is that of time. Bacon is very knowledgeable about the shortcomings of the Julian calendar and the problems of lunation, namely, that the year is not precisely 365-1/4 days long nor is a month measured exactly by 24-hour intervals. Every 130 years the calendar gains one day, and "after 4256 years the moon according to the calendar, will be called new when it is full of light.... Skillful

---

[44] *Ibid.*, I, 272-73. Bacon does not mean that celestial bodies influence one's moral life, however, but only physical bodies inferior to their own. It is perhaps worth noting in this connection that Robertus Anglicus cites as the final cause of astronomy its utility, esp. in medical practice where causes of diseases cannot be known if the physician is ignorant of "the motion and disposition of the supercelestial bodies" (THORNDIKE, p. 199).

[45] *Ibid.*, I, 205.

astronomers have no doubt that all these statements are facts. Moreover, every computer knows that the beginning of lunation is in error three or four days in these times, and every rustic is able to view this error in the sky.''[46] Bacon recommends to Pope Clement IV that astronomers be consulted and the calendar corrected so that Christendom will not be guilty of the terrible error of celebrating Easter (and thus Rogation, Ascension, and Pentecost as well) at the wrong time. Although the calculations of the Council of Nice, which established the dating of Easter, were accurate, the calendar has simply failed to keep pace.[47]

Astronomy is, then, a more comprehensive study for Bacon than it has become in more recent times. In *Opus Majus* Bacon's goal is to demonstrate that the art is not bogus magic but rather a justifiable science, the aims and results of which are not only compatible with Christian philosophy and theology but necessary to them. He cites Cassiodorus to explain the general benefits it holds for men:

> If we inquire after astronomy with a pure and disciplined mind, it floods our senses, as the ancients say, with great brightness. For such is the result when we turn the mind to the heavens and investigate with inquiring method that whole celestial frame, and with mental acuteness by contemplation gather in part what mysteries of such magnitude have veiled.... By these means, it seems to me, to know the climes, to understand the lengths of the seasons, to note the course of the moon for the determination of Easter, in order that the artless may not be confused in regard to it, — all this does not appear silly. There is also another advantage from such studies which is not to be despised, if we learn from them the suitable time for sailing, the time for ploughing, the dogstar of summer, and the mistrusted storms of autumn.[48]

Such eloquence was not to be denied. Astronomy continued to be a viable study despite her detractors. Bacon is sharp in his condemnation of false astronomers who give the art a bad name. The culprits are guilty of asserting particular ''necessities'' when in fact the science is such that it can deal only with generalities. ''The astronomer should not state a matter specifically but in general terms,'' he insists, ''as one who views something from a distance.''[49] Only false mathematicians predict necessity in particulars. Yet the heavens do influence the earth (Bacon has a whole section devoted to the properties of the planets, their houses, and the effects of their conjunctions in various signs),[50] and one does well to study their effects in retrospect:

---

[46] *Ibid.*, I, 296. In fact, Bacon's teacher, Robert Grosseteste, was the first Latin writer to make a systematic attempt to bring about the calendar reform. See CROMBIE, *Robert Grosseteste*, p. 97, esp. note 3.

[47] *Ibid.*, I, 303.

[48] *Ibid.*, I, 199.

[49] *Ibid.*, I, 264. Bacon is quoting from Ptolemy's *Centilogium*.

[50] *Ibid.*, I, 276ff. E.g., Jupiter and Venus are benevolent and fortunate planets; Saturn and Mars are malevolent and unfortunate; Aries, Leo, and Sagittarius are hot and dry houses, while Taurus, Virgo, and Capricornus are cold and dry, etc. Cf. Robertus Anglicus, Commentary on *De Sphaera* (THORNDIKE, p. 209). A student interested in pursuing medieval views on astrological problems would do well to begin with Robertus Anglicus, whose discussion of mansions, conjunctions, properties of planets, their influence on metals, fortune, health, climes, personality, parts of the anatomy, and so on, is fullsome and confident. His text was highly respected in such places as the Universities of Montpellier and Paris. The *Commentary* is dated 1271 ''when the sun was in the first degree of Taurus and Scorpio in the ascendent.''

One can examine history at past periods, and study the effects of the heavens from the beginning of the world, as in the case of floods, earthquakes, pestilences, famines, comets, prodigies, and other things without number, which have happened both in human affairs and in nature. After he has discovered these facts, he should consult the tables and canons of astronomy, and he will find that there are constellations corresponding in an appropriate way to the effects in each case. He should then study with the help of tables similar constellations in future time, either near or remote according to his wish; and he will then be able to express judgments on the effects, because they will be similar to those in the past, since if we assume a cause the effect is taken for granted."[51]

All in all, not very scientific. A great deal of observation and logical induction will be necessary before Bacon's major premise on the heavens' influence upon earth can be altered. But he does, in addition to summarizing intelligently the views of the past, advocate a consistently rational method of analysis and does, despite the numerous ideas about the influence of rays which seem so quaint to our way of viewing things, clarify for his own time the validity of this most speculative of the sciences. He still exhibits the tension between "physiciens et astronomes," Aristotelian and Platonic method, yet, especially in his discussion of optics, approaches both sides with a new method, and that is what will ultimately be revolutionary.

Among the great scholastics, St. Bonaventure, Albertus Magnus, and Thomas Aquinas also viewed adroitly the conflict between the mathematicians and the physicists. The mathematician-astronomers, St. Bonaventure noted, could reproduce celestial motions without "a single erroneous result,"[52] yet to him their devices were not necessarily representations of the truth of things as they are. He believed the methods of the physicists also constituted a path towards truth and hoped for a future reconciliation. It is easy to read both political tact and a forward vision into St. Bonaventure's position. A full reconciliation, however, had to wait four centuries, until the publication of Newton's *Principia* (1687). Albertus Magnus (1193-1280) published extensive compilations with considerable scientific content. Though empirically biased, he was not a mathematician and the details of astronomic calculation fell outside his ken. Nevertheless, he helped spread astronomical ideas, particularly the system of al-Bitruji in simplified form. In his works there is a profusion of references to the Islamic astronomers and also a profusion of incorrect attributions. Accepting a system with ten spheres, two devoid of either stars or a planet and each moved by a separate intelligence, he contributed to the information about the heavens; but he did not resolve any major problems.[53] Thomas Aquinas (1225-1274), Albertus's student, was also fully aware that the assumptions of the Ptolemaists need not necessarily be true, but that they did save the appearances and that no other known devices were able to do this. He believed one can, in fact one must, use the devices of epicycles and eccentrics, but one might also hold a

---

[51] *Ibid.*, I, 404.

[52] St. BONAVENTURE, *In Secundum Librum Sententiarum Disputata*, 14.2.2 as cited by DUHEM, *To Save the Phenomena*, p. 40.

[53] DUHEM, *Le Système*, III, 326-345; see particularly, p. 339.

contradictory Aristotelian metaphysics. For Aquinas, as for the others, the conflict remained unresolved, though he pointed out that "the apparent movements can, perhaps, be saved by means of some other hypothesis."[54]

During the later Middle Ages, astronomy remained essentially unchanged in most of its generalizations: Ptolemy continued to be the choice of most astronomers — "all the modern astronomers" according to John of Jandun (d. 1328)[55] — but the metaphysical foundations were trying to become Aristotelian. In the meantime, Alfonsine Tables spread out from Spain, more translations were made, astronomical instruments were improved, and the common calculations of astronomy were made by computing devices — the abacus, astrolabe, and a planetary computer. Yet although the 14th century became possessed of better instruments and more observations, there was little theoretical progress. There was definitely popularization: at the end of the century, Chaucer wrote his *Treatise on the Astrolabe* for his son, little Lewis (age 10!) to prepare him for Oxford. Chaucer draws on a compilation of Sacrobosco and Messahala.[56]

But despite popularization in the 14th century, no criticism of the hypotheses on which astronomy was based is successful. It is a subject they were not yet ready to deal with. The celestial physics of Aristotle reigned at the same time his terrestrial physics became increasingly subject to criticism. The scientific revolution had to begin on earth before it could reach the stars. A renaissance took place in the extension of the "impetus" approach to the motion of bodies. This theory which has a long history offers an alternate explanation of the cause of motion than that of Aristotle which required the mover to be in contact with the body it placed in motion. Jean Buridan (d. 1358), rector of the University of Paris in 1328 and again in 1340, a proponent of the impetus theory, was among the first to think of an extension of terrestrial physics to the heavens.[57] He avoided the need of a Mover for the sphere by assuming that God gave the impetus to the heavenly bodies. He was a Ptolemaist, but discusses a version of the system of Heraclides in which the diurnal movement of the stars is attributed to rotation of the earth.

Such discussions evince a freedom of thought that is new. Grant attributes much of this to the condemnation in 1277 by Pope John XXI on the advice of Etienne Tempier, the Bishop of Paris, of 219 propositions drawn from many sources which were interpreted as limiting the power of God.[58] Whether or not this thesis is correct, succeeding philosophers openly

---

[54] St. THOMAS AQUINAS, *De Caelo et Mundo* 2.17, in *Opera Omnia* (Misurgia, New York, 1949), XIX, 120, as cited by DUHEM, *To Save the Phenomena*, p. 42.

[55] JOHN OF JANDUN, *Acutissimæ quæstiones in duodecim libros Metaphysicæ ad Aristoteles et magni Commentatoris intentionem ab eodem exactissime disputatæ*, 12.20. See DUHEM, *To Save the Phenomena*, p. 43.

[56] See F. N. ROBINSON, *Works of Geoffrey Chaucer* (Cambridge, 1957), pp. 867-68. Cf. Derek PRICE, *Equatorie of the Planetis*.

[57] SARTON, *Introduction*, III, 543.

[58] Edward GRANT, *Physical Science in the Middle Ages* (New York, 1971), pp. 27-28.

discussed the hypothetical possitility of such astronomical phenomena as the movement of the earth. Buridan's discussion of a possible rotation of the earth is not unique; it was argued by William of Ockham and Francois de Meyronnes as well.[59] Even St. Thomas had discussed the idea, though he then discarded it, as had many since antiquity. But Buridan's was a sound discussion based on the relativity of motion and indicated that with a different physics the rotation of the earth could well explain all the phenomena. However, Buridan concluded that things are not that way: the earth does not rotate.

Nicole Oresme (ca. 1323-1382), whom Crombie has labeled the anticipator of "the Copernican revolution in astronomy,"[60] wrote a vernacular commentary on Aristotle's *De Cælo et Mundo* entitled *Le Livre du Ciel et du Monde*. Although he supported the Aristotelian earth-centered cosmos in general (though he took exception to the ban on epicycles and eccentrics), nevertheless, he advanced in elaborate terms the possibility of a system in which the earth turns. Through a careful discussion of the relative motion he disproves arguments against the rotation theory (e.g., if the earth moved there would be a great wind; or, if the earth moved an arrow shot straight up into the air would not come straight down), asserting that "it is impossible to demonstrate from any experience at all" that the earth does not rotate.[61] As an empiricist and logician he clearly had at his disposal and understanding all that was necessary for Copernican revolution. All that is lacking is a changed dispositon. He concludes:

> However, everyone maintains, and I think myself, that the heavens do move and not the earth: For God hath established the world which shall not be moved, in spite of contrary reasons because they are clearly not conclusive persuasions.[62]

Oresme is not overly dogmatic; and despite his characteristically medieval love of orderly tradition he does concede the opposite choice as distinctly possible.[63]

The Middle Ages draws toward an end with Ptolemy in the ascendant. It is a qualitative and amended Ptolemy, whose details are not always understood, but whose system was acknowledged as the one to be used, even if physically at odds with Aristotle's physics. The astronomical

---

[59] Marshall CLAGETT, *The Science of Mechanics in the Middle Ages* (Madison, 1959), pp. 584-85. See also G. McCOLLEY, *Isis*, XXVI (1936-37), 392-402. See WILLIAM OF OCKHAM, *Summule in Libros Physicorum*, IV, 19-21; François DE MEYRONNES, in his commentary on LOMBARD's *Sentences* II. dist. 14.*q*.5. Two medieval astronomers who seriously considered the hypothesis of diurnal rotation were Nicholas of Cusa and Celio Calcagnini (1479-1541), though Pliny had long before, without scientific justification, insisted upon the earth's rotation. See G. DUHEM, "François de Meyronnes et la question de la rotation de la terre," *Archivum Franciscarum Historicum*, VI (1915), 23-29.

[60] *Robert Grosseteste*, p. 203.

[61] *Le Livre du Ciel et du Monde*, trans. MENUT and DENOMY (Madison, 1968), p. 521.

[62] *Ibid.*, p. 537.

[63] *Ibid.*, p. 539.

references which permeate Dante's *Inferno* and *Convivio* evidence a Christianized Aristotelian cosmos, but in celestial physics Dante favors Ptolemy. Yet the dispute between physicists and the old astronomers was gradually resolving in the direction of physics, though not the physics of Aristotle; that would change too. With the challenge of Copernicus and the observations of Tycho Brahe, astronomy, like all the arts, would soon move from the realm of idea and metaphor toward the world of measurement and description. But the beginning of this change takes place in the 13th and 14th centuries where "the methodological revolution to which modern science owes its origin" takes place.[64] Curiously enough, the change grows out of theological studies which in their subject have nothing whatsoever to do with astronomy. It grows in ways to which the theologians themselves are completely oblivious. Although Augustine may have been skeptical of the value of astronomy, his general encouragement of rational inquiry into the nature of things which is inherent in his rational theology led in the 12th century, with the revival of Aristotle, to most sophisticated refinements in logical method. The significance to scientific inquiry of the new logic and its mathematical integrity can scarcely be overstressed. As Crombie observes, "The strategic act by which Grosseteste and his thirteenth — and fourteenth — century successors created modern experimental science was to unite the experimental habit of the practical arts with the rationalism of twelfth century philosophy."[65] What is perhaps most curious in the incremental change of disposition towards physical matters is that so many of the new Franciscan tradition of empiricists — Grosseteste, Bacon, Pecham, Middleton, and Duns Scotus, and even Kepler in his way — show strong residual neoplatonic influences. They seem to have wanted to express themselves in the old way in spite of themselves.

---

[64] *Robert Grosseteste*, p. 9.
[65] *Ibid.*, p. 10.

The Concept of God's Absolute Power at Oxford in the Later Fourteenth Century

The concept of God's absolute power has a brief but instructive history in the philosophy of the later Middle Ages. A concept that derives ultimately from the commonplace of God's omnipotence,[1] it is nonetheless a notion which has caused some difficulty among theologians and historians, both medieval and modern. Yet as a useful concept for the development of ideas in moral theology and ideas about God, the *potentia Dei absoluta* enjoyed its fullest bloom in the first half of the fourteenth century. During the second half of the century, the concept is known but used less and less as the decades pass until finally a theologian of consequence, Thomas Netter, writing around 1420, no longer uses the term at all. This essay will attempt to illustrate something of the development of this concept from the late thirteenth through the late fourteenth century, focusing on Oxford philosophers after 1350.

Bishop Etienne Tempier's ill-tempered Condemnation of 1277 cannot accurately be said to have caused any developments in philosophy, but it can be seen as an indicator of the reactions against certain trends in thirteenth-century thinking.[2] These trends were primarily the result of non-Christian additions to Christianity — specifically Aristotle and Averroes to Christian philosophy. In his prefatory remarks Tempier singles out for attention the Averroistic doctrine of the double truth, Andreas Capellanus' tract, *De amore*, an untitled book on geomancy, and several other unspecified books on magic and witchcraft.[3] The confused list of propositions that follows also contains many propositions which can be traced to pagan, as opposed to Christian, sources.

---

[1] For the origins of the concept see J. MIETHKE, *Ockhams Weg zur Sozialphilosophie* (Berlin, 1969), pp. 141 ff.

[2] Tempier's 219 condemned propositions are printed in H. DENIFLE and A. CHATELAIN, eds., *Chartularium Universitatis Parisiensis*, vol. I (Paris, 1889), 543-55.

[3] *Chartularium*, I, 543: "... vera secundum philosophiam, sed non secundum fidem catholicam, quasi sint due contrarie veritates... nigromanticos aut continentes experimenta sortilegiorum, invocationes demonum, sive conjurationes in periculum animarum..."

What many of the 219 propositions have in common is the imposition of some implicit or explicit limit upon God's power. Some propositions openly and clearly impose limits to God's capabilities, such as "That happiness cannot be immediately infused by God" and "That God could not make a greater number of souls" and "That God could not have made primal matter except from a celestial body."[4] Other propositions attribute to nature or to a natural process of causality certain events, thereby apparently removing some of creation from God's control. This tendency can be seen in the following propositions: "That when all the heavenly bodies return to the same point, which will be in 36,000 years, the same occurrences as now exist will return" and "That nothing happens by chance but all things come about by necessity, and that all future events which will be will be of necessity, and those which will not be it is impossible for them to be, and that nothing happens contingently, all things considered" and "That trances and visions happen only through natural causes" and "That fate, which is the disposition of the universe, proceeds from divine providence not immediately but through the mediary of the motion of higher bodies."[5]

We see that the emphasis in all these propositions falls on creation, rather than on the Author of creation. Implicit in them is a view of a God who created the universe as an engineer builds a computer: once he sets it going, he becomes a mere witness to the workings of his creation. His powers to interfere or tamper with the systems he has initiated are severely limited, and in some cases they do not exist at all. This emphasis, which does not characterize especially well the thirteenth century as we know it today, is nonetheless understandable. When one recalls that Aristotle's constant focus lay on the world of palpable phenomena, where the part played by any god was small, it is scarcely surprising that some of this focus should find its way into Christian thought just as it was grappling for the first time with the full corpus of Aristotle's work. When we look back today at the thirteenth century, this shadow of determinism seems hardly so threatening; but if we may judge by Bishop Tempier's Condemnation of 1277 — not to mention his earlier Condemnation of 1270,[6] then perhaps we can sympathize somewhat with a defensive reaction to a perceived threat to the fabric of Christianity. Clearly pagan philosophy is seen to shake the

---

[4] *Chartularium*, I, 545: 22. "Quod felicitas non potest a Deo immitti immediate. 27. Quod Deus non posset facere plures animas in numero. 38. Quod Deus non potuit fecisse primam materiam, nisi mediante corpore celesti."

[5] *Chartularium*, I, 544-54: 6. "Quod redeuntibus corporibus celestibus omnibus in idem punctum, quod fit in xxx sex milibus annorum, redibunt idem effectus, qui sunt modo. 21. Quod nichil fit a casu, sed omnia de necessitate eveniunt, et, quod omnia futura, que erunt, de necessitate erunt, et que non erunt, impossibile est esse, et quod nichil fit contingenter, considerando omnes causes. 33. Quod raptus et visiones non fiunt, nisi per naturam. 195. Quod fatum, quod est dispositio universi, procedit ex providentia divina non immediate, sed mediante motu corporum superiorum."

[6] *Chartularium*, I, 486-87. The editors note on p. 487: "Notum est istas assertiones esse pro magna parte averroisticas."

foundations of revealed religion by stressing nature and natural processes rather than the God of nature and his ways.

One cannot claim that the strategic concept of the absolute power of God was developed with Bishop Tempier's Condemnation as a manifesto, but clearly it was a reaction to a similar perception about the emphases and directions of Christian thought. William of Ockham was not the first to use the concept, but he is one of the first to explain its use clearly. When the subject comes up in his *Quæstiones quodlibetales*, dated in the early 1320's, he takes the time to explain:

> Concerning the first matter I say that God can do certain things according to his ordained power and certain things according to his absolute power. We should not understand this distinction to mean that God really has two powers, one of which is ordained and the other absolute. Because as far as the created universe is concerned there is only one power in God.... Nor should we understand this distinction to mean that God can do some things in an ordered fashion and others in an absolute fashion rather than in an ordered fashion. Because God cannot do anything in an unordered fashion. But the distinction must be understood to mean that 'to be able to do something' is sometimes taken according to the laws established and ordained by God, and God is said to be able to do those things according to his ordained power. 'To be able' may also be taken in another way to mean to be able to do everything that does not involve a contradiction, whether God ordains that he should do this thing or not, because God is able to do many things which he does not will to do.... And this meaning of 'to be able' relates to God's absolute power. Thus the Pope cannot do a given thing because of the law established by him, although absolutely he can do that very thing.[7]

Ockham stresses three points here. First, he makes it clear that God's absolute power is one of an ordered pair: the *potentia ordinata* (essentially, the laws of creation) and the *potentia absoluta*. To consider the one without the other is impossible, for both express aspects of one thing, namely God's power. Second, he points out that God does not do some things *de potentia absoluta* and others *de potentia ordinata*. Thus the distinction cannot be properly used to show how God usually behaves and how he may sometimes behave, for, as Ockham says, God can do nothing outside the order and system he has ordained. Finally, he shows how the distinction is to be understood: namely, as a statement about the nature of God. That statement may be summarized in the following manner: despite the nature of the created universe and the physical and biological laws by which nature takes

---

[7] Circa primum dico quod quædam deus potest facere de potentia ordinata. et quædam de potentia absoluta. Hæc distinctio non est sic intelligenda quod in deo realiter sint duæ potentiæ quarum una sit ordinata. alia absoluta. quia unica est potentia in deo ad extra quæ omni modo est ipse deus. Nec sic est intelligenda quod aliquæ potest deus ordinate facere. et alia potest absolute et non ordinate. quia deus nihil potest facere inordinate. Sed est sic intelligenda quod posse aliquid aliquando accipitur secundum leges ordinatas et institutas a deo et illa deus dicitur posse facere de potentia ordinata. Aliter accipitur posse pro posse facere omne illud quod non includit contradictionem fieri. sive deus ordinavit se hoc facturum sive non. quia deus multa potest facere quæ non vult facere. Secundum magistrum libro I sententiarum distinctione 43. Et illa dicitur posse de potentia absoluta. Sicut papa non potest aliquid secundum iuris statuta ab eo quæ tamen absolute potest." WILLIAM OF OCKHAM, *Quodlibeta septem* (Strasburg, 1491), VI, q. 1 (f. 91ʳ).

its course, God retains the power to do anything he pleases to do, except for a contradiction such as an irresistable force and an immovable object. Thus God remains capable of doing many things which he does not do, because he has voluntarily limited himself to act only *de potentia ordinata*.

Ockham offers this explanation in considering the question whether a man can be saved without grace.[8] The standard orthodox answer to this question is categorically negative — salvation and God's grace are so intimately linked that any other answer would fly in the face of elementary Christian doctrine. However Ockham offers one explanation of how a man might be saved without grace. He suggests that because of his absolute power God is able to dispense with secondary causes and to bring about the same results directly. Since grace is a secondary cause, it can be dispensed with and God can accept a given man directly into heaven.[9] He discusses this at some length and then adds the following:

> Second, I say that no man ever will be or can be saved, nor will he ever choose or be able to choose a meritorious act without grace, according to the laws ordained by God. And this I believe because of holy scripture and the sayings of the saints.[10]

Thus he provides a first class illustration of his explanation of the two powers: God could by means of his absolute power accept a man into heaven without first conferring grace upon him, but he will not in fact do so because he has ordained laws decreeing that salvation comes through grace alone.

Some twenty years after Ockham had written his explanation in his *Quæstiones quodlibetales*, Gregory of Rimini, commenting on the *Sentences* at Paris, offered a similar formula. Although somewhat longer than Ockham's, Gregory's theory clearly derives from and in places even echoes the work of his older contemporary:

> For God to be able to do this or that can be understood in two ways: one way according to his ordained power and another way according to his absolute power. Not that these are two powers in God, one ordained and the other absolute, nor do the school philosophers intend this meaning, but 'to be able de potentia ordinata' is correctly said to mean that, given the eternal law and the systematic ordering of things which is nothing other than the will of God by which he eternally wills, God can cause this or that or such or such to exist. However, 'to be able de potentia absoluta' is said to mean that which God can simply and absolutely do. On the other hand it is not said that de potentia ordinata God is incapable, given the current law and the system of order that now exists. But it is said de potentia absoluta that God is incapable of doing what simply and absolutely cannot be done. It is obvious that simply and absolutely and without

---

[8] "Utrum homo potest salvari sine caritate creata." *Ibid*.

[9] "Quidquid deus potest facere mediante secunda causa in genere causæ efficientis vel finis. potest immediate per se. sed caritas creata si sit causa sive efficiens sive dispositiva disponens ad vitam æternam erit causa secunda efficiens vel finis. ergo sine ea deus potest dare alicui vitam æternam..." *Ibid*.

[10] "Secundo dico quod nunquam salvabitur homo nec salvari poterit. nec unquam eliciet nec elicere poterit actum meritorium secundum leges a deo ordinatas sine gratia creata. Et hoc teneo propter scripturam sacram et dicta sanctorum." *Ibid*.

contradiction God is capable of many things which he does not do, given the current law and the will with which he wills that he should do something. And thus some things, although they are simply possible, are incompossible with the present divine order.... However, these things are only incompossible because that divine ordering is not necessary. That is, God need not have ordered creation as he did — indeed, it is possible for him to have ordained and willed the opposite; therefore, that which is only impossible given the system of ordering the universe (that is, it is incompossible to that order) is not absolutely impossible but possible, and simply speaking God can do it.[11]

Gregory's formulation restates Ockham's three points — that the two concepts form an ordered pair, that God does not behave in a manner foreign to the order he has created, and that the distinction is really a means of asserting the free and undetermined nature of God's will. However, Gregory also makes another point that is cloudier in Ockham, namely that the distinction has mainly to do with the range of possibility available to God before creation. Where the suspension points indicate an omission in the text, Gregory gives the example of Christ: Christ, he says, need not have been incarnate and need not have died; but, he adds, this could not be, given the ordering of things which God eternally maintains and which decreed that man should be redeemed by means of Christ's death.[12] That is to say, God might have decreed that man's salvation should be accomplished in some other way or that it might not be accomplished at all, but he did not. So the option to decree otherwise no longer exists *de potentia ordinata*, although it may be contemplated *de potentia absoluta*.

Gregory continues with a further explanation of the respectability of the distinction between God's two powers. An earlier distinction, he says,

---

[11] "...Deum posse hoc vel illud facere potest intelligi dupliciter: uno modo secundum potentiam ordinatam, et alio modo secundum potentiam absolutam. Non quod in Deo sint duæ potentiæ, una ordinata et alia absoluta, nec hoc volunt significare doctores, sed illud dicitur ad intellectum recte intelligentium posse de potentia ordinata quod potest stante sua ordinatione et lege æterna quæ non est aliud quam eius voluntas qua æternaliter voluit hæc vel illa et tale vel tale esse futurum. Illud autem dicitur posse de potentia absoluta quod simpliciter et absolute potest. Econtra, illud non dicitur posse de potentia ordinata quod non potest stante lege et ordinatione sua quæ nunc est; illud vero non posse de potentia absoluta quod simpliciter et absolute non potest. Patet autem quod simpliciter et absolute sine suppositione contradictionis Deus multa potest quæ non potest stante eius lege et voluntate qua voluit sic se facturum. Et hoc ideo, quia illa etsi sint simpliciter possibilia, sunt tamen incompossibilia ordinationi divinæ...Quamvis autem ista sunt incompossibilia quia tamen illa ordinatio non est necessaria, id est, non est necessarium Deum sic ordinasse, quinimmo possibile est ipsum ordinasse et voluisse oppositum; ideo illud quod solum est impossibile ex suppositione ordinationis, utpote ei incompossibile non est absolute impossibile sed possibile, et simpliciter loquendo illud Deus potest facere." GREGORY OF RIMINI, *Super Primum et Secundum Sententiarum* (Venice, 1522, reprint 1955), 162ᵛ P - 163ʳ A. I follow the punctuation given by William J. COURTENAY, "John of Mirecourt and Gregory of Rimini on Whether God Can Undo the Past," *Recherches de théologie ancienne et médiévale*, 39 (1972), 224-56 and 40 (1973), 147-74.The passage from Gregory appears in 40 (1973), 158-59, fn. 129.

[12] V.g.: "constat quod simpliciter loquendo Christus potuit non incarnari et non mori: iuxta verbum eius. potestatem habeo ponendi animam et iterum. oblatus est quia voluit. et tamen istud non poterat stante ordinatione sua qua æternaliter proposuit per suam mortem redimere genus humanum. sunt enim hæc incompossibilia. deus proposuit se moriturum et deus non morietur: referendo ad idem tempus." GREGORY OF RIMINI, *loc. cit*.

agrees substantially with that between God's ordained and his absolute power. This earlier distinction, for which he cites Anselm as his authority, lies between God's justice and his power. Many things that God can do by means of his power he will not do because of the demands of justice.[13] Gregory's attempt to provide a pedigree for the distinction between God's two powers suggests that perhaps in the twenty years since Ockham's formulation such apologetics had become necessary. Indeed, William Courtenay has shown at some length how Gregory, essentially a conservative Augustinian, felt that God *de potentia absoluta* could cause a past event not to have happened, while John of Mirecourt, writing only three years after Gregory, argued that even *de potentia absoluta* God was unable to rewrite the past.[14] Perhaps by the 1340's there was a sufficient lapse of time that theologians no longer felt any need to defend God against the determinism that Bishop Tempier feared, and for that reason it was not necessary to apply so rigorously the distinction between the two powers. Or perhaps there were other reasons as well, such as Nicholas of Autrecourt's apparent need for certainty.[15] In any event Gregory both explains and defends the distinction at greater length than Ockham.

In the twenty years between Ockham's explanation in the 1320's and Gregory of Rimini's in the 1340's, many philosophers used the distinction between God's absolute and his ordained power. Moreover, although it is not always evident from the quotations given by modern historians, the bulk of these thinkers used the distinction correctly.[16] It is true that a host of problems can be let loose through its misuse. For example, if one should by some error give the impression that God might actually use his absolute power on some unknown and unforewarned day, the concept of a whimsical, arbitrary, untrustworthy God would not be far to seek. By the same token a fearful sort of voluntarism could arise from too great an emphasis on God's actually using his absolute power. In such ways one can see that a God of tyrannical and capricious proportions might seize men's minds, and the fabric of Christian thought could be torn as badly by the remedy to pagan determinism as by pagan determinism itself. But in the event this is not what happened. Philosophers of the first half of the fourteenth century managed the concept adroitly, and it is only after the Black Death that we find some alterations in thinking at Oxford.

During the second half of the fourteenth century, at least among those philosophers I have examined, there is a tendency to avoid relying on the

---

[13] "Huic distinctioni concordat alia antiqua qua dictum est: quod quædam deus non potest de iusticia quæ potest de potentia. Cum enim nihil sit iustum: nisi quod est conforme voluntati divinæ: quæ est prima et summa lex iusticiæ: iuxta illud Anselmus...." *Ibid*.

[14] COURTENAY, "John of Mirecourt and Gregory of Rimini."

[15] COURTENAY, "John of Mirecourt," 39 (1972), 236, fn. 27, cites the case of Nicholas of Autrecourt.

[16] *Ibid*. In this footnote Courtenay presents his own short and clear definition of God's absolute power. He adds, "No thirteenth or fourteenth century theologian, with whom I am familiar, rejected the distinction for reasons of a-temporality or determinism, nor did they depart from the common usage,...."

distinction between God's two powers, and this shades into a misunderstanding of it. In the early fifteenth century Thomas Netter no longer even uses the terms *potentia absoluta* or *potentia ordinata*, and he gives no indication that he understands their meaning or usefulness.

MS. Oriel College 15 contains, along with the *Sentences* commentaries of Richard FitzRalph and Robert Holcot, some twelve questions of Nicholas Aston, who read the *Sentences* at Oxford in the mid-1350's.[17] These questions, all that has been identified of Aston's work to the present time, deal with a number of matters which a few years earlier might have summoned forth a philosopher's subtle use of God's absolute power. Aston declines the summons. For example, the third question asks whether the efficacy of a secondary cause is necessarily required for any action,[18] a question whose negative answer Ockham assumes as a commonplace in discussing the *potentia absoluta*.[19] Aston deals with the question at some length without ever mentioning the *potentia absoluta*. In fact in a tract occupying twelve large folios, he mentions the concept only once in passing, and on a second occasion when he might have mentioned it he explains God's power in some detail avoiding completely any mention of God's absolute power. This second instance arises in dealing with question 11, whether a proposition signifying the present non-existence of God involves a contradiction.[20] In the course of his discussion Aston deals briefly with divine power in such a way as to cause his reader to suspect that he is arguing silently against the idea of God's absolute power. Since divine power, he says, is simply infinite (because for another power to be greater than a power that is simply infinite includes a contradiction, as if there were a body greater than a simply infinite body), then divine power is capable absolutely in every positive thing which does not include a formal contradiction.[21] In his parenthetical denial that there can be another power greater than infinite power, one can see Aston avoiding any mention of God's absolute power, though there can be little doubt that he means just that when he says "another" power.

Even in dealing with the problem of whether a past event is necessarily a past event, a problem where both Gregory of Rimini and John of Mirecourt rely heavily on God's two powers,[22] Aston avoids the issue

---

[17] MS. Oriel College 15, ff. 210va - 222rb.

[18] "Utrum ad omnem actionem causæ secundæ efficiencia causæ primæ necessario requiritur." f. 213ra.

[19] See above, p. 213.

[20] "Utrum alia propositio significans præsente deum non esse contradictionem includit." f. 220vb.

[21] "... sed nunc de facto divina potentia est tanta quanta possibile est quod alia sit. Cum ipsa sit infinita simpliciter (quia quod alia potentia esse maior quam potentia simpliciter infinita contradictionem includit, sicut si esset aliquod corpus maius quam corpus infinitum simpliciter) ergo divina potentia potest in omne positivum absoluter quod formalem contradictionem non includit." f. 221vb.

[22] See COURTENAY, article cited.

altogether, and it is instructive to see how he does so. His method of proceeding is to pose the question positively, that every past event is necessarily a past event, and then to argue against it.[23] He gives twelve arguments to show that a past event is not necessary but rather derives from the divine will freely willing that it be a past event. He draws a brief conclusion from these twelve arguments and then poses ten arguments *ad oppositum* to show that the past is necessarily the past. Then there follows an *ad quœstionem* with its subsections, in which Aston gives his own opinion on the problem. His opinion is an extension of the conclusion to the twelve *quod non* arguments, namely that every past event is a past event because the divine will, acting freely, wills it to be a past event. Aston will not even allow that God, as beginner of temporal events, sets in motion a process which carries its own necessity with it. For him it is God alone who freely wills the past to be the past.[24] Thus necessity is ruled out, and God retains his freedom. Aston concludes by giving ten refutations to the ten arguments *sed contra*.

What is interesting about this handling of the question is that Aston seems to be just as eager as Ockham and and Gregory of Rimini to defend God's freedom, but by failing to distinguish the two powers of God he lays the way open for God to behave arbitrarily. What Aston affirms is that a given past event is such because God freely wills it to be such, but he seems not to notice that implicit in his argument is the fact that God might will it to be other. Because the question is designed to set necessity and God's free will in opposition to one another, and because he emphasizes primarily the impossibility of any necessity moving God to act, Aston seems to overlook the implication that if God freely wills the past then he may will a past event not to have taken place.

This is precisely the sort of problem that the distinction of God's two powers was designed to deal with. Gregory of Rimini argued on behalf of God's freedom that *de potentia absoluta* he could cause a past event not to have happened.[25] To be sure since he deals with his creation only *de potentia ordinata*, God will not cause a past event not to have happened —

---

[23] "Utrum omne præteritum necessario sit præteritum." f. 214vb.

[24] "...intelligo articulum sic: quod omne præteritum absolutum est præteritum a primo principio actualiter volente libere contradictione illud esse præteritum, quia si aliquod ⟨præteritum⟩ [MS. aliquod] absolutum esset præteritum et non a deo, sequitur ipsum fuisse et non fuisse. Ideo illo modo intelligendo articulum negatur ipsum tanquam falsum... ex hoc quod A est præsens semper erit verum in futuro quod A est præteritum; quia semper erit verum quod A fuit præsens, quare semper erit verum quod A est præteritum. Sed non ex hoc quod A est præsens sequitur quod deus volet A esse præteritum. Ergo A esse præteritum non dependet a voluntate divina actualiter volente illud esse præteritum, et consimiliter arguitur de quolibet absoluto præterito... Dico quod instantiæ illæ non procedunt, quia quod deus voluit esse præsens iam vult esse præteritum et econtra eadem volutione a parte dei sicut eadem volutione qua deus vult antechristum esse nunc et vult antechristum fore. Ideo dico quod si deus habeat actum circa obiectum aliquod semper voluit actum ut si vult me esse semper volet me fuisse." f. 215rb.

[25] COURTENAY, article cited.

but he does retain the freedom to do so. John of Mirecourt argued on behalf of the integrity of creation that even *de potentia absoluta* God could not cause a past event not to have happened.[26] He might have declined to create the universe at all, but having done so, John argued, he established some things, like time, which carry a necessity of their own with which God cannot tamper, even *de potentia absoluta*. It should be noted that both Gregory and John give equal and just measure to God and to the laws of the created universe. But by ignoring the distinction between God's two powers, Nicholas Aston has introduced a note of uncertainty about God, a possibility of a whimsical and arbitrary deity, upon whose will the integrity of the past is wholly dependent.

It is difficult to say why Aston chooses not to use a distinction which he evidently knows. Nor can one easily believe that anything in these twelve questions will tell us why he so chooses. If his full commentary on the *Sentences* is ever recovered, we may find some explanation there. But in the meantime, what should be noted is that Aston's unwillingness to use the distinction seems to be a harbinger of philosophical attitudes for the remainder of the century.

Active at Oxford from the mid-1350's to the early 1370's, John Wyclif was sufficiently convinced of God's inability to annihilate any substance or accident in the material world that his notion of God's power seems idiosyncratic. On one occasion he says that God cannot annihilate any substance without annihilating the whole created universe, and he cannot annihilate that.[27] In the same tract he rules out the possibility of God's annihilating any created thing on the grounds that annihilation is an evil act, of which God is incapable.[28] Again in response to the proposition that God's omnipotence necessarily includes his ability to annihilate, Wyclif responds that God's goodness and justice preclude his capacity to annihilate.[29] He goes as far as to concede that FitzRalph may be right in saying that God may annihilate if he wishes to do so, but what this means to him is not that God may retain an absolute power but rather that his ways are simply beyond human understanding.[30]

---

[26] COURTENAY, article cited.

[27] "Item deus non posset adnichilare substantiam aliquam, nisi adnichilet totam universitatem creatam; set illam non potest adnichilare: igitur nichil penitus adnichilare..." JOHANNIS WYCLIF, *De ente librorum duorum*, ed. Michæl Henry DZIEWICKI (London, 1909), p. 289.

[28] "Deus enim est illius naturæ quod non potest malum facere, dampnificando creaturam nisi occasione data, set scit benefacere ex seipso sine occasione data ex parte creaturæ: ideo nescit adnichilare, licet sciat creare..." *Ibid.*, p. 308.

[29] "...si deus sit bonus et iustus, tunc non est adnichilativus, quia adnihilacio est incompossibilis illi." *Ibid.*, p. 314.

[30] "Set satis est pro omnipotencia sua, ut exponit dominus Armakanus, quod potest adnichilare, si voluerit; et sic intelligendum est illud dictum Sophar, Job 11: Si subverteret omnia vel in unum coartaverit, quis contradicet ei... aut quis dicere potest, Cur ita facis? Quasi diceret: nemo potest eum racionabiliter increpare quicquid fecerit. Verumptamen ordinavit leges et consequentias eternas cum quibus non potest dispensare, cum ex eius immensitate bonitatis, et sapiencie sint incorrigibiles." *Ibid.*, p. 314.

Given this unwillingness to accept God's ability to annihilate, it is hardly surprising that Wyclif takes a restricted view of the distinction between God's powers. Moreover, although he gives evidence in his *De potentia Dei productiva ad extra*, that he has some understanding of the distinction, he rarely uses it in his philosophical and theological discussions. In this work he defines God's absolute power as that which extends to the possible in intelligible being, whereas his ordained power extends to the possible in actual being in time.[31] In other words for Wyclif the absolute power of God is confined to realms of thought alone and has little to do with God's retaining any freedom to do other than he has done. He notes that both Scotus and Bradwardine had maintained that God could cause something to exist and not to exist at the same time, but he relies on Henry of Ghent who maintained that God cannot do what cannot be done.[32]

What Henry of Ghent maintains is no different from what Ockham maintains: not even *de potentia absoluta* can God create simultaneously the immovable object and the irresistible force. But apparently Wyclif's refusal to allow God the power of annihilation, which his absolute power permits, has brought him to a point where he cannot consider the concept of God's absolute power as a responsible tool for the analysis of various theological and philosophical problems. For example, in arguing about the reality of points on the continuum in the *De logica*, Wyclif uses the idea of God's absolute power to prove his point. No theologian would deny, he says, that God *de potentia absoluta* can make a pointed (punctalem) substance and by annihilating every other thing except that, allow to remain a pointedness (punctualitas), or a point which is a substance. Thus, he concludes, a point can exist.[33] Even though he violates his own rule about admitting God's

---

[31] "Potentia absoluta est que terminatur ad possibilia in esse intelligibili et absolute possibili; potentia autem ordinata est que terminatur ad possibilia secundum suum esse existere pro alico tempore..." MS. Trinity College Cambridge B. 16. 2, ff. 123vb - 124ra. This manuscript contains the *De potentia Dei productiva ad extra*, ff. 123^r - 141^r. It has never been edited in its entirety, though Dziewicki has printed ff. 135rb - 138vb in his edition of WYCLIF'S *De ente, op. cit.*, pp. 287-315. I quote from J.A. ROBSON, *Wyclif and the Oxford Schools* (Cambridge, 1960), p. 184.

[32] "...doctores qui diffuse discutiunt si iam deus non potest facere illud simul esse et non esse, quia illud non potest fieri et econtra... quam materiam tractat doctor subtilis, super primo sententiarum, dist. q. et doctor profundus, libro primo, cap. 13. Doctor autem solempnis, Quodlibet suo 6°, qu. 3^a dicit quod omne impossibile ideo est impossibile quia deus non potest illud facere; et Quodl. 8°, q. 3^a dicit quod deus non potest tale facere quod illud non potest fieri." MS. cit., f. 124rb, quoted in Robson, p. 184, fn. 3.

[33] "Similiter, ut credo, nullus theologus negaret quin deus de potentia absoluta potest facere substantiam punctalem, vel condensando, vel noviter causando, vel tertio faciendo spiritum esse in situ punctali et annichilando omnem aliam creaturam preter talem spiritum servatum immotum; et tunc patet quod punctualitas vel punctus, que est substancia huiusmodi *esse* punctalis, est actus positivus in illa substancia, sive sit separabile sive inseparabile." JOHN WYCLIF, *Tractatus de logica*, ed. Michæl Henry DZIEWICKI, 3 vols. (London, 1893, 1896, and 1899), III, pp. 33-34. For fourteenth century discussions on the continuum, see John E. MURDOCH and Edward A. SYNAN, "Two Questions on the Continuum: Walter Chatton (?), O.F.M. and Adam Wodeham, O.F.M.," *Franciscan Studies*, 26 (1966), 212-88; V.P. ZOUBOV, "Walter Catton, Gérard d'Odon et Nicolas Bonet," *Physis*, 1 (1959), 261-78; Wolfgang BREIDERT, *Das aristotelische Kontinuum in der Scholastik*, Beiträge zur Geschichte der Philosophie und Theologie des Mittelalters, N.F. 1 (Münster i. W., 1970).

capacity to annihilate, Wyclif still blurs the distinction between the two powers, such that God's limitless capacities *de potentia absoluta* are called upon to prove the existence of a thing which can only exist in the created world.

Wyclif's failure to understand the nature of God's two powers may in part be the result of his conviction that God cannot annihilate any created thing. But it may also be part of a larger intellectual phenomenon of the later fourteenth century. One may make a hypothetical reconstruction of events: Nicholas Aston, studying in the 1350's, might have been in a position to hear a good lecturer discuss the distinction. Thus he might have known about the two powers of God but decided, for reasons of his own, to argue his questions without the help of this concept. Those who heard Nicholas Aston lecture would have realized what he was doing only if they took the trouble themselves to read Ockham or Adam Wodeham or Robert Holcot or someone from the recent past who had dealt with the issue. With Wyclif in the 1360's we find a man with a somewhat eccentric view of the distinction and apparently no need to correct it. Another document from the late 1370's or early 1380's, Stephen Patryngton's *Repertorium Argumentorum*,[34] provides additional evidence that philosophers were losing track of the precision and usefulness of the distinction between God's two powers.

Patryngton, a Yorkshire Carmelite with a distinguished career in his order, first appears in Oxford records in 1366. He received his doctorate in 1389.[35] While a student he compiled his *Repertorium*, a collection of over 1200 questions debated by masters and students during his stay at Oxford. Some of the questions are reported with full discussion, but the majority are simply stated, together with a very brief indication of how they may be answered. The questions seem not to be original with Patryngton but rather to have been taken down by him while listening to the lectures of others. Unfortunately, he does not name the vast bulk of those whose questions he quotes, but two philosophers who are named, Richard of Ferebrigus and John Wyclif, lead me to conclude that the work was compiled at least as late as the 1370's and probably, because of the anti-Wyclif stance, the late 70's or early 80's.[36] One of the manuscripts is dated 1393 by its scribe, a Florentine Franciscan studying at Oxford,[37] and we may therefore conclude that the questions were still current at that time.

---

[34] There are three manuscripts of the *Repertorium Argumentorum*. St. John's College Cambridge D. 28 (James 103); Venice, Biblioteca Nazionale San Marco fondo antiquo 2. 280; and Florence, Biblioteca Laurenziana, Plut. XVII, sin. cod. x. I quote from the Florence manuscript.

[35] A.B. EMDEN, *A Biographical Register of the University of Oxford to 1500*, 3 vols. (Oxford, 1957-59), s. v. Patryngton.

[36] For Richard of Ferebrigus see EMDEN, *Biographical Register*, s.v. Feribrigge.

[37] "Explicit compilatio quædam diversorum argumentorum recollectorum a diversis doctoribus in Universitate Oxoniæ, ordinata satis pulcre per Reverendum Fratrem [name omitted, blank in ms.] Sacræ Theologiæ Magistrum eiusdem Universitatis de Ordine Carmelitarum, scripta per me Fratrem I. Fey de Florentia Ordinis Fratrum Minorum in Conventu Oxoniæ anno domini 1393, die sequenti festum 40 martyrum ad laudem domini nostri Jesu Christi. Amen. Amen." f. 113ᵛ.

In three places God's absolute power is examined in detail, and in all three the question raised is similar: that whatever God can accomplish by means of his absolute power he can also accomplish by means of his ordained power. The first of these, which comes about a quarter of the way into the *Repertorium*, fails badly to convey its point because of a confusion of terms. Instead of contrasting the present dispensation of things *de potentia ordinata* with what might have been *de potentia absoluta*, the question speaks only of the law now current, that is God's ordained power, and contrasts this with itself.[38] The question is mercifully brief and unintelligible as well, except by reference to the other two questions.

The second of the three questions seems to pose the issue most clearly: that everything possible through God's absolute power is possible through his ordained power or through the law now current.[39] The discussion hinges upon an opposition: either the law now current has been God's intent from eternity or else we open the door to a host of arbitrary events, such as the damnation of Christ's humanity and the salvation of Lucifer, which would also have to be seen as God's intent from eternity. For if some other law were now in effect, then there would have to be some other truth than what we now have. This situation cannot be admitted because it is not the case. And thus, he concludes, we must hold onto the present law according to common sense and to the manner of scholastic discourse.[40] The third question, that whatever God can preordain by means of his absolute power he can also preordain by means of his ordained power,[41] is merely an extension of the second. It takes as its example the salvation of Lucifer and argues that since all God's decisions endure for eternity, then if God can decree by his absolute power the salvation of Lucifer, he can do the same by means of his ordained power.[42]

---

[38] 22. B. 10: "Quod de lege sive stante lege iam currente multa possunt fieri de ipsa lege sive ipsa lege stante arguitur. Nam de lege ista distinctione deus potest dimittere naturam assumptam et illam dampnare et multa alia huiusmodi quæ non potest facere de ipsa lege, igitur etc." f. 29ᵛ.

[39] 38. A. 1: "Quod omne possibile de potentia dei absoluta est possibile de potentia dei ordinata sive de lege currente iam arguitur." f. 36ᵛ.

[40] "Nam vel lex currens iam est ordinatio dei præsens, ut volunt doctores, et tunc sequitur, signato quocumque effectuali signali, sic erit; igitur de præsenti ordinatio dei sic erit sive de lege iam currente sequitur enim materia; vel humanitas christi dampnabitur igitur in præsenti et ab æterno deus præordinat illam dampnandam, et lucifer salvabitur. Igitur deus in præsenti sicut ab æterno præordinat illum salvandum, et ita de quocumque signato... Si alia lex iam currens non sit deo lex æterna et veritas increata seu potentia, tunc erit aliqua veritas creata vel igitur alia quam propositio vel complexum quo non potest dari cum nulla sit talis, et tunc vel naturaliter significans quod maxime videtur tenendum secundum communem sensum et modum loquendum scolaris..." f. 36ᵛ.

[41] 61. A. 2: "Quod quicquid potest deus præordinare de potentia absoluta potest et de potentia ordinata arguitur." f. 60ᵛ.

[42] "Nam de potentia dei ordinata iste demon potest prædestinari sicut salvari, ergo a pari etc. Antecedens arguitur: quia potentia ordinata nihil aliud dicit quam ordinationem dei; sed de æterna ordinatione dei iste Sathan sive Lucifer potest salvari; ergo de potentia dei ordinata. Minor arguitur: nam ista consequentia est necessaria: 'iste salvabitur ergo deus ab æterno

In other words what Patryngton reports is not merely an unwillingness to make a distinction between God's two powers, as we saw in Nicholas Aston's case, but rather an attempt to subsume the absolute in the ordained power. This attempt seems unrelated, at least as far as the argument goes, to Wyclif's reluctance to admit the possibility of God's annihilating something. It seems rather to hinge on a loss of understanding about the usefulness of making the distinction at all. What seems to dominate in Patryngton's report is a need to find in God a constancy which from eternity has been the same and will continue to be the same until Doomsday and beyond. The idea of a hypothetical power which might allow God to change his mind or the idea of God before creation confronting a range of possibilities — this concept seems foreign to the imagination of those Patryngton records. They seem rather to quail at the prospect of any dispensation different from the present one and so attempt to transform God's absolute into his ordained power. Moreover, over and over again in the *Repertorium* one finds questions that could be answered very well by reference to the two powers of God, but they are invariably handled without reference to the distinction.[43] In other words Patryngton testifies to a dead idea. Like a modern atomic physicist presented with a proposition from Newton, Patryngton's lecturers seem to realize that the concept of God's two powers is somehow important enough to mention, but they give no evidence that they understand it as anything more than a curiosity to be brought into line with current doctrine.

It is regularly with respect to basic doctrines, such as of creation, or the eucharist, that philosphical positions in the Middle Ages are made most clear. William Woodford, O.F.M., writing against Wyclif in the early 1380's, thus confirms this loss of understanding of the *potentia absoluta* in his *De sacramento altaris*.[44] Now Woodford was a contemporary of Wyclif at Oxford, perhaps even his *socius* when the two were reading the

---

præordinavit eum salvandum;' sed antecedens est possibile absolute, ergo consequens est possibile de eadem potentia; ergo de potentia dei absoluta possibile est quod deus ab æterno præordinavit istum ad beatitudinem; ergo possibile est de æterna dei ordinatione istum salvari." f. 60ᵛ.

[43] For example, question 8. B. 4: "Quod deus potest suplere vicem causæ materialis et vicem causæ formalis arguitur (f. 16ʳ). 24. A. 6: "Quod deus non possit producere creaturam aliquam quæ non sit magis imperfecta quam perfecta arguitur" (f. 31ʳ). 32. A. 10: "Quod deus non potest facere materiam sine forma" (f. 32ʳ). 38. B. 4: "Quod deus potest punire aliquem sine peccato sibi imputabili præmio durative arguitur" (f. 37ʳ). 51. B. 1: "Quod deus non potest revocare seu recreare aliquod tempus vel instans præteritum vel anticipare futurum arguitur" (f. 49ʳ). 88. B. 4: "Quod omne possibile est ei naturaliter possibile arguitur quia per potentiam suam naturalem quia per potentiam suam obbedietialem quam est omnis creaturæ ita naturalis ut deus non possit eam tollere manente natura nec creare sine illa" (f. 88ᵛ). 88. B. 4. is the entire article.

[44] Manuscripts of WOODFORD's *De sacramento altaris* are the following: MS. Bodley 703, MS. Cambridge University Library Additional 3571, MS. British Library Harleian 31, MS. British Library Harleian 42, MS. British Library Royal 7. B. iii, MS. St. John's College Oxford 144, MS. Exeter College Oxford 7. I quote from MS. Bodley 703.

Sentences.[45] Although a noteworthy and in many ways distinguished Franciscan, he was also a less imaginative and more orthodox man than Wyclif, and his *De sacramento altaris*, which includes a fairly substantial attack on Wyclif's eucharistic teachings, reveals some of Woodford's inadequacies.

The *De sacramento altaris* is divided into 72 sections, called *dubia*, and in the entire tract Woodford mentions God's absolute power only once, in Dubium 63. The topic under consideration in the *dubium* is whether there is in the eucharist some real substance in which the accidents of bread and wine may subsist,[46] and Woodford treats the topic at considerable length, dividing his answer into twenty subsections which he calls *veritates*. In the eighteenth veritas, almost at the end of his discussion of the question, he asserts — not for the first time — that the substance of bread ceases to exist in the process of transubstantiation. This time, however, he adds that this ceasing to exist occurs *de communi lege*, or as earlier philosophers would have said *de potentia ordinata*. Then he adds that the actual transformation into the body of Christ may be *de potentia absoluta*.[47] As his authority for this view he cites the fourth veritas of this dubium, where he cited the opinions of Duns Scotus, Durandus, and many other doctors to the effect that it may be possible for some of the substance of bread to remain after the consecration, simultaneously with the body of Christ.[48] Needless to say, this citation does not in any way substantiate his reliance on God's absolute power.

In fact it seems to me that in this instance we have a clear case of the misuse of the concept of God's absolute power, at least as Ockham had defined the idea. From Ockham we learn that the concept is not intended to explain how God sometimes behaves, where his customary mode of behavior is explained through his ordained power. As Ockham says, God can do nothing that is not ordained. Not even miracles are to be accounted for *de potentia absoluta*, for that notion is intended solely to describe the

---

[45] The following passage seems to testify to a socius relationship between the two men: "habuit [Wyclif] enim de consuetudine scribere responsiones ad argumenta per me sibi facta in quaternio quem sibi misi cum argumentis et remittere quaternium." f. 163[r].

[46] "Si in loco sacramenti sit alia substantia subiectans realiter accidentia sacramentalia." f. 157[v].

[47] "...in transubstantione panis in corpus christi panis substantia desinit esse quantum est de commune lege. Posset tamen de dei potentia absoluta panis transubstantiari in corpus christi et remanere in esse." f. 163[r].

[48] "Quarta veritas est quod possibile est panis substantiam simul remanere post consecrationem cum vero corpore christi. Hanc tenet doctor subtilis super quartum, durandus super quartum, et multi doctores. Et hanc ostendo primo quia possibile est panem assumptum a christo mediante corpore suo et sic panem esse corpus christi sicut christus est nunc homo. Secondo quia possibile est deum reproducere panem post eius conversionem in corpus christi in eodem loco quo prius sub aliis accidentibus similibus. Tertio quia possibile est deum convertere lapidem vel lignum in panem illum pro mensura pro qua panis ille convertitur in corpus christi, secumdum quod alias declaravi. Quarto quia possibile est panem esse multipliciter et in eodem loco et in diversis locis et sic simul remanere in esse et aliud converti." f. 158[v].

freedom God retains, without regard to his creation. It is not intended to describe any event within creation, for within the created world God voluntarily operates only through his ordained power.

It is true that Ockham, in his *De sacramento altaris*, attributes transubstantiation to divine power, but he is careful to avoid mentioning God's absolute power.[49] Moreover, he uses the notion of divine power or omnipotence only to deal with the problem of a substance — that is the bread — which has prior existence and no posterior existence and to discuss the issue of a substance's existing without accidents.[50] In discussing the eucharist in his commentary on the *Sentences*, he does not mention God's power,[51] and even in the *De sacramento altaris* he makes it clear that there is a mystery here which is not wholly intelligible. With Woodford, however, we face an intellect of considerably less perspicacity, and his use of God's absolute power seems to come as a last resort in his process of reasoning. He uses the concept to account for an event within creation, thus drawing upon a power that functions, if it can be said to function at all, only outside creation. At that point in his discourse he seems to have exhausted the rational approaches to the problem and yet not to have solved it satisfactorily. Rather than admit with Ockham that some aspects of the mystery remain mysterious, he has desperate resort to a concept that evidently he does not understand.

Thus a concept, developed in the early fourteenth century as a means of demonstrating God's limitless freedom, and incidently of demonstrating the extent of his grace in creating as he in fact created, had at Oxford by the middle of the century lost its efficacy and by the end of the century become misunderstood. Nicholas Aston argues around the problem, as if he knew of the existence of the *potentia absoluta* but was unwilling to use it. Because of his reluctance to admit God's ability to annihilate, Wyclif too puts a curious construction upon the *potentia absoluta* and its relation to the *potentia ordinata*. Stephen Patryngton reports a confused distinction between the two powers, reflecting an apparent unwillingness among Oxford theologians to admit the validity of God's absolute power and their need to see that power transformed into the more manageable ordained power. William Woodford simply uses the concept wrongly, without apparently realizing that God's *potentia absoluta* was never intended as a means of explaining unusual events in this world. Although he lies somewhat beyond the historical scope of this study, it is nonetheless instructive to note that Thomas Netter, writing in the early 1420's just after the Council of Constance, prefers to speak of

---

[49] *Tractatus venerabilis inceptoris Guilhelmi Ockam de sacramento altaris* (Strassburg, 1491).

[50] "Hoc est igitur a divina potentia negandum quin omnem rem absolutam priorem naturaliter possit deus facere et conservare sine re posteriori." f. 132ʳ. "Quod omnipotentia dei potest facere substantiam sine omni accidente absoluto formaliter inhærente sibi." f. 132ᵛ. Both quotations from OCKHAM, *De sacramento altaris*, ed. cit.

[51] William OCKHAM, *Opera Plurima* (Lyon, 1494-1496, reprint 1962). *Super quattuor libros sententiarum*, IV, q. iv, v, vi, and vii.

God's 'omnipotence' solely, even when he is addressing particularly
Wyclif's statements about God's absolute power.[52]

It is difficult to say just why this decline of an idea should have
occurred at Oxford when it did. Whether or not it also occurred with the
same intensity and the same configurations at Paris or elsewhere, I cannot at
this point say. It is true that many of Oxford's best scholars — Bradwardine,
Buckingam, Holcot, to mention only a few — died in the Black Death of
1348-49 or shortly thereafter. But others survived the plague — Richard
FitzRalph, Adam Wodeham, Nicholas Aston — and it is in any event
difficult to believe that intellectual traditions succumb to the same bacilli as
humans. Perhaps it is no more than a question of intellectual evolution: like
the wooly mammoth or sabre-toothed tiger, the idea appeared, thrived for a
time, and passed from the scene, leaving only fossilized remains. Perhaps it
was a case of men of Aston's generation feeling far enough removed from
the Paris of Etienne Tempier that they had no need to fear the same threats
to Christianity. More research is needed before we have a satisfactory
answer to this question. But it is beyond doubt that at the University of
Oxford in the fourteenth century we can trace the decline of one of the
bell-wether theological premises of the Middle Ages. Here is an instance
where the pursuit of a systematic logical analysis foundered, and led not so
much to clarity as to confusion.

University of Ottawa

---

[52] Thomas Netter WALDENSIS, *Doctrinale antiquitatum fidei catholicæ ecclesiæ*, 3 vols.
(Venice, 1757, reprint 1967). See volume I, Liber I, articulus I, capites 10-21, col. 71-122,
where Netter discusses the nature of God's power in reply to WYCLIF's *Trialogus*.

Postscript

Breaking Up the Synthesis:
From Plato's Academy to the "School of Athens"

A model for the so-called medieval synthesis might seem to be very simple. It would involve a belief in two related propositions, namely, that God is the Creator of all things, and that all things are ordered and therefore to be interpreted according to God's design. But by now the reader will see in how many respects it would be a mistake to construe lightly in such premises a prolegomenon to intellectual narrowness or naiveté. As Professor Eldredge's essay helps to make clear, few periods have been so diverse or subtle in their analysis of experience and its possible interpretations as the Middle Ages. From its beginnings, the so-called "intellectual synthesis" of the Middle Ages exists between various recurring tensions, disparities which continuously re-engage the mind and seek resolution. In fact, we now appreciate that it is hardly fair to speak of a "synthesis" at all — the development of medieval epistemology is much more fluid than that. Perhaps, however, we can arrive at a more fruitful generalization by imagining it as a dynamic, complex, and relatively continuous process of translation of a simple idea, a vertically organized referral from the objects of creation to a perfect eternal design. At the same time, we have seen that like all generalized models, this one was seldom without some form of challenge.

An organizing model for many of the oppositions we have seen may be found in classical form in the writings of Augustine and Boethius — an ever-shifting balance between realism and nominalism, the perpetual struggle between Platonic theology and Aristotelian logic, or the vexing problem of determinism and voluntarism as it pertains to Grace. And at the heart of these tensions lie the fundamental questions of medieval humanism. Although the synthesis seems at first to be anchored faithfully and theoretically in the two simple propositions, it is in fact the turbulent diversity within the scheme which involved medieval men themselves, characterized the intellectual life of their times, and now attracts our own attention. Particularly this is true of the many chapters in our study of medieval thought provided by the repeated recurrence of medieval thinkers to the old disputation of Plato and Aristotle. One of the most exemplary of these reiterations occurs as an important spiritual controversy of the thirteenth century. As much as anything else in the *itinerarium mentis* of medieval culture this controversy summarizes both the vision of the medieval synthesis and the nature of its historic fragility. Also, the controversy between theology and the sister arts in this period anticipates a popular reflection of its irresolution in the allied arts themselves more than two centuries later. In comparing the two moments we may obtain a clearer notion of what was at stake in the persistence of the referential model itself. In the thirteenth century this is nowhere better illustrated than in disputes over curricula in the English universities.

When John Pecham was raised to the Archbishopric of Canterbury in 1279, the real energy in Christian theology was being exercised not in the cloistered gardens of monks, but amidst the noisy controversies of Europe's university towns. In contrast to the relative calmness and order with which Pecham's predecessors had pursued their contemplative reflections, a spirit of intense and often raucous competition had developed between two principal factions of university thinkers. On the one hand there gathered enthusiastic proponents of neo-Aristotelianism, and on the other an alarmed coalition nervously defending a patristic tradition whose major emphases were thought to be threatened by the "new philosophy".[1] Very quickly the conflict between the "theology" of the Augustinian traditionalists at Oxford (and Paris) and the "philosophy" of the neo-Aristotelians grew so intense that Pecham and others felt it to involve all but the most basic items of faith.[2] Despite the fact that he himself was trained in Aristotelian logic and metaphysics (under Grosseteste at Oxford), on the matter of their intrusions into theology Pecham now became disturbed enough to accuse the Aristotelians of filling the church with idols (Aristotelian philosophical dogmas), and warned that this condition was the apocalyptic danger of the last days; if the doctrines of Augustine and the other fathers were scorned "the whole fabric of Christian philosophy [would] crumble."[3] Subsequent events, in fact, seemed to prove the Archbishop a fair prophet.

I. — PHILOSOPHY VS. THEOLOGY

Let us look more closely at the opposition which Pecham so excitedly describes. The antithesis he sets up involves a startling critical contrast: the "theology" of the Augustinian tradition, which he identifies as "the Christian philosophy", and the "philosophy" of the Aristotelians, which he identifies with "idolatry".

To make sense of this extremity we need first to remember that in the early middle ages a rigorous distinction between theology and philosophy

---

[1] See Decima L. Douie, *Archbishop Pecham* (Oxford, 1952); also M. Chenu, "La Première diffusion du Thomisme à Oxford," *Archives d'histoire doctrinale et littéraire du Moyen Âge*, III (1928), 185-200.

[2] At Paris and Oxford quite often the Augustinian traditionalists were, like Pecham himself, Franciscans, while the neo-Aristotelians were as frequently Dominicans. This, of course, added sharp fraternal rivalry to the philosophical disputation.

[3] Douie, 292-3.

had not yet been worked out. In part this *'ambiguity'* owed to the *synthetic* character of philosophical study at that time. As we see, even in applications of Boethius, before the twelfth century the art of "philosophy" usually involved the mastering of certain logical and dialectical techniques which could them be employed in the pursuit of theology, the study of Scripture and the fathers. The priority had been particularly established by St. Augustine who, in making considerable use of Plato and platonists in his own work, nevertheless makes absolutely clear the principle of subordination of philosophical sources and methods to his primary intellectual discipline, theology.[4] As with Plato, the emphasis is on transcendence. Until the twelfth century most of the great scholars of the Christian West had continued in this Augustinian sense of priorities, and their tradition had remained largely dominant even to Pecham's own day. Most of those scholars would also have agreed with Cassiodorus in his famous letter to Beothius, labeling Plato as theologian and Aristotle as logician (*Plato theologus, Aristoteles logicus*), and in the spirit of the first commandment deemed precedence of the logical over the theological evident idolatry.[5] Let Aristotle keep his place.

There follow two observations about the approach of Archbishop Pecham's "Augustinian tradition" to the subject of philosophy. First, in accord with its Augustinian heritage, their "Christian philosophy" was largely informed by categories which were ultimately Platonic, or which had a similarly transcendent character.[6] Second, philosophy in the Augustinian tradition remained ancillary to the demands of theology, queen of the arts.

---

[4] See his *On Christian Doctrine*, 2.40.60-63 tr. D. W. ROBERTSON, Jr. (N.Y., 1958), 75-78; or his *City of God*, especially Bk. VIII, ch. 10 (Loeb, Cambridge, 1940) III, 44; and Bk. XVIII, ch. 41 (Loeb) VI, 16. We need to keep in mind, of course, that the word "theology" is a more modern term which we now project back on to St. Augustine. He would not have called himself a "theologian," but rather, a student of "divinity" or "the Sacred Page." Our present use of the word "theology," here adequate for a description of Augustine's chief activity, was begun by Abelard in the twelfth century. Before it had been used to describe pagan beliefs or mythologies which included pagan interpretations of the divine, as for example "Plato theologus" in the following note. On the separation of theology and philosophy in this period see further David KNOWLES, *The Evolution of Medieval Thought* (London, 1962), 261 ff.

[5] *Cassiodori Senatoris Variæ*, XLV, 4, ed. Th. MOMMSEN, *Monumenta Germaniæ Historica: Auctorum Antiquissimorum* (Berlin, 1961), XII, 40. This division of titles began to be disputed in the last third of the twelfth century upon the discovery of the *Liber de causis*, attributed to Aristotle, though actually this turned out to be merely a concise re-working of the *Elementario theologica* of the neo-Platonist Proclus. See O. BARDENHEWER, ed. *Die pseudo-aristotelische Schrift über das reine Güte, bekannt unter den Namen Liber de Causis* (Fribourg, 1882).

[6] It should be observed here that medieval philosophers from the first half of the twelfth century produced numerous theories about the "reality" of classes, and not all of these fit very neatly into a scale between "nominalism" and "realism." John of Salisbury, who observed that there seemed about as many theories as heads, has left us a useful survey of contemporary opinion in the second book of his *Metalogicon* (ch. 17, with his own conclusions in ch. 20). But this particular aspect of the controversy was a small and relatively short-lived tip to the huge cultural iceberg composed by the Augustinian-Aristotelian crisis of vocabulary in the later Middle Ages.

In short, philosophy was yet not an autonomous activity. Pecham's list of "philosophical" champions is predictable:

> the sons of blessed St. Francis.... Alexander [of Hales].... St. Bonaventure and his kind, in whose treatises are to be found everything that pertains to sanctified philosophy, teaching with Augustine the eternal rule and unchanging light, in complete contrast to that new stuff.[7]

Pecham was not alone in his challenging of the neo-Aristotelian theologians. Shortly before his appointment to the Archbishopric, there had been a crisis at the University of Paris where, as at Oxford, the teachings of Aristotle and his Arabic commentators had been flourishing. In 1267, Bonaventure had criticized the neo-Aristotelian teachings in his *Collationes in Hexaemeron*, particularly as these ideas had been understood through the Aristotelian commentary of Averroes. Three years later, perhaps at Bonaventure's instigation, Étienne Tempier, the Bishop of Paris, condemned thirteen philosophical teachings of Averroes. The two leading proponents of Averroism, Siger of Brabant and Boethius of Dacia, had equated the good life with philosophy and natural wisdom without attempting, as Paul Vignaux has pointed out in Augustinian rejoinder, to reconcile their philosophy with "the theology of humility."[8] Boethius of Dacia, in his glorification of philosophy and natural things, asserts: "I call a philospher any man who, living according to the true order of nature, has acquired the best and ultimate end of human life."[9] Similarly, Siger insisted, "We have nothing to do with the miracles of God, since we treat natural things in a natural way."[10] Such an enthusiasm was not easily to be denied, and the teaching continued, arousing sufficient interest to engage the attention of Pope John XI, who on January 18, 1277, requested of Tempier the names of the Magisters teaching these errors. Tempier, instead of complying, condemned 219 propositions, some of which included doctrines which were clearly in accordance with the teaching of Thomas Aquinas, even though earlier Aquinas too had attacked Averroisms in his *De Unitate*. Within two weeks, Pecham's predecessor, Robert Kilwardby, followed suit and condemned the teaching of such propositions in England. The propositions condemned included such doctrines as the eternity of the world,

---

[7] "Præterea noverit ipse quod philosophorum studia minime reprobamus, quatenus misteriis theologicis famulantur; sed profanas vocum novitates, quæ contra philosophicam veritatem sunt in sanctorum injuriam citra viginti annos in altitudines theologicas introductæ, abjectis et vilipensis sanctorum assertionibus evidenter. Quæ sit ergo solidior et sanior doctrina, vel filiorum beati Francisci, sanctæ scilicet memoriæ fratris Alexandri, ac fratris Bonaventuræ et consimilium, qui in suis tractatibus ab omni calumnia alienis sanctis et philosophis innituntur; vel illa novella quasi tota contraria, quœ quicquid docet Augustinus de regulis æternis et luce incommutabili, de potentiis animæ, de rationibus seminalibus inditis materiæ et consimilibus innumeris, destruat pro viribus et enervat pugnas verborum inferens toti mundo?" (*Reg.* iii, 901.)

[8] Paul VIGNAUX, *Philosophy in the Middle Ages* (London, 1958), p. 88.

[9] VIGNAUX, p. 89.

[10] Quoted in Fredrick BAILY, *The Mind of the Middle Ages* (N.Y., 1958), p. 262.

the idea that God did not create *ex nihilo* but creates continuously from undefined matter, the impossibility of transitory things ever gaining immortality, the notion that God (though Creator and prime mover) now stands aloof from the universe and has no interest in individuals, the theory that all humanity is part of one intellect, the thesis that man's fate is written in the stars, and the proposition that there is no more exalted status than to occupy oneself with natural philosophy. All of these were extremities of neo-Aristotelian positions. Pecham, when he became Archbishop, reiterated the condemnations.

The condemnations reflect, nevertheless, something of the complex tensions within late medieval thought. If for St. Augustine and the early fathers philosophy had not seemed to be distinct from its mistress, theology, by the thirteenth century a veritable anthology of philosophical (and political) issues was forcing a distinction into open discussion. There were two choices of response for the leading figures of the intellectual world, who were often theologians. One choice is represented for Pecham in his list — men who continued with force to subsume philosophical practice and the study of the "mechanical arts" under the primary service of theology. The other, represented in part by men like Albert the Great and St. Thomas Aquinas, was concerned to recognize the cleavage, but then to construct a greater synthesis of theology and philosophy in which the two "sciences" would be harmonized. Theirs was an attempt to demonstrate that the realm of the theological should always be the realm of the logical, and it is an effort still often heralded as the signal glory of medieval intellectual history.

By the fifteenth century this great attempt at a "synthesis" had already begun to fall apart. Let us try to see some of the simpler reasons why this should have happened.

II. — PLATO VS. ARISTOTLE

As several of the authors in this volume have observed, it might almost seem that the real roots of the break-up of our medieval ideal reach all the way back to Plato and Aristotle in Athens; that theirs is in some sense the ancestry, and even the form of the medieval problem. This notion is both partly true and partly illusory — but the illusion is no less important than the reality in appreciating the history of this idea. It is not inappropriate for us to pause, therefore, for a brief recapitulation.

The most influential work of Plato's through the Middle Ages — indeed the only one readily available until the Renaissance (in a translation by Chalcidius) — was the *Timaeus*.[11] Most students of Western culture

---

[11] A standard modern edition of Chalcidius is edited by J. H. Waszink, *Timæus a Calcidio translatus commentarioque instructus* (Corpus Platonicum medii ævi — Plato Latinus, Vol. IV [London, 1962]). See also Tullio Gregory, "Note e testi per la storia del platonismo medioevale," *Giornale critico della philosophia italiana*, XXXIV (1955), 346-84. There was a translation of *Meno* and *Phædo* by Aristippus (d. 1162), not so widely available.

remember the *Timaeus* as an attempt to pick up the pieces of Plato's *Republic*. The *Republic* had tried to come to grips with a definition of man — of humanness — by asking a great political question: "What is the least change in existing society necessary to cure the evils affecting mankind?" The answer: A present or future heavenly kingdom — the ideal state of the philosopher king. Its practical applicability? In Plato's own experience the experiment with Dion and Dionysius had been an abject failure, and even toward the end of the *Republic* we see that Plato is less than fully hopeful — more parenthetic and more speculative. The desirability of an ethically responsible rule of reason seems to be everywhere threatened by an equally real apprehension of the human propensity for irrational behaviour. "The *Republic* is in consequence a *chiaroscuro* of aspirations to reason, the sun, the philosopher-king.... threatened by the irrational, the cave, the tyrannical Thrasymachus."[12] Accordingly, as Plato tries to continue the dialogue with his students at the Academy he reshapes his material. The discourse recapitulated at the outset of the *Timæus* is only an outline, ignoring practical aspects of implementation. The purpose of the *Timæus* is to discover the nature of humanness in terms of a remote past, the ancient days of Athens. It is a projection back to Genesis of those visions which could not any longer be reasonably argued for the future. And as twelfth century commentators at the school of Chartres were to read it, if the heavenly kingdom was indeed before, the imperfection that Plato describes as "now" must surely be some acknowledgement of a "fall."[13] Perhaps they were not really unfair to Plato in this suggestion.

At the risk of repeating mundanely what most readers will know too well, let us recollect briefly the basic principles of epistemology, metaphysics and cosmology which Plato elaborates in the *Timæus*, reminding ourselves of the way in which they resemble those of Pecham and his Augustinian tradition.

---

[12]From J. Patrick GRANT, the introduction to his *The Transformation of Sin: Studies in Donne, Herbert, Vaughan and Traherne* (Montreal and London, 1974), p. 6.

[13] See WILLIAM OF CONCHES glosses on the *Timæus*, ed. J. M. PARENT, *La Doctrine de la création dans l'école de Chartres*, études et textes (Paris and Ottawa, 1938), 142ff. For further general commentary see N. M. HARING, "The Creation and Creator of the World according to Thierry of Chartres and Clarenbaldas of Arras" (study and texts), *Archives d'histoire doctrinale et littéraire du moyen âge*, XX (1955), 137-216. The myth of the fall adduced by Plato in his *Symposium* is that of Aristophanes, whose perfect world was represented by an egg-like spherical man, androgenous, and complete in all respects, but who through unruly aspirations "fell," or was fractured. Ever after, Plato said, the two chief parts strive to be reunited again, and this *eros* longing after wholeness is both a primary evidence of the "fallen" condition and a chief characteristic of human experience. But it seemed clear to Plato that the perfect communion lost and now longed for was not to be obtained through the most obvious of erotic "unions"; rather, it seemed that at precisely that moment when union seemed to have been achieved one was most conscious again of the greatness of the division. Human completion was to be sought therefore not in the realm of the tangible, but of the intelligible. The children's rhyme "Humpty Dumpty sat on a wall," if considered in this context, turns out to be a rather "Platonic" myth of the fall, complete with appropriate forewarnings against Aristotle.

The first issue, we remember is the epistemological question. We can have, according to Plato, two kinds of information, 1) of the *tangible* — that is, of the visible realm of change and appearances, and 2) of the *intelligible*, which being mental and spiritual, is beyond the realm of changefulness. The first is the realm of opinion, the second of knowledge. What we must learn to do, as all remember, is to escape from worlds of shadow and belief to the world of Form and Light. How? Through the education of the philosopher-king, which will include arithmetic, to enable us to work with ideas alone in our heads liberated from sense experience; geometry, a study of the relationship of forms; and dialectic, the crucial and final step which liberates men from the cave of shadowy tangibles. Through the medium of this nascent *quadrivium* and *trivium*[14] one can become capable not merely of dealing with concepts in reasoning; one should also know and understand the Platonic Ideas (forms). The pilgrimage out of the cave is formally analogous to the pilgrimage St. Augustine will trace between the two Cities: from the realm of the tangible to the realm of the intelligible. And at that point where the student has emerged into the Light, embraced the intelligible, he has achieved the essence of perspective. It is as though he should come to know at precisely the same moment not only the right answer, but the right question. For Augustine, as for Plato, that event constitutes an epiphany, a kind of fundamental translation. The pilgrimage begun in the darkness of the cave, in fallenness, will have concluded in the light of revelation — of redemption.

The second question is the metaphysical: What is ultimately real? Obviously, for Plato, it must be the intelligible world of Forms, the realm of the One, the universal — not the realm of nature, the many, the tangible particulars of creation. And since the forms appear to have in common characteristics like permanence, stability, and intelligibility, Plato reasoned that behind them must be a Form of Forms, an Idea of the Good, which was the ultimate reality and source of reality for everything else.

Finally, the cosmology of the *Timæus* could seem precedent to the theology of creation in medieval Christian tradition. Its premises are built upon the epistemology of the *Republic*, and their consequence is what we would expect: if the Eternal Being is an intelligible reality and the temporal kingdom of Becoming is tangible, then since the world is a tangible, it must "come to be." Whatever comes to be must have a *Cause* — even though, Plato says, it is very hard to find — and if we accept that the work of any maker is only as good as its eternal model, and agree that creation is good and beautiful, then we should conclude with Plato that the Maker is Good and Beautiful.[15] For Plato's *Timæus* the beauty of the created realm is

---

[14] Cf. the medieval curriculum, composed of a *quadrivium* — arithmetic, geometry, astronomy and music — and a *trivium* — grammar, rhetoric, and logic. During the Middle Ages training in the arts of the *trivium* for the purpose of *disputa* was again called "dialectic."

[15] *Timæus*, ed. F. CORNFORD (Indianapolis, 1959), p. 17.

evident in its symmetrical composition by triangles — ultimately arranged, as some of Plato's successors were to say, in hierarchies of being.

The critical question in Plato's cosmology concerns "translating" the Form from the realm of Being into the *mimesis* of the realm of Becoming. Plato's answer: the Demiurge, which draws out the perimeters of space, the "receptacle or nurse of all becoming." We could express his model in this way:

$$\frac{\text{Being (Idea, Form) — intelligible}}{\text{becoming (acts, nature) — tangible}} \text{ Demiurge} \left.\right\} \left\{ \frac{\text{Subject}}{\text{Object}} \text{ Verb} \right.$$

We see that the model can be conceived of as both logical and grammatical: what Plato seemed to have done was to make of the realm of intelligible form (Eternal Being) a kind of subject, the kingdom of the tangible "becomings" (or nature) a kind of object predicated upon the subject, and his Demiurge, a transitive agent between subject and object (a translator, or grammatically speaking, a verbal agent) the channel of relationship between the two realms. Creation, in this framework, is mimetic, imitating not so much other tangible objects as eternal ideas.[16] The implication of developments of this notion for human creativity in the early Middle Ages was that the artist who shapes experience, who gives it form, was expected to produce not the form of nature, but the "Form" above the line of Plato's Demiurge — the form of the intelligible idea.

Now we see that this undergirding principle is still very much evident in medieval art before the twelfth century. That is why, for example, when we observe in early paintings of the Madonna and Child that the infant Jesus is depicted not as a dimpled baby, but rather as a miniature man with arms and hands in formal iconographic composition, we do not attribute to the medieval painter an inability to paint "real babies". Rather, we recognize that in accord with the style and artistic skill manifested elsewhere in the painting the artist was not attempting to give us a picture of the literal baby Jesus at all. Instead, he was painting an Idea, in this case, the idea of the creative *verbum dei* incarnate, the enfleshed Word of God, or the *lumen veritas* who is then depicted as the mature promise of enlightenment to persons willing to transcend the realm of the tangible through him. And the artist's own creativity is then also a translation, a referral for understanding analogous to the transitive agency of Plato's Demiurge or the Scriptural God-in-Christ. We have seen that in the thirteenth century this principle was still receiving vigorous articulation, as a matter of fact, in the overwhelmingly Augustinian and Platonic aesthetic of Archbishop Pecham's much admired contemporary, St. Bonaventure.[17]

---

[16] *Timæus*, p. 36.

[17] See BONAVENTURE's *De Reductione Artium ad Theologiam*, ed. and translated by S. Emma Therese HEALY (St. Bonaventure, N.Y., 1939).

We can readily appreciate that to St. Augustine and his successors a basically Platonic vocabulary must have seemed almost made to order for the burgeoning Christianity of the evangelists and St. Paul. But to anticipate the later medieval abandonment of this model, we should turn our attention briefly to what Aristotle, Plato's pupil, had already rejected in the model. Aristotle, all remember, could not believe that anything other than the measurable physical world could be in any useful sense "real." So he rejected Plato's Ideas. In his insistence on the changing, tangible world as the only "real" world, and yet in his desirousness of dealing with all of the categories that Plato raised, Aristotle achieved an apparently simple but masterful answer — redefinition. He simply redefined all of the major questions — epistemological, metaphysical and cosmological — with reference to observed nature only as the source of reference. Thus, his great work, the *Metaphysics* (and finally also his *Ethics*), has the effect of drawing all Plato's "real" categories down to inclusive redefinition, "naming," in the realm "below" the line of Plato's "translator," or Demiurge.[18] Whereas Plato had ranged freely from psychology and metaphysics and finally to eschatology and the myth of an after life (prototypically we might say that there is no discontinuity between philosophy and "theology" in Plato), the effect of Aristotle's redefinition is to make all practicable questions those of the immanent and objective realm — of philosophy in the objective sense. Thus, whereas the answers to the great questions — epistemological, metaphysical, cosmological, or even ethical — were for Plato really one (the Form, or the Idea), the answers for Aristotle were, of necessity, all different, and his metaphysic thus had the effect of separating the 'disciplines' of philosophical enterprise, making them in measure autonomous.

Subsequently in Athens the principal debates were between Platonists and those who, like the Stoics, agreed at least with the bias of Aristotle's *Metaphysics* and *Ethics*.

III. — ST. AUGUSTINE AND MEDIEVAL PLATONISM

This postscript can make no pretense, obviously, to a synoptic view of the history of western philosophy, or even of medieval epistemology. It is necessary to our perspective at this point, nonetheless, to gather in one or two points of medieval Platonic theology as they were modified and channeled in Augustinian thought.[19]

---

[18] E.g., the realm of nature is now found to contain both general and particular, change and permanence, and matter which is both intelligible and tangible. The student of medieval Aristotelianism will want to direct himself to the understanding of this effect by St. Thomas, in his own *Commentary on the Metaphysics of Aristotle*, which has recently been translated by John P. ROWAN (Chicago, 1961).

[19] This will involve our bypassing Proclus, Plotinus, and the Middle Academy, whose achievement of a Second Mind and World Soul interposed between Supreme Mind and human soul are significant for the development of Augustinian theology. There is, of course, much

We may get a fairly good idea of where it is that medieval Augustinians could blend Scripture with Platonism if we pause for just a moment to consider the main features of New Testament Christianity. First, the New Testament, like the Old, argues for an Absolute Being who is the source and who is to be identified with the True, the Good, and the Beautiful. Second, it posits the creation of a tangible world which was originally a perfect reflection of the qualities of the Absolute Being. Third, it insists that creation was accomplished by a medium — the *dabhar* of the Genesis account ("and God said..."), or the Word of Wisdom of the book of Proverbs 8:23 ("set up from everlasting, from the beginning, or ever the earth was") or the *logos* of the Evangelist John ("In the beginning was the Word..."), which becomes identified by Johanine theology as the translator between God's realm and man's. Fourth, the New Testament repeatedly speaks of a Holy Spirit, a third aspect of that same God, who imbues the world with love and leads men to an apprehension of Godhead and finally, to union with him through Christ, the "translator." Thus we have a Trinity, a symmetry of three which accords with the symmetries which characterize the whole Platonic universe. Fifth, a New Testament division of man into body, soul, and spirit parallels that in the *Timæus*. Finally, both describe a "fall" — to save the appearances.

Augustine's triarchies of human mind-soul-body, memory-intellect-will, wisdom-knowledge-senses, and the three persons of God are thus natural formations, as later will be Dante's *Inferno, Purgatorio, Paradiso* with its theological rhyme scheme (*terza rima*), and even the intellectual symmetries of the triptych. Augustine's interpretation of Genesis 3 is informed by Platonic vocabulary such that the Garden of Eden becomes a perfect world of forms occupied by a complete and archetypal Adam.[20] Tempted by Eve (his lower wisdom) Adam fell, and the reward of his sin was the curse of death, of suffering, of broken will and corrupted intellect. Adam's sons' inheritance of his sin is formulated as a Platonic and mystical identity with the archetypal father "in whom" (*in quo*) all participate, as well as in terms of the inherited original sin passed from generation to generation through human reproduction. Man's fall is not partial: in Augustine man's reason is regularly repudiated as a sufficient means of salvation, "a salvation which can be won only through the miraculous intervention of God himself in history."[21]

---

more complexity to any portion of panorama surveyed in this essay. For more detail on particular points the reader is directed to relevant specific sources, some of which are listed in these notes. See especially, with cf. to note 25, M. D. CHENU's essay, "The Platonisms of the Twelfth Century," in *Nature, Man, and Society*, 49-98 (for complete reference see n. 24).

   [20] AUGUSTINE, *The City of God*, XII. 22-28 (Loeb, Cambridge, 1940), vol. IV, 108-130; see also XIII.3.

   [21] GRANT, p. 9. *Contra Faustum*, XXXII.19; also in his treatise *Morals of the Catholic Church*, I. 7, 11-12, tr. R. STROTHERT (Edinburgh, 1872), 7-8, where Augustine says: "But how can we follow after him who we do not see? or how can we see Him, we who are not only men, but also men of weak understanding? For though God is seen not with the eyes but with the mind, where can such a mind be found?" Augustine's answer is that of St. Paul: "in

With regard to universals, finally, for Augustine as for Plato there is but one answer to the epistemological, metaphysical, cosmological — even ethical questions: not, in the Christian scheme, Plato's Idea, but the Word or *Logos* — Jesus Christ, the God who enters history, who in his creative role "translated" in the beginning and is seen as continuing to translate daily in the Sacrament of Holy Communion between the realms of Being and becoming.

For Augustine, the Maker of the Universe is not so hard to find. This is the mundane genius of Augustinian Platonic theology which was not lost on its thirteenth century exponents such as Alexander, Bonaventure, Grosseteste and the apprehensive John Pecham. A problem with unChristianized Platonism had been that it indeed seemed Plato had never clearly drawn the line of demarcation between the logical, epistemological and metaphysical implications of form (i.e., theory), while on the other hand he had failed to make clear the distinction between extramental reality and intramental processes.[22] (This problem was extended in Plotinian and Neo-Platonism and the Middle Academy: Plotinus was not a pantheist, but on the other hand, he left no absolute barrier between the degrees of being.)[23] As in some Eastern thought, the realms of subject and object tended to collapse. But in being able to insist on the explicit *translating* (demiurge) role of the historical God revealed in *Scripture*, early Augustinians were able to preserve the realm of Being as "Wholly Other," to maintain the distinction between subject and object, while in the *verbum* assuring that the one would not be autonomous from the other. All thought, thus, has similar access to the same goal: there is no legitimate autonomy for any aspect of "philosophy." And at the center of Augustine's own theology is a doctrine of Person on which the whole dialectic pivots, which formulates a more comprehensive theory of personality than either Plato or Aristotle, and which, historical and yet transcendent, moves to provide an ultimate reference point, a criterion for Meaning: this for Augustine was the real significance of the Incarnation.

IV. — THE NEW ACADEMY

Old problems are new problems: it is this very issue which brings us back to the Oxford and Paris of Pecham and Alexander. As Professor Windelband showed long ago, in making the problem of universals its own starting point, medieval scholasticism "hit with instinctive sagacity upon precisely the same problem which had formed the center of interest during

---

Christ." Noting that "in human things reasoning is employed.... But when we come to divine things this faculty turns away," Augustine refers finally to the Incarnation as the only answer where reason fails: "What more could have been done for our salvation?" See also *Nature and Grace*, v. 5; *Confessions*, VIII, *passim*.

[22] For a concise summary of the tradition and development of Platonism from its founder to St. Augustine, see KNOWLES, chapters 2 and 3.

[23] KNOWLES, p. 29; see section 19-30.

the great period of Greek philosophy.'' In fact, he continued, ''[even] the delight in logical dispute, as this developed after the eleventh century at the schools of Paris, finds its counterpart as a social phenomenon only in the debates of the philosophers at Athens.''[24]

So here too, in the medieval universities there were the inescapable Aristotelian objections. Growing out of fragments of Aristotelian logic (as much as from his *Ethics* or *Metaphysics*), the *particulars* of experience were designated by the new philosophers as the true first ''substances,'' *res non predicatur*. Since now the logical significance of universals was essentially that of affording the predicates in the judgment (and in the syllogism) it seemed to follow that universals could not be substances. What could they be then? Martianus Capella had offered that a universal was the comprehension of many particulars by one Name (*nomen*), by the same word (*vox*); universals thus become collective, generic names, sounds (*flatus vocis*) which serve as signs for a multiplicity of substances and their accidents. In its extreme form, as in Roscellinus, the truly real is the individual thing and that alone, apprehended in the world of nature, of tangible reality.[25] If we look at the ''line'' of the *Timæus*, we see that here again reality is now said to be found below the line, in the realm of Object. In a somewhat hazy but interesting philogical continuation of the grammatical analogue, it is interesting to note that during the ''platonic'' era of Christian theology translations of John 1:1 had tended linguistically to emphasize the verbal, transitive properties of John's *Logos*: *in principium erat verbum* produces *verba* (Sp); *verbe* (Fr — as distinct from *mot*), and later Italian *nel principio era la parola*. After the methodology of Aristotle is fully in its ascendency, as for example in the most famous Biblical translation contemporary with the painting we are about to examine, it becomes ''Im Anfang war das Wort....'' For Luther, the *verbum dei* is not *Zeitwort*, or even *die Tat*, but simply *Wort*. Noun. Name. Object.

The applications of these academic disputes to questions of theology were self-evident and momentous. For example, Berengar of Tours on these premises contested in the doctrine of the Sacrament the possibility of the transmutation of the substance while the former accidents were retained. Roscellinus reached the conclusion that the three persons in the Trinity were to be regarded as three different substances, agreeing only in certain qualities and workings.

In Aristotle's system there was not such a good analogy for the Biblical Fall. Can we speak of nature, the tangible reality, as having ''fallen?'' So Thomas Aquinas, greatest of the new philosophers, and consistent methodist

---

[24] W. WINDELBAND, *History of Philosophy* (London, 1908), p. 288.

[25] WINDELBAND, p. 296. But see here Henry VEATCH, *Realism and Nominalism Revisited* (Milwaukee Marquette V. Press, Aquinas lecture series #19), and cf. Eike-Henmer KLUGE, ''Rosellin and the Medical problem of Universals,'' *Journal of the History of Philosophy*, xiv (1976), 405-414 for a detailed rexamination.

that he was, separated, in his categories, the realm of nature from the realm of the spiritual ideal, or grace.[26] The effect of this appropriation of Aristotelian methodology was to lead him to what Augustine would have considered an incomplete view of the Fall: while the will of man is fallen, the intellect is not. Man's intellect becomes more or less autonomous, almost as a consequence. And once again the answers to the great epistemological and cosmological questions could no longer, as they had been for Archbishop Pecham, be one and the same. Philosophy, as a discipline of the intellect rather than of the spirit, had become self-governing. And at the universities of Oxford and Paris, which had in their beginnings aspired to be the manifestation of Augustine's "New Academy," there lay the crux of their more than merely "academic" division.

John Pecham had said that *if* the Augustinian tradition were to give way to the new philosophy, the "whole fabric of Christian philosophy would crumble." As it turns out the "if" of the new philosophy, at least, was not so much an "if" as a "when." The ascendency of the new Aristotelianism was inevitable. Grounded in a superior methodology, more accessible to the growing interest in mechanical nature, it captured the good young men at Paris, Oxford, and throughout Europe. Indeed, it is on the point of methodology that Pecham's tradition most readily gave ground. The first of Aristotle's gifts to medieval philosophy had been his logic, and after a thousand years it was so much the method of dialectic that most of the finally bewildered Augustinians never even became aware that their most urgent need was for a more consistent vocabulary, a distinct methodology.

Certainly the "Christian philosophy" which Pecham had known did crumble, and in its collapse had an effect on politics, philosophy, law and the arts no less momentous than its effect on the history of Christian theology. Here we have time, however, to look only at some of the implications for the categorizing and representation of "things seen".

It would be too easy to say simply that before the crisis, art was a *mimesis* of the reality above the line of the *Timæus*, after the crisis, a *mimesis* of observable nature below the line of the *Timæus* — though indeed that statement contains at least part of the matter. But the late medieval attention to what we might at first consider to be "observable nature" is not at first for itself, nor does it derive simply from neo-Aristotelian categories of preparation. That is a still more complex story, one which begins with a new attitude toward nature in the twelfth century, and, as we have seen, is carried forward by the Franciscan tradition in the thirteenth. Though in this attitude transcendence still operates to create a vertical organization of understanding, there is already a heightened valuation for the objects of

---

[26] For convenience, one might see the collection translated and edited by A. M. FAIRWEATHER, *Nature and Grace, Selections from the Summa Theologica of St. Thomas Aquinas* (London, 1954).

creation themselves.[27] In a sense, what happens is that the current leading from Being to becoming reverses, and, as in Bonaventure's Aesthetic, it is the rich experience of the created order which leads men to an apprehension of its eternal model. Immanence itself, however, does not predominate until vertical organization — the principle of reference — gives way to another order. Meanwhile, among the several implications of the crisis of universals for art we see that in a final transition from the old, unified and idealist view to the new pluralism art itself became something of a mirror, a *mimesis* of this later change in philosophical vision.

V. — THE SCHOOL OF ATHENS

One of our best illustrations for this point moves us ahead to the very end of the Middle Ages, and a room in the Vatican called the "Stanza della Segnatura". It is a place where popes from Nicholas V on signed encyclicals and bulls of moment. Pope Julius II commissioned Raphael to adorn it with frescoes. On the ceiling are four figures, Theology, Philosophy, Poetry, and Law.[28] The four walls were to accord. Commissioned in 1503, the paintings were finished by 1513 — a period of monumental significance in European intellectual history. The choice of Raphael to represent our question here is particularly appropriate, since his genius, by the admission of his biographers,[29] was not primarily inventive or anticipatory: rather, he was one who was always most open both to tradition and to the acceptance of new ideas. In this room, you may read them upon him as on a map.

---

[27] See the earlier essay by Professor Jeffrey. The best single collection of essays on this subject is that by M. D. CHENU, *Nature, Man, and Society in the Twelfth Century*, selected, edited, and translated by Jerome TAYLOR and Lester K. LITTLE (Chicago, 1968), of which the first essay, "Nature and Man — The Renaissance of the Twelfth Century" offers an excellent introduction. For a particularly Platonic point of view, see Tullio GREGORY, *Anima mundi: la filosofia de Guglielmo di Conches e la scuola di Chartres* (Florence, 1955), 175-246; also Winthrop WEATHERBY, *Poetry and Platonism in the Twelfth Century* (Princeton, 1972).

[28] E.g., the four ceiling medallions, philosophy (with its books "natural" and "moral"), jurisprudence, and theology, have pendant to them four transitional corner panels: between the "School of Athens," signifying philosophy, and "Parnassus," signifying poetry, the first small fresco shows two spheres — an opaque sphere within a transparent one — earth and heaven, with above them the muse of Astronomy, Urania, who as a scientific figure belongs to philosophy, but as a muse belongs to poetry; the corner between *Parnassus* and the *Disputa* has a depiction of "The Flaying of Marsyas" which has both poetic and theological significance (see Bruce Smith's essay in this volume — on Music — for a judicious explication); between the *Disputa* and *Jurisprudence* Raphael places appropriately "The Fall of Adam and Eve," which while primarily theological has obvious juridicial connotations; between *Jurisprudence* and *The School of Athens*, is a panel of the "Judgment of Solomon," which while primarily juridicial is also philosophical, in that Solomon was thought in many respects to be a model philosopher-king.

[29] A. P. OPPÉ, *Raphael*, ed. with intro. by Charles Mitchell (London, 1970); Askar FISCHEL, *Raphael*, trans. Bernard Rackham (London, 1964); Eugène MÜNTZ, *Raphael* (Paris, 1960); Andre-Charles COPPIER, *L'Enigme de la Segnatura* (Paris, 1928), esp. p. 36ff. While some might find Coppier's "un homme-carrefour" a little too harsh, most of his biographers consider Raphael to be "monumental" in the primary sense of the word.

XII.   ''The School of Athens'' — Raphael (Stanza della Segnatura)

XIII.   "The Dispute of the Sacrament" — Raphael (Stanza della Segnatura)

On the left as you enter is the fresco universally known as the *School of Athens*. It represents Philosophy. Striding forth from an array of Greek philosophers, representing at once the seven liberal arts and the perceived continuity between Old and New Academy, are the two still dominant forces in western philosophical tradition: Plato and Aristotle. Plato, modelled on Raphael's portrait of Leonardo, is old and bearded, with iconographic attributes of a Moses, and he is shown with his right hand pointing upward. In his left he carries (vertically) a copy of his *Timæus*. Aristotle, young and swarthy, spreads his arm confidently downward to describe the tangible world of experience. In his left hand, is a copy (held horizontally) of his *Ethics*. The painting is an epitome of the controversy.

But to be held in consideration with it is the opposite fresco, on the right of the door, representing Theology. It is called *Disputa del Sacramento*. Before anything else in this picture we cannot help but notice its Platonic-Augustinian structure. First, there in the horizontal chain of clouds is Plato's "reality line" from the *Timæus*, extending across the picture, dividing the realm of the Eternal from that of the Temporal.[30] Second, in the graceful ascent of sweeping circles and fundamentally tripartite triangular composition we see the clear formal imprint of an Augustinian and Platonic symmetry. The balances are perfect, in the hierarchies of angels, witnesses, and the unified number of Patriarchs in Judgment to the three persons of God.[31] This feature leads us naturally to the further observation that the circles also descend to corporeal men in the realm of their temporal existence. The action moves from Father to Son through the aegis of the Holy Spirit. The Spirit, the fresco illustrates, is made known in the Sacrament of the Eucharist, whose Host, cross-framed in the monstrance, is the avenue of the spirit's translation (or, in the vocabulary of the doctrine of the Blessed Sacrament, the agency by which at once the Body of Christ [the Host] enjoins the Body of Christ [his Church] and his Spirit becomes its spirit). In a word, what we have here is a pictorial representation of the medieval Augustinian Baptism of the *Timæus*, where the realm of subject and object are held distinct and yet in mutual commerce through the agency of the *Verbum Dei*. In a manner familiar from the twelfth century, we are offered in this representation of the sacrament of communion a visual correlative for the principle of referral itself.[32] The initial verses of the four

---

[30] One wonders if the incomplete building at the right is not, even if humorously, intended to suggest the character of the realm of "becoming".

[31] Even the banded rays which descend from the Father (the "One") are numerically part of the symmetry. I am indebted to Russell Peck for the observation that there are twenty-two rays in all, one for each letter in the Hebrew alphabet, i.e., not only "I am," but also "I am the Alpha et Omega." (note the Septuagint "translation.") Cf. ISIDORE, *Etymologiæ*, XVI, 26,10, who notes that 22 is the number of God's created works during creation week, the number of generations from Abraham to Jacob, the number of the books of the Hebrew Scriptures up to Esther, etc.

[32] As in Suger's famous design for the cathedral of St. Denis. See PANOFSKY, *Meaning in the Visual Arts* (Penguin, 1960), Ch. 3.

evangelists hold the Augustinian key to the problem of universals: "The book of the generations of Jesus Christ, son of God," "born in the days when Herod was King in Judah," "His Gospel," in which he is known to be both man and God, the unique translator between the eternal and the temporal: "*in principium erat Verbum....* and the Word was with God, and the Word was God" — the same which "became flesh and dwelt amongst men." The insistence here is upon an historical as well as transcendent character of referral. And so the old line of the *Timæus* is not an effectual barrier, but, an invitation to referral and an occasion of understanding as we see in the Host itself. The line between Eternal and temporal, as it were, is bridged by the cross. Thus, the pilgrimage from tangible to intelligible for which Plato hoped was, in the eyes of his Augustinian successors, freed for realization, for transformation, through referral to a concept of universal Personhood in which both realms were accessible and "real."

But we should not fail to recognize that the scene around the altar is depicted as a *disputa*, precipitated in large part by the developing crisis of which we have spoken. It is not an accident, I think, that in Raphael's arrangement of Church fathers he sets against the philosopher on the right a group less distinguished perhaps, of hermits and early fathers whose significance is clear. At the feet of St. Jerome rests his *Biblia*, his standard translation of what medieval thinkers accepted as the historical record of divine revelation of the *verbum dei*. There also are his letters, whose constant moral injunction to his protégés is to find the reference for their theology in those same Scriptures. On the other side are the traditional philosophers and theologians — St. Thomas, *Dante teologica*, Ambrose, Augustine, Bonaventure. (The placing of Bonaventure and Augustine in this group, if indeed the philosophy vs. theology controversy is integral to the "Disputa," might seem to be a confusion by Raphael. By Raphael's time, however, Pecham's neat orderings had become muddled with a great many other issues from the history of Italian spirituality which are too complex to detail here. And it will be remembered, further, that Augustine's *City of God*, the philosophy of a culture, was by then regarded by many as the beginnings of Christian "philosophy," while Bonaventure by the end of his life was as often thought to be a traitor to the Scriptural ideals of St. Francis which he had once espoused — St. Francis, it should be noted, is on the right in heaven. Thus as we further examine this picture, we see that the split between theology and philosophy is apparent even here.) It is not insignificant for Raphael's perspective that a desert father figure urges the unresponsive philosophers in the manner of his Platonic model. But in the structure of the fresco, we still have, at the center, the transitive agency of Augustinian Platonism, lending a subject-verb-object, trinitarian, triangular shape to the whole composition.

Consider again for a moment the *School of Athens*. It is a distinctly more modern painting. Here, there is no triarchy, but rather, polarity, a tension between two fundamentally opposed opposites: there is no eternal source of reference, no verbal synthesis, just tension.

XIV. "Parnassus" — Raphael (Stanza della Segnatura)

XV. "Fortiude, Prudence, and Temperance" — Raphael (Stanza della Segnatura).

But there remain two walls. Between the *Sacrament* and the *School of Athens* Raphael depicted the poets. *Parnassus*, actually Helicon, is a scene where, led on by a Sapphic *anima*, poets of the ages ascend to stand in the presence of a Bacchic Appollo's music. The ascent is uneven. For Homer, Vergil, Horace and Dante there is a kind of plateau, next to the muses, nearest the God. But as we look at their faces we see that Vergil glances askance at Dante, Horace is for some reason bemused, Homer blind but like Tireseus, stands with inner eye cast upward. On the other side a more modern group of poets, including Raphael's friend Sanazzaro, stand further from Apollo, eyes entirely away — a scene of some uncertain exchange. Who are the ones who look toward us so skeptically?[33] And at the bottom, as the path winds downward to our right, two seekers receive a wise old man's advice. He points, *not* up the hill, but ambiguously, away, across the floor. Does he point to the portrayal of Law on the fourth wall of the room? Or is it to Jerome and the Desert Fathers, left half of *Disputa del Sacramento*? This fresco has been adjudged to be a failure: Professor A.P. Oppé, one of the most distinguished students of Raphael, finds it "not only flat, but actually unsuccessful in its obvious attempts to escape from flatness" — Raphael's *Parnassus* exemplifies, in effect, the loss of a dimension.[34]

The fourth wall is now predictable. The representations are of *civil* and *ecclesiastical* law, Justinian and Gratian, a split which reflects the portraiture of both *law* and *philosophy* on the ceiling.

Here clearly is a room which reflects a keen sense of intellectual crisis, which feels the tensions which result from altercation and irresolution, and which is unsure of itself. This would seem apparent even in Raphael's treatment of the three virtues which crown the last wall. They are a strange lot, an enigmatic portrayal of Fortitude, Prudence and Temperance. Fortitude and Temperance are somewhat detached — Temperance holds her bridle not, as we might expect, to herself, but, looking the other way, thrusts it at Prudence. And this is not the Prudence of traditional painting who spins, garners, or girds herself: what is she doing? Gazing at herself in a mirror, illuminated not by the sun, but by artificial light. Prudent introspection? Or narcissistic internalizing? Two hundred years before she never would have been painted in this way. And the little cherub who points

---

[33] Are these, perhaps, followers of Ficino? Ficino (1433-99), an eminent "new" Neo-Platonist nearly contemporary with Raphael, had concluded, following the rediscovery of Aristotle, that "universals" would have to be sought out in the tangible realm of nature, the realm below Plato's "line", and thus could be generalized from the understanding of a sufficient number of particulars. Among his numerous disciples were many artists, including the great Leonardo da Vinci, as well as a number of minor poets. There has been a recent reprint edition of FICINO's *Commentarium in Platonem* (Torino, 1959).

[34] OPPÉ, p. 76. He adds, somewhat disturbingly, that this "failure amounts to a virtue in modern eyes," perhaps anticipating E.H. GOMBRICH, who in his *Symbolic Images* (London, 1972), p. 91, finds *Parnassus* "a perfect vision of *Numine Afflatur*, the divine inspiration of poetry."

heavenward, a reflection of Plato and the desert father, does not seem so convinced. While the "Stanza della Segnatura" is very much reflective of the tension and the change, as even the pun in its name would seem to suggest, it seems headed already in the direction of the change itself: *Segn / natura* (the sign of nature) is by 1500 very much in the ascendant. From this point on, in "things seen" we now see pretty much just that — a representation of what can be observed. The realm of ideal reality is no longer successfully incorporated in the shape of natural creation.

The loss of a viable Universal in art is akin to that discovered in all aspects of late medieval and early Renaissance culture. The difference between medieval advice to young princes and Renaissance courtesy books will become, for example, that the former ascribes to nobility independent truth and the character of God, while the latter moves from a spiritual definition to a definition of attributes. (We are on our way to Lord Chesterfield.)[35] The center of study in medieval universities will move from theology to philosophy, from moral to natural law, from metaphysics to physics. Not all these reorderings, or their concomitant changes — artistic, philosophical, educational, political — were to be smooth, or even merely confusing. In politics, for example, the symbolic and venerable "divine right of kings"[36] with its panoply of hierarchy and sanctified order abdicated to the parliamentary procedures of Cromwell's middle-class saints only when Charles I knelt at the headsman's block. In this symbolic event we see anticipated the turning point of modern European history, the civil war and regicide of the French Revolution, and measure the invisible depths to which the foundations of social and moral order had already been shaken in this earlier period of European history.

Among painters at the end of the Middle Ages, Raphael was apparently, or as far as we know, content to depict the problem and leave it at that.[37] But for a man of fierce intellectual integrity in a period of such

---

[35] In his *Advancement of Learning* Bacon will suggest that a new, scientifically based ethical system may be formulated only after a great many biographies have been written — case histories from which ethical principles may be derived not as intuition or revelation, but as the product of an analysis of numerous scientifically analysed particulars which, in their aggregate, will suggest "proper" principles. (We are reminded that Pope's "whatever is, is right," if not really a Boethian statement, is definitely Aristotelian.)

[36] The so-called "Divine right of kings" is actually a late formulation of medieval kingship and is not in a rigorous understanding of that phrase very ancient. The analogous hierarchical relationship implied by the phrase certainly was invoked, however, by medieval kings, and although no less than five English kings were deposed and murdered between 1307-1485, the old concept of sanctified kingship did not come under serious attack in this period. See also GRANT, *op. cit.*, p. 2.

[37] As opposed, for example, to his contemporary Hieryonomus Bosch, whose work is full of apocalyptic portent and a real despair for the principle of "referral for understanding" as it had been previously understood. See "Bosch's *Haywain*: Communion, Community and the Theatre of the World," *Viator*, IV (1973), 311-31, in which I have attempted to illustrate the tension in Bosch between despair for the principle and desire for its vocabulary.

XVI.   ''John the Baptist'' — Leonardo da Vinci

irresolution, his life had to attempt somehow to synthesize again or to unify the two realms which had come asunder, the immanent and the transcendent, the kingdoms of nature and grace. St. Thomas Aquinas had worked toward an all-embracing synthesis — his *Summa* — and seemed to many to have succeeded brilliantly. But as the years went by it became harder and harder to create a *summa*. Leonardo da Vinci, a master of most of Hugh of St. Victor's "mechanical arts", a "universal" man, was one who in his own way tried — and failed. Following the lead of Ficino, he hoped to find a universal which could emerge from the particulars — a universal below "Plato's line". But he was unsuccessful in convincing himself that this was the only realm of his real experience. Giovanni Gentile says about Leonardo, describing his response to the crisis:

> The unity of the [intelligible] illuminates his fantasy; and the intellect comes in to break up this unity into the endless multiplicity of sensible appearances. Hence the anguish and the tragedy of this universal man, divided between his irreconcilable worlds, leaves in the mind an infinite longing, made up as it were of regret and sadness. It is the longing for a Leonardo different from the Leonardo that he was, one who could have gathered himself up at each phase and remained closed off either altogether in his fantasy or in his intelligence.[38]

Lesser men could choose one fantasy or the other, late medieval scholasticism and empiricism, or the mystic way. Gentile, one of Italy's greatest modern philosophers, saw that Leonardo, steeped in Neo-Platonism but also one of the first mathematicians in the modern sense, had really sensed the problem with which modern man is now grappling. He understood that if a man starts with himself alone in the world of nature and logically and rationally moves through mathematics he never comes to a universal — only to particulars and mechanics.[39] The question becomes: how can finite man, bound forever to the circles of his tangible world, produce a unity which will cover the many particulars? Can he really create *ex pluribus unum*? If he cannot, how can the particulars have unity and meaning for him? *Eppure se muove*, Galileo was about to observe.[40] Or, how, as you come to doubt Aristotle's *telos*, do you get from his side of the line to a unity which is more than the sum of its parts — from the Lyceum back to the Academy? Leonardo, a much more acute and anticipatory genius than Raphael, spent his whole life trying to paint the universal, the soul. In Leonardo's work too, we find the heavy handed signal of referral, pointed heavenward. But the object of Leonardo's signal, as in his portrayal of John the Baptist, is the hand itself that points, not the vision to which it refers our attention. The soft eyes and ambiguous sexuality of the face behind may seem to invite us into a shady confidence — but not to any clear vision beyond the moment. It is thus the surface detail of the sign itself which is resolved in sharpest focus; the clearest reality is the Baptist's skin and bone.

---

[38] *Leonardo da Vinci* (N.Y., 1956), p. 174; see also *Il Pensiero Italano del Rinascimento*, in the Opere, 4th ed., (Firenze, 1968) XIV, 117-149.

[39] See F. SCHAEFFER, *The God Who Is There* (London, 1969), p. 61.

[40] With reference to his observation that the earth was not after all the "still point" and center of a Ptolemaic-Aristotelian universe: "And yet it moves!"

The natural world, when fully natural, no longer seemed to signify the spiritual: the traditional signs of referral — the icons and symbols of sanctity — no longer seemed to be natural. Because Leonardo could not accept an irrational 'solution' to this dilemma he would never let go of this hope of finding a unity which included both the universal and the particular, theology and philosophy, meaning and mathematics. But the problem remainded unsolved.[41] There seemed to be no Universals below the "line."

Archbishop John Pecham's thirteenth-century hypothesis thus becomes, in hindsight, a kind of prophecy. We look back to such a figure to find him standing in the middle of a panorama of intellectual history which extends from Augustine to Descartes, from *dubito ergo sum* to *cogito ergo sum*, from the philosophy of culture to the culture of philosophy. Pecham's struggle is an extremely useful vantage point for the student of the Middle Ages, for in it simplest continuing denominator that extraordinarily comprehensive and long-lived culture may be read as a diligent attempt to carry the intelligible values of the classical and Biblical past into an increasingly 'tangible', even technological world. For a long time, and perhaps especially during the twelfth and thirteenth centuries, men seemed to be succeeding. After Pecham, and by the time of Leonardo and Raphael, the attempt would seem to many to have failed — the order of reference lost. So if we see in Pecham's frenzied defence of the old tradition and his rallying of forces against the new philosophy a kind of stark-eyed terror, we need not wonder that it is there. It is because he all too clearly foresaw the defeat — and the despair — which must ensue from a victory of an independent philosophy, and, by extension, each other art, over theology. In the resulting divisions, the coherence of a referral for understanding would be lost. Behind him lay the modest successes of the twelfth century Augustinian "renaissance," the spiritual tranquility of a world where the forms of Augustinian 'Platonism' are still relatively consistent with the model, where God is wholly other, external, eternal, and yet is transcendent and intelligibly accessible through divine translation in space and time. In this tradition men could still see the trinitarian Deity reflected not only in "the lofty, the noble, and the grand" (Aquinas), but in the "smallest fleck of dust whirling in the sunlight" (Grosseteste). Body/soul/spirit; wisdom/ knowledge/senses; Being/translator/Becoming; Father/Spirit/Son; Subject/ Verb/Object — it was still, to evoke the terms of Professor Peck, a world of threes. But the world Pecham imagined to be coming was not a secure coherence of modest successes, but a renaissance of magnificent failures. For him, the world of threes was, in effect, soon to become a world of twos — as in "The School of Athens," irreconcilable twos — thesis — antithesis — struggling and waiting, perhaps for Hegel, and yet another world.

We verge at last on a new understanding of a familiar term: the desire for intellectual and cultural "synthesis" which had marked the heuristic

---

[41] As his two versions of the "Madonna of the Rocks" make especially clear.

imagination of the Middle Ages gradually gave way to an analytical mode of thinking. If we were to consider the shift in language noted by Professor Lopez, in which European languages we now describe as "synthetic" begin to lose some of their characteristic features, and in which temporal order and the definite article emerge to recharacterize language itself as increasingly "analytic", perhaps we might find, as speech turns to print, a linguistic corollary to the shift from imagination to description. From "creation" to "invention" (in the modern sense), the emphasis in thinking at the end of the Middle Ages turns from synthetic formulation toward analytic description. Emphasis once placed upon the relational and referential character of knowing falls increasingly upon analytic descriptions in which what is valued is the objective and empirical character of knowledge. A twelfth century aphorism such as William of St. Thierry's *amor ipse intellectus est* ("love itself is understanding") begins even by the sixteenth century to sound suspiciously like mystical twaddle. Far fewer folk, for understanding, can see themselves as "standing under" (*sub iaca*) in a vertical order of reference whose binding principle is love; — they seek instead to stand upon, to master the science of the visible: authority rests with the thing that may itself be seen, defined, empirically verified. In an anticipation of our own time, interpretation thus becomes increasingly synonymous with "control", epistemology with mastery.

The essence of the medieval idea of referral for understanding is that it operated on a vertical axis. This was as true, in its own formulation, for Franciscan aesthetic near the end of the Middle Ages as for earlier Augustinian articulations of the model. Accordingly, one discovers a vertical organization in medieval astronomy, music and numerology as readily as in Dante's poetry or the history of painting down to Michelangelo and Raphael. By the end of the period, however, artists begin to move toward still-life, landscape, and portraiture, and their principles of organization, now predominantly horizontal, are reflected in the growth of empirical method, of technological science, and of political as distinct from ethical theory. With all of these developments, as modern persons, we are familiar. Yet as language in all of our own disciplines tends to evolve and individuate more rapidly than ever, we may still find attractive the genius — and the ultimate simplicity — of the integrative verticality of the medieval model. In it, "things seen" may have both their own and yet another character: they are, and they signify. The peculiar grace of this referential understanding is that it opens up to diverse angles of enquiry a plane of shareable discourse, an axis of relationship in which the prevalent tendency to atomism is counterbalanced by an integral calculus for conversation and intellectual community. Here, perhaps, is an ideal not less attractive to us than it was to the men and women of the Middle Ages.

D.L.J.

INDEX
of
NAMES AND SUBJECTS

254

256

258

264

LIST OF WORKS CITED, ALSO BY AUTHOR
(includes Paintings).

BIBLICAL QUOTATIONS

LIST OF CONTRIBUTORS

John W. Abrams is Professor of History and Director of the Institute for History and Philosophy of Science and Technology at the University of Toronto. He researches and writes in the area of history and philosophy of science.

Lawrence Eldredge is Professor of English Literature at the University of Ottawa. He has written articles on Chaucer, medieval literature, and intellectual debate in Latin Literature of the fourteenth century.

John Freccero is Professor and Chairman of the Department of Italian Language and Literature at Yale University. He has written numerous distinguished articles in Latin and Italian Literatures, most recently on Dante and Petrarch.

Patrick Grant is Associate Professor of English Literature at the University of Victoria. He has written *The Transformation of Sin: Studies in Donne, Herbert, Vaughan Traherne* (1974); *After Images: A Chapter in the History of Ideas and Their Literary Implications* (1979) and numerous articles on English Literature and western intellectual history.

David L. Jeffrey is Professor and Chairman of the Department of English at the University of Ottawa. He is author of *The Early English Lyric and Franciscan Spirituality* (1975), the forthcoming *Chaucer & Wyclif: Hermaneutic and Narrative Theory in the Fourteenth Century* (1979), and articles on medieval literature and medieval art history.

Richard W. Kaueper is Professor and Chairman of the Department of History at the University of Rochester. He is the author of *Bankers to The Crown: The Ricardi of Lucca and Edward I (1973)* and articles in medieval court history and economic practices.

Robert S. Lopez is Sterling Professor of History at Yale University. He has published numerous books and articles, including *Medieval Trade in the Mediterranean World* (1955); *Naissance de l'Europe* (1962); *The Three Ages of the Italian Renaissance* (1970) and *The Commercial Revolution of the Middle Ages* (1971).

Russell A. Peck is Professor of English at the University of Rochester. He is the author of *Kingship and Common Profit in Gower's Confessio Amantis* (1978), ed. Gower's *Confessio Amantis* (1968), and of numerous articles on Chaucer, Middle English literature, and medieval aesthetics, especially number theory.

James R. Shaw is Associate Professor of Philosophy of Science at Vanderbilt University. He has written articles on late medieval philosophy of science, and currently is completing a book on Alberthus Magnus.

Bruce Smith is Associate Professor of English at Georgetown University and a Fellow of the Folger Institute. He is the author of articles on medieval and renaissance literature, music and drama.

David Wilkins is Associate Professor of Art History at Pittsburgh University. He has written articles and a monograph on Italian painting of the trecento and quattrocento especially.

Achevé d'imprimer
en février mil neuf cent soixante-dix-neuf
sur les presses de l'Imprimerie Gagné Ltée
Louiseville - Montréal.
Imprimé au Canada